THE AGING FAMILY

The Aging Family

New Visions in Theory, Practice, and Reality

Edited by

Terry D. Hargrave, Ph.D.

and

Suzanne Midori Hanna, Ph.D.

Routledge
Taylor & Francis Group
New York London

Published in 1997 by Routledge
711 Third Avenue, New York, NY 10017
2 Park Square, Milton Park, Abingdon, Oxfordshire OX14 4RN

First issued in paperback 2015

Routledge is an imprint of the Taylor & Francis Group, an informa business

Library of Congress Cataloging-in-Publication

The aging family : new visions in theory, practice, and reality/ edited by Terry D. Hargrave and Suzanne Midori Hanna.
    p. cm.
  Includes bibliographical references (p.) and indexes.
  ISBN 0-87630-841-8 (hard)
    1. Social work with the aged. 2. Family social work. 3. Aged—Care. 4. Aged—Family relationships. I. Hargrave, Terry D. II. Hanna, Suzanne Midori.
HV1451.A38 1997
362.6—dc21   96-54236
                                                                                   CIP

Copyright © 1997 by Routledge

All rights reserved. No part of this book may be reproduced by any process whatsoever without the written permission of the copyright owner.

ISBN 13: 978-1-138-86948-6 (pbk)
ISBN 13: 978-0-87630-841-7 (hbk)

To my grandparents, Junichi Hanaoka, Clara Dee Wade,
Lydia Debra Dunning, and John Hyrum Pollock,
for their faith in a better life.
And to my parents, Mervil Hanna and Peggy Marie Pollock,
children of immigrants and pioneers who provided a better life,
and now in later life bless us with their pioneering spirit.

Suzanne Midori Hanna

To my children, Halley Anne Hargrave and Peter Sloan Hargrave,
who have taught me to love and helped me to grow.

Terry D. Hargrave

Contents

Preface		ix
Prologue:	One Family's Struggle with Alzheimer's Disease	1
	Harvey Joanning	

Part I: Family Therapy and Later Life

Chapter 1	Integrating the Process of Aging and Family Therapy	19
	Suzanne Midori Hanna and Terry D. Hargrave	
Chapter 2	Aging: A Primer for Family Therapists	39
	Terry D. Hargrave and Suzanne Midori Hanna	

Part II: Models of Treatment

Chapter 3	Finishing Well: A Contextual Family Therapy Approach to the Aging Family	61
	Terry D. Hargrave and William T. Anderson	
Chapter 4	Solution-Focused Brief Therapy with Aging Families	81
	Marilyn J. Bonjean	
Chapter 5	A Developmental–Interactional Model	101
	Suzanne Midori Hanna	

Chapter 6	The Strength–Vulnerability Model of Mental Health and Illness in the Elderly .... Cleveland G. Shields and Lyman C. Wynne	131

Part III: Special Issues

Chapter 7	Changing Roles and Life-Cycle Transitions .... Mary A. Erlanger	163
Chapter 8	Marriage in Middle and Later Life .... Richard B. Miller, Karla Hemesath, and Briana Nelson	178
Chapter 9	Gender Issues and Elder Care .... Nancy L. Kriseman and Jacalyn A. Claes	199
Chapter 10	Alzheimer's Disease and the Family: Working with New Realities .... Janie Long	209
Chapter 11	Family Systems and Nursing Home Systems: An Ecosystemic Perspective for the Systems Practitioner .... Wayne A. Caron	235
Chapter 12	Reconciling with Unfulfilled Dreams at the End of Life .... Wayne E. Oates	259
Chapter 13	Dying and Death in Aging Intergenerational Families .... William T. Anderson	270

Part IV: Implications for the Future

Chapter 14	Future Directions for Family Therapy with Aging Families .... Suzanne Midori Hanna, Terry D. Hargrave, and Richard B. Miller	295

Name Index	....	309
Subject Index	....	317

Preface

Aging is a complex and fascinating process that encompasses many fields, including biology, sociology, psychology, and spirituality. It is by nature systemic, touching every part of the current and intergenerational family. Family members stand at various points along the continuum between youth and aging, growing older individually and together, and revealing through their process truths, both personal and universal. Yet, even as the therapeutic community gives lip service to the value of aging and the family, the various fields have been slow to examine and utilize the dimension of aging in the context of family. The field of family therapy is no exception.

The American Association for Marriage and Family Therapy has had a special caucus on aging for several years. First led by Marilyn Bonjean, then later by Suzanne Hanna and Denise Flori, members of the caucus would share their ideas and goals concerning the special needs and treatment of problems related to aging in the context of the family. As the work in the caucus progressed, it became evident that different theoretical approaches to dealing with the aging family were emerging and that many of the techniques being used were innovative and significant. A proposal was made to bring together our ideas into a family therapy volume entirely devoted to aging and its meanings. This book is the result.

From the outset of the project, there was a desire that the work reflect the status of the caucus. As such, this book represents the "work up to this point." Because dealing with aging families is a relatively new area in family therapy, there are noticeable gaps in the research. Issues of aging and ethnicity, illness, spirituality, and ethics, as well as certain theoretical approaches, are underrepresented or are not addressed fully. Clearly, there is more to be done, but we believe that this volume is an accurate representation of the current work in family therapy and aging and should give impetus to others to move on with research and exploration of other aspects of the aging process.

In Part I, we provide an introduction to both the work of family therapy and aging and the field of gerontology. Chapter 1 reviews the efforts that have been made to integrate aging and family therapy and how the field has dealt with problems associated with aging. Chapter 2 offers an overview of the information in the biological, psychological, and sociological fields of aging.

Part II reviews different theoretical approaches that members of the aging caucus have developed in working with aging families. Although many consider the therapeutic community as a whole to be moving away from theory, theory still serves us well in charting courses for integration. Terry Hargrave and William Anderson discuss their use of Contextual Family Therapy with aging families in Chapter 3, and Marilyn Bonjean explains a solution orientation to aging in Chapter 4. Suzanne Hanna puts forth her Developmental-Interactional Model in Chapter 5, and the section is closed by a discussion from Cleveland Shields and Lyman Wynne of the Strength-Vulnerability Model.

In Part III, some of the really tough issues associated with aging and the family are examined. Never before have people lived so long. This has caused the development and life cycle of the family to change. Mary Erlanger addresses some of these shifting roles and transitions in Chapter 7. The increase in individual longevity has also meant an increase in marital longevity. Richard Miller, Karla Hemesath, and Briana Nelson discuss aging and married relationships in Chapter 8. Much of the aging population is female and a huge percentage of the caregiving population is made up of women. Therefore, gender considerations have a dynamic effect in the aging process. Chapter 9, by Nancy Kriseman and Jacalyn Claes, focuses on some of these gender issues as they relate to aging.

Alzheimer's disease is perhaps one of the most heinous and devastating problems facing aging individuals and their families. In Chapter 10, Janie Long presents an in-depth look at the disease and how treatment has progressed. Another difficult area for families concerns what to do when self-care is no longer possible and nursing home placement becomes necessary. Wayne Caron is a pioneer in mapping out ways to help families face difficult placement issues, and he reports on his work with the Bibliography Project in Chapter 11. Wayne Oates addresses a much-neglected topic in Chapter 12—the emotional task of coming to terms with failures, heartaches, and regrets. Here the reader will find the wisdom of Wayne's many years of experience and insight as he gives us a view of aging from hearts and dreams of the eldest generation. In Chapter 13, William Anderson reviews

Preface

some of the issues that individuals and families confront as they deal with the final challenge—death and dying. Finally, Chapter 14 discusses the future of family therapy with aging families.

We acknowledge and appreciate the efforts and dedication of the chapter authors. Their work stands as a gift to the therapeutic community and will serve as encouragement for others to move into the arena of aging and the family. Also, we wish to acknowledge the courage and commitment of the many individuals and families with whom all of us in the aging caucus have worked through the years. In many ways, we have been helped and taught by them much more than they have been helped by us.

This book opens with a very personal piece by our friend and colleague, Harvey Joanning, in which he gives a firsthand account of his own experience with Alzheimer's disease. Although many of us in the caucus have known through our work with aging families the frustrations that aging produces, Harvey's story truly captures the essential elements of the loss, guilt, love, and care that are a part of later-life experience. It is not about a particular treatment; it is a moving story that offers great insight into the reasons why so many of us desire to work with families in later life. Alzheimer's disease hit Harvey's family at a younger age than is usual, but the themes that it brought with it resonate powerfully across generations.

Terry D. Hargrave

Suzanne Midori Hanna

THE AGING FAMILY

Prologue

One Family's Struggle with Alzheimer's Disease

Harvey Joanning, Ph.D.
Iowa State University
Ames, Iowa

Thou hast vanished from my reach leaving an impalpable touch in the blue of the sky, an invisible image in the wind moving among the shadows.

Rabindranath Tagore

"I CAN'T FIND THE BATHROOM"

June 13, 1989

I return home from my morning run to find Sue still in bed. This is unusual. She is a chemistry teacher at a community college and has an 8 o'clock class; it is 7 o'clock. I sit on the edge of the bed and ask, "Sue, why are you still in bed? Aren't you feeling well?" She has been crying. I am concerned. She looks at me, "I've got it."

"You've got what?"

"I've got what my mother had."

My stomach feels like an express elevator dropping 20 floors. Her mother died of Alzheimer's disease several years ago.

"What makes you think that you have Alzheimer's?"

"The dean called me into his office. Students have been complaining."

"Complaining about what?"

"Complaining that I repeat myself in class. That I've been going over the same lesson day after day. I can't remember whether I have."

"Why didn't you tell me this last night?"

"I was going to, but I didn't want to upset you. I wasn't sure what to do. But I've been up all night worried about it, and I am really scared."

Sue begins to cry again. I do my best to comfort her, but to no avail. We decide to visit the dean to get a clearer idea of what is happening and I call for an appointment. The dean will see us immediately. The two-mile drive from our home to the campus seems endless as Sue sobs.

We arrive in the dean's office at about 8:30 a.m. He reports, in Sue's presence, that students have been complaining. Her usual good teaching style is now a series of repeated lectures and confusion during the lectures, in class and in the lab. The dean is concerned but supportive. He has no idea how his comments are affecting Sue. He asks what he can do to help.

"I have Alzheimer's disease." Understandably, the dean looks shocked; Sue is only 42. The idea of a young woman's having this disease surely makes no sense. He looks at me questioningly. I tell him that it is possible because early-onset Alzheimer's disease runs in my wife's family. The dean encourages Sue to continue teaching with support. Embarrassed, she flatly refuses. The school assigns a substitute teacher.

Visits with physicians begin. We want to find out if Sue does have Alzheimer's disease. Our family physician gives her a thorough physical and finds no problem. However, when he gives her the Mini Mental Status exam, she misses more than half of the questions. She does not know who the president of the United States is, what day it is, or what year it is. I am profoundly shocked; I've had no inkling of her difficulty in these areas.

The doctor orders a CT scan; we wait anxiously for the results, talking about the outcome and how it may affect our lives. Ten days later, the doctor calls with encouraging news. All the tests came back negative, including the CT scan. There is no indication of any neurological disorder. He suggests that we write her problems off to stress and wait a few months to see if they recur. Relieved, Sue immediately takes his advice to heart. "At least it's not Alzheimer's disease, she says. Stress I can live with." Sue may be relieved, but I still feel a great deal of anxiety. I saw my mother-in-law go through similar episodes 15 years earlier.

July 8, 1989

Summer school is over. Sue and I take a short trip to Dubuque, Iowa, where her sister and brother-in-law live. Sue and Barb have always been very close, and it's been some time since we've had an opportunity to visit Barb and Jim overnight. In the morning, Sue gets up before I do and leaves the bedroom. Soon she returns.

"I can't find the bathroom."

I am startled. "Honey, it's right across the hall."

"It is?"

"Yes, it's right across the hall. Try again and see if you can find it."

She leaves and is gone at least another minute. I get out of bed and go into the hallway; she is wandering down the hall to the kitchen. "Sue, can't you find the bathroom?"

"No, is there one on this floor?"

"Yes, Honey, it's where it's always been, just down the hall." I take her down the hall and open the door to the bathroom.

"Yes, that's where it is. Now I remember."

I go back to our bedroom. I'm thinking, "Oh, my God, this is for real. It isn't stress, it's Alzheimer's."

How Sue is acting is precisely how her mother acted many years before. Her mother became forgetful and confused about where things were. This went on for a couple of years before it got to the point where people realized she was having serious problems.

We visit with Barb and Jim. I want to talk to them about Sue but I don't want to alarm them. I finally decide not to say anything; I'm not ready to accept the fact that my wife has such a serious disease. I also don't want to frighten Barb, who is only 15 months younger than Sue. Barb worries about developing dementia. My anxiety level is so high that my stomach is acidic and my intestines ache. These symptoms will become painfully familiar over the next few years.

On Sunday afternoon we leave Dubuque and go to White Pines State Park, a place we visited on our honeymoon. Bill, our son, is with us. Excited about going to this beautiful, wooded area, he is oblivious to anything out of the ordinary. On the drive to the park, I grow more and more anxious, although Sue seems quite at ease. That night I sleep fitfully, waking often, worrying about Sue.

On my morning run, images roll through my mind of what Sue's mother went through: her stay in a nursing home, her progressive forgetfulness and disorientation. "What am I going to tell the kids?" "How am I going to break this to them?" "What is going to happen to Sue?" "What is going to happen to me?" All in all, this weekend has been thoroughly frightening. It has left me concerned about my wife and emotionally devastated. I feel very alone because I know Sue does not want to talk about the possibility of having Alzheimer's disease and I'm not yet sure that she is sick.

When we arrive home, I walk into the house behind Sue watching for any sign of encroaching dementia. She seems alert, happy, and sure of where she is going. There is no evidence that anything is wrong. I continue to watch her for several days, constantly looking for some signs of dementia, but find little indication of it. At times she misplaces things, but she always finds them and is able to continue. She seems alert when talking with me, generally staying on the topic. Through the next few weeks, however, I notice that Sue will suddenly make a comment that seems to come out of nowhere—one that doesn't seem to connect to anything that's been happening or to anything we've been talking about. For instance, during a conversation about the alfalfa I am growing for our rabbits, she may inject a comment concerning an incident that took place with Barb when they were children, or something that happened with her roommate in college.

I desperately want to talk to Sue about my concerns, but she seems content and happy. I know that bringing up my fears will devastate her. Consequently, I despair in silence. Years from now, I will be glad that I didn't say anything because life will soon become a nightmare for her—and for all of us.

September 1989

I usually go to the university early, and so Sue continues taking Bill and Sarah to school in the morning and picking them up in the afternoon. This routine seems to be proceeding normally until my son says, "Mom has sure been acting weird lately."

"What do you mean?"

"She can't seem to find her way home. She gets lost all the time."

"What do you mean, she gets lost?"

"Well, she picks us up at school late. She says she can't get there because there's too much traffic, but we can see her driving around a block or two away. Finally, she'll get to the school and pick us up. Then on the way home she'll turn on the wrong street. A couple of times she's run a stop sign. We almost got hit the other day because she ran a stop sign right in front of a guy. She got mad at the guy, even though she ran the stop sign."

I don't want to deal with this information. "I think your mom is a bit preoccupied. Let me know if it continues."

Sarah comes to me with similar complaints. Sue has frightened her several times while driving. Sarah wants to know what's wrong with Mom, and why she is having such a difficult time driving. Again, I hesitate. "I am not sure, but I'll look into it."

Sue continues with many normal activities, a lot of cooking and baking—things she has always liked to do—and continues to read. She's always been an avid reader, but I notice that her reading rate has slowed down. She generally reads one or two books a week, but lately she continues to read the same book for three or four weeks. One day, I mention it. Later, I realize she is reading the same title again and again and again.

December 1989

The holidays are approaching and life is pretty happy, with the kids looking forward to Christmas. Sue is baking her usual assortment of goodies, but I notice that some of them don't taste quite right. Although I find this a little odd, I don't think too much of it. I find out why when Bill comes to me and says, "Mom was baking a cake yesterday and left some of the ingredients out. She's been doing that a lot lately. But when I tell her she is leaving things out, she gets mad at me and tells me to mind my own business." This is unlike Sue. She has always enjoyed having the children help her with cooking. The fact that she is getting angry with them bodes ill.

After Christmas, we decide to exchange some things at the mall. I remind Sue that she hasn't yet applied for her Iowa driver's license. She seems very reluctant to do so. I finally insist. Can Sue pass the exam? I think this will be a way to bring Sue's illness into the open if she is having problems. We drop her off at the exam center and come back 15 minutes later. We wait 45 minutes, an hour, an hour and 15 minutes. Worried, I decide to check on her. When I ask her how she is doing, she looks at me perplexed and in pain. "I can't answer these questions. They don't make any sense. I can't figure out the right answers."

With only two items to go, I encourage her to finish and she does. We learn that she has answered fewer than half of the questions correctly. I am stunned beyond belief. This woman was a national merit scholar in college. Until recently, she could do complex mathematics in her head and teach advanced chemistry classes! She has been driving for 20 years.

We are at home. She has little to say.

"Sue, what's on your mind?"

"I can't pass that exam. I'm going to lose my driver's license."

We have a long discussion that evening regarding Sue's fears. Not surprisingly, her concern about Alzheimer's disease emerges. "I'm afraid I've got this damned disease."

"Honey, it's possible, but let's not panic just yet."

"No, I've got it. I don't know what I'm going to do."

It is a very sad evening for both of us. We sit up through the night, talking about what may happen to her, what may lie ahead for both of us. The next morning I call the University of Iowa Department of Neurology and talk to Dr. Kuljis, who is involved with the Alzheimer's Information Network. He is very supportive and suggests that we come to Iowa City.

January 2, 1990

Sue and I get up early and drive three hours to Iowa City. Fortunately, Sarah is able to come with us. She is quite a comfort to Sue in her anxiety about this appointment. I also am glad to have Sarah along. I haven't slept much in the last couple of weeks.

The staff members at the Department of Neurology are excellent. They are used to working with Alzheimer's patients and are aware of our anxiety. Dr. Kuljis is especially respectful. He talks with Sue for a long time. It is obvious throughout the examination that she is having trouble with her memory. She becomes confused beyond the normal forgetfulness of aging.

While Sue is taking psychological exams, Sarah and I visit with Geri Hall, a nurse who works with families of Alzheimer's patients. She is extremely knowledgeable about Alzheimer's disease and is helpful in telling us what to expect. We talk for an hour. Much to my surprise, Sarah details more events that I have not been aware of, such as Sue's driving on the wrong side of the street and needing help in writing checks in the grocery store. Each time Geri asks a question about Sue's behavior, Sarah immediately answers, "Yes, my mom does that!"

Still in disbelief, I stop her at one point. "Sarah, are you sure?"

"Oh, yeah, we've been seeing this all fall. We have to call mom every day to remind her to come and get us."

I am in shock. I cannot believe that my wife is having all these problems and I say so. I also realize that I must not be the only spouse in my situation. Geri is reading my mind.

"This isn't surprising. Often Alzheimer's patients will hide their growing disability from their spouses because they are afraid to let others see what is happening to them."

With my mind much more open to the possibility of Sue's having this disease, I am now ready to look for the things my children have been talking about.

April 1990

We have been to Bethesda, Maryland, with the hope of participating in a research study on Alzheimer's disease, but the demands of the testing were too much for Sue. We are now spending endless hours talking about what is happening to her. These hours are tearful for her and anxious for me as we discuss what the future may bring. She confesses that she has been hiding her confusion from me, that she has been having difficulty remembering things, and that she has to write notes to remind herself what to do on a given day or during a given week. She even has to write notes to remind her where the notes are. It is increasingly difficult for her to manage the house. Sue wants to help but is unable to do much.

She has begun to show signs of clinical depression. She has difficulty sleeping and wakes up agitated. Her appetite is diminishing. She spends many, many hours just sitting there in despair or crying. Most of the time, I can comfort her and help her to get through her bouts of weeping. But as the weeks stretch into months, she grows more restless, more despondent, and more anxious. She starts to talk about wanting to die. This is a hard time for me. I have to comfort Sue through her depression and also keep myself together emotionally.

Comments about suicide become more frequent. Often she says, "You've married a dud. Nobody should have to be married to somebody like me. I'd be better off dead." I tell her how important she is to me and express my love and my desire for her to continue as part of my life. She doesn't want to hear optimistic words. She repeatedly asks me to help her commit suicide.

I came home from work one day to find Sue in the kitchen with a number of chemicals from her lab work spread on the table. "Sue, what are you doing?" Agitated, she looked at me and tried to remove the items. I took her into the living room to talk, to comfort her, and to get her to watch TV. I took the things she had on the table and hid them, figuring that she was trying to concoct a poison. Now I keep a close eye on her to make sure she does not harm herself.

May 1990

I'm on my morning run. I realize that I have moved from being my wife's spouse to being my wife's caregiver. Developmentally, Sue is a confused 15-year-old. She has to be helped to remember what needs to be done next in the day. I remind her to brush her teeth and to take a shower and tell her where to look for her clothes. She is still able to take care of her physical needs, but she has to have her day's activities laid out and be reminded of what to do next. She is mildly confused most of the time. I remember what Geri Hall told us in January. The stages of Alzheimer's disease are, first, *forgetfulness,* much like all of us experience as we grow older. This will eventually give way to *confusion,* which is distinguishable from forgetfulness because the patient not only forgets things, but becomes confused about what to do on a day-to-day basis. Eventually this leads to *ambulatory dementia* and then to *terminal dementia.*

As warmer weather comes, it seems to lift her spirits, as well as mine. I am becoming less anxious. I must be coming out of the initial shock of realizing that Sue is dying. I seem to be accepting the loss of my wife. Our children also are accepting the loss of their mother.

Cindy seems most affected by Sue's illness, probably because she is the oldest and has shared Sue's interest in science and math. Cindy and Sue would spend hours working on Cindy's homework. It is difficult for Cindy to lose her mother's emotional and intellectual support. However, Cindy is able to change roles as Sue's health fails.

Sarah deals with her mom's illness by looking to her friends for support. Sarah has always been very popular and has a well-developed social support system. Her boyfriend and his family are also very understanding and give Sarah shelter from the emotional stress at home.

Bill has always been closer to me than to his mother. Also, he was young, about 10, when his mother became symptomatic. In addition, he has always been very independent and intolerant of "mothering." Consequently, he has distanced from his mother as her symptoms have emerged.

We try to continue life as normally as possible. When Sue's roommate from college visited, Sue was delighted and enjoyed the visit tremendously. As they were leaving, the friend and her husband remarked on how fast Sue was deteriorating. I agreed. Through tears, they tried to be supportive. As I watched them drive down our lane, I realized that this was a new era. Dreading what was to come, I knew that the woman I'd been with for 20 years was no longer there.

I still try to keep us as busy as possible. During the summer, there will be ethnic celebrations and Old Threshers' Reunions. I'm an avid steam engine and antique tractor buff, so we'll go to as many different festivities as possible. As long as she is with me and we go only for the day, Sue seems content. But if we stay longer, she becomes agitated and wants to go home.

September 1990

Sue is complaining that she is lonesome and doesn't have anything to do. This is new behavior. Until now, she has seemed quite content to be home alone. Sue grows more disoriented. She usually stays at home now while I am at work. However, since she is more anxious when she is in the house alone, the children and I adjust our schedules so that there is always someone with her. For the most part, we succeed.

At times, I suggest that she do something outside the house, but she seems reluctant. She did attempt to work at a local greenhouse owned by a friend, but after a day refused to go back because the men were "looking at her funny." The men at the greenhouse weren't aware of her disability, but the two women she worked with were. They supported Sue, but she was unable to do even simple tasks, and it became an exercise in futility.

January 1991

I get in touch with some day care centers in Boone during the Christmas holidays. Sue has always loved small children, and I think that assisting at such a center might be helpful for her. I was referred to Theresa, who works with mentally retarded patients in a state hospital, including those with Alzheimer's. She offers to take Sue into her home while she sits with other people's children. We contact the parents of the children and explain the situation. As everybody agrees that it is worth trying, we approach Sue with the idea. We explain that Theresa has too many children to care for and wants to know if Sue would volunteer some time to help her. Sue is very excited at the possibility. I had taken this indirect approach because I did not want her to be offended that I was paying someone to care for her. Her pride and self-esteem has already suffered enough and my tactic helps Sue to save face.

The change has been a godsend for all of us. For the first time in a long time, Sue's spirits are lifted. She enjoys going to the day care center, and the children, who range in age from infancy to four years old, love her because she plays with them. They wait at the front door for Sue in the morning and hang onto her when we pick her up in the afternoon.

April 1991

Having Sue at Theresa's house has been helpful, but I have reached my emotional and physical limits. Sue's condition requires constant attention during the day, much of which Theresa provides at the day care center. But I am still left with 14 to 16 hours a day of caring for Sue at home. Our children do what they can to ease the burden. However, Sue is now my shadow, one step behind me and one step to my right at all times. It is very disconcerting to have someone constantly near you wherever you go in the house. I try to joke with her about it, but I am troubled nevertheless. The situation is becoming critical because she doesn't recognize our children.

"Are those our kids?"
"Yes, they are, Honey. That's Cindy, and Sarah, and Bill."
"Oh, that's right."
An hour or two later: "Who are those people in the other room?"
"Those are our children."
"Oh, that's right."

She becomes confused about the children and at times becomes mildly combative. They talk to her and remind her who they are, and then she backs off. Nonetheless, she has a particularly hard time recognizing our daughters and confuses Bill with me because we are about the same height and build. But if Bill speaks, she knows it is not me because his voice is higher than mine.

June 1991

Bill's voice has changed dramatically while Sue has continued to deteriorate, and she is having great difficulty telling us apart. Strangely, this helps make caring for Sue a little easier. Until now, I have been the only one who could get her to do things we want her to do. Bill now mimics what I do and can get Sue to follow his lead.

The confusion stage is moving to ambulatory dementia. Matters are particularly difficult for me because Sue is now hallucinating. She wakes me in the night and tells me there are people in the room. I turn on the lights, assure her there's no one there, and go around the room with her to show her that we are alone. She is satisfied and goes back to sleep for an hour, and then wakes me up again because she is frightened. I calm her down and she goes back to sleep for another hour, then wakes me up yet again.

For 27 days, I have had virtually no sleep. The human body is not designed to go that long without a good night's sleep. I've lost 20 pounds, have grown physically weak, and need medical assistance. My physician has prescribed medication that is helping me to sleep and allows me to go back to sleep after my wife wakes me up. I become so groggy from the medication that I do not wake up even when Sue is up walking or hallucinating.

August 1991

The medication is helping. I am able to regain my weight and my strength so I can continue to care for my wife. Sue has stopped hallucinating and is sleeping longer. Apparently she went through a change in brain function that led to the hallucinations and agitation. However, I am still extremely stressed, both physically and emotionally. Can I continue? I've started to think about placing my wife in a nursing home. I am torn between wanting to care for Sue and realizing that I cannot provide the care she needs. My children also need me as a parent.

Unlike last summer, Sue is now uncomfortable when not at home. I stay away only long enough to fulfill my duties at the university. Fortunately, my summer load is relatively light. However, the situation is getting to the point that I am going to have to make a move. After visiting nursing homes in the area, I have selected two homes with Alzheimer's units that I think can do a good job. I have put Sue on their waiting lists, hoping for an opening.

September 22, 1991

I awake at 3:30 in the morning to find Sue in a fetal position, moaning very loudly. I turn on the light and see that her eyes are rolled back in her head and that she is foaming at the mouth. She is having a grand mal seizure. I have seen seizure disorders before. I wake my son and ask him to call 911 because the seizure is quite severe. The ambulance arrives as she finally begins to regain consciousness. In total, her seizure lasts between 8 and 10 minutes. The emergency technicians help me take her to the hospital. Luckily, it is Monday, the day a neurologist visits our community hospital, and he gives Sue a full workup. By noon he calls me aside. "Your wife needs a nursing facility. You cannot care for her at home."

We take Sue home that day. By nightfall, I can see the neurologist is right. Sue has lost most of her remaining mental ability. She is completely disoriented, and does not know who or where she is, who I am, or who the children are. She later regains some of her ability, recognizing me and responding to my directives. However, I must help her with everything—to go to the bathroom, to take a shower, to get dressed. It is clear I have to do something soon. We are all exhausted. Sue no longer can go to the day care center, and when I bring women in to help, she will not tolerate their presence.

October 8, 1991

I go to work in the morning, leaving Sue with Cindy and a friend, Judy. At about 10:30, Cindy calls. "I can't handle Mom. She knocked me down and she knocked Judy down." Every time they approach Sue, she strikes at them violently. I immediately leave for home. A plasterer had been doing some repair work in our kitchen. This upset Sue. By the time I arrive, Sue is pacing and screaming. Cindy keeps her occupied while I call the nursing homes. The first has no opening and can't help me. The second has an opening and was about to call to see if I wanted to place Sue. If there is such a thing as divine intervention, it happened at this moment. It's hard to believe the home has an opening. Generally, Alzheimer's units in this area have very long waiting lists. But this unit has an opening and no one else on the list is ready to take advantage of it.

This is the most difficult day of my life. The children and I explain to Sue what is going to happen and why we can't care for her any longer. We tell her we are going to take her to a place where she can be cared for. She seems to be somewhat aware of what we are saying. She sees that we are upset. Everybody is crying. Sue probably picks up on the nonverbal communication as much as on the verbal because she starts to cry as well.

I talk with her for an hour. Finally, she agrees to go with us. We pack her belongings and take her to the nursing facility, which is about 15 miles away. She is calm and content on the way. She has always enjoyed rides in the country and it's a beautiful day. The nursing home is run by the Lutheran church. On the way into the facility, she asks, "Are we going to church?"

"No, Honey, this isn't a church, but it's run by the church."

"Oh, it's a Catholic church?"

"Honey, it's a Catholic home."

Sue has always been devoutly religious so I let her believe that it is a Catholic facility. I operate out of her reality to minimize confusion and anxiety.

When we arrive, a social worker meets us and takes us up to the unit. We walk into the unit and take Sue down the hall. As we walk, she realizes what is happening. We reach the room and unpack her bag. Sue turns to me and says, "I don't want to be here."

"Sue, you have to. I can't take care of you at home any more. You'll have to stay here." This is a terrible time for us. Both of us are crying, and Sarah is crying. Cindy, although she is upset, seems to handle the situation better than the rest of us. The social worker suggests that I leave while they keep Sue in the room. Cindy stays with her mother, talking to her long enough for Sarah and me to go. We wait outside.

I feel absolutely miserable. I have just left my wife in a place in which she does not want to be. I have just separated myself from the person to whom I have been very attached for 23 years, the person most central in my life. I say to the nurse, "What have I done? I can't do this to her."

The social worker is very supportive. "I know you love your wife, and if you love her, you will do this. You will leave her here because it's not right for you to take her home." Without that support and firmness, I would probably take Sue back home. The worker's determination allows me to go home without her.

On the trip back to Boone, Cindy drives, and Sarah sits with me in the back seat of the car. In the evening, several of my graduate students show up and say we are going to party. I look at them as though they are crazy because I have just left my wife in a nursing home! One of the young men is related to my wife. He knows what I have been going through because he went through the same thing with his father. They insist that I accompany them. Finally I go, thinking it crazy.

It is the best thing I could have done. We go to a local pizza parlor, sit, and talk. I eat something and have a beer with these guys. I haven't had a drop of alcohol in two years. My anxiety in dealing with Alzheimer's simply has resulted in a constantly acidic stomach, and the thought of alcohol has not appealed to me. But the beer this night tastes pretty good. It takes enough of the edge off my anxiety that I am able to fall asleep when I get home and I do not wake for 10 hours. For two weeks, I sleep 12 to 14 hours a day. I am so physically exhausted that my body needs this much time to restore itself.

I call a couple of times every day to see how Sue is doing, but the people at the nursing home discourage me from visiting. They want my wife to bond to this environment and are afraid that my visit will undo the progress they have made. When I finally do visit two weeks later, Sue is very angry with me and chases me off the ward. Surprisingly, her reaction does not bother me as much as I thought it would. The nursing staff had prepared me by warning that Alzheimer's patients are often angry with their families when first placed. Their anger is easily understood; they feel abandoned and alone.

Within six weeks, Sue adjusts. Specialists in Iowa City alert me to the fact that I placed Sue just in time. Doing so any later would have made it difficult for her to bond to the environment. I am thankful that the space opened for her when it did.

October 22, 1993

I have just returned from visiting Sue. It has been two years since I placed her. Her health has deteriorated tremendously. She sleeps most of each day. When she is awake, she sits in a chair and stares. I sat in front of her, talked to her, but received no response. Her eyes did track with me momentarily. The large doses of antiseizure medication leave her muscles wooden. Without it, she would be convulsing often. She cannot stand alone and must be lifted into her chair or bed. Her life expectancy is hard to determine but probably won't exceed one or two years. This terminal dementia stage begins when the patient is no longer able to move about. Ultimately, vital systems fail. Many victims die of pneumonia before this occurs.

Sue signed a living will three years ago to avoid prolonging her life. I want to keep her as comfortable as possible, but I have no intention of delaying the inevitable. I am preparing myself to make future decisions. There will be hard questions to answer. Do I have fluids and food withheld when she can no longer eat? Do I have her treated for infections that could be fatal? I know what I plan to do but actually doing it is another matter.

When I visit Sue, I no longer feel the sense of anguish that haunted me the first few months after placing her. Anguish has been replaced with numb sadness while I'm with her. This lifts when I leave. My children occasionally make comments about Sue as they deal with their sense of loss. To us, it feels as though she has already died. I have decided not to push the children to talk about their feelings; rather, I make myself available to listen if they choose to talk.

At times I wonder what Sue's funeral will be like for me. Will I be overcome with grief? I don't think so. Have I finished the grief process? I think

I have. Have I changed as a result of this experience? Most definitely! Despite the pain of losing Sue, I think I am a stronger person emotionally because of what I've been through.

Sue died on February 27, 1994. I was with her at the time and was relieved that she died peacefully in her sleep. The funeral was a more difficult experience than I thought it would be, but I recovered quickly. My children are doing well and continue to be a source of support for me and for each other. I welcome the opportunity to talk with others who are dealing with Alzheimer's disease. Periodically, I get calls from strangers who have been given my name by the Alzheimer's Association. Talking to them helps me deal with my own feelings and gives me the satisfaction of helping someone else.

I

FAMILY THERAPY AND LATER LIFE

1

Integrating the Process of Aging and Family Therapy

Suzanne Midori Hanna, Ph.D.
University of Louisville
Louisville, Kentucky

Terry D. Hargrave, Ph.D.
Amarillo College
Amarillo, Texas

The process of aging does not happen in a vacuum. Every family is connected to the aging process. Some family members experience it as they care for their eldest members because of some problem such as Alzheimer's disease or stroke. Some elders experience aging as they struggle to care for younger generations, providing financial assistance, housing, or child care. Still others experience aging as they view the legacy of past generations, watching as their families proceed through life in similar ways.

Traditionally, family therapy has given attention to the intergenerational family, but it has not really focused on the process of aging. Some founders of the family therapy movement based their approaches on intergenerational relationships (i.e., Bowen, 1978; Framo, 1981; Boszormenyi-Nagy, 1987a). More recently, Williamson (1991) stressed personal authority in the family of origin as an issue in successful adult development. However, these perspectives centered on the challenges of the middle or youngest generation,

only referencing the oldest generation in explaining current behav
emotional process in the family.

In family therapy literature, there are volumes devoted to individ
and launching; very little is directed toward later-life issues. Flori
reported that less than 10 percent of articles in leading family therap
nals focused on later-life concerns, with no trend toward a linear ir
over time. Furthermore, her analysis of clinically oriented articles re
that their emphasis was on the concerns of mid-life adults, followed by
of youth, and then those of elders. Similarly, in 1993 only three worl
at the American Association for Marriage and Family Therapy A
Conference concentrated on aging issues (Sprenkle & Bischof, 1994)
recently, Herr and Weakland (1979) were lone voices in family ther
they developed a strategic therapy for older adults and their families.
tually, Carter and McGoldrick (1989) also looked specifically at the s
and problems facing the family in later stages of the life cycle. In th
view of the literature, Richardson, Gilleard, Lieberman, and Peeler
indicate an increase in interventions for the aging family. Howevei
also note a great need for outcome research on treatment models dev
for older families.

Given that members of the younger generations are those most
seeking family therapy services, the relative lack of attention given to
of aging is not surprising. However, the pattern may also relate to the
practitioners. Family therapy in later life is about how the *therapist*
to later life, not just the family. For the field to fully stretch its applic
across all families, professionals must address their biases derived fro
sonal experience, their own aging process, and societal messages that p
uate myths about elders. Family theories of problems and solution
submit to the lens of elder sensitivity as part of theoretical refineme

Similar critiques of the field have helped family therapists to rec
dilemmas within families that stem from issues of gender, race, and c
Using each of these as a lens, family therapists have been able to a
important clinical challenges while respecting a wide array of ind
differences. As gender-sensitive and race-sensitive views were advanc
nicians were free to debate and to disagree, but once the issues were
things were never quite the same. As a result of this social process, clin
have been able to expand their ways of working with specific popu
and, in the process, have improved their models to the benefit of all

With respect to families in later life, there are dilemmas, challeng
opportunities that are unique to this developmental stage. However
practitioners are unaware of the issues, much in the same way as the
were prior to the opening up of dialogues about gender and race. As
graphics shift dramatically toward an older population, family rese
and clinicians now must become acquainted with and knowledgeable

Integrating the Process of Aging and Family Therapy 21

an aging cohort. Without this understanding, theories of family therapy will remain developmentally biased toward a point of view rooted in early stages of the life cycle. To evolve a field of family therapy that accounts for all corners of society (that is, all points of view within the system), practitioners must show that their applications are effective with older populations and sensitive to their concerns.

This book is intended to expand the trickle of dialogue that now exists on these issues. The remainder of this chapter outlines the "culture" of aging, those dilemmas and challenges specific to later life; those attributes of later-life families that put many mainstream family therapists to the test. In looking at the issues of this cultural group, elder sensitivity across all family therapy approaches can be assessed. Such examination helps the field to identify myths and disrupt stereotyping. It also becomes a catalyst for integration, as various models provide useful pieces of the final mosaic. Finally, consideration of these issues reveals the need for one piece of the clinician's mosaic to include the basics of gerontology. Such integration is similar to work by family therapists who have successfully addressed the problems of younger populations (i.e., addictions, anorexia nervosa, schizophrenia). After learning the basics about drug abuse or schizophrenia, these innovators integrated systemic thinking with traditional work to develop treatment approaches for specific populations. It is with a similar intent that this chapter proceeds. The time has come to integrate mainstream family therapy approaches with concerns of later life.

THE CULTURE OF AGING

It is important to remember that intergenerational families are changing even while family therapists are *learning* about them. This century has witnessed a dramatic increase in the generations that make up the family. Medical advances in combatting disease, increased longevity, and a general population increase have made four and five *living* generations a common phenomenon. As families approach the next century, intergenerational groups, with their corresponding problems and resources, are true pioneers as they learn to adapt to the new experiences called *family*. In turn, family therapists must pioneer new methodologies and discover ways of thinking that will help the changing family use their stresses to develop new strengths.

Anderson and Hargrave (1990) describe how a hypothetical five-generation family might look in the future:

> The 95-year-old great great grandmother has outlived her husband and many of her friends. She now faces the last stage of life and its ultimate challenge—letting go. Her 75-year-old widowed daughter

is dealing with caring for her 95-year-old mother and her own need for independence. The daughter must deal with such questions as, "Where should I live?," "When do I have to give up my driver's license?," "Am I still an adult, even though my 50-year-old-daughter has to provide some care for me?" The 50-year-old daughter, in turn, faces many challenges: helping her own adult children separate and establish themselves in occupations and homes, caring for her 75-year-old mother, working with her husband to prepare for retirement, and dealing with repressed sibling issues that tend to surface at this time. The 25-year-old son or daughter is looking for help to get started in life as he or she nurtures small children, attempts to purchase a home, and wonders how he or she will be able to support the growing number of elderly. Finally, the young children of the fifth generation watch the intergenerational processes and absorb, albeit silently, the profound lessons being manifested across the five generations. (p. 311)

Although this is not yet the norm, many contemporary families are already facing challenges of age not known to previous generations.

Traditionally, elders have been served by physicians, clergy, and social workers—those who are not trained primarily in psychotherapy. In service networks today, expertise continues to weigh in heavily on the side of advocacy and case management, rather than in the realm of clinical skills. Thus, family therapists are not easily found in areas that serve elders. When family therapists do begin treating problems from an elder perspective, issues related to loss, illness, roles, and legacy quickly challenge the utility of any single approach.

Changing Family Roles

Carter and McGoldrick (1989) point out that the launching-of-children stage, or middle adulthood, is perhaps one of the most challenging of the family life cycle. The family must renegotiate the marital dyad, develop adult relationships with children, create new relationships with in-laws and grandchildren, and care for their older members. At the same time, late adulthood requires the ability to function in spite of physiological decline. With younger generations, the task is to assume a position of support. This gradual change in family roles can be facilitated by increased communication and negotiation in the family unit. Most families negotiate this transition well, and older adults most often see their adult children as friends (Blieszner & Mancini, 1987).

With these changing roles also comes additional caregiving responsibilities for younger generations. These family members often underestimate the strain of caregiving as frailty in the elder increases. Consequently, some families do not organize themselves sufficiently to share the burden evenly. Among the caregiving issues that face an aging family are emotional coping; time management; relationship problems with spouses, children, and siblings; responding adequately to the emotional, physical, and financial needs of the elder; eliciting support; resolving feelings of guilt and inadequacy; and planning for the future (Smith, Smith, & Toseland, 1991). Caregivers experience more physical and emotional illness, they age prematurely, and they experience a lower level of life satisfaction (Johnson, 1988). In addition, the frail elderly do not like being dependent on their children (Myers, 1989). As a result, where caregiving is a major component of interaction, an aging family often experiences more interpersonal conflict and negative affect (Sheehan & Nuttall, 1988).

It is a popular societal belief that caregiving in the family leads to a "role reversal" with adult children and their older parents. However, Seltzer (1990) points out the negative implications of this concept—that older people experience a second childhood and should be treated like children. Even though older people may have some of the same physical needs as children, Brody (1990) maintains that adult offspring never become parents to their parents. Older adults should retain the respect and dignity of adulthood. Love for a parent should be different from the love one experiences for a child. Instead of a reversal, these transitions can be thought of as the reciprocity that evolves and completes family process through the life cycle. Family members care for each other in different ways at different stages in the life cycle.

Another important aspect of changing roles relates to gender dfferences and aging. Research shows that as women and men age, they become more androgynous in their gender roles. Women become more assertive and men become more accommodating (Gutmann, 1977). In addition, women live nearly six years longer than do men and are most often left without a partner or peer during their final stages of life. Sometimes the roles they assume evolve developmentally from the loss of complementarity they had known with a mate. They may develop new skills to compensate for the loss or they may feel isolated and incomplete. When working with families during such transitions, practitioners must view conflicts and the position of each family member in light of these changes over time, not solely in the present context. This is an area where gender-sensitive therapy can encourage greater flexibility and growth for all family members. In addition, it is important to remember that women constitute the majority of older people; thus, social services are often tailored to women and may overlook the needs of older men.

Later-Life Losses

An aging individual lives long enough to experience loss in many areas of life: death of a spouse, relatives, or close friends; loss of job and social status; diminished physical health; reduced income and standard of living; and the eminent fact of losing one's own life (Hargrave & Anderson, 1992). The accumulation of these losses, where grief over one issue is mixed with the grief over another, often results in a "bereavement overload" (Kastenbaum, 1977) where none of the issues can be resolved adequately. In our youth-focused society, there is little support for the aging person who experiences grief over loss. There is a tendency to isolate the older person by avoiding any talk about sadness and death. Therefore, the older family member is left alone with much of this grief (Butler & Lewis, 1991).

Another emotional issue closely associated with aging is the possible feeling of guilt. As an older person tries to consolidate his or her life meaning across the life span, it is quite common for the person to experience feelings of guilt and despair associated with lost opportunities, past failings, and circumstances that caused pain (Erikson, Erikson, & Kivnick, 1986). These feelings of guilt may cause an older person to drift into a state of hopelessness (Erikson, 1982), but they also can be used successfully to integrate past life experiences with the meaning of one's existence (Butler, 1963).

Such issues can greatly influence individual and family functioning as aging progresses. They can also combine with loneliness, fear, and isolation to produce severe emotional trauma and depression for some elders. However, it is not clear whether or not depression becomes more common with age since few studies include adults over the age of 70 (Newmann, 1989). In studies where older adults were included, increased age was not a correlate of depression (Lieberman, 1983). However, many of the life events associated with aging are significant precursors to depression, such as significant loss (Lieberman, 1983), less social support (Holahan & Holahan, 1987), loss of control over their environment (Maiden, 1987), and poor physical health (Jarvik, 1983). Most disturbing is the emotional trauma associated with the high rate of suicide among the elderly. At least one fourth of the suicides in the United States are committed by the elderly. White males are most at risk (Butler & Lewis, 1982). In addition, people over 65 are more than twice as likely to succeed in their suicide attempts. Practitioners must become acquainted with such risk factors in order to conduct competent assessments.

Chronic Illness

Physical health has a tremendous impact on the human condition and the function of the family. Perceptions of self, role maintenance, and living conditions are all somewhat dependent on health. At the turn of the century, most illnesses experienced by the aging population were classified as *terminal*. The advances of medicine throughout this century have greatly expanded the average life span and now most illnesses experienced by the elderly are *chronic*. Although a very small percentage of older people require long-term institutionalization for their health problems, over 86 percent experience chronic health problems that require health services and caregiving for daily needs by family members (Zarit & Zarit, 1982).

The need for more regular medical service is a significant characteristic of an aging culture. With its specialized language and protocols, the field of medicine can be thought of as a professional subculture in our society. Elders become inducted into this world through their increased needs, and they must learn to cope with the combination of benefits and deficits that accompanies medical settings, services, and procedures. Any critique of the medical profession would include an analysis of those aspects that can be disempowering for patients and their families, sometimes unintentionally robbing them of their sense of self-determination. With older people, this issue of disempowerment emerges because of developmental circumstances initially, but it can be compounded by the increase in medical services.

Chronic illnesses experienced by older people can also result in a loss of control and independence. Since maintaining a sense of personal control is one of the primary factors in life satisfaction among the elderly (Thomae, 1985), significant emotional stress can result from its loss. Chronic illnesses become a major factor influencing one's ability to live independently, often signaling the onset of major caregiving roles for the family. In addition, many younger family members may view the chronic illness of an elder as a problem they wish to avoid, rather than as a normative change to which all families must adjust. Thus, some loss of relationship may result as they cope with stress through increased distancing.

Chronic illness and its impact on the family also bring up serious ethical concerns. In a case where chronic illness incapacitates an elder member, when and how much of the family's emotional and fiscal resources should be contributed to prolonging life? Is it appropriate for an older person to consider physician-assisted suicide when there is little chance of recovery? When is it appropriate for the family to take over the decision-making process for the elder? These are but a few of the questions that the aging family will face when an elder is afflicted with serious illness.

Intergenerational Legacies

Every family has a sense of tradition and history, a heritage that each member can claim or reject. This heritage is the sense of identity that evolves from shared history and contributions made by each member. As death nears, family members either accept that life will go on through younger generations or they become rigid in the denial of death. If the response is denial, ineffectual roles may lead to unresolved issues that linger after death. Peck (1968) views this issue from the older person's perspective as negotiating *ego transcendence versus ego preoccupation*. When a person transcends ego, he or she realizes the worth of the intergenerational family and tries to pass on the elements of his or her wisdom to the younger generation as a legacy. Most older people contribute to the family by offering care, guidance, and nurturance to the younger generation (Erikson, Erikson, & Kivnick, 1986). On the other hand, ego preoccupation indicates that the older person does not see the value of his or her contribution toward meeting the needs of younger family members. Most grandparents see their grandchildren as extensions of themselves and as an expression of immortality (Timberlake, 1980).

The entire intergenerational group participates in the giving and receiving of legacies. Hargrave and Anderson (1992) view the time near death as one of the best opportunities for the family to settle old issues, resolve wounds, and develop love and trust. They suggest that the responsibility for such issues should be shared with the entire intergenerational family. When this happens, younger members have the opportunity to affirm their family legacies in some areas and to negotiate change with elders in other areas. As each generation develops acceptance of the other's position, intergenerational reconciliation takes place.

The transition to multiple family forms in our society serves as a challenge and a resource for developing intergenerational legacies. Multiple marriages and blended families may blur a family's ability to determine responsibility for caretaking, sibling contribution, and resolution of family problems. However, these new family configurations may also function as the tribes and communities of past eras, making more members available to share the burdens and blessings. With couples surviving much longer after the departure of children, there may also be more divorces and second marriages (Hargrave & Anderson, 1992). With these options, new issues come to the fore, such as visitation of grandparents, reactions of adult children to new marriages, questions of inheritance, and the adjustment to additional family members when previous emotional difficulties may be still unresolved.

These issues have already begun to change the culture of aging in our society. From debates on health care for elders to prenuptial agreements in later-life marriages, this generation is becoming a pioneering generation. As the experience of this culture gradually falls upon baby boomers, aging issues will have increasing influence on our society as a whole and on marital and family therapists specifically.

FAMILY THERAPY AS ELDER-SENSITIVE THERAPY

If taken one by one, early approaches to family therapy have some disadvantages when working with later-life families. For example, Structural Family Therapy tends to ignore longitudinal changes over time with a family, thus ignoring historical factors that play heavily into the development of legacies. Bowenian Family Therapy does not offer enough pragmatic thinking to intervene in crises brought on by chronic illness. Behavioral Family Therapy does not have a framework for addressing the phenomenology of losses experienced by elders. Experiential Family Therapy may be too direct for some families who prefer to cope with changing family roles in silent, persevering ways.

However, if these models of family therapy are grouped according to common elements, there is great collective value in what they offer. A review of concepts from these approaches reveals how the models view family process but not necessarily how they view the actual process of problem resolution. Nevertheless, if these concepts are examined separately from technique, traditional approaches to family therapy can be grouped as political, behavioral, or psychodynamic, with several approaches falling into more than one category, but none actually transcending all three.

Political Approaches

Approaches in this category include Structural, Strategic, Bowenian, and Contextual models of family therapy (Minuchin & Fishman, 1981; Haley, 1987; Bowen, 1978; Boszormenyi-Nagy, 1987). Although their intervention strategies are very different, all share an emphasis on family organization related to interpersonal boundaries (closeness/distance) among members and hierarchical responsibilities between generations. These issues of involvement, responsibility, power, and meaning are ultimately political in nature. Kantor and Lehr (1975) referred to the "psychopolitics" of the family, describing the interplay between family system issues and personal issues in family transactions. These models of family therapy strive to identify similar phenomena, though their language may be different.

Approaches that focus on structure or politics in the family help older families to address changing family roles in insightful ways. Some families may benefit from the pragmatics of structural-strategic approaches in adjusting to new roles, whereas others may gain from the thoughtful analysis of a Bowenian. Regardless of the style, all families are influenced by their own politics and clinicians must take these into account when developing workable strategies for change.

Behavioral Approaches

This category includes Behavioral, Structural, Strategic, and Mental Research Institute (MRI) related models of family therapy (Falloon, 1988; Minuchin & Fishman, 1981; Madanes, 1981; Weakland, Fisch, Watzlawick, & Bodin, 1974). For these models, data gathering must always include an emphasis on consequences of behavior among people and a description of interactions related to problems or solutions. These models have historically avoided any focus on past dynamics and have developed a variety of options that are problem-specific and direct in addressing a family's view of the problem. They are valuable for problem solving around the crises of chronic illness when introspection and analysis are not helpful. They help families to address the current problem in practical ways, to restore order in a brief period of time, and to develop plans for managing complex situations.

Psychodynamic Approaches

Models in this category focus on individual phenomenology within the family system and the impact of relational dynamics on family members' development. Models that have a stronger emphasis on psychodynamic information include Psychoanalytic, Bowenian, Contextual, and Experiential models of family therapy (Bowen, 1978; Boszormenyi-Nagy, 1987; Williamson, 1991; Whitaker & Keith, 1981; Satir, 1988).

Psychodynamic approaches provide a framework for helping families address the losses of seniors and the legacies they desire to leave. There are many issues between generations related to changes in the family over time. Such changes, rooted in history, affect the way family members think and feel about each other. Most approaches that address psychodynamic issues encourage intergenerational acceptance and empathy. They foster growth and development of individual family members and encourage the reconciliation of past differences.

In working with older families, attention to political, behavioral, and psychodynamic elements of the context is important. As underscored here, early approaches focused on one or two of these categories, but none of them alone was broad based enough to incorporate all three. It may have been because of this that constructivists began to integrate elements across models during the postmodern era. In clinical work with the elderly, a review of the literature reveals a pattern of integration in which practitioners simultaneously address two or three of these basic elements.

FAMILY THERAPY AND AGING: INTEGRATIVE TRENDS

Contemporary models of family therapy draw from multiple models to fit specific populations. These integrative models represent creative innovations that bypass many limitations of the early models. Those that have been developed with an aging population are sensitive to the issues of family roles, losses, legacies, and illnesses. They can be categorized as problem-solving, developmental, and educational approaches.

Problem-Solving Approaches

As mentioned before, Herr and Weakland (1979) were the first to make systemic therapy applications to the aging family. Their approach, like most problem-solving therapies, came out of the Mental Research Institute (MRI) tradition. The MRI approach to therapy focused on how problems were "maintained" by families through interactions and communications. Through intervening behaviorally, the MRI approach facilitated modification and change in the family (Segal, 1991). Most of these changes in the family fell under the rubric of *second-order change,* or modifications in the boundaries, alignments, power hierarchies, and relational level that are part of the basic organization of the system (Watzlawick, Weakland, & Fisch, 1974).

The MRI approach and later strategic family therapies centered on such interventions as reframing, jamming, and paradoxical injunctions, which made the necessary second-order changes so "symptoms" or problems experienced by the family became unnecessary or difficult to maintain (i.e., Fisch, Weakland, & Segal, 1983; Haley, 1986; Madanes, 1984). Bepko (1984) described strategic interventions with a demanding and unpleasant older person in an institution. Other models utilized strategic interventions to treat depression and conflict (Eisenberg & Carrilio, 1990; Bogo, 1987; Ratna & Davis, 1984).

In a similar approach, the Brief Family Therapy Center proposed a therapeutic focus that was not concerned with problems or complaints and how they were maintained, but rather with what resources and solutions made the problem better (deShazer, 1982). This approach of "doing more of what works and less of what doesn't" generated a model of solution-focused brief therapy. The model has been widely applied to different situations and problems, including alcoholism, adolescent difficulties, marital issues, and depression. Bonjean (see Chapter 4) has applied the model to aging individuals and families facing a variety of problems, including managing care for Alzheimer's patients, living transitions, grief due to multiple losses, and problems associated with chronic illness.

Other therapeutic approaches are reported that do not come out of a traditional MRI, strategic, or solution-focused model, but try to behaviorally confront and change specific problems associated with aging. These approaches deal with a variety of aging problems, including depression (McQuellon & Reifler, 1989; Blazer & Siegler, 1981), death and grief (Carni, 1989; Williams, 1989), alcoholism (Rathbone-McQuan & Hedlund, 1989), caregiver stress (Brody, 1985; Dobson & Dobson, 1985; Duffy, 1984), dementia (Gwyther & Blazer, 1984), and suicide prevention (Osgood, 1989).

Developmental Approaches

The developmental approaches to family therapy have derived their theoretical base from developmental life-cycle models (Carter & McGoldrick, 1989; Falicov, 1988) or existing family-of-origin theories (i.e., Framo, 1992; Boszormenyi-Nagy, 1987; Williamson, 1981). Like problem-solving approaches, these models have sought to alleviate stress in the family by (1) realigning structure and power in the family, (2) understanding family system development, and (3) improving relational bonds among family members and the intergenerational group as a whole. Carter and McGoldrick's (1989) seminal work on the family developmental life cycle outlined six stages of development. Their model discussed not only the key emotional process that organized transactions in the family, but also key transitional tasks to be achieved at each stage. Walsh (1989) was among the first to discuss the implications of later-life developmental transitions, such as retirement, grandparenthood, and retirement, in a therapeutic context. Benbow et al. (1990) expanded the final stage from Carter and McGoldrick's model and used it to focus on resources, transitions, adaptive capacities, and generational support in helping older individuals negotiate change.

Hanna (1986, 1995) uses the developmental-interactional model (DIM) to conceptualize aging problems and to facilitate change. The DIM combines intervention strategies from structural and strategic therapies while exploring life-cycle development, past relationships, and family resources (see Chapter 5). In a similar vein, Jerrome (1994) uses the developmental history of the family and the social history of different cohorts in society to understand elderly parents and their adult children, moving them in therapy toward closer emotional bonding.

Integrating the Process of Aging and Family Therapy

One of the key components of developmental models that have been based on existing family-of-origin theory is not only to relieve immediate family distress, but also to work to build intergenerational harmony for family members. In these therapies, much of the therapeutic emphasis with the aging family is on gaining strength and appreciation for the family as the older person and younger generations transition into such changes as moving, caretaking, and death. Many of these approaches utilize the therapeutic technique of life review (Butler, 1963) to access history with the older adult and pass along the story to younger generations. Besides engaging the older person in verbal reminiscence, several creative approaches have been used in life review therapy, including plays and dramas (Kaminsky, 1984), audiotaping (Myers, 1988), and video (Hargrave, 1994). Wolinsky (1990) utilizes life review and past history in marital therapy with older couples.

Several models use the family past in guiding interventions with the aging group. Quigley and Womphrey (1988) employ past history to foster understanding between elder and caretaker and prevent possible elder abuse. McEwan (1987) reports on resolving long-term issues in the intergenerational family utilizing a contextual family therapy model (Boszormenyi-Nagy, 1987) as do Jones and Flickinger (1987). The contextual model has also been used to rectify long-standing issues of perceived imbalance and violations of trust and justice in the family (Hargrave & Anderson, 1990, 1992; Anderson & Hargrave, 1990). These authors use a three-stage therapy model of life validation, life review, and intervention to achieve a therapeutic end in the family. This model is presented in detail in Chapter 3.

Family therapists may address developmental issues by encouraging younger generations to focus on these issues with their elders or by working with elders to address these issues with their children. Rather than encouraging further introspection or distance, family therapists are in a unique position to utilize significant relationships as a context for achieving personal integrity for individual family members.

Educational Approaches

Much of the work with aging families has been designed to educate them concerning the stresses and impacts that aging forces on the group and then provide information and direction concerning support to mediate the impact. Most educational approaches primarily focus on increasing knowledge and skill among caregivers, providing direction on accessing community and social services, and easing family emotional stress during transitions and loss (Myers, 1988). These approaches are usually problem or group specific, such as education and support for caregivers of Alzheimer's or dementia patients (e.g., Zarit, Anthony, & Boutselis, 1987; Lazarus, Stafford,

Cooper, Cohler, & Dysken, 1981), dealing with caregiver conflict and emotional strain (e.g., Sheehan & Nuttall, 1988; Dobson & Dobson, 1985; Hartford & Parsons, 1982), or managing transition to a long-term care facility (e.g., Rodway, Elliot, & Sawa, 1987).

The stress and impact of aging can be most profound when an aging member has Alzheimer's disease. Caregiver depression is of special interest in connection with Alzheimer's. Shields (1992) relates that negative affective responses from the family are significant predictors of caregiver depression. Other predictors of caregiver depression have been found in the way caregivers deal with boundary issues (Boss, Caron, Horbal, & Mortimer, 1990). In addition, caregiver and family burden in caring for an Alzheimer's elder has been the subject of several articles (Barber, 1988, 1993; Barber, Fisher, & Pasley, 1990). Finally, Boss, Caron, and Horbal (1988) deal with caregiver grief issues in dealing with the ambiguous loss of a family member with Alzheimer's disease.

Although a few of the educational approaches have been directed to individual families (e.g., Banks, Ackerman, & Clark, 1986; Blazer & Siegler, 1981; Gwyther & Blazer, 1984), most work in this area reflects effort directed at several families in a group that share common problems (Richardson et al., 1994). Caron has developed a family group approach to assist the elder and the family in the transition to an institutional care facility. In this approach, the family members work in groups to define important life characteristics that will help the institution grasp some of the personhood and dignity of the elder while at the same time helping the family support and appreciate the elder's contribution to the family. His approach is discussed in detail in Chapter 11.

Like many other medical and therapeutic modalities, family therapy has recast its models to include medical considerations along with those that are social and psychological. This multidimensional approach to treating the individual and family has come to be known as the biopsychosocial model (McDaniel, Hepworth, & Doherty, 1992). The application of the biopsychosocial model to aging individuals and the family has been the subject of several articles and books (i.e., Butler, Lewis, & Sunderland, 1991; Engel, 1980). Since a significant percentage of the aged population experiences chronic illness (Hargrave & Anderson, 1992), many of the applicable models of treatment come from this chronic illness research. Most notably, Rolland's (1987) work details a topology for chronic illness using factors to describe psychosocial consequences of an illness. These illness factors include the *onset* of the illness, the expected *course* of the illness, the practical and physical *outcome* of the illness with regard to a person's ability to function, and the *time phase* of the illness.

Educational approaches make good sense heuristically because of the application of interventions and services to specific stresses and problems. These approaches also involve emotional support of the aging group from people who care about and understand the complexity of the problems they face. In addition, educational approaches offer aging families an opportunity to be enlightened about the challenges of aging so they can anticipate and prevent problems from overwhelming the group. In some cases, there have been outcome measures applied that reflect increases among caregivers in morale and knowledge (e.g., Whitlach, Zarit, & Eye, 1991; Gilleard, 1990). However, there is a lack of the family-oriented research that is needed to determine the long-term effects of such group work in helping the family cope with the problems and challenges of aging (Richardson, Gilleard; Lieberman, & Peeler, 1994).

As a group, problem-solving, developmental, and educational approaches represent the first wave of family therapy innovations on behalf of older adults and their families. They are pragmatic and relevant. They address political, behavioral, and psychodynamic aspects of the aging process. In addition, some are sensitive to larger system issues that interact as services outside the family are needed. However, if one were to look at the field in general, there is no question that contemporary approaches to family therapy are turning more toward integrations that incorporate constructivist thinking and indirect narrative techniques (Todd & Selekman, 1991). These are areas that need to be developed on behalf of aging families.

CONCLUSION

The terrain of aging presents a complex and powerful opportunity to the family therapy field. This complexity requires the field to address changing family roles, later-life losses, intergenerational legacies, and chronic illnesses through models that address political, behavioral, and psychodynamic issues. The power of such an opportunity can be understood in light of early systemic thinking, which acknowledged that families were groups of people whose relationships implied influence as well as connection. Intervening on behalf of one meant intervening indirectly on behalf of all.

As our society becomes ever more systemic in thought, understanding systemic connections becomes more commonplace. Attention to the global economy is an example of how more attention is being paid to the interrelatedness of all aspects of the human condition. Recycling bins encourage the average citizen to think about systemic links between behavior and its consequences. Thus, as family therapists are invited to provide services to elders, their sphere of influence expands in profound ways because of this universal interrelatedness. Stepping between generations, the practitioner meets older families at the final crossroads where their behavior may affect generations to come. As family therapists move toward an integration with aging issues, the challenge brings with it an opportunity for personal growth and practice refinement.

REFERENCES

Anderson, W. T., & Hargrave, T. D. (1990). Contextual family therapy and older people: Building trust in the intergenerational family. *Journal of Family Therapy, 12,* 311-320.

Banks, M. E., Ackerman, R. J., & Clark, E. O. (1986). Elderly women in family therapy. *Women and Therapy, 5,* 107-116.

Barber, C. E. (1988). Correlates of subjective burden among adult sons and daughters caring for aged parents. *Journal of Aging Studies, 2,* 133-144.

Barber, C. E. (1993). Spousal care of Alzheimer's disease patients in nursing home versus in-home settings: Patient impairment and caregiver impacts. *Clinical Gerontologist, 2,* 3-30.

Barber, C. E., Fisher, B. L., & Pasley, B. K. (1990). Family care of Alzheimer's disease patients: Predictors of subjective and objective burden. *Family Perspective, 23,* 289-309.

Benbow, S., Egan, D., Marriott, A., Tregay, K., Walsh, S., Wells, J., & Wood, J. (1990). Using the family life cycle with later life families. *Journal of Family Therapy, 12,* 321-340.

Bepko, R. A. (1984). Strategic therapy with a "nasty" patient. Special Issue: Dementia assessment. *Clinical Gerontologist, 3,* 5-20.

Blazer, D. G., & Siegler, I. (1981). Evaluating the family of the elderly patient: Depressive disorders. In D. G. Blazer & I. Siegler (Eds.), *Working with the family of the older adult.* Monterey Park, CA: Addison-Wesley.

Blieszner, R., & Mancini, J. (1987). Enduring ties: Older adults' parental role and responsibilities. *Family Relations, 36,* 176-180.

Bogo, M. (1987). Social work practice with family systems in admission to homes for the aged. *Journal of Gerontological Social Work, 10,* 5-20.

Boss, P., Caron, W., & Horbal, J. (1988). Alzheimer's disease and ambiguous loss. In C. Chilman, F. Cox, & E. Nunnally (Eds.), *Families in trouble* (pp. 123-140). Beverly Hills, CA: Sage.

Boss, P., Caron, W., Horbal, J., & Mortimer, J. (1990). Predictors of depression in caregivers of dementia patients: Boundary ambiguity and mastery. *Family Process, 29,* 245-253.

Boszormenyi-Nagy, I. (Ed.). (1987a). *Foundations of contextual therapy: Collected papers.* New York: Brunner/Mazel.

Boszormenyi-Nagy, I. (1987b). The context of consequences and the limits of therapeutic responsibility. In H. Stierlin, F. B. Simon, & G. Schmidt (Eds.), *Familiar realities: The Heidelberg Conference* (pp. 41-51). New York: Brunner/Mazel.

Bowen, M. (1978). *Family therapy in clinical practice.* New York: Jason Aronson.

Brody, E. M. (1985). Parent care as a normative family stress. *The Gerontologist, 25,* 19-24.

Brody, E. M. (1990). Role reversal: An inaccurate and destructive concept. *Journal of Gerontological Social Work, 15,* 15-22.

Butler, R. N. (1963). The life review: An interpretation of reminiscence in the aged. *Psychiatry. 26,* 65-76.

Butler, R. N., & Lewis, M. I. (1982). *Aging and mental health: Positive psychological approaches.* St. Louis: Mosby.

Butler, R. N. & Lewis, M. I. (1991). *Aging and mental health.* New York: Merrell.

Butler, R. N., Lewis, M., & Sunderland, T. (1991). *Aging and mental health: Positive psychosocial and biomedical approaches.* New York: Macmillan.

Carni, E. (1989). To deal or not to deal with death: Family therapy with three enmeshed older couples. *Family Therapy, 51,* 59-68.

Carter, B., & McGoldrick, M. (1989). *The changing family life cycle: A framework for family therapy.* New York: Gardner Press.

deShazer, S. (1982). *Patterns of brief family therapy—an ecosystemic approach.* New York: Guilford Press.

Dobson, J. E., & Dobson, R. L. (1985). The sandwich generation: Dealing with aging parents. *Journal of Counseling and Development, 63,* 572-574.

Duffy, M. (1984). Aging and the family: Intergenerational psychodynamics. *Psychotherapy, 21,* 342-346.

Eisenberg, D. M., & Carrilio, T. E. (1990). Friends of the family: Counseling elders at family service agencies. *Generations, 14,* 25-26.

Engel, G. L. (1980). The clinical application of the biopsychosocial model. *American Journal of Psychiatry, 137,* 535-544.

Erikson, E. H. (1982). *The life cycle completed: A review.* New York: Norton.

Erikson, E. H., Erikson, J. M., & Kivnick, H. Q. (1986). *Vital involvement in old age.* New York: Norton.

Falicov, C. J. (1988). *Family transitions: Continuity and change across the life cycle.* New York: Guilford Press.

Falloon, I. (Ed.). (1988). *Handbook of behavioral family therapy.* New York: Guilford Press.

Fisch, R., Weakland, J., & Segal, L. (1983). *The tactics of change: Doing therapy briefly.* San Francisco: Jossey-Bass.

Flori, D. (1989). The prevalence of later life family concerns in the marriage and family therapy journal literature (1976-1985): A content analysis. *Journal of Marital and Family Therapy, 15*(3), 289-297.

Framo, J. L. (1981). The integration of marital therapy with sessions with family of origin. In A. S. Gurman & D. P. Kniskern (Eds.), *Handbook of family therapy* (pp. 133-158). New York: Brunner/Mazel.

Framo, J. L. (1992). *Family of origin therapy: An intergenerational approach.* New York: Brunner/Mazel.

Gilleard, C. J. (1990). Self-help information for caregivers: Does it help? *Geriatric Medicine, 20,* 13-14.

Gutmann, D. (1977). Notes toward a comparative psychology of aging. In J. Birren and K. Schaie (Eds.), *Handbook of the psychology of aging*. New York: Van Nostrand Reinhold.

Gwyther, L. P., & Blazer, D. G. (1984). Family therapy and the dementia patient. *American Family Physician, 29,* 149–156.

Haley, J. (1987). *Problem-solving therapy* (2nd ed.). San Francisco: Jossey-Bass.

Hanna, S. M. (1986). *Structured family treatment for the elderly chronically ill: A training manual for project support.* Madison, WI: Independent Living.

Hanna, S. M. (1995). On paradox: Empathy before strategy. *Journal of Family Psychotherapy, 6,* 85–88.

Hargrave, T. D. (1994). Using video life reviews with older adults. *Journal of Family Therapy, 16,* 259–268.

Hargrave, T. D., & Anderson, W. T. (1990). Helping older people finish well: A contextual family therapy approach. *Family Therapy, 17,* 9–19.

Hargrave, T. D., & Anderson, W. T. (1992). *Finishing well: Aging and reparation in the intergenerational family.* New York: Brunner/Mazel.

Hartford, M. E., & Parsons, R. (1982). Groups with relatives of dependent older adults. *The Gerontologist, 22,* 394–398.

Herr, J. J., & Weakland, J. H. (1979). *Counseling elders and their families: Practical techniques for applied gerontology.* New York: Springer.

Holahan, C. K., & Holahan, C. J. (1987). Self-efficacy, social support, and depression in aging: A longitudinal analysis. *Journal of Gerontology, 42,* 65–68.

Jarvik, L. F. (1983). The impact of immediate life situations on depression: Illnesses and losses. In L. D. Breslau & M. R. Haug (Eds.), *Depression and aging.* New York: Springer.

Jerrome, D. (1994). Family estrangement: Parents and children who "lose touch." *Journal of Family Therapy, 16,* 241–258.

Johnson, R. P. (1988). How to stay young in a fast aging world: Part II. *Co-Op Networker: Caregivers of Older Persons, 4,* 1–4.

Jones, S., & Flickinger, M. A. (1987). Contextual family therapy for families with an impaired elderly member: A case study. *Clinical Gerontologist, 6,* 87–97.

Kaminsky, M. (1984). *The use of reminiscence: New ways of working with older adults.* New York: Hawthorn.

Kantor, D., & Lehr, W. (1975). *Inside the family: Toward a theory of family process.* San Francisco: Jossey-Bass.

Kastenbaum, R. (1977). *Death, society, and human experience.* St. Louis: Mosby.

Lazarus, L. W., Stafford, B., Cooper, K., Cohler, B., & Dysken, M. (1981). A pilot study of an Alzheimer patient's relatives discussion group. *The Gerontologist, 21,* 353–358.

Lieberman, M. A. (1983). Social contexts of depression. In L. D. Breslau & M. R. Haug (Eds.), *Depression and aging.* New York: Springer.

Madanes, C. (1981). *Strategic family therapy.* San Francisco: Jossey-Bass.

Madanes, C. (1984). *Behind the one-way mirror.* San Francisco: Jossey-Bass.

Maiden, R. J. (1987). Learned helplessness and depression: A test of the reformulated model. *Journal of Gerontology, 42,* 60–64.

McDaniel, S. H., Hepworth, J., & Doherty, W. J. (1992). *Medical family therapy: A biopsychosocial approach to families with health problems.* New York: Basic Books.

McEwan, E. G. (1987). The whole grandfather: An intergenerational approach to family therapy. In J. Sadavoy & M. Leszcz (Eds.), *Treating the elderly with psychotherapy*. New York: International Universities Press.

McGoldrick, M., & Carter, B. (1989). *The changing family life cycle*. New York: Allyn & Bacon.

McQuellon, R. P., & Reifler, B. V. (1989). Caring for depressed elderly and their families. In G. A. Hughston, V. A. Christopherson, & M. J. Bonjean (Eds.), *Aging and family therapy: Practitioner perspectives on Golden Pond* (pp. 97-116). New York: Haworth Press.

Minuchin, S., & Fishman, H. C. (1981). *Family therapy techniques*. Cambridge, MA: Harvard University Press.

Myers, J. E. (1988). The mid/late life generation gap: Adult children with aging parents. *Journal of Counseling and Development. 66*, 331-335.

Myers, J. E. (1989). *Adult children and aging parents*. Dubuque, IA: Kendall/Hunt.

Newmann, J. P. (1989). Aging and depression. *Psychology and Aging, 26*, 150-165.

Osgood, N. J. (1989). A systems approach to suicide prevention. In G. A. Hughston, V. A. Christopherson, & M. J. Bonjean (Eds.), *Aging and family therapy: Practitioner perspectives on Golden Pond* (pp. 117-131). New York: Haworth Press.

Peck, R. C. (1968). Psychological development in the second half of life. In B. L. Neugarten (Ed.), *Middle age and aging*. Chicago: University of Chicago Press.

Quigley, C., & Womphrey, J. (1988). Violence can never be justified. *Community Care, 16*, 20-21.

Rathbone-McQuan, E., & Hedlund, J. (1989). Older families and issues of alcohol misuse: A neglected problem in psychotherapy. In G. A. Hughston, V. A. Christopherson, & M. J. Bonjean (Eds.), *Aging and family therapy: Practitioner perspectives on Golden Pond* (pp. 173-184). New York: Haworth Press.

Ratna, L., & Davis, J. (1984). Family therapy with the elderly mentally ill: Some strategies and techniques. *British Journal of Psychiatry, 145*, 311-315.

Richardson, C. A., Gilleard, C. J., Lieberman, S., & Peeler, R. (1994). Working with older adults and their families: A review. *Journal of Family Therapy, 16*(3), 225-241.

Rodway, M. R., Elliot, J., & Sawa, R. J. (1987). Intervention with families of the elderly chronically ill: An alternate approach. *Journal of Gerontological Social Work, 10*, 51-60.

Rolland, J. S. (1987). Chronic illness and the life cycle: A conceptual framework. *Family Process, 26*, 203-221.

Satir, V. (1988). *The new peoplemaking*. Palo Alto, CA: Science and Behavior Books.

Segal, L. (1991). Brief therapy: The MRI approach. In A. S. Gurman & D. P. Kniskern (Eds.), *Handbook of family therapy, Volume II* (pp. 171-199). New York: Brunner/Mazel.

Seltzer, M. M. (1990). Role reversal: You don't go home again. *Journal of Gerontological Social Work, 15*, 5-14.

Sheehan, N. W., & Nuttall, P. (1988). Conflict, emotion, and personal strain among family caregivers. *Family Relations, 37*, 92-98.

Shields, C. G. (1992). Family interaction and caregivers of Alzheimer's disease patients: Correlates of depression. *Family Process, 31*, 19-33.

Smith, G. C., Smith, M. F., & Toseland, R. W. (1991). Problems identified by family caregivers in counseling. *The Gerontologist. 31*, 15–22.

Sprenkle, D. H., & Bischof, G. P. (1994). Contemporary family therapy in the United States. *Journal of Family Therapy, 16*(1), 5–24.

Thomae, H. (1985). Psychology of aging: Personality and its attributes. In J. C. Brocklehurst (Ed.), *Textbook of geriatric medicine and gerontology* (pp. 105–121). Edinburgh: Churchill Livingston.

Timberlake, E. M. (1980). The value of grandchildren to grandmothers. *Journal of Gerontological Social Work, 3,* 63–76.

Todd, T., & Selekman, M. (1991). *Family therapy approaches with adolescent substance abusers.* Boston: Allyn & Bacon.

Walsh, F. (1989). The family in later life. In B. Carter & M. McGoldrick (Eds.), *The changing family life cycle* (2nd ed.) (pp. 311–332). New York: Gardner Press.

Watzlawick, P., Weakland, J., & Fisch, R. (1974). *Change: Principles of problem formation and problem resolution.* New York: Norton.

Weakland, J., Fisch, R., Watzlawick, P., & Bodin, A. (1974). Brief therapy: Focused problem resolution. *Family Process, 13,* 141–168.

Whitaker, C., & Keith, D. (1981). Symbolic-experiential family therapy. In A. S. Gurman & D. P. Kniskern (Eds.), *Handbook of family therapy.* New York: Brunner/Mazel.

Whitlach, C. J., Zarit, S. H., & Eye, A. V. (1991). Efficacy of interventions with caregivers: A reanalysis. *The Gerontologist, 31,* 665–672.

Williams, F. R. (1989). Bereavement and the elderly: The role of the psychotherapist. In G. A. Hughston, V. A. Christopherson, & M. J. Bonjean (Eds.), *Aging and family therapy: Practitioner perspectives on Golden Pond* (pp. 225–241). New York: Haworth Press.

Williamson, D. (1981). Personal authority via termination of the intergenerational hierarchical boundary: A "new" stage in the family life cycle. *Journal of Marital and Family Therapy, 7,* 441–452.

Williamson, D. S. (1991). *The intimacy paradox: Personal authority in the family system.* New York: Guilford Press.

Wolinsky, M. A. (1990). *A heart of wisdom: Marital counseling with older and elderly couples.* New York: Brunner/Mazel.

Zarit, S. H., Anthony, C. R., & Boutselis, M. (1987). Interventions with caregivers of dementia patients: Comparison of two approaches. *Psychotherapy and Aging, 2,* 225–232.

Zarit, S., & Zarit, J. (1982). Families under stress: Interventions for caregivers of senile dementia patients. *Psychotherapy, 19,* 461–471.

☙ 2 ❧

Aging: A Primer for Family Therapists

Terry D. Hargrave, Ph.D.
Amarillo College
Amarillo, Texas

Suzanne Midori Hanna, Ph.D.
University of Louisville
Louisville, Kentucky

A great upheaval has been brewing on the horizon for years and the initial waves of turbulence have already begun to wash through our society. Warnings about tumult that the phenomenal increase in aging will bring have been sounded by researchers for a long time, but only now is society realizing that we cannot run or hide. We live in an aging world. Consider a few of the undeniable indicators:

- Average life expectancy in the United States is 74.9 years (United States Bureau of the Census, 1989).
- Forty-two percent of the 31.2 million older Americans are 75 or older (United States Bureau of the Census, 1990).
- Median age in the United States has steadily increased and will be over 40 in less than 20 years (Social Security Administration, 1990).

Just as the cohort known as the "baby boomers" caused us to vastly expend the educational system in the 1950s and 1960s, redefined work and family life in the 1970s and 1980s, they will revolutionize the definitions and limits of aging in the 21st century. In a time of sparse economic resources, ever-fewer governmental supports, more chronic illnesses, and skyrocketing health care costs, the challenges that an aging society produces can seem overwhelming. But we must face these challenges simply because we have no other choice. Just as death is an inevitable part of every person's life, so aging—a long period of aging—will be more of a consideration with our population.

Along with the challenges that come with an aging population, there is also tremendous opportunity. In the last part of this century and continuing into the next, we will witness the reversal of many long-held prejudices and ageist beliefs about older people. We have the opportunity for the first time in our history to become a truly intergenerational society that benefits from the wisdom of elders that potentially empowers families. Perhaps we even will learn to allow older people as a group to become more productive and valued contributing members to our society and families. But even if we do not realize or seize the opportunities that aging brings, our aging population will be a factor that we must recognize in our everyday relationships.

As family therapists and family researchers have long recognized, there are tremendous developmental impacts and intergenerational considerations that affect the family. As with other successful integrations of different fields, it is important to start with a macro view of the population and its common themes. Then, it is possible to address those themes from a systemic view, deciding which family theory fits the dynamics and which theory of change fits therapeutic goals. Gerontologists usually view aging in terms of four distinct processes: (1) chronological aging, (2) biological aging, (3) psychological aging, and (4) social aging (Hooyman & Kiyak, 1993). Chronological aging refers to the number of years a person has been living from birth. Biological aging focuses on the physical changes that reduce efficiency in the human body. Changes in mental functioning, adaptive capacity, personality drives, and motives are the focus of psychological aging. Social aging refers to the roles and relationships an older person maintains with family, friends, and the world in general. While therapists are primarily focused on psychological and social aging, it is necessary to have some understanding of all four areas to fully appreciate the therapeutic challenges that an aging population presents.

DEMOGRAPHICS AND CHRONOLOGICAL AGING

The aging population of the United States and of the world is rapidly increasing. There is, however, substantially more to this increase in the aging population than simple longevity or general population increase. In addition, factors that greatly affect the demographic picture include changes in the relative number of older persons, increases in the oldest old category, decreases in dependency ratios, ethnic aging trends, and the aging population redistribution.

Increases in Life Expectancy

In 1900, average life expectancy was a little more than 47 years. Life expectancy has steadily increased to the current average of 74.9 years and is expected to increase to 77.6 by the year 2005 (United States Bureau of the Census, 1989). There is a pronounced gender difference in the number of aging individuals. In 1900, an average life expectancy for a 65-year-old man or woman was about 12 more years. Now women who reach age 65 can expect to live an additional 18 1/2 years, whereas 65-year-old men will live an average of 15 additional years (National Center for Health Statistics, 1988). Therefore, as a cohort ages, the ratio of males to females becomes greater. There are 83 men to every 100 women between the ages of 65 and 69, but only 40 men to 100 women among those elders age 85 and older (United States Bureau of the Census, 1990).

Medical advances in treating and curing acute diseases are primarily responsible for this increase in longevity. Influenza and pneumonia had been principal killers among the population, with the very old and the very young especially at risk. Today, with the advances in medical technology and the wide acceptance of early treatment, few die of these acute diseases but are much more likely to suffer chronic illnesses (Hooyman & Kiyak, 1993).

Aging Population Growth and Relative Number Increases

The United States Census Bureau in 1900 reported that the total population of the country was 76 million and that only 3 million of these people were age 65 and older. As a group, the elderly accounted for only 4 percent of the total population and were equally divided between men and women. The Census Bureau now reports that of the total population, 31.2 million are age 65 and older. Thirty-two percent of this older group are age 75 to 84 and over 10 percent are age 85 and older (United States Bureau of the Census, 1990). Older people now constitute over 12 percent of the population, with females making up 60 percent of this group. By 2010, the projected population of older people over 65 is expected to represent about 14 percent of Americans.

For some time now, the group of those 85 and older has increased more rapidly than any other age group (Rosenwaike, 1985). The number of elderly in this group has increased over 300 percent since 1960 (AARP, 1990). If current projections hold, this number will continue to increase with the tremendous influx of "baby boomers" starting in the year 2030 to make up approximately 5 percent of the *total* population in the United States (Hooyman & Kiyak, 1993).

This same demographic change is also occurring in the general world population. The older population grew by 30 percent in the decade of the 1970s alone (Longino, Soldo, & Manton, 1990). By the mid-1980s, there were over 290 million people over the age of 60. By the year 2025, demographic experts estimate that the world population will contain over 761 million persons over the age of 65, with one out of every seven people in the world being over age 69 (United Nations Secretariat, 1989).

The dramatic decline in the birth rate in this country continuing after the mid-1960s, combined with the high birth rates from 1900 to 1916 and 1946 to 1964, has contributed to a major increase in the median age. Median age increased from 28 in 1970 to over age 33 by 1990 (Social Security Administration, 1990). In the mid-1980s, one in every nine Americans was over 65. Assuming that the course of fertility continues relatively unchanged, by 2020 one in every five Americans will be over 65. Most of this increase will occur between the years 2010 and 2020 when the baby boom cohorts reach this category. The large 1950s birth cohorts mean that by 2040, one out of every five of the aged will be concentrated in the oldest age category (United States Bureau of the Census, 1987).

Dependency Ratios

Among the greatest concerns regarding the growth of the elderly population generally and of the oldest old category specifically is the proportion of the population that is employable compared with the number who are too young to work or are retired. This is known as the dependency ratio and the numbers have increased steadily so that there are fewer and fewer employed persons to support the elderly (United States Senate Special Committee on Aging, 1990). Currently, there are only five working people to every older person as compared with 10 to 1 in 1910. By 2010, the dependency ratio is expected to be about four working people to every person over age 65 (United States Bureau of the Census, 1988).

If these numbers hold true, there will be a tremendous burden placed on the working population. Simply stated, the fewer the number of workers to support each person over age 65, the higher will be the percentage of each working person's income that must be allocated to support each elder. Support programs such as Social Security run the risk of being taxed beyond the capability to provide assistance for the aging population. The probability of the working cohort not being able to provide such assistance appears to be high.

Ethnic Aging Trends

In general, the ethnic minorities in the United States have a higher mortality rate under age 65 and higher fertility rates. This contributes to a lower percentage of nonwhites in the aging category as compared with the population in general. Thirteen percent of all whites are age 65 and older, whereas only 8 percent of blacks, 6 percent of Pacific Asians, 6 percent of Native Americans, and 5 percent of Hispanics are in this range. However, the next century will see the percentages of ethnic minorities 65 and older increase at a more rapid rate than that of the white population (Hooyman & Kiyak, 1993). Gender patterns of aging ethnic minorities are similar to that of the white aging group. Women generally live longer than men and increasingly outnumber them as they age. Aging ethnic minority women are also more likely to remain widowed and live alone than their male counterparts.

Older Population Redistribution

Regionally, the Northeast has the highest percentage (13.6 percent) of its population that is age 65 and older. However, there is only one northeastern state among the list of states with the highest populations of older people (California, New York, Florida, Pennsylvania, and Texas). The highest proportions of older people to total state populations is very different. Florida has the highest proportion of older people, followed by Pennsylvania, Rhode Island, Iowa, South Dakota, Missouri, and Nebraska. Seventy-four percent of the older population lives in cities while only 26 percent live in rural areas (United States Bureau of the Census, 1989).

Relocation for people over age 65 is relatively low. Only 23 percent of the elder population moves as compared with 48 percent of the younger population. Longino, Soldo, and Manton (1990) have identified three types of moves that older people make. First, moves are most often made by relatively healthy and financially stable older people who are seeking more desirable physical surroundings, greater living amenities, or a friendship maintenance network. Second, moves are made to be closer to a caregiving adult child, and these people usually are debilitated physically to the point that they need assistance in carrying out everyday chores and functions. The third type of move is made when physical limitations are such that care or oversight of care by kin becomes essential.

BIOLOGICAL AND PHYSICAL AGING

Biological aging refers to the process of change in the individual that lowers the probability of survival and the capacity for self-regulation, repair, and adaptation to environmental demands (Birren & Zarit, 1985). The reasons that we age are not quite clear, but two theories are predominant. One theory holds that aging is genetically programmed at birth the same way that puberty is, with differences in longevity due to the genetic inheritance from the parents. The other theory is that aging and the physical decline of the individual are attributable to the environmental hazards and the effects of disease on the human system. Although there is research on both sides supporting the different theories, it is clear that the effects of aging on cellular structures make themselves felt in every system of the body (Zarit & Zarit, 1987). Physically, older people age at different rates and have a variety of limitations. However, it is helpful to understand some of the basic biological deteriorations that come with aging. The ability to anticipate the effects of these processes on family life enables the clinician to assume a metaposition from which to guide families through their adjustment to these changes.

Sensory Perception

Aging affects every sensation in the body so that the older person must receive greater environmental stimulation to achieve the same impact that was made at lower sensory levels at a younger age. Among these sensory declines, the reduction of vision is perhaps the most pronounced among the aging group. More than half of the cases of blindness in the United States develop after age 65 (Rockstein & Sussman, 1979). Sharpness of vision and adaptations to light fall off significantly with age, possibly affecting the older person's ability to drive, read, work, and manage household functions.

Over half of the elder population reports hearing loss, with loss in men being more frequent and significant than in women (United States Bureau of the Census, 1989). This loss often results in physical withdrawal from many social situations because of the frustration associated with understanding little of what is being said. Taste and smell sensations also lessen due primarily to the decrease in density of taste buds in the mouth and the decrease in the number of nerve fibers in the nose (Newman & Newman, 1983).

Cardiovascular System

Researchers have long recognized that the changes in the fibrous connective tissue in the body called *collagen* are dramatic as people age. Collagen tends to lose its elasticity with age. Although changes in collagen affect the entire body, the cardiovascular system is especially vulnerable. Fat is deposited on the heart's surface as collagen surrounding the heart stiffens. There is a gradual increase in the size of fat tissue and a decrease of muscle bulk in the aging heart, accompanied by a decrease in cardiac output. This means decreased blood flow to the rest of the body and a reduction of oxygen levels in the blood. Arterial walls also stiffen with the changes in collagen and fat deposits are more likely to form in the arteries (Zarit & Zarit, 1987).

Cardiovascular diseases are by far the leading causes of death among older people, but the reduced flow of oxygen-rich blood to the brain, other vital organs, and extremities of the body contributes to a variety of health complications (Bigner, 1983).

Respiratory System

The loss of elasticity in collagen also has a dynamic effect on the respiratory system as people age. Lack of elasticity in the connective tissues contributes to lower capacity for inhaling and exhaling. Also, muscle atrophy, a weakened diaphragm, and poor posture contribute to this lower lung capacity. Reduced ability to inhale and exhale has a direct effect on the oxygen supply to the blood, which in turn has its effect on the rest of the body. Some of the more frequently occurring respiratory disorders in older people include emphysema, bronchitis, and pneumonia (Zarit & Zarit, 1987).

Musculoskeletal System

Although muscle atrophy has long been considered part of the aging process, there is now substantial research that indicates that if older adults remain active and continue vigorous exercise, they can retain muscle size and strength (deVries, 1983). This finding suggests that muscle atrophy may be due to a decrease in physical activity among older people rather than the fact of passing years. Besides minor height changes due to spinal cord compression and poorer posture, most of the skeletal changes occur in the structure of the bone. The skeletal system of older people tends to become less dense and more porous, which makes the bones more likely to fracture. Older adult women are particularly prone to lose calcium in their bones, which may lead to osteoporosis. Common problems, such as back pain and arthritis, may make it difficult for older people to be mobile or to perform basic tasks, including cooking, cleaning, or activities related to personal hygiene.

Nervous System

How the brain works and its role in learning, perception, memory, and language are relatively little understood. The effects of aging on the brain are especially vague since most of the current knowledge regarding this part of the body is based on research with animals (Willott, 1990). It is not clear whether deterioration in the nervous system is due to genetic factors, to the environment, or to disease.

Nevertheless, several conclusions about the effects of aging on the brain can be drawn. First, it seems that as aging progresses, there is a decrease in the number of neurons in certain regions of the brain, with the frontal lobe being most at risk (Brody, 1973). These neurons are essential components of brain activity and are particularly prone to loss in the regions used for movement, perception, and language. Second, the structure of neurons, especially around the synapse, changes with age. This altering of structure may be responsible for a decrease in electrical activity in the brain and may affect the release of neurotransmitters that are responsible for the neuronal communication in the brain. Third, the dendritic connections between neurons that allow neurons to transfer information to each other seem to decrease in number in some regions of the brain as aging occurs (Willott, 1990). Finally, there is a general decrease in the weight of the brain. This may be primarily due to a decrease in the blood flow and oxygen to the brain, which, in turn, results in a loss of fluid in the brain (Hooyman & Kiyak, 1993).

Strokes, Parkinson's disease, organic brain syndrome, and Alzheimer's disease are four of the more common nervous system disorders associated with aging. Strokes are the third leading cause of death among the aged and may result in severe physical and mental disability for those who survive (Bigner, 1983). Parkinson's primarily affects motor activity, whereas organic brain syndrome and Alzheimer's affect memory, orientation, emotional stability, and rational thinking.

For older people who do not suffer from disease, changes in the nervous system have minimal effect on their lives. Reaction time and brain activity slow, but such changes are not as dramatic as once thought. There is evidence to suggest that there is some decline in memory and fluid intelligence, but these declines may not be profound. There is substantial research that does suggest that older people can combat the effects of memory loss with continued mental activity and by adapting new memory strategies (Zarit & Zarit, 1987).

PSYCHOLOGICAL AGING

Chronological age and physical health are normally what people consider when they think about aging. However, it is clear that there are tremendous psychological issues to consider. The focus of much of the literature on gerontology and aging has been on the psychological well-being of older people. Most of this work has tried to describe the correlates and determinants of why some older people are satisfied and well adjusted during the aging process while others struggle with depression, dissatisfaction, and maladjustment. There also have been several theories or approaches directed at understanding the psychological components that influence an aging person's personality, drives, and motives.

Development

Developmental theorists believe that as individuals develop throughout the life span, there are different stages that present themselves in a somewhat uniform sequence. Young children tend to develop language skills at around the same age and adolescents reach puberty within a defined age range. Most developmental theorists have seen that each stage of the life span presents certain biological and social tasks that must be negotiated if psychological well-being is to be achieved. If the tasks are successfully negotiated, the individual internalizes the success psychologically and displays more competence in dealing with future developmental challenges. If, however, the individual is unable to handle the pressures and strains at a certain stage, successful development will be curtailed and the likelihood of negotiating future life tasks will be diminished. Several developmental approaches have focused on aging and later life.

Perhaps the most influential developmental theorist was Erik Erikson. Erikson (1963) believed that the individual's drive to deal with environmental or social crisis is the energy force behind development. At each life stage, the individual is presented with psychosocial crisis. If an individual can deal successfully with the crisis the environment presents, then development is enhanced. However, Erikson maintained that each psychosocial crisis at each stage has to be addressed and successful resolution of that stage has to be achieved in order to deal with the next life stage.

Erikson conceptualized eight separate stages of psychosocial crises: *trust versus mistrust* (infancy), *autonomy versus shame or doubt* (toddlerhood), *initiative versus guilt* (preschool childhood), *industry versus inferiority* (school-age childhood), *identity versus role confusion* (adolescence), *intimacy versus isolation* (young adulthood), *generativity versus stagnation* (middle adulthood), and *ego integrity versus despair* (later adulthood).

The last stage of *integrity versus despair* has no future crisis to present to the aging individual, but is an evaluation and culmination of the seven previous stages. Ego integrity is achieved when an elder has come to grips with the contribution he or she has made to society. If an older person is able to reconcile this difficult crisis, a sense of peace and integrity about identity is achieved. If the older person is unable to reach this point of reconciliation, then a sense of loss, disappointment, and dissatisfaction results.

Peck (1968) sought to define and delineate the last stage in Erikson's model by extending the life stage of old age into three psychological conflicts. Peck maintained that negotiation of these three themes is essential if an older individual is to reach the last stage with a sense of integrity. The first theme identified was *ego differentiation versus work role preoccupation*. In this conflict, an aging person loses his or her ability to perform work and tasks the way they were performed in younger years. Successful aging requires that an older person redefine his or her sense of personal worth from what he or she "*does*" to what he or she "*is*" as an individual. The second conflict is *body transcendence versus body preoccupation*. As the body deteriorates, an older person must conceptualize happiness outside of the context of good health, building on resources that transcend physical comfort. The final conflict is *ego transcendence versus ego preoccupation*. As death nears for the older person, he or she will either adapt to the realization that life will go on through others or will become rigid in the denial of death and try to hang onto life through inappropriate or dysfunctional means. When a person transcends the ego, he or she realizes the worth of family and tries to give the elements of wisdom to younger generations.

Also influenced by Erik Erikson's theory, Robert Butler (1963) maintained that older people go through a universal process of life reminiscence or *life review* in an effort to reconcile their past experiences with their expectations and values. This process is brought on by the knowledge of approaching death. This life review can be historical and evaluative in nature, but also may focus on past unresolved issues in the individual's life. Therefore, Butler maintained that life review is particularly difficult for individuals who have unresolved issues. Life review has been and continues to be one of the primary therapeutic tools used in therapy with older people.

Personality

Personality refers to the patterns of feelings, thoughts, and behaviors that are distinctive to a person across time and situations (Matlin, 1992). Researchers and theorists vary widely in their explanations of personality, from patterns being determined by unconscious drives and forces to behavior being governed by context and situations. Some personality theorists have tried to focus more on describing personality as a compilation of traits instead of searching for an explanation of why some personalities are the way they are. Actually, there is very little that can be rigidly stated about the variations and dynamics that contribute to the expression of human personality; however, actively seeking to understand the consistent expression of individual personality lends insight to that which holds potential to help individuals and families function better.

Neugarten, Havighurst, and Tobin (1968) developed a personality topology from the famous longitudinal Kansas City studies. Their research suggested that personality was a crucial factor in successful aging and that people become more individualistic and differentiated with age. They categorized personality into four major types: (1) integrated, (2) armored-defensive, (3) passive-dependent, and (4) disorganized.

Integrated personalities are generally able to accept their strengths and weaknesses, to maintain intimate relationships with family and others, and are well adjusted during aging. Most older people with integrated personalities experience high degrees of life satisfaction. Older people with armored-defended personalties see advancing years as an enemy against which they struggle. They attempt to maintain activities that reflect middle-age roles and try to stave off the process of aging by using an array of defense mechanisms. Passive-dependent personalities have difficulty achieving commitment to caring for themselves cognitively, emotionally, socially, or physically. They are very dependent on caregivers and have low or medium levels of life satisfaction based on how successful they are in getting people to care for them. Older individuals with a disorganized personality type have lost their ability to contribute substantially to a role, usually because of some sickness or disease. They generally display poor emotional control and have deteriorated cognitively and physically.

These personality types closely paralleled those found by Reichard, Livson, and Peterson (1962) in their study of older men. They proposed five personality types: (1) mature, (2) rocking chair, (3) armored, (4) angry, and (5) self-hater. Mature personalities are those who adjust well to aging. Rocking chair types are more passive than mature types, but are satisfied to be more disengaged as aging occurs. Armored types are highly self-controlled and seek to maintain middle-age activities. Angry personality types are frustrated by the aging process and tend to lash out and blame others. Self-hater types are poorly adjusted to aging and tend to focus blame inward.

Predominant Psychological Issues

Older people experience myriad changes and losses that accompany age. Job loss or change, family role transition, deterioration of health, declining financial power, and the death of a spouse are just a few of the major losses that are common to the aging process. With these losses comes the tremendous potential for depression. Depression is the most common psychiatric problem among the elderly and at least one quarter of the suicides reported in the United States are committed by people over age 65 (Schefft & Lehr, 1990).

Schefft and Lehr (1990) also point out that there are enormous threats to the independence of older people, such as loss of physical and financial strength, which reduce the amount of control they can exercise over their homes and lives. There is evidence to suggest that as a group, older people utilize fewer coping strategies in managing their environments. With fewer coping mechanisms, personal control is reduced. Illnesses bring special psychological challenges to aging individuals. An older person may fear the unknown or feel guilt about being a burden to the family or to caregivers. In addition to these stressors, organic brain and emotional problems caused by dementia, stroke, or Alzheimer's disease can cause tremendous behavioral and emotional disruption. Resulting confusion and disorientation may lead to fear, rage, withdrawal, or impulsiveness.

SOCIAL AGING

There are significant challenges to social roles and relationships during the process of aging. An aging population changes the society in general and the family specifically in ways that have never been considered or researched in our history. Truly, this is the century of old age—and it is a path that has never been charted. To understand the challenges, we must grasp some of the complex roles that come with aging, the intergenerational impact of aging on the family, and the emotional bonds in the aging family.

Social Roles During Aging

Retirement

Employment in our society has a special importance in terms of productivity and contribution. Retirement, especially for men, can mean a particular loss of meaningful social roles and relationships that can contribute to relational stress and lowered self-esteem. Retirement demands that the individual negotiate new boundaries and meanings in relationships, including those with a spouse and adult children, as well as adjust to the stress of reduction of income (Walsh, 1989).

One of the most stressful adjustments during retirement is the demands placed on the marital dyad of an older couple. In the years of employment, an older couple most often will maintain separate spheres of influence and activity. Retirement requires the couple to share the same field. They often compete for the activity, influence, meaning, and satisfaction derived from the field. This retirement activity field very often is the couple's home and the extended family (Walsh, 1989). The couples who are able to negotiate and share this field, and redirect interests into new spheres of influence, can successfully sustain their marital dyad through the retirement stress. However, for couples who cannot share this activity field, the marital distress will likely focus on overinvolvement with the younger generations.

Life satisfaction after retirement tends to be connected with such factors as health, voluntary nature of retirement, income, family situation, type of former occupation, work values, and self-esteem (George, Fillenbaum, & Palmore, 1984). Those who have poor health or a history of adjustment difficulties throughout life are most at risk of having trouble with retirement (Braithwaite, Gibson, & Bosly-Craft, 1986). Those retirees with lower occupational status tend to have more financial difficulties and fewer opportunities to pursue a variety of satisfying and important nonwork activities, which, in turn, contributes to a lower level of life satisfaction (Calasanti, 1988). Many retired persons take a more active interest in the younger generations of the family. Satisfaction and self-esteem in retirement are greatly affected, depending on the willingness and openness of the younger generation to this involvement. Also, since over 10 percent of all people over 65 have a surviving parent (Brody, 1985), the retired person may find that he or she has traded work or a career for a demanding caretaking role. This caretaking can also cause tremendous emotional and financial stress on a retired older person's limited resources.

Widowhood

Since loss is one of the dominant themes of old age, the experience of losing a spouse is probably very different for the elderly than it is for younger people. Women are much more likely to experience widowhood than men, living longer as widows than their male counterparts (Treas & Bengtston, 1987). Women are less likely to remarry and to have more limited financial resources than men (Butler & Lewis, 1982).

Erikson, Erikson, and Kivnick (1986) identified two primary adaptations connected to widowhood. The first adaptation is to being alone after decades of being married. Those older people who adapt to being alone often organize their lives differently and utilize their resources to make the best of their situations. They tend to demonstrate competence and self-confidence in starting a "new" life. Elders who experience the grief of being alone as overwhelming often become depressed and locked into a "permanent mourning" style, which becomes a predominant theme throughout the rest of their lives. The second adaptation of widowhood involves coming to terms with the feelings that surround the death of a spouse (Erikson, Erikson, & Kivnick, 1986). Older individuals who have been married for many years often report the experience of spousal death as a "partial death" for themselves. Although most older people reach the point where they do not focus on the myriad feelings that were a part of their lives with their spouses, they never seem to finish the partial reexperiencing of the mourning associated with the death.

Besides the grief and mourning associated with widowhood in old age, the death of a spouse may bring severe financial problems or may require the surviving spouse to relocate from the home. The remaining spouse, who may have been partially cared for by the partner, may not be able to function independently. Finally, widowhood may force the surviving spouse and family to deal with the emotional, financial, and legal concerns associated with the possibility of remarriage (Walsh, 1989).

Grandparenthood

Eighty percent of older people have children. Of these, 94 percent are grandparents and almost 50 percent are great-grandparents. Three quarters of grandparents see their grandchildren at least every two weeks and half see them every few days (Smyer & Hofland, 1982). Since older people become grandparents at different stages of life, the meaning of grandparenthood is varied. Midlife grandparents tend to focus on interactional activities with grandchildren, whereas later-life grandparents may see grandchildren as opportunities to extend a legacy of care and nurturing to the family (Myers, 1989).

There have been inconsistent findings on the roles of grandparents. Some research suggests that grandparenthood is peripheral to the older person as a source of identity and satisfaction (Wood & Robertson, 1976). Other research maintains that the role is essential to the emotional identity of the older person (Kivnick, 1982). Where grandparents take an active role in the interaction with the younger generations, a variety of boundary shifts become necessary in the family. Grandparents must provide a source of love and nurture for the younger generations without neutralizing or challenging the responsibility or authority of the parents. Many parents become annoyed at grandparents' "advice" on childrearing or may even become jealous of the efforts of the older person to be a good grandparent in areas where the person might have been lacking as a parent. In many cases, grandparents and grandchildren may form such a strong coalition that the parental dyad is viewed by both with animosity (Walsh, 1989).

In many instances, grandparents have sole responsibility for the care of their grandchildren. It is estimated that nearly 3 million children now live exclusively with a grandparent (Milkner & Roe, 1991). Most often, grandparents take over responsibility because the parent is unable to provide care and nurturing because of substance abuse. Also, the rise of single-parent families often necessitates financial and physical help from grandparents. Many older people who looked forward to retirement and leisure years are pressed into service to raise their grandchildren (Hooyman & Kiyak, 1993).

The Intergenerational Family Impact of Aging

As Butler (1985) suggests, we live not only in the century of old age, but also in the century of the intergenerational family. The emotional field of the family at any given moment comprises at least three, and often four and five, generations of the family system (Carter & McGoldrick, 1989). A traditional focus of the family has been on the middle generations. However, with the prevailing demographic makeup of the family population, there are very few families that do not qualify as "aging families," at least in an intergenerational sense.

Family theorists have long talked about the family life cycle much in the same way that individual developmental theorists have discussed age-appropriate tasks. In a systemic view, McGoldrick, Heiman, and Carter (1993) discuss the interaction of biology, family history, cultural history, and current events in the life cycle of the individual and the family. Although they point out that describing a "normal" family life cycle is difficult, they do suggest a developmental cycle of an intact middle-class American family, highlighting the processes and changes that must occur during the family's expansion, contraction, and realignment of relationships in order to support an individual member's development in functional ways. The developmental stages they describe are (1) "between families—young adulthood"; (2) "the joining of families in marriage—the young couple"; (3) "families with young children"; (4) "families with adolescents"; (5) "families at midlife—launching children and moving on"; and (6) "the family in later life" (McGoldrick, Heiman, & Carter, 1993).

During the last two stages of the life cycle, the family comes into regular contact with the impact of aging. During the fifth stage, "*families at midlife—launching children and moving on,*" the family experiences multiple system exits and entries. Aging affects the family at this stage in that the system must deal with the potential disabilities and eventual death of the oldest generation. Also, it is at this stage of the family life cycle that the care of the elders is likely to fall on the middle, or what is increasingly known as the sandwich, generation (Dobson & Dobson, 1985).

In the final stage of the life cycle, *the family in later life,* the system must accept the shifting generational roles and focus the family power on the central and younger generations. The oldest generation must move into a supportive role for the middle generation, willing to use the experience and wisdom resources it possesses for the good of the family. The elders must protect the family by maintaining as much independence as possible without demanding that the younger generation overfunction for them or deny them the opportunity to provide nurture. Finally, the aging family must deal with the deterioration and death of its eldest members (Carter & McGoldrick, 1989).

Emotional Bonds in the Aging Family

The period in which aging affects the family is not only the latest in the family life cycle, but it is also the longest (Brody, 1985). Along with the potential resources and strengths in intergenerational families, there are also difficult tasks with which to cope. The emotional bonds of the family contribute significantly to how the aging individual, and the family, will deal with the challenges of aging. Myths concerning the emotional bonds in aging families abound. In order to understand the complexity and resources of the aging group, the myths and stereotypes of our society must be identified and counteracted.

A common myth about the emotional bonds in the aging family concerns the decay of the extended family. This belief maintains that there once was an extended American family in which intergenerational ties were much closer and that elders were once respected and given care by the family. American society, however, has never had multigenerational households in significant numbers (Treas, 1983). Built on the faulty premise of the America that "once was," another myth holds that relatives of aging individuals have little interest in and little contact with their elders. In actuality, almost three quarters of the older population has regular contact with their children (Shanas, 1980; Cicirelli, 1981). Several studies have looked for a connection between the frequency of contact and the well-being of the aging parents (Blau, 1981; Lee, 1979). Dowd and LaRossa (1982) suggest that contact contributes to a greater sense of closeness and emotional wellness.

Another common myth about the bonds in the aging family concerns the reciprocity of emotional and physical exchange patterns among aging individuals and their children. Many believe that elders are a strain on the intergenerational family and take much more than they are able to give; however, most research indicates that older parents give more assistance to their adult children than they receive (Riley & Foner, 1968). Exchange patterns work both ways in the intergenerational family and are characterized best as mutual aid (Myers, 1988).

Most research suggests that affection between generations is a central part of the emotional bonds in the aging family (Quinn, 1983; Mancini & Blieszner, 1989). Aging adults are selective in how they give attention and resources to their families. They often give most of their attention to the adult children with the greatest needs, the single children, and those divorced with children (Aldous, 1987). Some research reveals such themes as power struggles, patterns of assigning blame and disappointment centering on the failure to achieve (Hess & Waring, 1978).

CONCLUSION

As professionals dealing with families, we know the challenges and complexities of helping and changing any family. When viewing the complex chronological, biological, psychological, and social aspects of aging, it is difficult not to feel overwhelmed by the prospect of doing therapy with an aging family. And yet we cannot escape the fact that our society is aging and that an increasing number of families with aging issues as a presenting problem will be seeking help. It behooves us as professionals, therefore, to understand the challenges and to strive to master the techniques of working with this growing population.

REFERENCES

American Association of Retired Persons. (1990). *A profile of older Americans 1990*. Washington, DC. AARP.

Aldous, J. (1987). New views on the family life of the elderly and near elderly. *Journal of Marriage and the Family, 49*, 227–234.

Bigner, J. J. (1983). *Human development: A lifespan approach*. New York: Macmillan.

Birren, J. E., & Zarit, J. (1985). *Concepts of health, behavior, and aging: Cognition, stress and aging*. Englewood Cliffs, NJ: Prentice-Hall.

Blau, Z. S. (1981). *Aging in a changing society*. New York: Watts.

Braithwaite, V. A., Gibson, D. M., & Bosly-Craft, R. (1986). An exploratory study of poor adjustment styles among retirers. *Social Science and Medicine, 23,* 493-499.

Brody, E. (1985). Parent care as a normative family stress. *The Gerontologist, 25,* 19-29.

Brody, H. (1973). Aging and the vertebrate brain. In M. Rockstein (Ed.), *Development and aging in the nervous system* (pp. 121-134). New York: Academic Press.

Butler, R. N. (1963). The life review: An interpretation of reminiscence in the aged. *Psychiatry, 26,* 65-76.

Butler, R. N. (1985). Health, productivity, and aging: An overview. In R. N. Butler & H. P. Gleason (Eds.), *Productive aging: Enhancing vitality in later life* (pp. 1-13). New York: Springer.

Butler, R. N., & Lewis, M. I. (1982). *Aging and mental health: Positive psychological approaches.* St. Louis: Mosby.

Calasanti, T. M. (1988). Participation in a dual economy and adjustment to retirement. *International Journal of Aging and Human Development, 26,* 13-27.

Carter, B., & McGoldrick, M. (1989) *The changing family life cycle.* Needham Heights, MA: Allyn & Bacon.

Cicirelli, V. G. (1981). *Helping elderly parents: The role of adult children.* Boston: Auburn House.

deVries, H. A. (1983). Physiology of exercise and aging. In D. S. Woodruff & J. E. Birren (Eds.), *Aging: Scientific perspectives and social issues* (2nd ed.). Monterey, CA: Brooks/Cole.

Dobson, J. E., & Dobson, R. L. (1985). The sandwich generation: Dealing with aging parents. *Journal of Counseling and Development, 63,* 572-574.

Dowd, J., & LaRossa, R. (1982). Primary group contact and elderly morale: An exchange/power analysis. *Sociology and Social Research, 66,* 184-197.

Erikson, E. H. (1963). *Childhood and society* (2nd ed.). New York: Norton.

Erikson, E. H., Erikson, J. M., & Kivnick, H. Q. (1986). *Vital involvement in old age.* New York: Norton.

George, L., Fillenbaum, G., & Palmore, E. (1984). Sex differences in the antecedents and consequences of retirement. *Journal of Gerontology, 39,* 364-371.

Hess, B., & Waring, J. M. (1978). Changing patterns of aging and family bonds in later life. *Family Coordinator. 27,* 303-314.

Hooyman, N. R., & Kiyak, H. A. (1993). *Social Gerontology* (3rd. ed.). Boston: Allyn & Bacon.

Kivnick, H. Q. (1982). Grandparenthood: An overview of meaning and moral health. *The Gerontologist, 22,* 59-66.

Lee, G. R. (1979). Children and the elderly: Interaction and morale. The case of the United States. *Aging and Society, 5,* 19-38.

Longino, C. F., Soldo, B. J., & Manton, K. G. (1990). Demography of aging in the United States. In K. F. Ferraro (Ed.), *Gerontology: Perspectives and issues* (pp. 19-41). New York: Springer.

Mancini, J., & Blieszner, R. (1989). Aging parents and adult children. *Journal of Marriage and the Family.*

Matlin, M. (1992). *Psychology.* Fort Worth, TX: Harcourt Brace Jovanovich.

McGoldrick, M., Heiman, M., & Carter, B. (1993). The changing family life cycle: A perspective on normalcy. In F. Walsh (Ed.), *Normal family process* (2nd ed.) (pp. 405-443). New York: Guilford Press.

Milkner, M., & Roe, K. (1991). *Preliminary findings from the grandmother caregiver study of Oakland, CA.* Berkeley: University of California Press.

Myers, J. E. (1988). The mid/late life generation gap: Adult children with aging parents. *Journal of Counseling and Development, 66,* 331-335.

Myers, J. E. (1989). *Adult children and aging parents.* Dubuque, IA: Kendall/Hunt.

National Center for Health Statistics. (1988). *Health, United States, 1987.* Washington, DC: U.S. Government Printing Office.

Neugarten, B. L., Havighurst, R. J., & Tobin, S. S. (1968). Personality and patterns of aging. In B. L. Neugarten (Ed.), *Middle age and aging* (pp. 173-177). Chicago: University of Chicago Press.

Newman, B. M., & Newman, P. R. (1983). *Understanding adulthood.* New York: Holt, Rinehart & Winston.

Peck, R. C. (1968). Psychological development in the second half of life. In B. L. Neugarten (Ed.), *Middle age and aging.* Chicago: University of Chicago Press.

Quinn, W. H. (1983). Personal and family adjustment in later life. *Journal of Marriage and the Family. 45,* 57-73.

Reichard, S., Livson, F., & Peterson, P. G. (1962). *Aging and personality: A study of 87 older men.* New York: Wiley.

Riley, M. W., & Foner, A. (1968). *Aging and society, Volume I: An inventory of research findings.* New York: Russell Sage.

Rockstein, M. J., & Sussman, M. (1979). *Biology of aging.* Belmont, CA: Wadsworth.

Rosenwaike, I. A. (1985). A demographic portrait of the oldest old. *Milbank Mermorial Fund Quarterly: Health and Society, 63,* 187-205.

Schefft, B. K., & Lehr, B. K. (1990). Psychological problems of older adults. In K. F. Ferraro (Ed.), *Gerontology: Perspectives and issues* (pp. 283-293). New York: Springer.

Shanas, E. (1980). Older people and their families: The new pioneers. *Journal of Marriage and the Family, 42,* 9-15.

Smyer, M., & Hofland, B. F. (1982). Divorce and family support in later life. *Journal of Family Issues, 35,* 61-77.

Social Security Administration. (1990). *Social security bulletin: Annual statistical supplement.* Washington, DC: U.S. Government Printing Office.

Treas, J. (1983). Aging and the family. In D. S. Woodruff & J. E. Birren (Eds.), *Aging: Scientific perspectives and social issues* (pp. 92-108). Los Angeles: University of California Press.

Treas, J., & Bengtston, V. L. (1987). The family in later years. In M. B. Sussman & S. K. Steinmetz (Eds.), *Handbook of marriage and the family* (pp. 625-648). New York: Plenum Press.

United Nations Secretariat. (1989). *World population prospects, 1988.* Population Studies no. 106. Department of International Economic and Social Affairs. New York: United Nations.

United States Bureau of the Census. (1987). Estimates of the population of the United

States, by age, sex, and race, 1980 to 1986. *Current Population Reports.* Series P-25, no. 1000. Washington, DC: U. S. Government Printing Office.

United States Bureau of the Census. (1988). Household economic studies. *Current Population Reports.* Series P-70, no. 13, U. S. Department of Commerce.

United States Bureau of the Census. (1989). Projections of the population of the U.S. by age, sex and race: 1988–2080. *Current Population Reports.* Series P-25, no. 1018, U. S. Department of Commerce.

United States Bureau of the Census. (1990). Marital status and living arrangements. *Current Population Reports.* Series P-20, no. 1450, U. S. Department of Commerce.

United States Senate Special Committee on Aging. (1990). *Developments in Aging: 1989.* Washington, DC: U.S. Government Printing Office.

Walsh, F. (1989). The family in later life. In B. Carter & M. McGoldrick (Eds.), *The changing family life cycle* (2nd ed.) (pp. 311–332). New York: Gardner Press.

Willott, J. F. (1990). Neurogerontology: The aging nervous system. In K. F. Ferraro (Ed.), *Gerontology: Perspectives and issues* (pp. 58–86). New York: Springer.

Wood, V., & Robertson, J. (1976). The significance of grandparenthood. In J. Gubrium (Ed.), *Time, roles and self in old age.* New York: Human Sciences Press.

Zarit, J. M., & Zarit, S. H. (1987). Molar aging: Physiology and psychology of normal aging. In L. L. Carstensen & B. A. Edelstein (Eds.), *Handbook of clinical gerontology* (pp. 376–386). New York: Pergamon Press.

II

MODELS OF TREATMENT

~ 3 ~

Finishing Well: A Contextual Family Therapy Approach to the Aging Family

Terry D. Hargrave, Ph.D.
Amarillo College
Amarillo, Texas

William T. Anderson, Ed.D.
Texas Women's University
Denton, Texas

INTRODUCTION

In doing therapy with an aging family, we believe that it is necessary for the therapist to have a theoretical framework in which to organize information concerning the family and guide eventual interventions that will help the family change. This chapter discusses one such theoretical framework based on the constructs of contextual family therapy (Boszormenyi-Nagy & Krasner, 1986) that we have found helpful. The work discussed here grew out of an initial project to explore family therapy techniques with aging families where the elder lived in a personal care facility. Personal care facilities generally provide such services as meals, cleaning, and supervision but do not provide nursing or medical care. Over a two-year period, we worked with 29 families. In some of the cases, we only worked with the older person, but in most we worked with at least part of the family in some capacity. The average number of sessions undertaken was nine, although we met with one family for 33 sessions. The youngest family member who attended the sessions was eight years of age; the eldest was 93. Through the diverse and complex problems that these aging families faced, we developed a therapeutic model, which we have reported on over the last several years (i.e., Hargrave & Anderson, 1992; Anderson & Hargrave, 1990; Hargrave & Anderson, 1990).

THEORETICAL BACKGROUND

The therapeutic approach of contextual therapy is a comprehensive approach to psychotherapy that integrates several psychological and developmental theories (Boszormenyi-Nagy & Krasner, 1986). It emphasizes the healing of relationships through growth in familial commitment and trust by developing loyalty, fairness, and reciprocity. Contextual therapy is based on the premise that there are four dimensions of relational reality that must be considered in therapy (Boszormenyi-Nagy & Krasner, 1986):

Facts

Facts are anchored in existing environmental, relational, and individual components that are objectifiable. They include genetic input, physical health, basic historical facts, and events in the person's life cycle.

Individual Psychology

The individual's psychology is the subjective internal psychological integration of his or her experiences and motivations. This psychology produces subjective influences on relationships as individuals strive for recognition, love, power, and pleasure, and are motivated by aggression, mastery, or ambivalence.

Family or Systemic Transactions

Family or systemic transactions are the communication or interaction patterns of relationships. These transactions produce the family's style of organization, which defines power alignments, structure, and belief systems.

Relational Ethics

Relational ethics deals with the subjective balance of trustworthiness, justice, loyalty, merit, and entitlement among members of a relationship. As members of the relationship interact in an interdependent fashion, relational ethics requires them to assume responsibility for consequences and strive for fairness and equity in the process of give and take.

The key element in the contextual approach is the dimension of relational ethics. This dimension is best described as a balance of fairness in the family relationships between the entitlements and obligations of each member of the family. This is an instinctive contract among family members based on trust that the family is committed to meet the individual member's needs and that the individual members will do what is necessary to maintain the existence of the family (Boszormenyi-Nagy & Krasner, 1986; Boszormenyi-Nagy & Ulrich, 1981).

When individuals in the family take part in mutual investment in one another in a balanced fashion, a sense of trustworthiness is developed. This resource of trustworthiness is seen as the essential element in building intergenerational strength and loyalty (Boszormenyi-Nagy, 1986). Trustworthiness allows individual family members to contribute to one another with a free sense of giving without threats or manipulation. As members give to one another in a responsible, nonexploitative way, they earn a sense of worth and self-delineation. Family strength and balanced individual emotional health are the result in such families (Boszormenyi-Nagy & Krasner, 1986).

When there is imbalance or injustice in this contract, or ledger, family dysfunction often occurs (Boszormenyi-Nagy & Spark, 1984). Individual members who are unjustly hurt through lack of nurturance by the family will often seek their care or nurture in a self-justifying manner referred to as destructive entitlement (Boszormenyi-Nagy & Krasner, 1986). Destructive entitlement can manifest in many ways, including paranoid attitudes, hostility, and emotional cutoffs, and such behaviors are often directed at innocent parties, such as spouses and children (Boszormenyi-Nagy & Krasner, 1986).

The primary premise of the contextual family therapy approach is that there is a need to mobilize trust in the balance between give and take in the family. Through balanced and trustworthy actions, the therapist is able to help the family change dysfunctional patterns and address unresolved emotional issues (Boszormenyi-Nagy & Krasner, 1980). The main therapeutic method in this effort is that of multidirected partiality (Boszormenyi-Nagy & Krasner, 1986). Multidirected partiality means that the therapist validates each family member's corresponding concerns, loyalties, and experienced injustice. The therapist supports each family member based on the notion that every person has a justifiable reason for actions, roles, and beliefs. Therapy in the contextual approach becomes a process of speaking openly about and negotiating ledger issues, exploring loyalties, examining cutoffs, exposing relational corruption, undoing stagnation, and intervening to promote family trust and justice (Boszormenyi-Nagy & Ulrich, 1981).

THEORETICAL CONSTRUCTS

The contextual framework is essential to understanding the goals of therapy with aging families. Although there may be certain types of situational stresses, such as time management, financial circumstances, or coping issues, we view the relational dimension or the emotional field of the individual and the family as the root of most symptomatology or dysfunction. Therefore, the first and primary goal in therapy, like contextual therapy, is to help move the aging family toward rejunctive efforts to balance the intergenerational ledger of individual entitlements and family obligations.

Therapeutic Goals

In aging families specifically, it is necessary to recognize the psychological reality that exists within each person. Although there are many individual and relational aspects to this reality, we feel that there are two primary issues that aging families must come to grips with in order to finish well. *First, aging families must deal with the psychological and relational stress associated with loss.* Adjusting to the economic, physical, and emotional losses in old age presents a profound obstacle to the family. The physical deterioration of one's body and one's diminishing material wealth signal that the end is coming. These emotional losses are profound because they entail much more than losing a person; they also involve losing relationships. Losses move the family to the realization of ultimate loss—letting go of life. To negotiate this loss well, the older individual and family have to see that there is a spiritual transcendence long after physical life is terminated. This transcendence exists in intergenerational linkage. The older person has now done his or her part to perpetuate the family for generations to come. Refusal to deal with these losses means denial, a sense of futility, and sometimes extreme efforts to hold on. So the first goal of therapy is to help the older person and the family let go.

The second therapeutic goal is to help members of the aging family reconcile themselves with the past. Even in healthy families, reconciliation with the past takes place as older individuals and their families take stock of lost opportunities, hurts, and regrets that occurred during the life cycle. But aging families usually take part in this activity willingly. Despairing older people and symptomatic or dysfunctional families either refuse to look at these past issues or find it too difficult to deal with the past. Older people and aging families need to do the work of communicating about, reconciling with, and forgiving the past. In these actions, the groundwork for trustworthy relations is constructed for the intergenerational family.

Overview of the Therapeutic Process

We believe that the intergenerational ledger concept of the relational ethics dimension of contextual therapy is the best framework within which to address these two goals in therapy. However, we also believe that working with aging families involves the use of specific techniques. Although the contextual framework and the intergenerational ledger are used to organize and conceptualize family issues and problems, we also have integrated techniques from other therapies to facilitate the building of trust in the family. We have integrated these techniques to cover three broad stages of therapy with aging families: *life validation, life review,* and *interventions.* Again, each stage is used within the contextual framework and is aimed at the rejunctive effort of balancing obligations and entitlements in the last stage of life.

Life Validation

The beginning stage of therapy is called life validation (Asnes, 1983). The therapist uses a general *macrohistorical* knowledge of events to gain access to the older person's *microhistorical* perspective of his or her life. These initial sessions, usually with the older person alone, give the therapist the initial opportunity to join with the elderly client. As the older person talks about his or her individual history and perspective of development, the therapist has the opportunity to give credit and be partial in recognizing the client's background, history, and contribution. When the therapist takes this position of initial validation, the older person recognizes the therapist as an advocate; trust is formulated in the therapeutic relationship. The life validation stage also gives the therapist an initial opportunity to access the intergenerational family relationship ledger from the older individual's developmental perspective. Usually, this initial stage of therapy will last one or two sessions.

In choosing the historical events to use in the life validation process, therapists should try to refer to periods that are easy to recall and are at different individual and family developmental stages. For instance, a cohort of 80-

year-old people would have the following historical events associated with their developmental life cycle: World War I (childhood), ratification of the 19th Amendment and the Great Spanish Influenza Epidemic (adolescence), the Great Depression (young adulthood), World War II (early middle adulthood), the Korean conflict and the Cold War (late middle adulthood), and the assassination of John F. Kennedy (retirement).

Life Review

In Erikson's (1963) stages of psychosocial development, the last stage of old age is characterized by a struggle with ego integrity versus despair. The older person who faces the end of life and reflects upon the way that he or she has developed, accomplished goals, and maintained dignity will develop a sense of integrity and wisdom. One who looks upon his or her life as wasted and unfulfilled will despair in the hopelessness of being unable to change the past and not having enough time to live life differently. But from both perspectives, older people review their lives. One of the most influential therapies with older people, and certainly the best researched, is life review (Butler, 1963). As a person approaches death and reckons with personal invulnerability—at any age—a universal process of reminiscing about the past occurs. Life review in older people may result in greater self-awareness and wisdom or in excessive guilt, agitation, and despair. The review and reminiscence process seems to be especially intense around areas of past conflicts, regrettable choices, or hurts inflicted on others. Butler (1963) conceptualized the life review "as a naturally occurring, universal mental process, characterized by the progressive return to consciousness of past experiences, and, particularly, the resurgence of unresolved conflicts; simultaneously, and normally, these revived experiences and conflicts can be surveyed and reintegrated."

In the second stage of therapy, the therapist details the intergenerational family ledger issues using the life review. Contextual therapy concepts, such as fairness, trust, loyalty, and entitlement, are extremely evident as details of past events are revealed in the life review. Although the life review process can be done with just the older person, important details can be given by the entire family. Having the entire family present offers two benefits. First, as the older person talks of the past and the family understands, entitlement is earned; responsible and reciprocal interactions take place. This enhances trust in the family. Second, as the family interacts about the past, it clarifies not only ledger issues, but also systemic or transactional patterns in the family. Life review gives the therapist another opportunity to credit and be partial to family members, but the information in this stage of therapy is much more detailed than in the life-validation stage. Conflicts are clarified and resources are strengthened during this stage. The therapist can begin to hypothesize about family ledger imbalances and to look for specific points of therapeutic intervention.

Interventions

With the valuable background information gained in the first two stages of life validation and life review, the therapist moves the family to the third stage of therapy, called intervention. This stage lasts until the family therapy is terminated. The key element in constructing interventions is the ability of the therapist to encourage and coach the family to use its relational resources to address the imbalances in the ethical dimension. Therefore, with the knowledge of family ledger imbalances gained in the first two stages of life validation and life review, the therapist suggests interventions that will correct imbalances and build additional trust and resources in the family.

It is important to realize that when interventions are successful, the problems associated with aging do not dissipate. As we have seen, aging presents a variety of problems with which both strong and weak families must deal. Interventions are designed to relieve symptomatology and dysfunction. In addition, they are designed to strengthen the family so that the intergenerational group can deal successfully with the stresses and tasks that are ahead. Therefore, interventions are not simple problem-solving approaches. Rather, they are endeavors to build the family resources so that finishing life well can be accomplished.

There are three primary types of interventions that we use in this approach. The first is the contextual therapy technique of multidirected partiality (Boszormenyi-Nagy & Krasner, 1986). In any relationship, there is a balance between individual entitlements, or what an individual takes from the relationship, and family obligations, or what an individual contributes to the family to maintain relational existence. Multidirected partiality occurs when the therapist credits each family member's concerns in the relational balance of this exchange. A therapist's crediting or taking sides with each family member in turn motivates the family member to initiate trustworthy giving to others. Giving fair consideration to family members stimulates them to give fair consideration to others and the process of forging trustworthy actions begins a spiraling reciprocation in family relationships.

The second type of intervention we use is best called balancing obligations and entitlements (Hargrave & Anderson, 1992). Our society tends to treat older people as though they are useless because they are unable to perform in their old roles. It is our contention that older people have a valuable contribution to make to the intergenerational family, not because of what they do, but simply because of who they are. The eldest generation is replete with opportunities and resources to impart the emotional love, security, and trust that any relationship requires. In this type of balancing intervention, we try to coach the family in accessing their resources to meet the needs of the family. We especially use this intervention with older people who have shut down their giving to the family. For instance, an elderly woman in the early stages of Alzheimer's felt she was a burden to her family. In response to the feeling, she withdrew from relationships and came to resent her only daughter for her daughter's efforts to take care of her. Instead of focusing on the mother's unacceptable behavior, we chose to focus on the daughter's need for love, respect, and appreciation from her mother. When the mother saw the daughter's need, she immediately responded with tender and loving words of encouragement. This contribution, in turn, built a sense of entitlement with the mother so that she felt secure and accepting of the daughter's necessary help.

The third type of intervention we use is the work of forgiveness (Hargrave, 1994; Hargrave & Anderson, 1992). This intervention is designed to address the basic questions of love and trust in the family and rebuild relationships after severe family violations have occurred. We conceptualize forgiveness as two distinct efforts, one of exonerating and one of forgiving. Exonerating means that the victim is able to lift the load of culpability from the victimizer while making significant connection and identification, whereas forgiving means that the victim and victimizer are actually able to restore a loving and trustworthy relationship. Each step contributes to the process of forgiveness and each is appropriate in different situations and different relationships. We encourage the work of forgiveness through a four-station process of insight, understanding, giving the opportunity for compensation, and overt forgiving. Accomplishing the work of forgiveness is tough in therapy, but it is perhaps one of the supreme manifestations of finishing life well because it involves the work of a family willing to rebuild a relationship and trust one another even after severe damage.

THE THERAPEUTIC PROCESS

The Role of the Therapist

Adult children of the older person most often will be the ones to make the initial call or contact about therapy. The motivation to seek help for the older person is stimulated by several causes, which may be related to depression, anxiety, sleep disorders, disorientation, stagnation, stress, grief, symptomatology, or regret. The therapist first and foremost should be an advocate for all the generations and individuals in the family—whether they are present or not. One of the initial ways this is accomplished is to offer *respect* for each generational position. Here, we feel the age of the therapist is important. Whenever possible, the therapist should allow the older person to be the teacher about his or her life. Even the most despairing older adult has had a tremendous life experience simply due to having lived 70 or more years. Letting the older person and the family teach and recall various periods with respect recognizes an older person's wisdom of years. Also, it is essential to listen to the situation and stories of the family without reframing or giving alternative meanings. The family tells the story in certain ways because it is a reflection of the relational ethics dimension and the family ledger. To reframe or try to change meaning violates the family's perception of their relationships. The therapist should speak to adults in the room as equal adults. This models for the family the fact that even though the therapist may be young, he or she is able to relate to each adult generation on an adult level. This is important for the older generations in recognizing the contributions of the therapist, but it is also important to younger adults, who will witness, perhaps for the first time, how to take adult positions with older family members. A common mistake of therapists working with older people for the first time is to talk to them as if they need help in understanding everyday language.

During the middle stage of therapy, the advocacy role of the therapist shifts slightly from the emphasis of being taught to include more overt partiality toward individual family members and a role as commentator on family interaction and relational issues. As family members realize that their individual issues will be credited by the therapist, they are more willing to listen and credit other members' issues. Therefore, the overt partiality shown by the therapist serves as a model of giving and trust for the family. As the therapist comments on family interaction and relational issues, the family is encouraged to explore their own resources in addressing some of the problems in the family.

During the intervention stage of therapy with aging families, the role of the therapist shifts to that of an intergenerational coach. Although there clearly are interventions and directives suggested by the contextual therapist, the interventions that we are discussing here are much more directive and may entail more involvement on the part of the therapist. We suggest for two primary reasons more directive coaching by the therapist during interventions than what is usually found in the contextual approach. First, the intergenerational aging family interacts much like a *disengaged* family (Minuchin, 1974); that is, family members are not as involved in day-to-day activities with each other. In an aging family, this usually is not due to impenetrable or rigid boundaries, although these may also exist, but occurs simply because the intergenerational family members seldom live together.

This lack of interaction and time together to work things out makes it difficult for the family to explore new relational options. Many times, the therapy session will be the longest period the family spends together at any one time. These families simply need more direction from the therapist.

Second, there is the element of past and future. Most aging families have had imbalanced relational issues for decades; discovering new options may be difficult without the therapist's suggesting new methods of intervention. There is also a limited future for the aging family. The oldest generation only has a certain amount of time to build intergenerational trust. These members cannot realistically expect to have a decade or even several years to explore trustworthy relations. As a directive coach, the therapist can help the family address old wounds sooner and point clearly to new balances of family interactions.

There are certainly more concerns in doing therapy with a family whose eldest participating member is 85 years old than in one where the eldest member is 40 years old. Many of these issues are very practical in nature. Therapists, for example, must be more sensitive to room lighting to ensure the best opportunity for the older person to see. Since many older people experience hearing loss, therapists must speak clearly with sufficient volume. If older clients wear hearing aids, other noises, such as air conditioners and heater fans, must be kept to a minimum. Even the sitting area must be considered. Firm, slightly elevated, but comfortable seats are of great assistance to the older person. All of these considerations express sensitivity toward aging members and foster positive interaction.

Assessment

Assessment is the key to discovering the relational resources necessary to construct good interventions that will help the family build trustworthy relations through intergenerational balance. However, it is important to remember that assessment is a continuing activity throughout the therapy process. The therapist should assess the family and have initial "hunches," but these ideas should be held tentatively with room for modification as therapy proceeds. Since there are four dimensions to the relational reality of the aging family system, assessment should proceed through these four organizing factors.

Assessment of Facts

Some facts may be changeable, such as medical conditions, and others may be irreversible, such as growing up in an adoptive family. No matter what the facts, it is important that the therapist assess and give fair consideration to how the facts have shaped the family.

The medical facts are usually the most common context for assessment done with older people in our society. Indeed, such facts are important as one assesses an older person, because they will have a strong impact on how the individual feels about him- or herself and how the rest of the family interacts. For instance, if an older person cannot walk or does not have the manual dexterity necessary to dress, this affects his or her ability to maintain an effective self-image and it will have impact on the family as well as on other social relationships. Cognitive assessment of the older person is also necessary. While there are elaborate procedures for psychological assessment of an individual's cognitive status, we are essentially interested in memory and affect. An older person may have Alzheimer's disease or organic brain syndrome, but in early or moderate stages, the person will still have access to some memory and have quite dynamic affect.

One of the more essential areas of assessment concerns the medications being taken and physical condition of the older person. Most older people seek medical advice from a variety of physicians for numerous physical ailments. Family members are usually very supportive of the elder member seeking the help of several physicians in dealing with their problems. Often, physicians will prescribe medications for the conditions and the older person may end up taking several medications for an array of ailments for years at a time. Sometimes the prescribing physicians are not aware of the full medication regime and the older person becomes overmedicated. Further, some medications may actually work against the conditions that other medications are working to correct. Some medications will cause extreme behavior in older people, such as depression, hallucinations, and tremors. It is important for the therapist to assess the effects of the medication regime and work with the physicians and the family to medicate the older person only when necessary and helpful. Up to 43 percent of older people misuse drugs in some way (Raffoul, Cooper, & Love, 1981). No amount of therapy will cure anxiety or depression if the cause of the problem comes in the form of daily medication.

However, not all of the assessment of facts is on a medical level. The therapist must also be sensitive to the circumstances that have shaped the individuals and the family. For instance, the loss of parents, extreme poverty, malnutrition, child abuse, poor school attendance or performance, adoption, psychiatric illnesses, and criminal records may all be a part of the factual dimension (Boszormenyi-Nagy & Krasner, 1986). Predetermined or irreversible facts will have a dynamic effect on individual development. Therefore, the facts of the family through various stages of the life cycle must be traced. A good method of tracing these developmental facts is by creating a family genogram (McGoldrick & Gerson, 1985). Genograms allow the therapist to organize important factual information by creating a family tree in the first few sessions. Besides being a good assessment tool, genograms can be used in the intervention process. Genograms also serve as a joining technique for all family members.

Assessment of Individual Psychology

The individual psychology dimension is a subjective realm that involves learning, conditioning, behavior, and development. It is difficult for any one psychological theory to account for all of these different modalities, but it is necessary for the therapist to gain some appreciation and insight into the personality and development of each individual in the family. Here, it is important not to classify individuals into diagnostic categories that may overemphasize behavioral tendencies (Boszormenyi-Nagy & Krasner, 1986). The essential assessment area of individual psychology for the therapist is to learn how responsible individuals in the family are and what interventions will work best with the family.

It is important for the therapist to understand some of the developmental issues that have contributed to each family member's psyche. As we have mentioned before, these will often become evident during the life validation and life review stages of therapy and are understood best in terms of Erikson's psychosocial development. Erikson, Erikson, and Kivnick (1986) have illustrated how each psychosocial crisis has various potentials for the psychic development of individuals. An adapted form of this illustration is found in Table 3.1. Adaptive strengths are present in the individual if the psychosocial crisis is negotiated in realistic balance. Maladaptive tendencies are found in individuals who are imbalanced at one end of the psychosocial crisis—for instance, too trusting or too autonomous. The malignant tendencies are found in individuals who are unable to negotiate the crisis. This framework is important to assessment because it enables the therapist to credit each family member's individual position and perspective in the relational reality. It also gives the therapist crucial insight into what issues will be most important to each family member, thereby making the therapist more of an advocate for each person in therapy.

Assessment of Family or Systemic Transactions

In assessing the family or systemic interactions, it is central for the therapist to understand the communication process and power alignments in the family. These communication patterns and power hierarchies give key information on how to go about intervening with the family in order to change behavioral patterns that serve as barriers to balancing the intergenerational ledger.

The first area of this dimension encompasses family members' involvement with one another. In other words, is the family *disengaged* or *enmeshed*

A Contextual Family Therapy Approach

TABLE 3.1
Adaptive Tendencies of Psychosocial Development

Maladaptive Tendency	Psychosocial Crisis	Malignant Tendency	Adaptive Strength
Sensory maladjustment	Trust vs. mistrust	Withdrawal	Hope
Shameless willfulness	Autonomy vs. shame/doubt	Compulsion	Will
Ruthlessness	Initiative vs. guilt	Inhibition	Purpose
Narrow competence	Industry vs. inferiority	Inertia	Virtuosity
Fanaticism	Identity vs. role confusion	Repudiation	Fidelity
Promiscuity	Intimacy vs. isolation	Exclusivity	Love
Overextension	Generativity vs. stagnation	Rejectivity	Care
Presumption	Integrity vs. despair	Disdain	Wisdom

Adapted from an illustration appearing in Erikson, Erikson, and Kivnick (1986).

(Minuchin, 1974). Disengaged families generally are uninvolved with each other. There may be a general lack of caring among members, making it very difficult to get them to interact with one another. Family members are disconnected from each other's thoughts and emotional processes. Members of enmeshed families are generally overinvolved with one another. There is usually a disregard of individual or personal boundaries, which reduces the sense of self-identity. Family members will think, speak, and act on another member's behalf. Self-delineation in these families may be so vague that problems for one family member may cause unbearable pain for another. Whereas it is difficult to get disengaged families to interact with one another, enmeshed families make validation tough because individual responsibility gets lost in a global emotional field of members feeling and acting on one another's behalf.

The second concern in assessing this dimension relates to family communication. Communication, whether manifest in verbal or nonverbal behavior, specifies family meanings and rules. Important to well-functioning families is the clarity of communication matching metacommunication (Bateson, 1972), or verbal matching nonverbal. If communication is unclear, there is high potential for *double-bind* messages (Bateson, Jackson, Haley, & Weakland, 1956). For instance, an older mother may insist that her daughters show love and care for her but then berate them because they do not let her be independent. When the daughters in turn distance themselves to let the mother be independent, they are accused of not caring. Such messages hinder responsible family interactions. Another aspect of communication that requires attention is the level of honesty in the family. Members of some families may be hesitant to talk honestly with one another and will avoid painful or emotionally charged subjects. In these families, members sometimes will talk about other members when they are not present, make important family decisions alone, and actively deceive one another.

A final consideration in assessing this dimension involves the power hierarchy and alignments in the family. In order to intervene and learn from families in a constructive manner, the power structure of the family must be understood. Often this power structure will be made overt in the communication patterns of the family. For instance, one person is responsible for the group communication. A person in this position may speak for others, may tell them how to interpret communication, and may monitor communication. This person would be extremely powerful. Generally, power can be understood in terms of which persons make things happen in the family or prevent things from happening in the family.

It is important to realize that with any family, but especially with an intergenerational aging family, the family system is not the only system that operates. More complex community and social systems become more important as an aging family requires additional resources. Boundaries and communications among neighbors, friends, social services, medical services, and support agencies become so intermixed at times that appropriate expectations are unclear (Wolinsky, 1990).

Assessment of Relational Ethics

The assessment of the fourth dimension of relational ethics is the most important component in the relational reality of the family. The intergenerational processes of fairness, reliability, and trustworthiness are key to this dimension (Boszormenyi-Nagy & Krasner, 1986). An initial step in assessing this dimension is to determine equity in the balance between what an individual is obligated to give to the family and what the individual is entitled to receive. This equity is ferreted out in dialogue with the family and is evident as members talk about fairness, being cheated, or being underbenefited or overbenefited.

People who have given too much without receiving their just entitlement feel that they have been cheated of their fair share. They may then become cynical to the point that they are unable to recognize the efforts of other family members to give to them. They may discount the gestures of others as being too meager and tend to depend on their own self-sufficiency. They do, however, still hold family members responsible to fulfill entitlement. This puts the family in an awkward position of the individual's refusing to take what the family offers, but holding the family responsible for its inability or unwillingness to give enough. Such situations provide evidence for the assumption of severe deterioration in the level of trustworthiness in the family.

On the other hand, family members who consistently overbenefit from the family and do not fulfill obligations may experience guilt. People in this position may feel fearful and helpless in dealing with life. They may have taken so much from the family that they feel as if they owe too great a debt to others. They have been cared for all their lives without giving reciprocal care. Now they may believe that there is no other option but to continue the same pattern. Generally, these people lack a clear sense of identity and self-esteem; they are irresponsible in fulfilling their familial roles.

In working with aging families, this emotional field in the relational ethics dimension is the most essential object of therapy. If there is a rejunctive effort to balance justice in the family by the way of fair giving and taking, trustworthiness is established and the family and older person can actively work on finishing well. If the emotional field is not addressed effectively, then the family continues harboring the same imbalances, which results in little modification in dysfunctional actions.

TREATMENT APPLICABILITY AND CASE EXAMPLE

In aging families where there is an imbalance of fairness in the family that has prompted emotional distress, the intergenerational group may be void of trust resources. A lack of trust resources can often result in destructive family action toward one another and dysfunction becomes evident. In these types of families, an approach that utilizes the tenets of contextual therapy is very effective. It is reasonable to anticipate that this type of therapeutic approach through the three stages would last between 6 and 10 sessions. However, depending on the level of family distress, therapy might be long-term and take up to 30 or 35 sessions.

Case Example: Missing Margaret

In the following case example, a 71-year-old woman had periods of hysteria and was so filled with anxiety about her family's safety that she refused to be left alone. She would call her 37-year-old daughter repeatedly during the day to make sure she and her family were safe. She eventually refused to let the husband go to the bathroom by himself because she was fearful that something would happen to him. Although the family reported that she had always been anxious, she was becoming more dysfunctional and it was causing great distress in the family. In addition, she was having severe lapses of memory and the family was concerned that she was developing Alzheimer's disease. Recently, she was finding it difficult to keep her balance while walking.

The father, mother, and daughter all attended the first session. In assessing the family, the therapist was very interested in the mother's slurred speech, memory lapses, and inability to keep her balance while walking even though she had no apparent injury. He questioned the family about the medications the mother was taking. The father revealed that his wife had been given Valium by her family physician and that he had been "directed" to give her the medication "when she needed it." In the father's opinion, she was constantly filled with anxiety so she was always in need of medication. The mother was severely overmedicated and the therapist suspected that this was the cause of her physical ailments. The mother was sent to a physician for a thorough physical examination where it was confirmed that overmedication was responsible for the physical problems.

The second session took place two weeks later after the mother had fully recovered from the medication effects. Although her memory and balance had returned, her anxiety level was still very high. The therapist started the second session by utilizing the technique of life validation to build trust with the mother.

Therapist	Tell me a little about your life. You would have been entering the work world or marrying around the time of the Great Depression?
Mother	I worked as a teacher and librarian. I didn't marry until I was in my 30s.
Daughter	Mama was known the world over as having the most organized library in any school.

Therapist	Oh, really?
Mother	I was always able to hold things together. The school principal would depend on me to organize and administrate much of the school schedule because he knew I could get it done.
Therapist	So you could get things done, even though you didn't have the power of a principal.
Mother	Everybody knew that I meant what I said. They just didn't cross me.
Daughter	(*laughing*) It was because they were all scared of you. Even the principal was scared.
Therapist	So you were extremely organized and important to your school.
Mother	I'm very proud to say, Yes. I was chosen to set up libraries all over this state because the administration knew that it would be done right. I had a very good reputation.

The therapist had validated the woman's career and she felt her self-esteem rise as a result of the exchange. This helped bind the therapist to the woman for later work. The woman talked about her organization in such a way that indicated that she was almost tyrannical in her administrative style—an indication that was overcontrolling. However, the therapist did not reframe or challenge this characteristic at this stage. He was more interested in joining with the mother.

Toward the end of the first session when the therapist was asking the mother about her childhood, she revealed that her young sister has been killed when she was a girl while they were playing in the front yard. The therapist hypothesized that this early trauma might have played a role in the mother's anxious and overcontrolling behavior to counter fear. At the next session, the therapist entered into the life review stage of therapy, asking the mother to recount this past trauma. Once the mother confirmed that the event had shaped her life, the therapist asked her to explore the incident more carefully.

Therapist	Get a mental picture of you and your sister, Margaret.
Mother	All I can see is me standing on the curb and that Model T touring car—with the sliding glass windows up. The lady was learning how to drive. I remember seeing that car come down the private drive. They shouldn't have been on the private drive. She came, and she saw the children. We were playing "catch the streetcar." It ran right by, you know, on the side of the house. And we were out there playing like we were going to catch the streetcar. And as the car came down, Margaret

	stepped off the curb and it frightened the woman. She lost control of the car and hit Margaret.
Therapist	When Margaret got hit, did you see it happen?
Mother	Yes, I was standing right by her. We were holding hands, and the force knocked Margaret's hand out of mine and took Margaret instead of me.
Therapist	And when you see this, are you seeing it like you were watching a movie or do you see it like you were inside yourself?
Mother	(*pause*) I can only see a picture of Margaret with her hand held out when she was holding mine and we were standing together. Mama or someone had taken a picture of us like that. They inked me out and left Margaret, just a picture of Margaret standing in the picture. And this hand is out, you know, and I'm not with her. It's out waiting for me, but I'm not with her.
Therapist	And you're left alone.
Mother	I'm left alone, and I wish I could cry.
Therapist	You lost Margaret. Was it your fault?
Mother	No, I don't believe so. She stepped away from me. I just miss her. I guess I've always missed her, and that's why I've probably ruined my daughter's life. I have always been terrified if I couldn't see my family, or if they went anywhere, I walked the floor until they came home.
Therapist	What were you afraid of?
Mother	I was afraid they wouldn't come back.

Here the woman made the connection herself between her overcontrolling behavior and her current anxiety. During the rest of the therapy session, the therapist encouraged the father and daughter to refer to this incident and remind the mother overtly of the trauma when she became overanxious about them. The mother was calmer with the insight and reported that she felt her burden lifting.

During the next two sessions, when the therapist would encourage the family to talk about past life events that shaped their relationships, the therapist noticed that there was an extreme hesitancy to talk honestly with the mother. The therapist hypothesized that this was an effort to protect the mother from pain and protect the family from engaging her at a point where she would overcontrol. The therapist, in the fifth session, initiated a balancing obligations and entitlements intervention with the family. He started by questioning the daughter about her protecting behavior.

Therapist	You seem to protect your mother from the truth.

Daughter	I have to. I'm the one who always keeps it together. I'm the one they depend on. But lately, I don't know if I can take it any more.
Therapist	Things are difficult?
Daughter	My husband's mother is very sick. My children need attention. I am just about to the end.
Therapist	What could your mother do to help?
Daughter	(*almost laughing*) I've never really considered it. She is always so worried about everything. If I got her involved, it would just be one more thing to take care of.
Therapist	I'm not sure your mother is that fragile. If she could help you, what would you want?
Daughter	(*starts to cry*) Just to be there. Like my mother-in-law. She is so sick but is always concerned about me. She always gives me kind words. I wish it was like that between us.
Mother	I can see how important she is to you.
Therapist	Could you help your daughter?
Mother	I certainly could try.

At this point, the therapist helped the mother and daughter identify specific things that the mother could do that would demonstrate love and concern. The mother called the daughter and engaged her in conversation about her and tried to be supportive. She also started making clothes for the grandchildren. Through the next four sessions, the therapist and family explored new ways for the mother to give to the daughter. As the mother gave to the daughter, her anxiety continued to be reduced. In addition, the mother and daughter developed a closer and more intimate relationship.

CONCLUSION

We utilize a contextual family therapy approach as a model to conceptualize trust building and problems in the older family. Through the process of life validation, life review, and interventions, we try to motivate change in the elder family by moving them toward trustworthy interactions. Any therapeutic effort that forges this type of intergenerational trust makes the family stronger and will eventually produce a healthier intergenerational group. While it is true that not all families will completely resolve long-standing problems, we believe that all families can improve on their histories in the last stage of life to initiate the type of bonds that will help them finish life well.

REFERENCES

Anderson, W. T., & Hargrave, T. D. (1990). Contextual family therapy and older people: Building trust in the intergenerational family. *Journal of Family Therapy, 12*, 311-320.

Asnes, D. P. (1983). The life validation approach in psychotherapy with elderly patients. *Journal of Geriatric Psychiatry, 16*, 87-97.

Bateson, G. (1972). *Steps to an ecology of the mind.* New York: Ballantine.

Bateson, G., Jackson, D., Haley, J., & Weakland, J. (1956). Toward a theory of schizophrenia. *Behavioral Science, 1*, 251-264.

Boszormenyi-Nagy, I. (1986). Transgenerational solidarity: The expanding context of therapy and prevention. *American Journal of Family Therapy, 14*, 195-212.

Boszormenyi-Nagy, I., & Krasner, B. (1980). Trust-based therapy: A contextual approach. *American Journal of Psychiatry, 137*, 767-775.

Boszormenyi-Nagy, I., & Krasner, B. (1986). *Between give and take: A clinical guide to contextual therapy.* New York: Brunner/Mazel.

Boszormenyi-Nagy, I., & Spark, G. (1984). *Invisible loyalties.* New York: Brunner/Mazel.

Boszormenyi-Nagy, I., & Ulrich, D. N. (1981). Contextual family therapy. In A. S. Gurman & D. P. Kniskern (Eds.), *Handbook of family therapy* (pp. 159-186). New York: Brunner/Mazel.

Butler, R. N. (1963). The life review: An interpretation of reminiscence in the aged. *Psychiatry, 26*, 65-76.

Erikson, E. H. (1963). *Childhood and society* (2nd ed.). New York: Norton.

Erikson, E. H., Erikson, J. M., & Kivnick, H. Q. (1986). *Vital involvement in old age.* New York: Norton.

Hargrave, T. D. (1994). *Families and forgiveness: Healing wounds in the intergenerational family.* New York: Brunner/Mazel.

Hargrave, T. D., & Anderson, W. T. (1990). Helping older people finish well: A contextual family therapy approach. *Family Therapy, 23*(1), 9-19.

Hargrave, T. D., & Anderson, W. T. (1992). *Finishing well: Aging and reparation in the intergenerational family.* New York: Brunner/Mazel.

Hargrave, T. D., Jennings, G., & Anderson, W. T. (1991). The development of a relational ethics scale. *Journal of Marital and Family Therapy, 17*, 145-159.

McGoldrick, M., & Gerson, R. (1985). *Genograms in family assessment.* New York: Norton.

Minuchin, S. (1974). *Families and family therapy.* Cambridge, MA: Harvard University Press.

Raffoul, P. R., Cooper, J. K., & Love, D. W. (1981). Drug misuse in older people. *The Gerontologist, 21*, 146-150.

Wolinsky, M. A. (1990). *A heart of wisdom: Marital counseling with older and elderly couples.* New York: Brunner/Mazel.

4

Solution-Focused Brief Therapy with Aging Families

Marilyn J. Bonjean
ICF Consultants, Inc.
Milwaukee, Wisconsin

The therapist asked Mrs. Glenn, her client, how she could be helpful and the client and therapist began the therapeutic process of collaborative solution construction. Mrs. Glenn replied: "If I were 50 again, it would be different." She explained, "But I'm not 50, I'm 75 and I have some heart problems. My husband is in a nursing home because he had a stroke four years ago and I couldn't take care of him at home. Now my daughter is having mental problems. She has been in and out of the hospital and I don't know what will happen. She has two children and they need care. I can do a little for them but I can't bring them up if that is what's needed. If I were younger, it would be different, but at 75 I have to be realistic about the future and the choices I have."

Therapist Figuring out a realistic plan for helping your family certainly isn't easy. I know you are very worried about them and trying to find the right thing to do. Are there certain parts of this situation we should start examining together?

Mrs. Glenn (*in a tearful voice*) Yes, I'm just frantic they will expect me to take care of the children completely. I don't think I can manage a teenager. I need to figure out how to talk to my daughter's doctor.

Therapist	I'm sure it is frustrating trying to figure out the hos communication. However, you would feel better if y have a useful conversation with your daughter's phy that right?
Mrs. Glenn	It would be a start, but I think he blames me for my d problems. I tried to be a good mother, but she has h rough time.
Therapist	It is hard to talk to someone you feel blames you, a ers do get blamed for a lot. Have you ever had any (tions with the physician that you thought went a litt

Solution-focused brief therapy is an effective approach to help adults achieve their goals. Mrs. Glenn has begun to form a relation: the therapist that will serve as the context for finding solutions th her. She is beginning to define goals and will now be assisted in e: any exceptions to the situation she has identified as a problem. As t pist adapts to the client's language, world view, and values, a stanc that the client has the ability to solve problems and the therapist's facilitate this discovery of inherent strength and aptitude.

Behaviorally describing problems occurring in the present an goals that, when achieved, are clearly credited to the client's eff(firming. The client is free to express intimate feelings if comforta so, but the emphasis is placed on behavioral changes rather than o: A brief, solution-focused approach helps older adults experience results from therapy fairly quickly and enhances their commitme therapeutic process.

THEORETICAL BACKGROUND

Solution-focused brief therapy developed from the work of fam pists at the Brief Family Therapy Center in Milwaukee, Wisconsi member of that group for five years. In the first book describing waukee group's work, Steve deShazer (1982) traces the history of b tion-focused therapy dating back to Milton H. Erickson. In *Spe niques of Brief Hypnotherapy,* Erickson (1954) described a brief the uses neurotic symptomatology to meet the unique needs of the c utilized, with very good success, whatever clients brought to tl solve problems without trying to find and solve causative underl adjustments. Erickson viewed clients as having within their socia the resources for changes to occur. The therapist and client toge use these resources to solve problems. Erickson emphasized respecting the abilities of clients and the responsibility of the therapist to help focus these abilities toward behavior to achieve client goals.

A further influence on solution-focused brief therapy was that of the Brief Therapy Center established at the Mental Research Institute (MRI) in Palo Alto, California. In *Brief Therapy: Focused Problem Resolution,* Weakland, Fisch, Watzlawick, and Bodin (1974) set forth some ideas about problems, how they are maintained and how change happens.

These ideas were also being examined at about the same time by the original Milwaukee group at the Brief Family Therapy Center (BFTC), which gradually developed a brief method focused on the solution rather than on the problem. DeShazer described this process (Cade, 1985):

> Over the last three or four years we have shifted significantly from a concern with problems, complaints, and how to solve them, to a concern with solutions and how they work. Over this time, we have become convinced that solutions, from case to case, have more in common than the problems they solve. We used to think that solutions had to bear a fairly high degree of correspondence to the problems and complaints brought in by families or clients. We have now come to the conclusion that very little correspondence may be necessary. (p. 5)

In 1988, Eve Lipchik and I established our joint practice, ICF Consultants, Incorporated, to continue to explore the relationship between therapist and client, the role of emotion in this model, and the application of the model to various issues, such as aging, domestic violence, and medical family therapy. As a gerontologist and family therapist, my work has often been with older families or in settings with chronically medically ill adults and their families. I have continued to utilize and develop the brief solution-focused model because the clients with whom I work often have little time for change to occur before very dramatic transitions take place, such as loss of family support, placement in a nursing home, or increased health problems. They have been disempowered by multiple losses, failing control over their bodies, and involvement in hierarchical relationships with community helpers and agencies. This model emphasizes client strengths and the importance of the therapist's adapting to create a fit with the client's values, language, and world view. The essential elements in therapy are the primacy of client goals and measures of change meaningful to the client. The approach empowers clients and engenders hope for both the clients and therapist.

THERAPEUTIC MODEL

Therapeutic Assumptions

Therapy models are based on certain assumptions about the nature of the person, problem formation and maintenance, creation of change, the role of the client, and the role of the therapist. Making assumptions explicit allows the therapist to discuss behaviors with clients. The assumptions underlying solution-focused brief therapy are well described by Walter and Peller (1992).

Assumption One

Therapy that focuses on the positive, on the solution, and on the future facilitates change in the desired direction. Many other professions are also emphasizing the importance of positive visualization and mental rehearsal. In medicine, sports, and business, the study of excellence or success is a developing trend.

Assumption Two

Exceptions to every problem can be created by the therapist and client, which can then be used to build a solution. This may seem an impossible task in therapy, perhaps because the concept of exceptions and solutions is not broad enough. An exception can be any fluctuation in the problem situation itself, variations in coping ability, increased acceptance—anything that implies change for this client. Solutions may be choosing to remain in a difficult situation rather than feeling trapped or utilizing a community resource so that caregiving is a little less strenuous physically. Finding a solution often does not mean dramatic differences, but enough change to meet the client's goals.

Assumption Three

Change is occurring all the time; it is a constant. As human beings, however, our brains screen out much of the environmental fluctuation. We see only a fraction of what is in our environment. We are not apt to find exceptions to problems or possible solutions, just as by design we are unaware of the blind spot in the eye. The brain is designed to respond to important events for our survival, not the total complexity of the world (Ornstein & Thompson, 1984). The collaboration of the therapist and client can broaden the perception of variations in the client circumstances.

Questions asked by the therapist can help the client notice and/or interpret occurrences differently. For example, Mrs. Clark came to therapy because she was enraged at her husband. He had Alzheimer's disease and would often argue with her over things that happened, which were clearly caused by his memory problems, such as losing items or only half completing projects. She wanted him to admit his fault. When she observed times that they argued less, she discerned it was when she did not push for admission of fault. There was some variation in their arguments. She also noticed the changes in her husband from a very self-confident man to one who needed to guard his self-esteem. The therapist's questions helped her identify a method of changing the arguments by not pushing as hard as she would have before her husband became ill and concentrating instead on preserving his self-esteem.

Assumption Four

Small change leads to larger change. Difficulties are often solved one step at a time. Any change by one person in an interactional system will influence others in that system and the continuous systemic reactions will reinforce continued change. Older adults with multiple losses may have little tolerance for more change since even positive changes are stressful. Incremental steps will be easier for the client and can lay a foundation for more steps over time.

Mrs. Gold had become very depressed after her husband's death and her health had deteriorated. She had always been an avid walker, but had given it up because she knew that walking her usual three miles was impossible. As she worked with the therapist, Mrs. Gold decided that taking walks would be a sign to her of returning to more of her old self. She began by sitting on her front steps, then walking to the first tree in front of the house, and finally increasing the length of her walk. As she resumed walking, people along the way greeted her and her social contact and support increased. The therapist encouraged her to go slowly, trusting that these positive changes would become cumulative and self-reinforcing.

Assumption Five

Cooperation is inevitable. Client behavior that is not illegal or harmful to self and others, is accepted as part of the client's thinking about how to influence the environment for what is believed to be in his or her best interest. When a client goes about change slowly or questions suggestions of the therapist, it is informative to the therapist to match the pace of change and assist the client through his or her unique manner of changing. Resistance is the reaction of the client to misunderstanding or inflexibility on the part of the therapist.

Mr. North was a retired executive accustomed to running his own corporation. He came to therapy at the insistence of his children, who were concerned about his possible remarriage after the death of their mother five years earlier. Mr. North made it clear to the therapist that he knew about hiring consultants since he had often done so for his business. He wanted the therapist to consult with him on improving the communication between himself and the woman he was currently dating. He thought this should be done by the therapist's describing various alternative behaviors he could try so that he could evaluate them one by one. Instead of disagreeing with Mr. North, the therapist complied with his request. She also, however, asked him questions to identify his most successful communication style so that any suggestion would fit for him. This raised issues regarding the pros and cons of each choice. Mr. North agreed and a cooperative relationship was established.

Assumption Six

People can resourcefully create change. They can make changes in their circumstances, belief systems, or perceptions of their circumstances. This model emphasizes a nonpathologizing approach so that the therapist can help facilitate change toward goals rather than assess character or behavioral defects.

Mrs. Biddle was very upset. She was in danger of losing her home care because she criticized each aide who was sent to her home. She explained to the therapist that she had always been very careful in her work and could not tolerate the way various aides did the job. She could not just let them do careless work. Mrs. Biddle and the therapist discussed her former occupation as a florist and Mrs. Biddle explained that she was very good at keeping competent employees. The therapist asked her how she treated and managed the employees. Mrs. Biddle described how she had trained each employee to do well and then praised him or her. The therapist then asked her to begin to think about the aides as her employees and design training for them. As Mrs. Biddle began to feel more in control with the aides, she became less critical and was better liked by the home care agency.

Assumption Seven

Meaning and experience are constructed between the individual experience and the interactions among people. People share their experience in language and symbol and so meanings evolve and change in interactions.

Assumption Eight

Actions and descriptions are circular. How a situation is described influences the actions that will be taken in that situation. When descriptions are changed, different actions become possible. For example, Mrs. Eastman and her daughter came to therapy because the daughter wanted to improve communication with her mother. As therapy progressed, Mrs. Eastman was able to explain to her daughter that she thought they did communicate because they talked with each other. The daughter had a different definition of communication. She thought they should share feelings and that her mother did not want to be close to her because so few feelings were shared. Mrs. Eastman was able to explain her upbringing, which had not encouraged the exchange of emotion, and her view that a mother's role was to listen to her daughter to show caring. With this new understanding of what communication meant and what behaviors indicated caring to both women, the mother and daughter could construct a solution that respected both points of view.

Assumption Nine

Both the therapist and client are experts. The therapist will bring a knowledge of human development, models of change, information about community resources, an ability to assist clients in focusing their energy on problem solving, alternative viewpoints of client problems, and solutions for consideration. The client will bring a viewpoint of personal circumstances, a definition of the problems and their solution, strengths, problem-solving abilities, and a preferred manner of going about change. It is in the interaction between client and therapist that something can happen that will influence the client viewpoint and/or circumstances so that the client will determine that goals have been met and that the problematic situation is "better enough" for termination.

Therapeutic Process

Solution-focused therapy is based on a systemic epistemology. Epistemology is the study of how we know what we know. How we think is tied to what we believe we know. Traditional psychotherapy models are based on linear epistemologies that consist of discrete elements assumed to have existences of their own, independent of contexts and relationships. One element acts upon another to produce an effect that stops and starts. *A* causes *B*. Systemic epistemologies recognize patterns and relationships influenced by context. *A* and *B* are in relationship to each other and are recursively influenced by each other. Since we live in a continuous flow of sensory experience, we make sense of it by drawing distinctions. We say that *A* is different from *B* and so draw a boundary. We can draw these boundaries in many different ways (Keeney, 1983). One way is to include only the biomedical aspects of problematic situations of a client; another is to include only the psychological aspects of the situation, and still another is to focus only on the social components. A useful approach is to consider the recursive influence of all three of these elements as the client and therapist interact together. The multiple descriptions that can result from considering these levels of experience produce a rich, flexible consideration of areas of possible solution.

Problems are formed as clients punctuate or interpret their experience in ways that cause them discomfort or pressure from the surrounding community. A change in punctuation can lead to different behavior or different behavior to new punctuation. Insight is not seen as necessary for change. The goal of developing insight can mean that there is a correct view, which the therapist knows and should help the client find. If we live in a continuous flow of experience, then punctuation of experience is arbitrary. There is no correct insight to achieve.

Some clients, however, value insight and believe that to achieve their goals, they will need an explanation of their problems. If this is so, the therapist can assist the client in finding an explanation that is plausible for the client so that the punctuation of change can take place. Since problems are viewed as part of a particular context that maintains them and gives them meaning, a small change is all that is necessary if it alters the defining context. Attempted solutions have often been drawn from the same frame as the problem and have just served to perpetuate problem patterns. Separating the problem from the solution allows us to concentrate on differences and on possible change. The solution is not seen as emerging from the problematic situation, but from a totally different situation to be described and understood. The therapist, therefore, will focus on the solution—a more positively viewed future—by asking questions that elicit a description of the desired state. This allows goals to become clear so the client and therapist have a direction for therapy. Examples of such questions are: How will you know when you no longer need to come to therapy? If a miracle occurred and your problems disappeared, what would be different? Who would notice? How would it affect you and them? How would you know if things were better? When that happens, who would be affected and how?

Often clients have experienced some fluctuation in the intensity or occurrence of the problem. This is investigated by asking whether anything in this positively envisioned future happens at all now. If so, the therapist can investigate the conditions under which exceptions happen and how more of these circumstances can occur. Some clients will not identify any exceptions to their problems. If this is the case, the therapist can examine with them what will need to happen for a small change to occur. Clients who can identify exceptions or show enthusiasm for working on small changes are usually easier for the therapist to work with than those who are ambivalent about change or envision no positive future. Scaling questions can be useful for some clients to achieve a subjective measure of their present location on the change continuum and mark progress toward goals. Scaling would involve the therapist's asking the client, "On a scale of 0 to 10, where 0 represents the worst and 10 the way things will be when problems are resolved, where would you place yourself now?" Berg (1991) suggests many uses of scaling questions that can assess the client's self-esteem, self-confidence, investment in change, willingness to work hard to bring about desired changes, prioritizing of problems to be solved, perception of hopefulness, and evaluation of progress.

In the solution-focused approach, clients are invited to recognize what they are already doing to move toward their goals. This invitation is much more attractive to clients when their feelings of frustration, failure, grief, depression, and so on are acknowledged and accepted by the therapist. Asking clients how they have managed to continue to cope as well as they have in difficult circumstances both recognizes the difficulty of the problem and underscores the exceptions. Struggling with clients to get acknowledgment of exceptions is seldom useful. A respectful curiosity about differences or coping ability over a period of time is usually much more helpful to change.

Questions about exceptions or positive futures may be very difficult for some clients to answer. They are being asked to focus on positive emotions when they may feel bad and it is more congruent for them to talk about problems (Kiser, Piercy, & Lipchik, 1993). Clients may try to protect themselves from disappointment or the consequences of change. Solution-focused therapists have tended to encourage translating feelings into observable behaviors. In essence, the therapist asks the client how he or she will act when feeling better. For some clients, this task is too difficult. In these instances, the sharing of feelings with another human being who understands and accepts them is a beginning step in change.

The power of the therapist's empathetic human presence should not be underestimated in gradually helping clients express feelings in ways that are likely to lead to greater satisfaction in daily life. When clients remain ambivalent about change, it is useful for the therapist to explore the reasons they have for going slowly. Sometimes the ambivalence results from considering change in either/or terms (Lipchik, 1993). Either I am a good daughter and visit my mother in the nursing home every day or I am a bad daughter and stay away to take care of myself. Considering a both/and position may help the client out of this dilemma so that she can visit and also do more self-care.

Acknowledging that the client's autonomy extends to all aspects of change is important so that decisions about not changing now or changing slowly are respected. Even when clients make a decision not to change, they may be in a more satisfying position because they have weighed the consequences and chosen not to do something. Each client is a unique person with special circumstances. This is especially true as we age since we have so many opportunities for becoming different from each other. I believe that crafting approaches that fit for each client is an important component of respect.

Other solution-focused therapists disagree. DeShazer (1985) offers techniques for specific conditions and utilizes a variety of generic interventions. He believes it is necessary only to find an adequate fit of intervention to problems for any change in the recurrent pattern to occur. The interesting and exciting part of therapy for me is the unexpected changes clients make that I could never hope to account for by a generic intervention. Putting undue importance on any certain question asked at any certain time puts the focus of change with the therapist rather than with the client.

Assessment

To be most useful to older adults, I utilize a solution-focused approach that is biopsychosocial. The co-occurrence of physical and mental health problems for older adults is well documented. Therefore, physical and pharmacological factors must often be examined as part of the change process. The psychological challenges of aging are unique, as are those of other life stages. In later life, an individual often struggles with issues of integrity, dependency, and social connection, trying to make sense of a lifetime of experiences. At earlier ages, individuals work to define themselves, whereas in later ages they are attempting to maintain a sense of personhood. Mastery over the environment becomes paramount in older age. Mental health needs are often expressed by older adults within a family milieu, such as to sense belonging; to integrate past, present, and future life experience; to adapt or adjust to changing demands from both internal and external sources; and to be supported in managing final life transitions in preparation for death (Eyde & Rich, 1983). Questioning clients about physical health, medications being taken, the involvement of family members or significant others, and the presence of community agencies begins a description of the resources available to achieve the elder's goals.

Solution-focused therapy is characterized by examining with clients their goals and those the therapist or others think are important. If outside influences, such as agency goals, are affecting the elder, these are discussed and their impact on the elder's goals are also considered. Elderly clients bring so much life experience to therapy that they have their own preferred method of going about change. They often have some experience of when the issue or situation that brings them is a little less intense or somewhat different.

Being oriented toward the future and that part of the change continuum in which problems are less intense or less frequent shapes the role of history in this model, the type of questions asked, the focus of the therapist, and the way in which interventions are formulated and shared with clients. It also stimulates hope in clients that change has already begun and can continue in a collaborative relationship with the therapist toward those outcomes important to the client.

In the solution-focused model, social control is left to other forces, except in cases of illegal activity or endangerment of the client or others. In these circumstances, the therapist is bound by professional ethics and legal stipulations to meet certain standards of society and to assist clients in meeting these standards.

In other models, assessment consists of gathering information about the client to make a comparison with a social norm or to discover issues from the past that may have an impact on the client now. Assessment in these models may take several sessions. In the solution-focused model, assessment is ongoing and means gathering information to create an understanding between client and therapist so the therapist can adapt or create a fit with the client. That is the responsibility of the therapist. When clients do not do what the therapist thinks they "should," it is because they believe another behavior is what they "should" be doing at the time.

For example, when a client who had been diagnosed as chronically mentally ill for 30 years was reevaluated and new medication utilized, she improved dramatically and a whole new way of approaching life was necessary. The client spent much less time sleeping or feeling too lethargic to be active in her family life or community. Learning to manage these new situations of responsibility was her goal. This seemed almost overwhelming to the client, who had handled problems in the past by taking her medication and going to sleep. As the therapist explored situations and focused on how the client was successful in handling interactions to her satisfaction, the client would often add information about a mistake or possible future problem. She demonstrated her ambivalence about change, which was both welcome and frightening. Instead of attributing this to resistance, the therapist understood that the client needed to go slowly and consider the good and bad in each situation.

The therapist learned to look at both aspects, satisfactory outcomes and mistakes, with the client rather than push for the client to do something else. They worked slowly, acknowledging how frightening it was to do something so different after 30 years. A cooperative relationship was established when the therapist did not push the client but found a pace that allowed for growth but did not produce too much anxiety.

Role of the Therapist

The therapist who is solution-focused selects certain areas of interest in the information given by the client. The therapist is interested in the client's values, language, and world view. Of additional concern are any exceptions to the problematic situation the client presents, a description of a future in which the problem has changed enough to meet the client's goals, and the consequences to the client of these changes. Focusing refers to an activity the therapist initiates through questions and concentration of attention with which the client collaborates as therapy progresses. The client increasingly attends to those portions of experience that support change as the therapist's questions introduce alternative perspectives on the client's experience. The therapist's orientation, focusing on what can improve, is important for older adults. Restoring control over the personal future can give hope and purpose, which are essential to well-being. The realistic awareness of the finitude of life may lead to experiencing time differently for older adults, in some ways increasing the urgency to solve problems and create more positive futures. Change, however, will come from the client and not from interventions by the therapist. Thinking otherwise may inhibit change because it denies client autonomy. The therapist is like a midwife facilitating a birth—assisting in the client's natural tendency to keep changing.

Abilities and strengths are emphasized rather than pathology. Since ageism is so prevalent in Western society, older adults often feel powerless or discounted. When the therapist has a strong belief that power is in the client, the older person's autonomy is encouraged. Empowering clients is a precondition to further change. Older adults have a long, rich life history from which they can glean examples of previously solved problems and successful changes. When approaching therapy, these past positive behaviors may have been forgotten as the present difficulty is emphasized. The therapist may need to see past a frail or aged body to the strength of spirit clients have developed. Life is the best teacher—not therapy. The therapeutic collaboration of client and therapist allows for reviewing the lessons older clients have learned from life and applying them to present problems.

Accepting the client's view of the world is an empathetic activity of the therapist. The therapist, however, does have a different view of the world. Acceptance of the client's view is not the same as adopting it. The different perspective of the therapist allows a useful collaboration and recombination of the client's view for change to occur. Clients come to understand better that the therapist is trying to be cooperative when their values and attitudes are respected. For example, when a male client explained that he felt very guilty because he had argued with his adult son just before the son died in an auto accident five years earlier, the therapist did not challenge the client's guilt feelings. The therapist asked how the client would know when the guilt feeling was better. The client replied that he probably would always feel somewhat guilty, but it would be useful to not think of the argument several times each day. The therapist asked the client what effect this would have on others. The client replied that it would make a difference to his other children. One of his sons had accused him of not caring about his remaining children because he constantly talked about the dead son. His wife was also upset because he seldom initiated sexual activity with her and had trouble maintaining an erection. The therapist asked if any of these thoughts lessened a little now. The client stated that only when he concentrated on his grandchildren and being a good grandfather did this happen. They then discussed ways of giving attention not only to grandchildren, but also to remaining adult children.

By accepting the client's view of his own guilt, the therapist and client began a collaboration in which the client could move from being a passive victim of guilt to being a responsible guilty party who could then engage in constructive activity and begin a new cycle of behavior that might relieve a certain amount of his guilt. Since the client was having sexual difficulties, the therapist also suggested a referral for a physical examination to gather information about any underlying medical problems. The therapist utilized the pace of change the client found useful. Such information is gathered from client responses as change behavior ebbs and flows.

When clients seek outside help, they enter into a relationship in which both the problem and potential improvement are open to redefinition by an outsider—the therapist. Negotiating the statement of problem and the goals to be achieved is essential. This collaborative framing offers a direction for the therapeutic work together and defines when this work will be finished. Problems need to be defined in solvable terms. Clients may have a story to tell in more or less detail about how and/or why they have come to seek outside consultation, but the most important question the therapist will ask is not "What is the problem?" but "How will you know when the problem is solved?" The definition of the solution in very realistic terms is important. It cannot mean magically taking away all the client's painful circumstances, but it can mean improvement.

For example, an elderly woman came to therapy with her daughter and son-in-law. She had been referred by her home health nurse due to rising tensions at home. Mrs. Green had suffered a stroke eight months before. She had gone through a rehabilitation program and was now living with her daughter and son-in-law. When they were asked how they would know when the problem was solved, they said it would be when Mrs. Green was happy. Asked what would make her happy, Mrs. Green replied, "I would be happy if I could be like it was before the stroke." In order to help her reach her goal, the family had been helping Mrs. Green with her home exercises, but a conflict had developed over the amount of time the family would devote to this. She wanted unlimited attention and the family wanted some limits. Mrs. Green's desired future of removing all effects of the stroke is something psychotherapy could not accomplish. An achievable goal needed to be negotiated. The therapist told Mrs. Green that she wished she could take away the stroke, but since this was not possible, she wondered what else would make the future a little more pleasant. Mrs. Green stated that less tension around her exercises would be useful, and her family agreed. Therapy could now proceed to envisioning together what that would be like—how each would know if there was less tension and whether a little of this lessening of tension sometimes happened now.

CASE EXAMPLE

When therapy begins, some clients have already started different behaviors by seeking consultation from an outsider, the therapist. In the first and subsequent sessions, the therapist assists them in continuing this change toward the goals that have been collaboratively defined. The following is an example of typical features of a first session. Mrs. Lily, 80 years old, and her two daughters, Mrs. Downer, 55 years old, and Mrs. Capitol, 58 years old, have come for consultation. Mrs. Capitol had made the appointment because they all had been arguing more than usual.

Session One

Therapist	As a beginning, it is helpful for me to understand what brings each of you here and how talking together can be useful to you. I need to understand what you'd like to accomplish.
Mrs. C	Well, I called because we've all been arguing a lot more lately. I'd like that to stop.
Mrs. L	I didn't want to come, but the girls insisted. If they keep trying to push me around, the arguing is going to continue. I'd like them to stop telling me what to do.
Mrs. C	Mom, you know we care about you, but you don't seem to care about yourself as much lately. You don't eat properly, and you stayed home from church the last few weeks. I'd like to know what's wrong.

Asking about outcomes at the beginning of the session tells clients that the therapist is interested in their goals and begins the assessment process

Solution-Focused Brief Therapy with Aging Families

focused on the future, not the past. The various interacting goals of family members are present for consideration early in the session. The therapist can now gather a little information about the context in which solutions will emerge. The therapist and clients can explore the multiple levels of the biopsychosocial system; information about living arrangements, social activity, and physical status may be useful to constructing solutions.

Therapist	Mrs. Lily, why do you think your daughters are so concerned about you?
Mrs. L	Well, I live alone, and they think I can't take care of myself anymore. I fell down a couple months ago, and now they are watching me like spies. I just hate it.
Therapist	Of course, no one likes to feel watched even if it is well meant. Did you go to your doctor after you fell?
Mrs. L	Yes, she said I was okay. Nothing broken. But my blood pressure was high, so she gave me some medication. I brought it in a bag like you asked.
Mrs. D	Mom, I don't think you're taking the medication properly. When I visit you, your pills are all over the place.
Therapist	Have you noticed any change since this medication?
Mrs. C	Yes, we fight with each other about everything Mom should do.

The therapist will ask clients to bring a list of medications or their containers in a bag so that medication interactions can be considered. When a physical assessment is available, the therapist may want this information to understand the biological context of the client. If this is not available, a referral to a geriatrician may be useful.

Therapist	When you were getting along better before the fall, how was that different from now?
Mrs. C	Well, my sister and I had disagreements, but they weren't constant like now.
Mrs. D	Yes, we're very different people, but we had realized that and were able to just let each other be different, but now I'm worried about Mom. I want her care to be right.
Mrs. C	Yes—that means your way.
Mrs. L	Now girls, don't fight. I've been taking care of myself just fine. You are both making me so nervous with your disagreements.
Therapist	Mrs. Lily, what would you like your daughters to do?
Mrs. L	I'd like them to let me figure out what is best. After all, I am the mother here, not the child.

Therapist	If your daughters were to let you figure out things, what will you do?
Mrs. L	Well, I would know if I took my pills. When they come over and start questioning me, I get so angry I don't remember what I did.
Therapist	Anything else?
Mrs. L	Yes, I'd be on the phone less, talking to them. Ever since I fell, they keep calling me.
Mrs. C	But Mom, you don't tell us if you need things, and I worry.

Threats to the health of parents may raise anxiety in adult children and reawaken tensions that had been dormant among family members. Respecting the hierarchy of authority in intergenerational relationships is important so that older adults can retain personal autonomy and their role in the family system.

Therapist	Mrs. Lily, you have done something right in raising your daughters—they are very concerned about you. I'm wondering how the girls could feel more assured that you are okay and you could feel less controlled.
Mrs. C	Well, my sister always goes over and tells Mom what to do.
Mrs. D	No, I don't—but Mom needs suggestions. You never really get involved. Because I'm not working, you think I can just do everything.
Mrs. C	No, you just do everything.
Therapist	I want this to slow down a little. I understand that both of you think differently about how your mom should be helped. You said before that you were each different and had learned to accept that. Mrs. Lily, do you see your daughters as different from each other?

The therapist now guides the conversation to a consideration of how each daughter will approach the other and her mother with respect for that person's way of doing things. This is aimed at the goal they stated of wanting arguments to be reduced. As the first session ends, the therapist will have obtained a statement of the goals and a definition from the clients of how they will recognize progress as well as completion of the goals. Exceptions will be explored if the family can identify some in the present and/or past. If no exceptions can be identified, they may talk about coping methods or consider the small steps that could lead to a change.

At the end of first sessions, I often compose a reflection on the session during a short break and return to share it with the family. This reflection will contain a summary of main points, compliments, and suggestions for noticing, thinking about, or trying certain behaviors, as well as considering community services or gathering information. These are only suggestions and are based on material obtained from the family in the session.

Therapist   As I understand the issues and concerns we've been discussing, it seems to me that all of you care a lot for each other and are really disturbed by the level of tension in your family. You all want this fighting to stop. However, you each also want to keep your independence and not be controlled by anyone else. I would suggest, Mrs. Lily, that you think about how you want your daughters to be involved in helping you, like driving or shopping trips. Perhaps both of you (*to the daughters*) could think about what you would be willing to do. It might also be useful to consider someone outside the family for certain things. I have this packet of resources for each of you to examine. We can talk more about them next time.

Session Two

When the family returns for the second session, the therapist asks about change that is the focus of interaction.

Therapist   What has been happening during the last week that you would like to continue?
Mrs. C   Well, I thought it went better for a day or two.
Therapist   What exactly happened that you thought was better?
Mrs. C   We fought a little less.
Mrs. L   Yes, I'm a lot less nervous when they get along, but after a few days, they were back at it again.

The therapist will focus on change and any slight exception to the problematic behavior. Often change will happen in an oscillating fashion. Any exception will be carefully explored. This family could now examine what each believes she did to help create a difference and how more of this could happen.

Mrs. C   It seemed to help when my sister and I talked over what we would each do for Mom.
Mrs. D   Yes, I knew what my sister was doing so I got less angry when Mom told me what was happening.
Mrs. L   They didn't talk to me about this, and I don't like decisions made without me.

Now the session can proceed with problem solving around the daughters' respecting their mother's independence.

Therapist As I understand it, you have all found a way to have less arguing and tension by talking over what each of you will do. Mrs. Lily, you want to be part of deciding who will do what. Perhaps you will want to consider involving a public health nurse to check on you instead of your daughter doing everything. She could help you set up your pills and help you remain in control.

Session Three

Therapist In our last session, we talked about the ways in which you were cooperating with each other and discussing how to be helpful. How has that continued?

Mrs. L I called an agency and had someone come to the house to interview me. I think I would like to have someone come to help me with some housekeeping and to check my pills. Maybe then I could do other things with the girls.

Mrs. C Well, Mom, we are just concerned for you.

Mrs. L I know, but what would really make me feel better is going shopping or to lunch with both of you. Since I fell down, I have been more afraid—but not about pills—about dying. I'd like to have more time to do things with my girls—but not just pills and doctors—some fun.

Mrs. D Is that why you sometimes haven't gone to church and seem so preoccupied?

Mrs. L Probably.

The family together planned how they would be more emotionally available to each other. The daughters may not be getting along better, but that was not the goal of therapy. Arguments were be reduced, which was the goal, so that Mrs. Lily had the emotional support she was seeking, as well as the independence. Both daughters were reassured that their mother was safe.

Therapy ends when the goals clients have expressed are met to their satisfaction. In termination, these goals will be reviewed and the methods clients have used to reach them will be reinforced. The focus will be on client competence and a more positive future.

CONCLUSION

As Miller (1994) points out, the major impact of solution-focused therapy is on the therapist and not on the clients. A theoretical model is the philosophy that guides the therapist in establishing the therapeutic relationship and the focus of treatment with the client. Each therapist adopts a model that both helps the client toward useful change and fits the therapist's values and world view. I have continued to utilize and develop the solution-focused model because its basic assumptions are consistent with my beliefs about the nature of person and the occurrence of change. It has also continued to have advantages for me in my work with aging families.

Client outcomes are consistent with those provided by an effective therapy model (Cummings, 1977; Garfield, 1986). Quality assurance studies at ICF Consultants, Incorporated, show that the average length of treatment is five sessions and that 87 percent of clients report satisfactory goal attainment and maintenance at the time of our yearly follow-up. The hopeful, future orientation of this model makes working together with clients enjoyable for me. In very difficult circumstances with aging families, valuing small, incremental goals allows me to experience progress with clients and continue to see possibilities for change to explore with them. Establishing and maintaining a cooperative relationship challenges me to explore my own emotional reactions and grow toward more sensitive collaboration. Expanding the area of solutions beyond the psychological to the biological and social allows me to interact collaboratively with other professionals involved with my clients so that they, too, are part of solution construction.

Assisting aging families in their growth provides me with opportunities to learn useful approaches to my own life transitions. It has especially taught me the importance of wisdom shared between generations and the healing that can be an elder's legacy. It continues to be a privilege to participate in that process and a solution-focused orientation assists me in that participation.

REFERENCES

Ahlers, C. (1992). Solution-oriented therapy for professionals working with physically impaired clients. *Journal of Strategic and Systemic Therapies, 11*, 53–68.

Berg, I. K. (1991). *Family preservation: A brief therapy workbook.* London: B.T. Press.

Cade, B. W. (1985). The Wizard of Oz approach to brief family therapy: An interview with Steve deShazer. *The Australian and New Zealand Journal of Family Therapy, 6,* 95-97.

Cicirelli, V. G. (1983). Adult children and their elderly parents. In T. H. Brubaker (Ed.), *Family relationships in later life.* Beverly Hills, CA: Sage.

Cummings, N. (1977). Prolonged (ideal) versus short-term (realistic) psychotherapy. *Professional Psychology, 8,* 491-505.

deShazer, S. (1982). *Patterns of brief family therapy: An ecosystemic approach.* New York: Guilford Press.

deShazer, S. (1985). *Keys to solution in brief therapy.* New York: Norton.

Erickson, M. (1954). Special techniques of brief hypnotherapy. *Journal of Clinical and Experimental Hypnosis, 2,* 109-129.

Eyde, R., & Rich, J. (1983). *Psychological distress in aging.* Rockville, MD: Aspen Systems.

Friedan, B. (1993). *The fountain of age.* New York: Simon & Schuster.

Garfield, S. L. (1986). Research in client variables in psychotherapy. In S. L. Garfield & A. E. Bergin (Eds.), *Handbook of psychotherapy and behavior change.* New York: Wiley.

Gurean, B., & Goisman, R. (1993). Anxiety disorders in the elderly. *Generations,* Winter/Spring, 27.

Keeney, B. (1983). *Aesthetics of change,* New York: Guilford Press.

Kiser, D., Piercy, F., & Lipchik, E. (1993). The integration of emotion in solution-focused therapy. *Journal of Marital and Family Therapy, 19,* 233-242.

Langton, S., & Langton, C. H. (1983). *The answer within: A clinical framework of Ericksonian hypnotherapy.* New York: Brunner/Mazel.

Lipchik, E. (1993). Both/and solutions. In S. Friedman (Ed.), *The new language of change: Constructive collaboration in psychotherapy.* New York: Guilford Press.

Lipchik, E. (1994). The rush to be brief. *The Family Therapy Networker,* March-April, 35-39.

Miller, S. (1994). The solution conspiracy: A mystery in three installments. *Journal of Systemic Therapies, 13,* 18-37.

Ornstein, R., & Thompson, R. F. (1984). *The amazing brain.* Boston: Houghton Mifflin.

Tobin, S. (1991). *Personhood in advanced old age.* New York: Springer.

Walter, J., & Peller, J. (1992). *Becoming solution-focused in brief therapy.* New York: Brunner/Mazel.

Weakland, T., Fisch, R., Watzlawick, P., & Bodin, A. (1974). Brief therapy: Focused problem resolution. *Family Process, 13,* 142-168.

5

A Developmental–Interactional Model

Suzanne Midori Hanna, Ph.D.
University of Louisville
Louisville, Kentucky

The Developmental–Interactional Model (DIM) of family therapy is an integrative approach to working with individuals, couples, and families that combines elements of structural-strategic family therapy with life-cycle and intergenerational approaches. This blend of influences suggests that all problems can be conceptualized with a relational and developmental component. The relational component refers to interpersonal interactions related to the problem. The developmental component refers to changes in these interactions and in the problem over time.

The goal of this model is to help significant relationships function in a way that will resolve the presenting problem. Applied to families in midlife and later life, clinicians use this model to assess relational dynamics over time, determining how these transitions relate to a family's problem-solving capability. Problems are categorized as situational, transitional, or chronic. Typically, therapeutic investigations uncover family strengths and commitments that aid in problem resolution. By hearing a family's unique story, the therapist is able to explore possibilities that fit into the context of the story and facilitate cognitive-behavioral changes in the family or network.

BACKGROUND

The DIM evolved from work with an older population. The setting was a community agency that offered older persons outreach and such services as transportation, home-delivered meals, and respite care. Project Support was one of the services, providing in-home family counseling for the chronically ill, including those with Alzheimer's disease and other dementias (Hanna, 1986). Treatment was provided by graduate students in social work, psychology, and nursing who had requested a field placement or practicum in family therapy. This community-based context was different from a mental health or psychiatric context in that the population was not always looking for counseling or therapy. Thus, the role of the therapist had to be carefully constructed, based on families' expectations for help.

Traditionally, the role of the therapist has been influenced by certain unspoken expectations that the practitioner should identify and label psychosocial problems, ultimately to prescribe a cure. However, it is only recently that therapy has been viewed as having value for any population other than the mentally ill. Consequently, many older people have not been inclined to think of themselves or their families as candidates for psychological treatment. In addition, many have lived much of their lives having nonclinical resources for coping with the stresses of life and do not consider themselves to be in need of therapy just because they or a family member have a chronic illness. In community-based settings, older people are often looking for respite services or help with household chores, rather than psychosocial interventions.

Likewise, family members of someone ailing do not see themselves as lacking personal resources or needing "treatment." During the development of the DIM, many people protested (and rightly so) that they did not have fears, anxieties, low self-esteem, or dissatisfaction with life like the "people who need therapists." Because of this, it was important to acknowledge this legitimate reality for those who wanted "help" but not "therapy." In addition, the evolution of family therapists occurred with marital, child, and adolescent problems. These were often addressed in the literature as problems responsive to interactional interventions (Bodin, 1981; Minuchin & Fishman, 1981). However, the influence of chronic medical conditions or impending death was rarely discussed. Therefore, the role for family therapists with an older population had to include an understanding of these added dimensions.

The concept of "consultant delivering psychoeducation" evolved to address this shift in therapeutic tradition. It enabled clinicians to acknowledge their own professional expertise while allowing families to define how psychologically oriented the intervention would be. Some families referred to Project Support were comfortable with a traditional therapeutic process, while others needed more pragmatism and less pathologizing. The consultant role was consistent with the influence of social construction on the field of family therapy. This influence focused on the importance of a family's "lived experience" and the "expert" knowledge that comes from this experience (White & Epston, 1991). The therapist became a collaborator by combining professional problem-solving knowledge with family knowledge about how to define help. Some families were comfortable with a traditional therapeutic approach, but it soon became apparent that the consultant role was effective with all types of families. Students learned to glean expert knowledge from clients and to avoid the trap of ultimate authority. Since most consultants were young graduate students and most families were middle-life and older adults, this stance was also respectful of the age differential that often existed in the therapeutic system.

As the model evolved, "therapy" for this population was conceptualized as consultation and education to prolong, maintain, and improve the quality of one's life in the face of chronic illness and the tasks of caregiving. Just as diabetic or heart patients would receive a basic education in how to care for themselves, it was assumed that families with chronic illness were entitled to a basic education in how they could best care for each other (McCubbin, 1980; McCubbin, Patterson, McCubbin, & Wilson, 1983). Thus, the approach developed for this population was one in which social service workers combined a therapeutic focus with an educational focus on the practical, daily aspects of their needs. Following the direction of psychoeducation, it was explained that early intervention in the healthiest of families could:

1. Minimize the negative impact of chronic illness on others.
2. Provide low-cost health promotion to lower the incidence of chronic illness in the caregiver.
3. Delay the family's dependence on institutional care.
4. Provide efficient, short-term support.

Besides dilemmas in defining the therapist's role, there were also dilemmas in using traditional family therapy approaches. Because the sense of time changes for those in middle and later life, ahistorical appoaches in the field (i.e., structural-strategic) were not making use of normative tendencies for older persons to reminisce. This author also found that older families became frustrated when practitioners did not understand how their relational history affected service needs. Thus, intergenerational assessments led to greater understanding of each member's dilemmas. This sense of understanding increased the likelihood of success by helping consultants to individualize their interventions.

At the same time, historical approaches to family therapy (i.e., intergenerational) often assumed more past conflicts than some of the presenting problems warranted. When families had no previous history of therapy and defined their problem in situational terms that were unique to their illness or later-life stage, structural-strategic interventions offered pragmatic solutions when long-standing conflict was not an issue. These interventions were also helpful in cases where neither generation wanted to address historical issues. Thus, a flexible integration developed, allowing equal access to historical and interactional factors, but slanting the emphasis based on the family's needs. The balance and variation between these two realms led to the label "Developmental–Interactional Model."

THEORETICAL ASSUMPTIONS

All problems have a relational component. Family theories distinguish themselves from psychodynamic theories by their focus on relationships (Haley, 1976). Behavior is viewed as the response to one or more relationships, and thus must be understood within the context of those relationships. The impact of problems on family relationships is addressed and the impact of relationships on problems is considered a therapeutic resource. Solutions materialize by examining significant relationship changes and by using the examination to discover personal and relational resources that will support targeted outcomes. The following example illustrates this point.

> Living alone at age 78, Mr. James was having trouble caring for himself. Service providers wondered why his four adult children did not intervene. Family history revealed a pattern of proud independence by this father who had repeatedly refused help from concerned children after the death of his wife. When consulted, his children expressed their confusion and helplessness, not knowing what to do when the "head of the house" told them he was doing fine and didn't need to live with them. With this additional information, the situation turned from one with an ailing, lonely man to one in which an entire family was frustrated by patterns and roles that were not effective for the transitions in their stage of the life cycle.

It is unlikely that this information would have come forth from speaking only to Mr. James. In family therapy, it is crucial to get information from or about as many participants as possible. The focus on significant family members clarifies needs of the individual within an interpersonal context (relational component). In this case, family relationships provided a natural support for targeted changes. The additional information (historical and interactional sequences) clarified the situation for service providers, who helped the adult children change the way they related to their father (cognitive/behavioral change).

The therapist learned that Mrs. James had played a significant interpersonal role in the family prior to her death (historical sequence). In fact, she was the mediator in most conflicts between the children and Mr. James (interactional sequence). However, since the problem was one of negotiating a transition among current relationships, problem resolution was facilitated by focusing on how siblings were organized and what hindered their ability to intervene successfully on their father's behalf. The family therapist was tempted to explore long-standing resentments among family members; however, since these were not included in the clients' definition of the problem, a structural approach, informed by family history, was chosen and proved to be effective.

Structural family therapy assumes that in order to help individuals and families, one must look at how family life is organized (Minuchin & Fishman, 1981). In the DIM, family structure is defined as the pattern of leadership (power and responsibility) that organizes the family and influences perceptions, feelings, and behavior. The goal of this approach applied to aging families is to restructure relationships to achieve a balance of power and responsibility as the family pursues its goals. As the James siblings began to work as a team, they developed a new pattern of leadership, which was separate from but respectful of their father's previous role. As their sense of teamwork improved, they were able to negotiate new roles successfully in their relationships with him.

All problems have a developmental component. This suggests that the past relates to the present, either through macrostages of development or through microcycles of interaction over time. Healthy family life is thought of as a progression of tasks that are mastered from one stage to the next. Structural-strategic and life-cycle approaches to family therapy suggest that problems develop when families do not successfully negotiate tasks of a new life-cycle stage (Haley, 1973; Carter & McGoldrick, 1989). Thus, a functional family life cycle can be thought of as successful interactions that facilitate family development over time. If problems occur, these are seen as the result of interactions that have not successfully addressed certain tasks in a current or earlier stage of the life cycle. The problems in the James family were thought of as the effects of aging, since new roles were needed for a new stage in the life cycle. This macrostage began as the parents' physical health changed and was accentuated by Mrs. James' death.

The developmental component can also be understood through the lens of intergenerational approaches to family therapy. Here, it is the past that explains how family members develop attitudes, thoughts, and feelings about self and others. These approaches involve adults' exploring parent–child–sibling issues from their family of origin that may have a developmental bearing on their present family relationships (Kramer, 1985). In working with elders and their adult children, there are often circumstances that merit an exploration of micropatterns over time with particular focus on how the family addressed earlier transitions, such as adolescence, the empty nest, and other milestones. Such developmental history may be tapped for examples of successful coping strategies or for the identification of unresolved issues that are restraining necessary changes (Boszormenyi-Nagy & Krasner, 1986). In the work of Michael White (1983), the focus would be on the intergenerational patterns of thought that might be restraining a successful transition.

The James children were aware of the intergenerational issues, but did not want to address them with their father. Since Mrs. James had always helped the family to cope through indirect strategies, the therapist also helped them address the issues indirectly by suggesting new patterns that enabled them to be more involved with Mr. James, but without the stress of confrontations. In this way, a knowledge of previous coping strategies was used to find a level of intervention most comfortable for the family. At the same time, historical issues that kept siblings from working together were addressed directly, enabling a new pattern of mutual support and leadership to develop.

Each person and each family is unique: thus, effective solutions will make use of this uniqueness. This perspective applies to families the basic approach that Milton H. Erickson contributed to psychotherapy and strategic family therapy:

> Each person is a unique individual. Hence, psychotherapy should be formulated to meet the uniqueness of the individual's needs, rather than tailoring the person to fit the Procrustean bed of a hypothetical theory of human behavior. (Zeig, 1985, p. vii)

Applied to aging families, this assumption is helpful in addressing the variety of presenting problems, which necessitates theory integration. Most settings do not have multiple service providers who can specialize in a specific problem category; thus, practitioners working with elder services encounter a range of levels of severity and problem types. Problem definitions may vary according to those who are doing the defining: children in middle life, "What should we do about Dad?"; older adults, "I don't need outside help"; service providers, "Why don't they help him?" Problems also range from the situational (i.e., medical problems, chronic illness) to the transitional (i.e., grief and loss) to the long-standing (i.e., chronic mental illness, resentments, unresolved losses, personality conflicts). Thus, the particular generation or system defining the nature of the problem must influence the treatment plan.

In addition to the uniqueness of the problem, family stories bring uniqueness into the therapeutic process and should be appreciated as a resource for problem solving. This encourages the consultant to search for and find strength in the face of adversity, which exists in every family. Such recognition becomes the foundation of the therapeutic relationship. From it, specific interventions are formulated that build on acknowledged successes. Following the Ericksonian tradition, five additional ideas are useful in working with elders, emphasizing flexibility and noncoercive interaction as important elements in formulating a successful treatment plan. (Lankton & Lankton, 1983, pp. 11–27).

1. People make the best choice they can see to make for themselves at any given moment.
2. Teach choice; never attempt to take choice away.
3. The resources the client needs lie within his or her own personal history.
4. Meet the client at his or her model of the world.
5. The person with the most flexibility or choice will be the controlling element in the system.

As an assessment is conducted, each family's adversity is appreciated and their unique strengths are recognized. Differing points of view are respected and the consultant explores these within the family as they relate to potential solutions.

OVERVIEW OF THE PROCESS

The DIM involves a sequence of interviews that gather relevant information in a structured format. The structure is designed to minimize client anxiety and to provide a concrete sense of direction for the therapist. It begins with two to four assessment sessions, which lead to a series of two to four intervention sessions. In reality, assessment and intervention cannot be delineated as separate stages because proper assessments facilitate therapeutic process, making them interventions as well. For example, negotiating the attendance of multiple family members for the purpose of assessment is an intervention that affects the system. Also, as the consultant gathers information, each question becomes an intervention when used to strengthen the therapeutic relationship or facilitate change. However, since the DIM has a specific order to the process, it is described here as having two parts: an assessment stage and a problem-solving stage.

Assessment Stage: Tasks

Identify and Involve the Hierarchy

A crucial question that must be asked and answered is, "Who has the power in the family and will that person or persons attend the first session?" If the initial telephone contact suggests that important parties may be difficult to involve, the first session is usually held with those who are willing to attend. In this instance, the assessment process is used to explore the dynamics of nonattendance and to discuss the engagement of those who have influence in the system. Particularly in later-life extended-family networks, there are issues related to legal guardianship and shifts in roles that often result in a change of power or dependency. Those who have the most influence may be key family members who appear to be leaders in making decisions or caregiving, or they may also be outside the immediate family, such as physicians or even grandchildren. If power is localized in one member, the consultant will want to give support to this person while also listening fairly to other family members. If power appears to be shared, the consultant will want to label and support the family's ability to cooperate.

Sometimes, the person with the most power is not vocal or may distrust anyone who is not inside the family circle. For example, in cases where elder abuse or neglect is suspected, the suspected abuser may be present but defensive or uncooperative. These people can be engaged during the assessment process by looking for clues to their biases, attitudes, and frame of reference. By taking a sympathetic stance and positively connoting their efforts, consultants seek ways of understanding this person's experience until cooperation is achieved.

When those seeking services are those with the *least* power in the family, the primary therapeutic goal becomes that of coaching them to engage other family members in the consultation process. This should be accomplished before proceeding with the problem-solving stage. When leaders of the fam-

… ily or reluctant members are difficult to engage, the consultant relies on the first two assumptions of the DIM for direction:

1. What relationship is influencing their behavior?
2. Where in the development of that relationship is an entry point for intervention?

In these instances, the assessment conducted with those who feel powerless will focus on an understanding of those perceived as having more power. The goal is to address the conflict. If this is unsuccessful, the goal becomes one of teaching negotiation skills to resolve the conflict. These skills should empower family members to break impasses with the established hierarchy.

If elder abuse is alleged and consultants are meeting with victims alone, identifying and involving the hierarchy must identify ambivalence that the older person may have about taking action and changing the power differential. Ironically, victims of elder abuse often retain their power to maintain the status quo out of fear or a sense of obligation, thus disempowering would-be helpers outside the situation. In such cases, the entire assessment process may be conducted with the victim alone. The goal is to understand and accept the ambivalence of the victim without pressure until a point of intervention is discovered that helps the victim resolve the dilemma and take steps toward safety. This movement paves the way for others in the network to become involved.

Learn the Family's Story

This is accomplished by constructing a genogram and a time line of significant events in the family (Hanna & Brown, 1995). During an assessment, the consultant develops a cooperative, positive relationship with the family and gathers information that is used in the psychoeducational process. This is accomplished by seeking to understand all family members and providing equal support to all.

Following the primary assumptions of the DIM, problem solving can best be accomplished when the facilitator has a knowledge of the interpersonal worlds of those seeking help. Therefore, one of the main tasks in this stage is to provide a rationale for gathering such information, and then to gather successfully information that will provide a systemic view of the family story. This systemic information must include (1) sequences of interactions around the presenting problem, (2) differences in family relationships over time, and (3) roles that family members have historically adopted in these relationships. As the story unfolds, the consultant looks for answers to these questions as a prelude to the problem-solving process. These questions lead the consultant to "systemic empathy," in which the history of the family integrates the experience of the group with the experience of individuals.

Validate and Reframe the Family's Story

Another key role for the consultant is one of clearly describing the process that family members have experienced. The following questions are used to guide the consultant in providing a description to the family.

1. In what stage of the life cycle is each participant?
2. What is the family's usual coping style?
3. What role in the family did the identified patient play before the onset of the problem?
4. How are power and responsibility distributed among relevant family members?
5. How much accumulated stress is each member coping with?
6. What other changes have occurred over time in relationships between these people?

There are at least two types of processes that families are experiencing. The first is the process of adjusting to or coping with an aging member. It is important for the consultant to acknowledge what is happening from a developmental and psychological point of view, and to offer reassurance and commitment to helping the family with their current stress. The second is the therapeutic process involving the family and consultant. In enlisting cooperation, it is important for the consultant to describe family participation as a strength and as evidence of how much they care for each other. The consultant's role can be described as helping people assess resources and options for meeting challenges that confront them. The family's role can be described as providing valuable information to the consultant so that the most appropriate resources and options can be discovered.

Assessment Stage: Techniques

Genogram

This is a three-generational diagram of a family group that identifies all family members and their current life circumstance. It should be drawn when family members are present. Basic information includes names; ages; years of birth, death, marriage, divorce; causes of deaths; present location; occupations; and ethnic and/or religious roots. Relational information includes family structure and intergenerational dynamics (Hanna & Brown, 1995).

To assess the nature of family structure, the therapist asks the following questions.

1. Who has the last word when important decisions are made?
2. Who interacts with whom in making decisions?
3. How do other family members relate (agree/disagree) to those who make the decisions?
4. Which additional subsystems of family members may influence decisions? How does this influence occur?

To assess intergenerational dynamics, the consultant asks the following questions.

1. How is your family unique from other families you know?
2. How are Mother and Father unique from each other?
3. What makes each sibling unique from each other?
4. How does each sibling relate to Mother, Father, and other siblings?
5. Are there other people who affect the way you currently relate to each other?

The method of interviewing for genogram construction is circular and reflective, consisting of exploratory questions that help the family identify patterns of communication, power, affect, and individuality. The line of questioning allows the group to compare their perceptions and to discuss patterns that shape general family functioning (Penn, 1982). At the conclusion of this interview, the consultant should be able to summarize questions 1-4 as part of the goal to validate and reframe the family's story.

Time Line of Important Events

The history of the family is an important key to understanding the impact of their current situation (Hoffman, 1983). Many times, a family crisis involves developmental issues that either necessitate or are a part of family changes. A change in family roles, cohesion, or balance of power among members may be a significant crossroad. When families view their history together, they are able to understand what is happening to them and how they can best cope. It is possible that their present situation is affected by earlier developmental stages of which they are unaware. Therefore, a family history helps to integrate the past with the present (Hiebert, Gillespie, & Stahmann, 1993).

In the DIM, family history is diagrammed on a horizontal time line with family members present. The following questions elicit nodal events through time, behavioral sequences during nodal events, and individual perceptions and meanings derived from these experiences.

1. What was the first (or next) significant event you shared as a family?
2. When this happened, how did each of you react? What was the sequence of these reactions?
3. After it ended, what conclusions did you draw about yourself and others?

Each event is listed in order on the time line as the family reminisces. Reactions and conclusions are summarized as the discussion continues. The process allows family members to hear differing perceptions while reminiscing about shared events.

Because medical issues are so central to an aging population, it is assumed that increased medical service is inevitable. Therefore, when medical problems are a part of the presenting problem, the following questions should be added to the end of the time line.

1. Are there disagreements or dilemmas over the best course of action?
2. Are there positive or negative emotions toward health care providers?
3. What frustrations and satisfactions have been experienced with the quality of health care?
4. How dependent is the family on the word of medical authority?
5. What are the general patterns of relating to medical personnel?

Positive Connotation

This intervention develops rapport and communicates support. The goal is to help families evolve new perceptions of old behavior so that fewer criticisms are made and conflicts are resolved. Because it is possible for several people to have different perceptions of the same event, such connotations can help people create new realities and, therefore, new feelings about current or past experience. For example, if someone suspected of elder neglect is present, the consultant can look for ways to construct a new picture of the situation with positive connotation. The alleged offender may be characterized as respecting the older person's independence or being cautious about how to intervene in the right way. By focusing on possible dilemmas that may be implicit, positive connotation can focus on important issues in a nonthreatening way.

One of the characteristics of a positive connotation is that it makes explicit the good intentions of behavior that may be identified with the problem. It also reduces shame by legitimizing feelings and attitudes to which people sometimes feel entitled, but that are usually social unacceptable to admit (i.e., revenge, desire for attention, praise). By the time a genogram and time line summarize the family's story, there are usually instances where positive connotation can provide a retelling of the story in order to help those in the system to reconceptualize their relationships. The following case illustrates how misunderstood behavior is related to client dilemmas.

> Mrs. Stevens, 61, was referred by the Adult Day Center because the social worker there was concerned that Mrs. Stevens was "in denial" since she was exhausted, but still not willing to entertain plans for the long-term care of her husband, 65, who had been diagnosed with Alzheimer's disease. Mrs. Stevens stated in the consultation that she did not believe she needed any help at this time. Thus, the problem was defined as a misunderstanding between the social worker and client. The goal of the consultation was to provide the social worker with a better understanding of Mrs. Stevens (respect for the hierarchy). The behavior that had been labeled as "denial" was positively connoted as an insightful sense of timing. This was documented with examples from the family's story when Mrs. Stevens had intuitively known when it was time to make a change in the status quo.

Metaphor

One of the most effective ways of speaking to people in their own language is through the use of metaphor. Metaphors help us to comprehend complex and evolutionary processes through a comparison to familiar elements in the natural world. When certain life crises are unexpected and bring uncertainty, the use of metaphor can provide a mental map of what people can expect to encounter in the future. For example, metaphors related to travel can help the family see that their inability to cope with the current stress is not because of any personal deficit, but is due to a lack of prior life experience. This can be illustrated by describing the family as a group of people who have traveled extensively with each other through many lands. However, because of the nature of their tribe, they were prone to stay in warm climates. Now that a storm has occurred (external circumstance beyond their control), it is understandable that they are caught without proper clothing (chaos created by the crisis). The consultant is merely a travel guide who is prepared to help the family acquire the needed resources to continue their journey (psychoeducation).

Another useful metaphor that explains the concept of prevention and health is a principle of auto mechanics. Most people understand that automobiles must have the oil changed periodically to maintain the life and function of the engine. The idea of respite for caregivers can be compared to changing the oil in a car. It must occur periodically, even when the car appears to be running well. Such a process comes under the category of preventive maintenance.

Agricultural images are also effective for helping people understand processes of healing and growth. The concepts of winter frosts, barren fields, spring planting, and autumn harvests can be compared to human beings who go through periods of tragedy, healing, hope, and moving on to a new life. Similar metaphors are effective in describing the process of personal growth that involves an individual going through a period of confusion as one behavioral pattern becomes obsolete and a new approach is developed. Since an aging population is often encumbered with extra medical issues, the consultant may want to employ medical and physiological metaphors that equate emotional healing with physical healing, and the consultation process with that of patient education, exploratory surgery, and the six-month checkup. Conflict can be described as an infection that prevents healing (or grieving) from taking place.

Consultants are encouraged to draw on a wide range of experience for other effective metaphors. Animal images, ethnic stories, art, and drama serve as communicators of systemic processes. The family's ethnic and cultural background often contains suitable metaphors. When men are primary caregivers, athletic metaphors may be helpful. When middle-class professionals are involved, language may involve philosophy and science. Opportunities to use metaphor will often occur as a family's story is told and the consultant searches for ways to validate and reframe their experiences. As relational issues are identified, desired changes may also be described through the use of metaphor.

These techniques represent an expansion of data gathering from individual to family system to community and a summary of major transitions from past into the present. The consultant reflects on the information with positive connotations and metaphor. At the conclusion of this stage, the consultant should be able to summarize questions 5 and 6 on page 110 to validate and reframe the family's story. The assessment process becomes a psychoeducational process that lends perspective to the current predicament and acknowledges the family's uniqueness. By reflecting on the information in a positive and supportive way, the consultant builds trust and credibility with the family.

Many times, the genogram and time line help grieving families to rediscover the richness of their lives by focusing their awareness on those aspects of life that can never be taken from them, such as experiences with loved ones and learning from family relationships. Heritage, culture, ethics, and values are also examples of the aspects of life that endure beyond life itself (White, 1988). Regardless of the type of family being treated, focusing on their history in a manner that highlights esthetics can enable a family to cope and find meaning in their pain. When assessments are conducted with this in mind, they often become interventions that minimize the need for additional problem solving. Families that respond well to such intervention often desire to spend several sessions going over important events, rather than rushing through their entire history in one session.

Problem-Solving Stage: Tasks

Address Structural Issues

In cases that encompass an aging family, *isolation* often is an issue that needs attention even after the hierarchy is involved. In cases where chronic illness is a factor, caregivers move into isolation due to unforeseen circumstances, personal style, or both. In the DIM, if caregivers are not comfortably sharing their responsibility with at least one person outside formal support services, they are considered too isolated. If the patient does not have at least two significant others who could be called upon for support, he or she is considered too isolated.

If isolation is an issue, the goal is to help family members broaden their support network. It is crucial that each consultant understand the impact that isolation has on the family's subsequent need for institutional resources. Even though it is tempting to engage an individual in problem solving over practical concerns, unless the caregiver can learn to involve others, the ability to give long-term care will be limited in proportion to the caregiver's isolation. If all attempts have been exhausted to involve others in the first session, the consultant may meet with an individual, but the primary goal remains finding a way to engage others. In the case of Mrs. Stevens, caregiver for her husband with Alzheimer's disease, there were three adult children and she was able to discuss important issues with one daughter, a nurse. Since issues of hierarchy and isolation could be ruled out, the consultant was able to intervene with the social worker, encouraging Mrs. Stevens to continue plans at her own pace, as supported by her family. As the impasse with the service provider was broken, Mrs. Stevens felt more support and empathy from the larger system and began to explore respite services for herself.

Another structural issue centers on *transitions of power and responsibility* that occur in aging families. In some families, there is a skew in the balance of power and responsibility due to the fact that those doing the most work are given the least decision-making power. Very often, adult children see themselves as having a right to share equally in decisions regarding their aging parent, but as a sibling group, there may be those who assume little or no responsibility for major caregiving tasks. Usually, gender is an influence because females provide most of the care for parents and in-laws. Thus, if they have taken primary responsibility, but have no power, their own wellbeing is at the mercy of siblings, sometimes miles away, who have not been involved in day-to-day transitions. These transitions leave a caregiver in the difficult position of having to help those absent to understand the complexity of those present. When important medical or treatment issues arise, caregivers may be outnumbered by other family members and left powerless because others disagree.

When there is an imbalance between power and responsibility, the goal is to help those with responsibility to share it or those with power to delegate it. When families lose their existing hierarchy due to the death or incapacity of a member, imbalance is often the unintentional first step toward transition. Consultants can validate and reframe the family's story in light of these transitions. Then, the future becomes an opportunity to restore relationships.

Address Historical Issues

In many cases, structural issues will either be ruled out during assessment or they may not change due to the influence of historical issues. For example, *misunderstandings* are problems in understanding that have occurred as a result of unclear communication in the past. Family members may misunderstand another's intentions or actions. Long-standing resentments may result. These resentments are usually tied to events in the family's history and can be addressed during assessment if identified on the genogram or time line. Once identified, misunderstandings of another's intent can be clarified and new relationships can be negotiated.

Historical issues also take the form of *intergenerational patterns of thought and behavior*. Sometimes problematic behavior is a survival pattern that is no longer useful in the current situation. At other times, patterns of thought evolve from family traditions and loyalties. These are addressed by exploring ways in which the original issues can still be respected in light of new behaviors or attitudes.

Match Intervention to Type of Problem

As the consultant begins to make these decisions, some basic questions are asked. *First, is the problem situational, transitional, or chronic?* In answering

A Developmental–Interactional Model

this question, the consultant must consider whether or not the family has a history of difficulties, whether they have sought counseling services previously, and whether they have met some developmental challenges without formal outside intervention. Usually, older families and their problems will fall along a continuum in this area.

Second, does the family need direct or indirect interventions? In the DIM, the more situational the problem, the more direct will be the intervention. The more chronic the problem, the more indirect will be the intervention. Table 5.1 provides a summary of direct and indirect interventions that have been used with later-life relational issues. Direct interventions are those that are considered straightforward, with therapist intentions and rationales made explicit.

Psychoeducation, some rituals, directives, and questions are direct interventions, depending on the level of disclosed intent. Indirect interventions are considered more strategic in nature, designed to break an impasse perceived by the consultant to be impeding the process. Indirect interventions are designed to help clients "save face" in some way and are often an intervention on the thinking of the clinician, as their implementation usually requires a shift in thinking, since the impasse is often between consultant and client. Paradox, metaphor, some rituals, directives, and questions are generally considered indirect, either due to their level of disclosed intent or due to the outcome being left to the control of the client (Wright & Leahey, 1984).

Situational problems are those that involve one-time medical crises, the onset of chronic illnesses, or the development of conflicts that have not existed in the past. Families with situational problems may have been successful in completing developmental tasks of earlier stages in the family life cycle and may have solved past difficulties without any formal social services or psychotherapy. If they have used counseling services in the past, those problems were successfully resolved and do not have a bearing on the current difficulty.

For situational problems, the assessment process alone provides perspective and mobilizes a family's creativity, minimizing the need for further intervention. If psychoeducation about nonnormative stressors and direct suggestions are included during the assessment process, the family may be ready to terminate soon after the assessment is complete. If further psychoeducation and problem solving are necessary, they are usually accomplished in two to four sessions.

Families with situational problems welcome structural and intergenerational approaches when they focus on support and education. The process is enlightening and healing. They find a sense of power from hearing a consultant affirm their family's strengths through the recounting of history,

TABLE 5.1
Summary of Direct and Indirect Interventions

Hierarchy

Direct Interventions

Provide psychoeducation about transitions, how they affect power structures in families, and what the possible solutions are.

Teach communication and negotiation skills.

Give directives for someone to take charge.

Take charge and give others assignments.

Develop rituals to transfer power.

Indirect Interventions

Ask questions related to the process: How did you come to be the one in charge? What would happen if things were different? What would be difficult about having to share this responsibility?

Ask questions related to coping with transitions: If things were to change, how would you cope? How have you coped with other transitions in your life? What strengths did you rely on? What were the results of using these strengths?

Isolation

Direct Interventions

Provide psychoeducation about caregiving, chronic illnesses, grief, and loss, emphasizing how isolation occurs and its effects and possible solutions.

Give directives aimed at lessening isolation and sense of burden (i.e., spending more time with other people, asking others for help).

Make referrals for more services.

Indirect Interventions

Introduce paradox (i.e., explore the advantages of isolation): How is it helpful to the person? How would they cope with the additional stresses of nonisolation?

Address the stresses of nonisolation instead of the benefits.

Develop rituals of celebration to increase social support.

Power and responsibility

Direct Interventions

Provide psychoeducation on the topic, explaining how imbalance

Indirect Interventions

Ask questions to explore family roles: Have each of you always

Direct Interventions (continued)

occurs, why it is common in aging families; options for addressing or preventing imbalances.

Give directives to help some share their burden and others to compromise in decision making.

Clarify expectations and rules around caregiving tasks and decision making.

Misunderstandings

Direct Interventions

Ask permission to become a facilitator, arbitrator or mediator. Use communication skills to clarify each side's issues.

Track interactions over time to locate the point in time when the misunderstanding began.

Give directives, helping parties relive a past experience in the way they wished it had occurred at the time (i.e., things they wish they had said or done).

Develop rituals to resolve past conflicts. Help family members plan and carry out an event or a series of activities that will interrupt old patterns or lay to rest unresolved losses.

Intergenerational Patterns

Direct Interventions

Label patterns as they are identified on the genogram and time line.

Indirect Interventions (continued)

taken this particular position in the family, where you were either not involved or were very involved? How did the pattern develop?

Ask questions to explore the possibility of change: Have things ever been different? What were things like before? What would happen if things changed again?

Develop rituals to redistribute the balance of power and responsibility.

Indirect Interventions

Ask questions about exceptions: What times have there been when the conflict didn't keep you apart? What were you doing differently during those times?

Ask questions to focus on the future: How would you like things to be at the time of your death? What will things be like in five years, if these things don't change?

Indirect Interventions

Prepare for paradox with questions that deconstruct the pattern and address dilemmas regarding

Direct Interventions (continued)	*Indirect Interventions* (continued)
Negotiate family-of-origin work to target needed changes within the family.	change: How did you come to think or act in this way? Which people and experiences have encouraged you in this direction? If you were to go in a different direction, what would be the reaction of those who are important to you?
Explore each person's sense of entitlement (i.e., what is thought to be fair/unfair, what he or she thinks is deserved) (Boszormenyi-Nagy & Krasner, 1986).	
Enlist other members of the network to support changes within the family of origin.	Introduce the paradox, "Don't change ... yet."
	Ask questions that focus on coping strategies: Would changes mean rejection or significant conflict for you? How would you cope with such adversity if you were to change these patterns?
Develop rituals to simultaneously honor and change family patterns.	

and they are open to organizational shifts because they are candid, realistic, and flexible when it comes to meeting new challenges. When families encounter situational crises due to the unforeseen nature of progressive illnesses, they usually will not require strategic interventions because the issues of trust and control are resolvable through open discussion.

The difficulties of the James family and Mrs. Stevens were both considered situational. Even though there had been past conflict between Mr. James and his children, they had completed normative developmental tasks until the time of Mrs. James' death. The Stevens family had also completed earlier developmental tasks and their pain was related to the loss and confusion accompanying Mr. Stevens' Alzheimer's disease. In addition, neither family was interested in a traditional counseling experience, but both were very receptive to the psychoeducational approach, which provided a model for how other families solved problems similar to theirs and what problem-solving strategies would work best for them.

Transitional problems are those that are clearly related to normative life-cycle transitions, such as adjusting to adolescent children, launching, retirement, or death. Families with transitional problems have usually completed developmental tasks from some earlier life stages, but may have reached an impasse during a current transition. They may have lived for some time with the difficulty instead of seeking outside help to resolve it, or they may have sought services that were not helpful or did not address the developmental difficulty.

For transitional problems, the assessment should reveal how long the family has been having difficulty (i.e., recent death or unresolved launching issues). In these cases, the assessment will facilitate engagement and stimulate the creation of new thinking, but more time may be needed for the transition to be completed. Grief and loss may take a toll on the healthiest families; therefore, consultants must be flexible with their expectations for change related to transitions. The timing of trauma recovery cannot be controlled by either consultant or family; it can only be acknowledged as a factor and respected for its influence on the change process. In these cases, sessions during the problem-solving stage may be spread out with a number of weeks between sessions, enabling rhythms of the family to proceed naturally. The adjustment to death, in particular, may need only sparse preventive work, rather than regular sessions. The latter may unintentionally convey a need for progress to follow therapy's timetable, rather than the timetable of the family's healing forces.

Transitional problems may also need indirect interventions, depending on the nature of the difficulty. If a long-standing launching issue leads to addressing the dependency of an adult child, the intergenerational patterns restraining the launching process may need to be addressed through metaphor, paradox, and ritual. These situations often find the adult child as primary caregiver. Dilemmas are often complicated when other siblings have evolved away from assuming responsibility for parents, but, at the same time, have grown to resent the power and/or dependency of the remaining sibling. Such schisms in families warrant a careful examination of historical evolutions, deliberate empathy with each member's position, and strategic solutions that help families to transcend their impasses. Thus, a combination of direct and indirect interventions is often needed in such cases. The case of Joyce and her mother illustrates this combination.

> Joyce, 38, was an unmarried only child whose mother, Alice, 80, had come to live with her during the final stages of cerebella taxia, a degenerative disease of connective tissue. After seven years of watching her mother's deterioration, Joyce developed uncharacteristic anger, rage, and fatigue. She was referred by the adult day center due to her fears that she was becoming abusive. In addition, Alice was expressing a desire to die and this made Joyce feel very guilty for her anger. Hierarchical issues were easily ruled out in this family, but isolation was identified as a significant factor. Although

professional caregivers came into the home while Joyce was at work, over the seven years her own personal and social life had dwindled until she had no one in whom to confide. Extended family lived hundreds of miles away and were visited annually. Joyce had not turned to them for support, given their geographic distance.

A family history revealed the successful launching of Joyce 20 years earlier, Alice's two marriages, and her devoted caregiving for two husbands during their chronic illnesses. This family tradition had encouraged Joyce to develop the intensity and exclusivity that contributed to her isolation and exhaustion. An intergenerational focus helped Joyce to understand her isolation as an attempt to fulfill family tradition. Her rage was positively connoted as an expression of starvation, signaling the need for first aid. She began making distinctions between the circumstances of Alice's earlier devotion in caregiving (surrounded by extended family) and her present circumstance (isolated). This helped her psychological isolation and potential abuse, enabling her to ask for more help and to take music classes once a week. However, some time was needed, given Alice's impending death, before she was able to think about a social life beyond the world of caregiving. She remained determined to keep Alice at home and to do everything she possibly could for her.

A year after the initial assessment, Joyce called for another consultation to discuss the effects of Alice's continued deterioration. At this time, Joyce remained determined to be the best daughter she could be, by her definition, since Alice now had no capacity to communicate. Joyce was particularly agonized by Alice's suffering, and was sure there must be more she could do. The consultant wondered, paradoxically, if Alice thought that Joyce was not ready for her to die. After eight years, is it possible that Alice worried about what Joyce would do without her? The suggestion mobilized Joyce. The thought that she was a burden to her mother was unbearable. She went home and had a one-way "conversation" with Alice. "Don't worry about me, Mom. I'll be O.K. You don't have to suffer like this on my account. I have things I want to do. I'll be fine." Within two days, Alice died. Joyce reported feeling completely at peace, knowing she had taken good care of her mother.

The combination of psychoeducation and paradox was used respectfully in this transitional case. Although Joyce remained attached to the care of Alice in a way that was still isolating, the influence of impending death

A Developmental–Interactional Model

suggests a dynamic different from the "enmeshment" one might encounter in younger families where overinvolvement occurs. In addition, the uncertain timing of death makes the effect of future-oriented interventions (constructivist or strategic) much different for aging families. Thus, Joyce was affirmed for her devotion and that devotion was ultimately used to help her reconceptualize the situation. This transitional case also illustrates how interventions may be sparsely spread over an extended period, rather than trying to force quick, strategic turnarounds at the outset.

Chronic problems are those that have their roots in the long-standing difficulties of adult family members and existed before the onset of problems related to aging or illness. Families with chronic problems sometimes have drug or alcohol abuse, histories of childhood difficulty, or long-standing conflict within the family. These preexisting conditions may have already been the subject of past psychotherapy, but have not been resolved sufficiently to neutralize their impact on a later-life concern.

In cases of chronic problems, the assessment will help consultants to understand the complexity of the multiple problems with which the family has dealt. In these instances, other service providers may be fully involved. Very often, referrals for more service come from the exasperation of these providers. However, it is important for consultants to consider the influence of other providers as a potential issue of hierarchy. If families have become "professional clients," many providers may be addressing the same problems without coordination of services. When the consultant discovers such issues, the problem should be limited to that which no other provider is addressing. Consultants may also define their role as one of helping the family to coordinate, rather than replicate, services.

In most cases, indirect interventions are most helpful for families with chronic problems because they represent a departure from traditional services, which are often direct and nonrelational in scope. In addition, indirect interventions have been found to effectively bypass resistances encountered with traditional approaches (Wright & Leahey, 1984). Todd and Selekman (1991) make the following point.

> Straightforward requests for change seem less successful with chronic, demoralized cases. Such families seem to react poorly to zealous optimism and pushy methods. At least initially, it seems important to mirror their skepticism and avoid extreme directiveness. Neutral, systemic methods, split team or reflecting team dialogues, and at times, even paradoxical methods are more promising than direct efforts to convince families that they have the power to change. (p. 321)

The case of Mr. and Mrs. Mills illustrates the use of indirect interventions.

This elderly couple, both with chronic illnesses, were referred for treatment when they sought housekeeping help. They were concerned about the lack of success of their sons, ages 29 and 27. Both sons were living at home; their daughter, 25, was the only child who had completed school and obtained a job. The parents expressed concern to the consultant that their sons had become a great burden and they wanted them to move out. The younger son and the daughter refused to attend the meetings, so the consultant met with the parents and older son.

A family history revealed the following details. Mr. Mills, a veteran of World War II, had been discharged from the army for psychiatric reasons and had married Mrs. Mills shortly after returning home. A history of further psychiatric treatment followed for him, along with periods of joblessness. He expressed bitterness about not being awarded more veteran benefits, and felt he had been dealt an injustice by the military system. It was also learned that their older son had been in the military, serving two tours of duty in Vietnam. However, during his second tour, he developed serious emotional difficulties and returned home. Periods of joblessness have also followed for him.

During consultations, questions were raised about the younger son, since he was in the home at the time of the meetings, but would not come out of his room. The consultant learned that he was diagnosed as schizophrenic and was in regular weekly therapy with a local psychologist. Because the consultant began to see herself as one of many service personnel who were involved with this family, a picture began to form of a couple that had developed an "extended family" out of veteran and community resources. Care was taken so that she would not become an extension of that pattern. An effective intervention would have to address the unresolved trauma around the father's and son's military experiences. A positive connotation would have to be communicated with respect to the parents' caretaking of their children. A further reframing would have to take place regarding the lack of success exhibited by the sons. Finally, the larger social service network would have to be reframed and prescribed as the extended family for this nuclear family.

The consultant designed a family ritual in which she asked the parents and older son to participate (Selvini Palazzoli, Boscolo, Cecchin, & Prata, 1977). At the outset, she described the parents as being good parents because of the way they tried to provide everything possible for their children. She described the children as wanting to return their love by trying to provide certain emotional supports. The family was described as one that was very close, whose members cared a great deal about each other. She explained how the children cared so much about their parents that they did not want to abandon them, and how they were also just following the example that had been set for them by their dedicated parents.

In addition, the consultant joined Mr. Mills in his feelings toward an unjust system and, as a representative of a similar system, expressed a desire to help him compensate for the injustice dealt him many years before. To accomplish this, she designed a family ritual, which was initiated when she awarded Mr. Mills and his son each a Purple Heart, in recognition of the part of themselves that they had lost in war. She designed a brief statement, which she asked them to read ceremoniously and discuss at certain prescribed times during the coming month. Along with this, the ritual also prescribed certain times and places for the family to meet in order to maintain their solidarity, as the older son had obtained an apartment. Before the ritual was prescribed, the son had moved into an apartment of his own, but continued coming to meetings. It appeared that the family was really asking for support of a process that had already begun before the consultation. By prescribing the family's enmeshment in positively connoted terms, the consultant removed the source of their ambivalence by supporting the secure end (closeness) that left them psychologically free to pursue the other end (distance) without the fear of total abandonment.

A month later, the family reported following through with the ritual in a modified form. Mr. Mills indicated that the Purple Heart ceremony had been very meaningful to him. He continued to carry his Purple Heart with him in his wallet, and the family had several discussions about it. His son was feeling positive about his living arrangement and was continuing to look for a job. Mr. and Mrs. Mills continued to be involved with the psychologist on behalf of their younger son's problems, but were also now seeking activity in their local church group, rather than relying so heavily on community service workers for support and interaction.

This consultation was completed in six sessions over a nine-week period. While the younger son's symptoms were not addressed, a central dynamic that explains the symptoms was focused on with the hope of starting the change process. Outward signs of progress began to manifest themselves during this time and the consultant offered support that did not take the form of traditional social service or mental health intervention. Because this family could be classified as a chronic situation, it was more efficient to use the time in strategic, empowering interventions, rather than to try to correct a lifetime of psychological ills.

As the various stages of the DIM proceed, presenting problems become known in the context of relational factors that provide the "big picture" (i.e., hierarchy, isolation, power and responsibility, misunderstandings, intergenerational patterns). As the specific factors are identified, problems are categorized along a developmental continuum and interventions are based on the nature of the problem and clients' expectations for treatment. The intervention targets relevant relational factors while addressing the presenting problem.

Problem-Solving Stage: Techniques

Paradox

Among the many techniques in family therapy today, paradox is one of the most controversial. However, as Milton Erickson so richly illustrated, paradox can be employed with respect and compassion (Lankton & Lankton, 1983). Paradox is defined as a directive that may seem opposite to that which common sense (or the therapist's sense) would dictate. For example, when someone expresses sadness, it may seem paradoxical to encourage the person to "hold on" to the sadness. However, such a prescription can enhance the grieving process by allowing the person to cherish the past and to give proper time for wounds or losses to heal.

Another rationale behind the encouragement of emotions that families may already be feeling (anger, resentment, guilt) is that by doing so, they feel validated and understood. To prescribe an emotion is to give the person permission to feel what he or she may be ashamed to feel openly. Since the masking of shameful feelings can underlie conflict, encouragement of such feelings provides a necessary expression that, paradoxically, also helps to diffuse the intensity of emotion. Therefore, guilt may sometimes be encouraged because this is how a family shows that they still care. Anger can be encouraged because this is how a family expresses pain.

Thus, the DIM uses paradox as an important form of empathy (Hanna, 1995). Attempts to talk through feelings rationally can be misunderstood by clients as a subtle message that they should not feel a certain way, or that there is something unfortunate about the way they feel. Since this model acknowledges the uniqueness of each family and each person, all emotions are considered expressions of uniqueness. The DIM grants each person an understanding of and respect for the emotions they feel. There will be many times when it will be appropriate to state, "The feelings you have are understandable. Hold on to them until you have learned something from them. They may be useful to the healing process. Don't let them leave—yet" (Watzlawick, Weakland, & Fisch, 1974). In the case of Joyce and Alice, paradox was respectful of Joyce's devotion and even encouraged her to be more devoted. This led to insight, which came from using natural influences within the family rather than thinking of them as adversaries (Lankton & Lankton, 1983).

Ritual

The use of ritual gained popularity in family therapy when the Milan team published early accounts of their work with Italian families (Selvini Palazzoli, Boscolo, Cecchin, & Prata, 1977). Imber-Black, Roberts, and Whiting (1988) have also used rituals extensively to address a wide variety of family problems. With aging families, rituals are often needed to facilitate transitions, many of which are being pioneered by these families, since previous generations did not live long enough to experience the transitions that have become necessary in recent years. Once the relational components are identified, the type of ritual can be specified. For example, with issues related to changes in hierarchy, rituals are used to transfer power and authority. With issues related to isolation, celebrations increase social support. With issues related to power and authority, rituals are used to redistribute the balance. If a traditional intergenerational approach is appropriate for the presenting problem, rituals are also designed to address nodal events along the time line that mark some unresolved difficulty. In the case of Mr. and Mrs. Mills, the ritual combined the tasks of launching with earlier themes of injustice to address historical influences. In other cases, the ritual may be the assignment of a project to help with some situational or developmental transition (see Caron, Chapter 11 for an example of a ritual that facilitates nursing home placement). In an older population, rituals related to mourning and respect for deceased loved ones are often therapeutic.

EVALUATION OF THE MODEL

The judgment of the treatment success of the DIM is based entirely on clients' reports of their relationship to presenting problems. In situational cases, psychoeducation will enable them to mobilize sufficient resources to adjust and cope with illnesses or losses. Thus, while a problem such as Alzheimer's disease will not go away, the family's relationship to it will change. In transitional cases, new developmental tasks will be completed and the family will reconceptualize the presenting problem based on this successful transition. For example, a couple may develop a new routine in retirement and no longer contemplate divorce. In chronic cases, any shift of focus on the presenting problem must be initiated by the family. Resolution of the presenting problem may become the impetus to address other long-standing problems if the DIM has provided a process that is different from the family's other experiences in treatment. What might start off as an issue of caregiving may evolve into therapy for historical sibling rivalries. However, this is most likely to occur when the consultant starts by working with the family's definition of the problem.

An advantage of the DIM is that clinicians with varying levels of expertise can use parts of the model before referral is necessary. It provides beginning practitioners with an integrative approach to family therapy while enabling them to deliver quality service. Thus, social service workers who want to learn family therapy skills can begin with the DIM. By learning to construct a genogram and time line, they are able to address hierarchical issues during the assessment stage and to provide psychoeducation. If transitional or chronic cases need more complex interventions, a referral can be made to a more advanced family therapist. When experienced family therapists use the DIM with chronic cases, the assessment stage lays a foundation for indirect interventions during the problem-solving stage.

During the time of Project Support, the DIM was used successfully with cases involving caregiving issues, elder abuse, chronic illness, marital and family conflict in later life, and issues related to grief and loss. In a survey of 19 cases seen during the first two years of the program, 63 percent of the families reported positive change as a result of consultations (Johnson, 1988). The average number of visits per family was 7.88. Positive change was related to the number of people involved in sessions ($T = 2.889, P = .05$). The average number of people involved in families reporting positive change was 6. The average number of people involved in families reporting no change was 3.

The DIM has also been effective with clients of all ages and with different family configurations. The structured order of the model helps consultants determine the level of difficulty before deciding on specific interventions. Since the assessment process by itself is a legitimate intervention for less difficult cases, short-term therapy is easily accomplished at this stage alone. Then, when circumstances warrant, further interventions during the problem-solving stage address more chronic problems. Maintaining a balance between the interactional and the developmental enables the clinician to focus on pragmatic solutions while including aspects of history that have been important to the family. This balance also positions the family therapist to be flexible. Rather than fit the client to the model, the DIM is an attempt to remain flexible, ultimately enabling information brought by the family to determine the direction of therapy.

REFERENCES

Bodin, A. (1981). The interactional view: Family therapy approaches of the Mental Research Institute. In A. S. Gurman & D. P. Kniskern (Eds.), *Handbook of family therapy: Vol. 1* (pp. 267–309). New York: Brunner/Mazel.

Boszormenyi-Nagy, I., & Krasner, B. (1986). *Between give and take: A clinical guide to contextual therapy*. New York: Brunner/Mazel.

Carter, B., & McGoldrick, M. (1989). *The changing family life cycle* (2nd ed.). Needham Heights, MA: Allyn & Bacon.

Haley, J. (1973). *Uncommon therapy: The psychiatric techniques of Milton H. Erickson.* New York: Norton.

Haley, J. (1976). *Problem-solving therapy*. San Francisco: Jossey-Bass.

Hanna, S. M. (1986). *Structured family treatment for the elderly chronically ill: A training manual for Project Support*. Madison, WI: Independent Living.

Hanna, S. M. (1995). On paradox: Empathy before strategy. *Journal of Family Psychotherapy, 6*(1), 85–88.

Hanna, S. M., & Brown, J. H. (1995). *The practice of family therapy: Key elements across models*. Pacific Grove, CA.: Brooks/Cole.

Hiebert, W., Gillespie, J., & Stahmann, R. (1993). *Dynamic assessment in couples therapy*. New York: Lexington Books.

Hoffman, L. (1983). A co-evolutionary framework for systemic family therapy. In J. Hansen & B. Keeney (Eds.), *Diagnosis and assessment in family therapy*. Rockville, MD: Aspen Systems.

Imber-Black, E., Roberts, J., & Whiting, R. (1988). *Rituals in families and family therapy*. New York: Norton.

Johnson, M. (1988). *Empirical review of Project Support*. Unpublished manuscript.

Lankton, S., & Lankton, C. (1983). *The answer within: A clinical framework of Ericksonian hypnotherapy*. New York: Brunner/Mazel.

McCubbin, H. (1980). Family stress and coping: A decade in review. *Journal of Marriage and the Family, 42*, 855–871.

McCubbin, H., Patterson, J., McCubbin, M., & Wilson, L. (1983). Parental coping and family environment: Critical factors in the home management and health status of children with cystic fibrosis. In D. Bagarozzi, A. Jurich, & R. Jackson (Eds.), *Marital and family therapy: New perspectives in theory, research and practice*. New York: Human Sciences Press.

Minuchin, S., & Fishman, H. C. (1981). *Family therapy techniques*. Cambridge, MA: Harvard University Press.

Penn, P. (1982). Circular questioning. *Family Process. 19*, 267–280.

Selvini Palazzoli, M., Boscolo, L., Cecchin, G., & Prata, G. (1977). Family rituals: A powerful tool in family therapy. *Family Process, 16*(4), 445–454.

Todd, T., & Selekman, M. D. (Eds.). (1991). *Family therapy approaches with adolescent substance abusers.* Needham Heights, MA: Allyn & Bacon.

Watzlawick, P., Weakland, J. H., & Fisch, R. (1974). *Change: Principles of problem formation and problem resolution.* New York: Norton.

White, M. (1983). Anorexia nervosa: A transgenerational systems perspective. *Family Process, 22*(3), 255-273.

White, M. (1988). Saying hullo again: The incorporation of the lost relationship in the resolution of grief. Adelaide, Australia: *Dulwich Centre Newsletter,* Spring.

White, M., & Epston, D. (1991) *Narrative means to therapeutic ends.* New York: Norton.

Wright, L., & Leahey, M. (1984). *Nurses and families: A guide to family assessment and intervention.* Philadelphia: Davis.

Zeig, J. (Ed.). (1985). *Ericksonian psychotherapy: Volume I. Structures.* New York: Brunner/Mazel.

~ 6 ~

The Strength–Vulnerability Model of Mental Health and Illness in the Elderly

Cleveland G. Shields, Ph.D.
University of Rochester Highland Hospital
Rochester, New York

Lyman C. Wynne, M.D.
University of Rochester
Rochester, New York

INTRODUCTION

Family-life-cycle theory is an important component of most theories of family functioning. Theories of family functioning assess the ability of family members to carry out appropriate developmental tasks and to manage developmental transitions, such as establishing an enduring relationship, beginning child rearing, and leaving home. Few of these theories, however, concern themselves with the new and continuing developmental tasks faced by families with aging members. Recent writings on the family life cycle (Walsh, 1989), books on family-of-origin therapy (Framo, 1992; Williamson, 1991), and therapy with late life-families or their concerns (Hughston, Christopherson, & Bonjean, 1989; Walsh & McGoldrick, 1991) have begun to fill this void. Although biomedical and social policy studies of aging are rapidly proiferating, most gerontology research is empirically driven, not conceptually based (Zarit, 1990). Except for a few scholars (Boss, Caron, & Horbal, 1988; Niederehe & Fruge, 1984; Niederehe & Funk, 1987; Zarit & Zarit, 1982), little research is being done from a family systems perspective.

The purpose of this chapter is to describe family-life-cycle issues for the elderly and to apply a developmental perspective to mental health and illness in the elderly. First, we describe the major elements of family-life-cycle theory and how these apply to the elderly. Second, we reformulate the stress-vulnerability model (Goldstein, 1990; Cicchetti, 1990; Richters & Weintraub, 1990; Sameroff & Seifer, 1990; Rutter, 1990) that has been used in studies of mental health and illness at earlier stages of the family life cycle in order to broaden the conceptualization of mental disorders in the aged.

THEORETICAL BACKGROUND

We conceptualize the life cycle as consisting of two interacting life cycles: the individual life cycle and the family life cycle. The individual life cycle can, for the present purposes, be conceptualized in a condensed way as consisting of two components: *biological health* (Wynne, Shields, & Sirkin, 1992; Wynne, Sirkin, & Shields, in press) and *personal themes*. The family life cycle has four components: *larger systems factors, family events, family themes,* and *interpersonal processes.* The psychosocial components of the family life cycle have been discussed in detail for younger families (Carter & McGoldrick, 1988; Falicov, 1988; Walsh, 1982). Yet older family members often are faced with a different set of events and themes in their lives than are younger family members (Lieberman & Peskin, 1992). We first describe, therefore, the personal and biological health issues of the individual life cycle of a person in later life. Second, we describe our conceptualization of the family life cycle and the events, themes, larger systems, and direct interpersonal processes relevant to later-life families. Finally, we describe the interaction of the individual and family life cycles.

Individual Life Cycle

Biological Health and Illness

A key word in understanding the health of the elderly is heterogeneity. While it is true that older persons are at greater risk for many acute and chronic illnesses, it is also true that there is no simple description of the health or illness of the elderly. Rolland (1987) has developed a psychosocial

The Strength–Vulnerability Model

typology of illness using four factors to describe the psychosocial consequences of an illness. These factors and their descriptors are as follows: *onset* (acute or gradual); *course* (progressive, constant, or relapsing/episordic); *outcome* (incapacitating or nonincapacitating: fatal or shortened life span, or nonfatal); and *time phases* (crisis to chronic to terminal). Rolland (1987) has stated that by using these factors, one can "generate a typology with 32 potential psychosocial types of illness" (p. 206). All 32 types of illness may not exist, but the concepts remain valid: the relationship of health, illness, functioning, and age are complex and varied. Many elderly live healthy and active lives; a number are slowed by illness, but are not disabled; and only a minority are functionally impaired due to serious illness.

Family researchers studying the elderly need to include not only measures of the research subjects' diagnosed symptomatic illness, but also measures of health perceptions and functional impairment, as well as other measures of the psychosocial consequences of illness (i.e., Ware & Sherbourne, 1992; Ware, 1987; Franks, Campbell, & Shields, 1992; Franks et al., 1992). Illness is transactional; that is, it is experienced in the context of family and other relationships (Wynne, Shields, & Sirkin, 1992; Wynne, Sirkin, & Shields, in press). Therefore, the meaning and consequences of illness for the individual need to be assessed in relation to its impact on the family and the family's reciprocal impact on the course of the illness.

Personal Themes

This would include those issues relevant to the elderly that have contributed to a person's repertoire of skills available in later life. Among these are historical issues, such as education, occupational skills, employment history, ethnicity, race, and religion, as well as developmental issues, such as Eriksonian developmental crises, personality characteristics, and psychiatric history. Education and work history are primary determinants of economic resources, which greatly affect the comfort and security of an older person. Many elderly persons have strong ethnic identifications if they are immigrants or children of immigrants (Gelfand, 1982; McGoldrick, Pearce, & Giordano, 1982). Cultural values and self-identity commonly are strongly tied to ethnic communities and minority group status.

Central to understanding the individual life cycle is the developmental perspective provided by Erikson's eight stages of the individual life cyle (Erikson, 1950; Erikson, 1968; Erikson, Erikson, & Kivnick, 1986). It is overly simplistic to think only of the final two stages of Erikson's model as pertaining to the elderly. Instead, earlier themes and dilemmas reemerge in new ways in later life. For example, trust versus mistrust sets the stage for one's sense of hope in future generations. Unresolved conflicts around autonomy versus shame may help determine an elder's ability to ask for and make use of help when facing functional decline. The resolution of intimacy versus isolation epigenetically prepares the person in later life for coping with the inevitable losses that accompany aging, and for the developmental crisis of generativity versus self-absorption. How are the commitment of the elderly and their connection to the next generation shaped? Are they able to nurture young parents in their families and mentor younger colleagues at their work, or does their place in history seem threatened by the emergence of new leadership? Finally, the issue of integrity versus despair is faced as the elderly begin to evaluate their lives. Are they able to accept their failures and celebrate their successes or are they overwhelmed by the events of their lives? Do they embrace their "one and only life cycle and ... the people who have become significant to it" (Erikson, 1968, p. 139) or do they reject it and wish they had another life. At this stage, as in earlier stages, personality characteristics and psychiatric symptoms may be viewed as indicators of unresolved developmental crises.

Family Life Cycle

Larger Systems Factors

There are many factors in our society that affect the health and functioning of later-life families. For example, the health care system, Social Security and retirement income, housing, the economy, and societal attitudes toward aging all affect the aging group. Inadequacies in the United States health care system, particularly in long-term care, may result in extreme burdens for spouses and adult offspring who take on the responsibility of caring for their ill family member with little or none of the professional care resources that might be provided through long-term care programs. A high percentage of the elderly live in poverty or near poverty and thus reside in substandard housing, have no car, cannot afford public transportation, and survive on inadequate diets. Few elderly make use of such government programs as energy assistance, food stamps, public housing, or housing rental assistance (HHS, 1991).

Family Events

Later-life-family events are the foreseen and unforeseen gains and losses that happen over the life span but often accumulate especially in later life. These include such events as marriages of children, births of grandchildren, deaths of elderly parents, deaths of other family members, death of a spouse, divorces, remarriages, retirement, illness, and disability. Events that are expected to happen, such as the death of elderly parents or birth of grandchildren, may be easier to cope with than are unexpected events, such as the death of children, the birth of grandchildren to teenage parents, or the death of parents with young children still in the home (Carter & McGoldrick, 1988).

Family Themes

Family themes are the issues families must resolve together over the life cycle. Steinglass, Bennett, Wolin, and Reiss (1987) have developed a model of the family life cycle emphasizing specific family developmental themes in the early, middle, and late phases of the family. Early-phase families face the task of forming their family unit under the watchful eye of their families of origin. They must fashion an identity for their family unit that takes into account each partner's loyalties to his or her family of origin and an identity that sets boundaries as to who is in and who is out of the new family unit. Mid-phase families are settled in their life commitments and have developed enough stability in their family environment to support their members' growth and development. A family shifts into late-phase concerns when gains and losses turn the family members' attention from maintaining their identity through their stability and work to transmitting the essential elements of that previously formed family identity to newly forming family units in their extended family. Thus, in late-phase families, identity reemerges as a central theme; however, this time the focus is on distilling, clarifying, and transmitting the family's identity or legacy to those newly forming family units.

Steinglass et al. (1987) emphasize that these phases are not necessarily chronological nor are they exclusive. For example, older family members who remarry will need to set boundaries and determine their identity as a new family unit (early-phase issues), while also seeking clarification and transmission of the legacy of their family identity to their newly married children, nieces, or nephews.

Interpersonal Processes

These processes of relational development are described by Wynne (1984): attachment/caregiving, communication, problem solving, and mutuality. Attachment/caregiving is the bond of affection in relationships. Communication is the ability to create shared understanding and meaning among people. Problem solving is the ability to devise solutions to problems and follow through with them. Mutuality signifies faithfulness to the relationship and the capacity to reinvent it as circumstances change over time. In enduring relational systems, primarily in families, these processes build epigenetically, that is, positive attachment/caregiving is needed before useful communication can happen. Competent communication is essential for effective problem solving, and effective problem solving is a prerequisite to support the maintenance of relationships over a lifetime.

Developmental Changes in Intergenerational Relationships

Family relationships change over time, especially the relationship between parents and children. The balance of attachment/caregiving of parent to child necessarily changes as offspring enter adulthood. Parents are no longer responsible for the care of their children, and adult offspring are challenged to give up the desire to be cared for by their parents. The bond between parent and child shifts from the responsibility of caregiving to a bond of affection and shared history. The shift is made from a hierarchical parent-child relationship to a more nonhierarchical adult-adult relationship. This developmental milestone is a central concept for Williamson (1981, 1982a), who called it the development of personal authority in the family system. Others have called it filial maturity (Blenkner, 1965; King, Bonacci, & Wynne, 1990). With the increasing life span and fewer children conceived per couple, people will have more family members in the generations before and after them than they will have in their own generation. Butler, Lewis, and Sunderland (1991) describe this as the change from the horizontal family to the vertical family with the result that intergenerational family relationships will become even more salient in the future.

Under these circumstances, the day is likely to come when elderly parents need help from their adult offspring, either with decision making or with hands-on care. For adult offspring to take on such a caregiving role with their parents requires another shift in the attachment/caregiving balance. Such a shift may be difficult to accomplish if the shift to an adult-adult relationship from a hierarchical parent–child relationship has not taken place earlier. The importance of this development milestone is made even more poignant by the research of Pillemer and Finkeher (1989) on adult offspring caregivers of elderly parents. They found that adult offspring caregivers who had remained dependent on their parents throughout their adult life are more likely to abuse their elderly parents than are those who have not remained so dependent.

Interaction of the Individual and Family Life Cycle

It is axiomatic that most individuals live in families of one sort or another and that families themselves are composed of individuals. Families and their individual members influence each other both positively and negatively. There are times when an individual's life-cycle stage and his or her family's life-cycle stage may be in conflict, whereas at other times the needs of the individual and the needs of the family mesh well (Carter & McGoldrick, 1988).

THERAPEUTIC APPLICATIONS OF THE STRENGTH–VULNERABILITY MODEL

Building on the interaction between the individual and family life cycles, we propose that the strength–vulnerability (SV) model be applied to the study of mental health and illness in the elderly. This model is an extension of the vulnerability stress models that guide much of the research in psychopathology in children and young adults (Rolf, Masten, Cicchetti, Nuechterlein, & Weintraub, 1990).

Proposition One

The individual life cycle and the family life cycle interact to create four factors: *strengths, vulnerabilities, health-enhancing factors, and risks.* These four factors are the primary concepts of the model. (See Figure 6.1).

Proposition Two

Strengths, vulnerabilities, health-enhancing factors, and risks function directly, indirectly, and interactively to influence the mental health and illness of individuals and the functioning/dysfunctioning of marital and family units.

Strengths are processes internal to the individual that promote healthy functioning and protect against psychopathology. These processes have been inadequately emphasized in the vulnerability literature, which has focused on the precursor pathology. Strengths are the personal competencies and wisdom, in the elderly, that have accrued through a lifetime of successes and successful coping with life's challenges. Strength processes include such personal characteristics as psychological and physical well-being, intelligence, intact cognitive functioning, hopefulness, a positive philosophy of life, and a sense of purpose in life.

We define *vulnerabilities* as processes internal to the individual that work to increase the likelihood of developing illness and distress. The origins of vulnerability processes are both genetic and biologically or psychologically

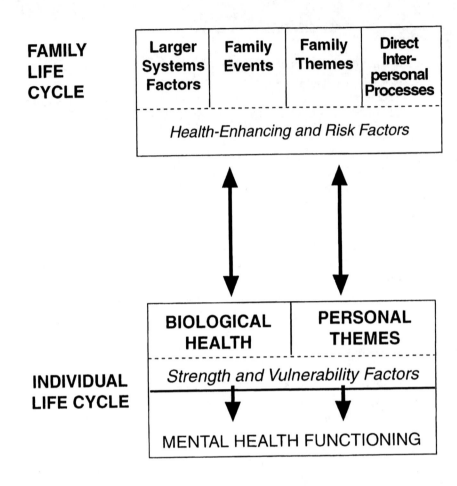

FIGURE 6.1. Strength–Vulnerability Model of Mental Health and Illness.

acquired through life experience and events (Gottesman & Shields, 1972). Vulnerabilities are predispositions or susceptibilities that increase the liability to illness; they are not in themselves clinically diagnosable illnesses or disorders. Some vulnerabilities may be indexed by measurable or observable premorbid characteristics. For example, low intelligence indexes vulnerability to a variety of difficulties and forms of distress and illness. Some forms of vulnerability are inferred when persons exposed to the same stressor or the same pathogen differ in whether or not they become ill or in how readily they recover. However, as we have emphasized, strength and health-enhancing factors also contribute to the equation.

The Strength–Vulnerability Model 139

Health-enhancing factors are external to the individual, promote healthy functioning, and are those statistically important environmental influences that often are protective, fully or partially, against pathology. Health-enhancing processes in the elderly include effective family problem-solving skills, family emotional closeness, suitable employment and financial stability, and large social and family networks. Health-enhancing processes can be converted into internal strengths, such as high self-esteem, insight, and feelings of attachment.

Risk factors are external to the individual and are those hazards measurable in the environment that increase the statistical likelihood (combining the interacting with vulnerabilities) that an individual will develop and continue to have psychiatric or physical illness or impairment. Risk processes are such things as death of a close famly member, economic downturn, illness of spouse, high expressed emotion from a spouse or caregiver (Leff & Vaughn, 1985), or an inadequate relational system for providing caregiving and problem solving (Doane, Hill, & Diamond, 1991).

In addition, a distinction is needed between genetic *risk* (assessed statistically in terms of the presence or absence of a disorder in biologic family members) and genetic *vulnerability* (assessed as characteristics, such as impaired cognitive functioning, in the index individuals themselves). A genetic family history of an illness is a *risk* factor; for instance, a statistically increased likelihood of illness based on data from a person other than the index individual. However, any evidence measurable in the index person (e.g., mood lability, attentional deficits) are *vulnerability* factors (which also can be evaluated as an increased statistical likelihood of illness). Thus, one can speak of genetic *risk* and *vulnerability*, depending on the source of the data.

Expanded from Zubin and Spring's (1977) formulation of the relation between vulnerability and life event stressors, Figure 6.2 is a graphic display of how we see these four processes at work in the life of an individual. The likelihood of illness is maximized if a person possesses low strengths and high vulnerability and the family and environment provide low health-enhancing factors and high-risk factors. The likelihood of illness is minimized if the opposite is true—that is, if the person possesses high strengths and low vulnerability and the family and environment provide high health-enhancing factors and low-risk factors.

This model can also be seen as a strength–vulnerability model for relationships themselves. Marriages and families, as relational systems, can be conceptualized as having strengths and vulnerabilities in neglecting or taking advantage of the health-enhancing events and in succumbing to or warding off the risk processes they encounter through time. The four

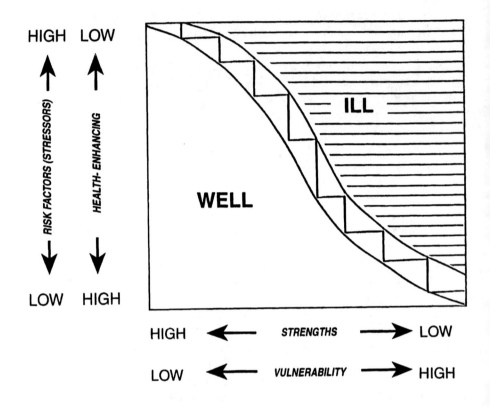

FIGURE 6.2. Relation of Vulnerability, Strength, Health-Enhancing, and Risk Factors.

strength–vulnerability processes at the family level can, in turn, act as health-enhancing or risk factors for the individuals within the family. (See Figure 6.2).

Strength Processes in the Elderly

In many cultures, it is the older persons who are sought for leadership and advice. While there are cognitive changes due to aging that are often the subject of negative stereotypes of older persons, the fact remains that major leadership posts in most governments, corporations, and many other organizations are held by older persons. This has led psychologists to study cognitive expertise in addition to cognitive skills. Salthouse (1990) discussed the evidence and theory for the differences in these abilities. Although certain cognitive skills may begin declining as early as the third decade of life, cognitive knowledge and expertise are thought to increase through much of adulthood. Salthouse suggests that the most promising explanation for this is that increasing life and professional experience more than compensates for losses in cognitive skills, such as processing speed or conceptual comprehension. Simonton (1990) reviewed the literature on creativity and wisdom in aging and showed that while many empirical measures of creativity (defined as divergent thinking) show age-related declines, productivity in many fields show increases, peaking at ages 40 and 50, with little dropoff thereafter. The major hypothesis in this research is that creative achievement requires more than the ability to think quickly and devise new ideas. Instead, creative achievement seems to be an interaction between the ability to think creatively and the wisdom acquired from enduring in a field. Baltes, Smith, and Staudinger (1991) have begun to examine the acquisition of wisdom through the life span with the goal of validating the belief that older persons actually possess more wisdom about life. Psychosocial theory (Erikson et al., 1986) suggests that if persons resolve various life crises as the challenges arise, they will acquire wisdom in later life.

Older persons with higher education and socioeconomic status show far fewer cognitive changes with aging (Albert, 1988; Schooler, 1990) than do other members of their aging cohort. Even in adults who show cognitive changes not resulting from a brain disease, interventions that teach memory or other cognitive techniques significantly improve their performance (Albert, 1988; Arenberg, 1993).

The research of Costa and McCrae (Costa & McCrae, 1984a; Costa & McCrae, 1984b; Costa, McCrae, & Norris, 1984; McCrae & Costa, 1984) has shown that facets of extroversion, such as friendliness, assertiveness, and cheerfulness, are robust predictors of well-being and psychological adjustment in later life. In an adult twin study with subjects ranging in age from 20 to 56 years old, Kendler, Kessler, Heath, Neale, and Eaves (1991) found that the healthy coping mechanisms of "turning to others" and "problem solving" are strongly explained by genetic factors, presumably related to temperament. These coping strategies significantly buffer the depressogenic and anxiogenic effect of stressful life events.

Lieberman and Peskin (1992) showed that there is no single appropriate response to loss in the elderly. In fact, those elderly who showed the least grief at the death of a spouse were the best adjusted at a one-year follow-up. They also suggested that there is evidence that many elderly use times of change, the loss of a spouse, or other major losses as times to make personal transformations that can enrich their lives.

Vulnerability Processes in the Elderly

There are five main sources of vulnerability factors: genetics, personality, physical health, brain changes, and cognitive changes. Plomin and McClearn (1990), reviewing the research from behavioral genetics, showed that genetics accounts for 30 to 50 percent of the variance in personality measures, except for hostility, assertiveness, belief in luck, and agreeableness. Behavioral genetic research in the elderly is just beginning, so few studies have examined the genetic effects of psychopathology in the elderly (Heston, 1991) although some new studies are being published (Gatz, Pedersen, Plomin, Nesselroade, & McClearn, 1992; Pedersen, Gatz, Plomin, Nesselroade, & McClearn, 1989). In younger subjects, genetics has been shown to account for less than 50 percent of the variance in personality and psychopathology, which means that over 50 percent of the variance is unaccounted for (Reiss, Plomin, & Hetherington, 1991), much of which is thought to be due to nonshared environmental factors. The nonshared environmental variance includes biological factors, such as obstetrical complications at birth; a variety of illnesses and nutritional problems that alter vulnerability; unique relationships with parents, siblings, friends, spouses, and partners; and distinctive events in a person's life. Personality research (Costa & McCrae, 1984a) has shown that facets of neuroticism (anxiety, hostility, self-consciousness, impulsiveness, vulnerability) are predictive of poor psychological adjustment and a lower sense of well-being in later life.

As people age, the risk of medical illness increases. Health status and functional status (the ability to take care of one's personal daily needs) are predictors of psychological distress (Arling, 1987; Kennedy, Kelman, & Thomas, 1990). Physical health status is highly correlated with life satisfaction and psychological distress (Revicki & Mitchell, 1990). Physical dependency and pain are highly associated with depression (Williams & Schulz, 1988). The presence of a major illness, or the belief that one has cancer, is associated with increased vulnerability for suicide among white males (Conwell, Rotenberg, & Caine, 1990). Albert (1988) notes that changes in cognitive functioning are highly correlated with changes in brain structure, which are found through neuroimaging. Aging is linked to certain changes in cognitive ability, such as the slowing and accuracy of information processing (Cerella, 1990), increases in semantic errors, and decreases in the ability to attend to two tasks, visual-spatial comprehension, concept formation, and abstraction. Sensory and primary memory remain intact, but there are decreases in secondary memory, most of which are attributed to differences in encoding and retrieval (Albert, 1988). In the previous section, we discussed how education and socioeconomic factors mediate and cognitive interventions may reduce many of these cognitive changes.

Health-Enhancing Processes in the Elderly

The importance of the family and social environment for the mental and physical health of the elderly should not be underestimated. Plomin and McClearn (1990) have shown that environmental factors account for more variance in psychopathology and personality traits than does genetics. As noted above, most studies of family or social environment variables have examined risk factors more than health-enhancing factors. We review here a few studies that have shown relationships between family and social environmental factors and positive outcomes.

Schooler (1990), reviewing psychosocial factors affecting cognitive functioning in aging, found that adults who live and work in environments that require independent thinking and decision making show higher intelligence and more cognitive flexibility into late life than do those elderly who do not work in such environments. The primary health-enhancing factor discussed in the literature is social support. For example, social support aids recovery from hip fracture (Cummings et al., 1988). Social support is related to decreases in mortality for men after controlling for social class, health status at baseline, cardiovascular risk factors, alcohol intake, physical activity, and body mass index (Hanson, Isacsson, Janzon, & Lindell, 1989). The more embedded one is in one's network, the lower is one's blood pressure (Goodman & Pynoos, 1990). The unavailability of confidants (spouse, friend, other) is a major predictor of depressive symptoms (Seeman, Kaplan, Knudsen, Cohen, & Guralnik, 1987). However, one study reported earlier death of patients on renal dialysis who were members of well-functioning African-American families (Reiss, Gonzalez, & Kramer, 1986). The author's explanation was that it was more difficult for well-functioning families with members who were working each day to accommodate to the long-term care demands of a chronically ill family member.

We propose that family attachment/caregiving, communication, and problem-solving skills are very important health-enhancing processes for negotiating change in families as their members age. In view of Schooler's (1990) findings on environmental complexity and cognitive functioning, we propose that the complexity of family communication, including the freedom to speak one's mind in one's family, to make decisions, and to take part in decision making in one's family, may lead to greater cognitive functioning, better health functioning, and thus better mental health. Marital interaction research supports the view that greater complexity in communication is predictive of marital stability (Gottman, 1979).

Risk Processes in the Elderly

Risk processes are those environmental processes that increase the susceptibility to mental illness by acting as stressors that may convert vulnerabilities into clinically manifest illnesses. Caring for an ill, elderly relative puts great strains on both the elderly caregivers and other family members. Cognitive impairment in the patient increases the mental health consequences for primary family caregivers more than any other patient variable (Baillie, Norbeck, & Barnes, 1988; Dura, Stukenberg, & Kiecolt-Glaser, 1990; Scharlach, 1989). It is the negative family interactions that put caregivers at greater risk for depression (Pagel, Erdly, & Becker, 1987; Shields, 1992; Williamson & Schulz, 1990). Fifty percent of family caregivers to those with Alzheimer's are clinically depressed (Gallagher, Wrabetz, Lovett, Del Maestro, & Rose, 1989; Gallagher, Rose, Rivera, Lovett, & Thompson, 1989). The multiple roles of a caregiver can act as both risk and health-enhancing factors (Stoller & Pugliesi, 1989).

The loss of a confidant increases the risk for depression (Emmerson, Burvill, Finlay-Jones, & Hall, 1989). Widowhood and multiple losses are risk factors for suicide in older white males (Conwell & Caine, 1990; Conwell, Rotenberg, & Caine, 1990). Social support serves as a buffer or blunt the effects of financial strain on depressive symptoms (Krause, 1987). Spouses of cancer patients who report that they have lost social support from the patient have lowered immune functioning (Baron, Cutrona, Hicklin, Russell, & Lubaroff, 1990). Retirement brings changes in social support. Retirees report the same quality of social support, but their social support network from coworkers decreases (Bossé, Aldwin, Levenson, Workman-Daniels, & Ekerdt, 1990). As persons age, their nonfamily social support network decreases, but their family support remains steady and their satisfaction with their children increases (Field & Minkler, 1988). The percentage of nonfamily support decreases and the percentage of family support increases with age (Palinkas, Wingard, & Barrett-Connor, 1990).

Negative family interactions are associated with poor adjustment or poor recovery from illness. Norris, Stephens, and Kinney (1990) found that negative family interactions were associated with the poor adjustment and slow recovery of daily functioning of stroke victims. Franks et al. (1992) found that older adults who reported that their families of origin were critical of them were more likely to be depressed. Negative social interactions are highly associated with well-being (Rook, 1984). Weddell (1987) found that the mood of stroke patients is highly related to the expressed emotion of key relatives (frequent critical comments and overinvolvement).

There is a negative bias in our society toward aging that even the elderly share about other elderly, although not about themselves (Schulz & Fritz, 1987). Public policy is moving to withdraw public support for elderly health needs and putting more of the burden on the family (Walker, 1987). The problem is that these moves may overwhelm the coping and caregiving strengths of many families.

We propose that the changing dynamics of relationships brought on by retirement, illness, children moving, and other life-cycle events can constitute a risk process. Families may have difficulty adjusting and changing roles. Families that have always functioned well, with clearly defined roles for each member, may become stuck and unable to negotiate changes in later life.

IMPLICATIONS OF THE STRENGTH–VULNERABILITY MODEL FOR CLINICAL RESEARCH ON AGING FAMILIES

A Model, Not a Theory

The strength–vulnerability model is a model, not a complete theory (Burr, 1991; Burr, Hill, Nye, & Reiss, 1979; Jacob, 1987; Shields, 1986). The model becomes a theory when it is applied to explain specific phenomena. The major components of the model are the individual and family life cycle from which arise the four primary concepts of the model: strengths, vulnerabilities, health-enhancing factors, and risks. The central proposition of the model is that strengths, vulnerabilities, health-enhancing factors, and risks work additively and interactively to affect the mental health or illness of individuals in the family. In addition, the model can be applied to the family or marital unit itself, using the four concepts to examine overall family or marital health.

The model guides an investigator through the process of deduction to the development of variables from the individual and family life cycle in order to assess strengths, vulnerabilities, health-enhancing factors, and risks. The model also encourages investigators to immerse themselves in the phenomena under study, to create inductively new variables not previously considered to assess the four factors of the model.

Implications for Theory Development and Research

In gerontology, most studies of a subject's social environment have focused on the positive consequences of social support (Baron, Cutrona, Hicklin, Russell, & Lubaroff, 1990) ignoring the negative consequences of conflicted relationships. Newer studies have begun to examine conflict in relationships (Pearlin, Mullan, Semple, & Skaff, 1990; Pearlin & Schooler, 1978; Shields, 1992). In terms of the SV model, most studies have examined health-enhancing factors in the environment but not risk factors. Similarly, most of the literature that examines qualities of the individual, such as personality factors, biological health, and other variables, focuses on vulnerability factors, not strengths. For example, there are many studies that examine vulnerabilities (Arling, 1987; Baron, Cutrona, Hicklin, Russell, & Lubaroff, 1990; Cattell, 1988; Cartwright, 1990; Col, Fanale, & Kronholm, 1990; Croog, Levine, Testa, et al., 1986; Christozov, Predov, & Petrov, 1987; Depner & Ingersoll-Dayton, 1988; Eisen, Miller, Woodward, Spitznagel, & Przybeck, 1990; Eisen, Woodward, Miller, Spitznagel, & Windham, 1987; Hopkinson & Doherty, 1990; Kennedy, Kelman, & Thomas, 1990; Kirsling, 1986; Palinkas, Wingard, & Barrett-Connor, 1990; Raffoul, 1986; Revicki & Mitchell, 1990; Weintraub, 1990; Williams & Schulz, 1988). Few studies, however, examine strengths (Decker & Schulz, 1985; Doherty, Schrott, Metcalf, & Iasiello-Vailas, 1983; Farmer, Locke, Moscicki, Dannenberg, Larson, & Radloff, 1988; Kendler, Kessler, Heath, Neale, & Eaves, 1991; Vitaliano, Katon, Maiuro, & Russo, 1989). The SV model explicitly directs investigators to examine factors of the individual and their environment that have both positive and negative consequences.

A significant feature of the SV model is that it encourages an examination of the interplay of individual, family, and larger systems factors. The model is rooted in a biopsychosocial tradition as it stresses the importance of the interaction of biological health, individual mental health, and family functioning. A particular research project may seek to establish the relationship of certain family factors to clinically significant outcomes, and that is appropriate, but the model requires investigators to discuss their findings from the perspective of multiple factors—even if their project is limited to examining only certain factors. Ultimately, the model fosters multivariate research because it advocates that investigators include multiple factors whenever possible and examine their direct, indirect, and interactive effects. Newer statistical methods make such studies more feasible than in the past.

The SV model takes the concepts of disease, illness, and disorder seriously (1992). It encourages the examination of both the effect of family factors on the course of illness (mental or medical) and the effect of illness on family functioning. There is a constant interplay between family functioning and illness. Serious chronic illness in the elderly can have a devastating impact on family functioning. At the same time, a history of poor family functioning can severely limit a family's ability to cope with a chronic illness and may place a person at greater risk for developing a chronic illness (House, Landis, & Umberson, 1988; House, Robbins, & Metzner, 1982). By taking illness seriously, the SV model encourages the study of the reciprocal effects of illness on family functioning and family functioning on the course of illness.

This section closes with a case example from the first author's research. This couple was assessed with the Camberwell Family Interview (Leff & Vaughn, 1985), with a marital history interview developed for this research, and with several marital interaction tasks common to marital research (Gottman, 1994; Noller & Fitzpatrick, 1988). This case demonstrates the use of the SV model for clinical assessment. Assessment with the SV model can be applied either to the individual or to the couple and family unit. A strength of an individual can be seen as a health-enhancing factor for a family and a strength of a family can be seen as a health-enhancing factor for an individual. The lens can shift depending on the focus of the research or the focus of the treatment. For example, in my research I am interested in predicting which caregivers are most at risk for depression and, therefore, I use the SV model to conceptualize the individual strengths and vulnerabilities of the caregiver and the health-enhancing and risk factors of the spouse-patient and the marriage. As family therapists, we often focus on improving the functioning of the family or couple and will conceptualize individual factors as health-enhancing or risk factors for marital and family relationships. However, this lens easily moves back and forth because poor marital or family functioning can be conceptualized as a risk factor for depression in a family member and depression in a family member can be conceptualized as a risk factor for poor marital functioning.

CASE EXAMPLE

We Couldn't Be Happier: Seeing Cancer Through Rose-Colored Glasses

Mr. and Mrs. Stein, ages 58 and 65, respectively, have been married for 15 years. This is a second marriage for each and they state that they are deeply in love and happy. Mrs. Stein is receiving chemotherapy after undergoing a mastectomy for breast cancer. They each reported very unhappy and highly conflictual first marriages. They have a close and supportive relationship with Mrs. Stein's daughter, but a strained relationship with Mr. Stein's sons. Mr. Stein is retired, having sold his share of a profitable business. Both spouses report that their parents were not happily married.

We asked the Steins to describe how they met, fell in love, and decided to get married. They told humorous stories about how they met and how their courtship proceeded. They also described each other in glowing terms, but never mentioned any fears or anxieties they may have had. Mr. Stein was dating several women at the time and Mrs. Stein had only been divorced for a short while. Mrs. Stein talked about how he was a "playboy with a fancy sports car" and how she beat out all the other women for his affections. Mr. Stein said that gradually he decided to drop the other women and only date Mrs. Stein. During this story, their affect was always light and cheerful with no mention of the anxieties and doubts each undoubtedly had.

During Camberwell Family Interviews and during couple interviews, both spouses stated that they never fought. If one of them was upset, the other would leave that person alone until he or she calmed down. Mrs. Stein told how her husband would come home from a bad day at work, and if he appeared the slightest bit irritable, she would stay away from him until he had worked it out of his system. Each spouse said that there was nothing he or she would want to change about the other. They each denied having any disagreements with the other or any current issues or problems that were unresolved.

Five months prior to this interview, Mrs. Stein had noticed a small lump in her breast. She did not tell her husband about it, but she did go to her physician. She had a mammogram, after which the physician recommended that she have a needle biopsy. She reported that she came home and cried, but that she did not tell her husband. She stated that she did not want to worry him, "He had enough to worry about at his business." When she had the biopsy, there were complications and her whole breast area was bruised. She stated that she still did not want to tell her husband, but she would no longer be able to hide it from him. They said that when she told him and he saw the bruise, they cried together. She is now undergoing chemotherapy and feels convinced that she is cured. She reports no symptoms of depression, but wonders how it would be if she were feeling worse physically.

Assessment of the Couple

Strengths

Mr. and Mrs. Stein are positively attached to each other. They care a great deal about one another and each spends a great deal of time thinking about how to make the other happy. They share hobbies and activities, which gives them pleasurable time together. They are very affectionate with each other, and during research interaction tasks, they listened attentively to each other.

Vulnerabilities

Although they cried together after Mrs. Stein showed her husband her bruised breast and told him that she was going to have surgery, they do not normally discuss the problem when one of them is upset. They do not work out their upset feelings together, but give each other space to deal with the feelings alone. Mr. Stein never told his wife that he was angry with her for not telling him earlier about the cancer, although he did extract a promise from her not to hide things like that in the future.

Health-Enhancing Factors

Mr. Stein is a highly educated and successful businessman. Both he and his wife exercise regularly. They are secure financially. Both enjoy hobbies that are intellectually challenging (amateur astronomy and acting in local musical theater). The couple has a good relationship with Mrs. Stein's daughter and visit her regularly.

Risks

Mrs. Stein's cancer is a major stressor for this couple. Mr. Stein has heart arrhythmia, which is currently controlled through medication. The first marriages of both spouses were highly conflictual and unhappy. Although neither spouse has any history of depression, both avoid expressing vulnerable emotions, such as sadness, fear, hurt, or anger. Both continue to feel deep hurt from both their families of origin and their first marriages, and they now go out of their way to avoid painful conflict. Relations with Mr. Stein's sons are strained. He still pays alimony to his ex-wife, which means that he maintains a limited contact with her.

Overall Assessment

The Steins are a positively attached, happy but not intimate, conflict-minimizing couple. They care very deeply about each other and are happy with their marriage as it is. They both fear outbreaks of strong emotion, which they associate with bad experiences of negative emotion, both in their families of origin and in their first marriages. Mr. and Mrs. Stein employ conflict-avoidance or deescalation maneuvers whenever one of them is emotionally upset, which usually precludes the partners' talking in any depth about emotional issues between the two of them. If Mrs. Stein's cancer should recur, this marriage could be at risk. The couple would either have to learn to express vulnerable emotions or they will become distant and lose the feelings of closeness they have now. However, because the spouses have positive attachments to each other, if the cancer were to reoccur, family consultation or therapy would have a good chance of success in helping them learn to share their more vulnerable emotions and become comfortable with conflict.

RESEARCH UTILITY AND TREATMENT APPROACHES

In this research, we are attempting to identify those couples most at risk for depression in a spouse or most at risk for disruptive marital conflict. The SV model provides a conceptual map that has guided us in choosing constructs and variables to assess. Since a core proposition of the SV model is that the three constructs of the model interact, we have to be sure to develop and include variables assessing each of these constructs for every source of data in the study—the couple, each spouse, the children, and the health care system.

Separately we have written about treatment approaches based on this model (Shields, King, & Wynne, 1995). We have described five levels of intervention drawn from the interpersonal process model of Wynne (Wynne, 1984). Level 1 is consultation, level 2 is supportive therapy with active problem solving, level 3 is focused on structuring and teaching communication skills, level 4 centers on establishing adult–adult relationships between adult offspring and their parents, and level 5 works on developing positive attachment in relationships with histories of negative attachment. Therapy with the Steins would probably be at level 3, teaching them to communicate more openly and with greater emotional depth. Because they tend to avoid unsettling and vulnerable emotions, they may avoid facing important issues between them and thus short-circuit their problem solving. Therapy would build on their strengths as a couple, particularly their strong positive attachment to each other, while intervening at the point of vulnerability, their avoidance of strong emotions. In addition, the couple's relationship with Mrs. Stein's daughter could be drawn on as a health-enhancing factor, at the same time acknowledging the risk factors of their unhappy family-of-origin experiences and their unhappy first marriages.

CONCLUSION

We have presented a model for theory building for family systems research and therapy with later-life families. The model is an extension of family life-cycle models to later life and a reworking of concepts from the vulnerability-stressor research literature. This model is needed to guide theory development, research investigations, and therapy with later-life families. We have tried to incorporate elements of existing models that we have found to be helpful and have reworked other parts to cast the model into a family systems framework that emphasizes not just vulnerabilities and risks, but also the strengths of individuals and the health-enhancing qualities of families and larger systems. In particular, the model is rooted in the biopsychosocial tradition (Engel, 1977; Engel, 1980).

There are similarities between our model and other existing models. In particular, there are similarities between the SV model and the series of family-stress models derived from the original ABC-X model developed by Reuben Hill (1958) and expanded and revised by Boss (1988); Lavee, McCubbin, and Patterson (1985); and McCubbin and McCubbin (1987). The original model included four concepts: A—stressor, B—resources, C—perceptions, and X—outcome. Later versions of the model include additional concepts, such as change, adaptation, and coping. Major differences include that the SV model is based on the family life cycle, that it identifies more explicitly family systems concepts to be incorporated, and that it discusses the interplay between the individual life cycle and the family life cycle. In addition, there are similarities among Wynne's (1984) epigenetic model of relational development and direct interpersonal processes, which is a central element of the SV model; Olson, Sprenkle, and Russell's (1979) circumplex model; and Doherty and Colangelo's (1984) and Doherty, Colangelo, and Hovander's (1991) family FIRO model. Wynne's attachment/caregiving, communication, problem-solving, mutuality, and intimacy sequence of relational development is similar to Olson's concepts of cohesion, communication, and adaptability, and to Doherty and colleagues' (1991) concepts of inclusion, control, and intimacy.

We encourage the use of the SV model to develop researchable theories with later-life families. Elsewhere, we have written about the application of the SV model to family therapy with later-life families (Shields, King, & Wynne, 1995). Since the model was partially developed from the vulnerability-stress models that guide research into psychopathology in adolescents and young adults, it is probable that it is applicable as a basis for theory, therapy, and research with families in life-cycle stages other than later life.

REFERENCES

Albert, M. S. (1988). Cognitive function. In M. S. Albert & M. B. Moss (Eds.), *Geriatric neuropsychology* (pp. 33–56). New York: Guilford Press.

American Association for Marriage and Family Therapy. (1989). *Annual Conference Program.* San Francisco, CA: AAMFT.
American Association for Marriage and Family Therapy, (1990). *Annual Conference Program.* Washington, DC: AAMFT.
American Association for Marriage and Family Therapy. (1991). *Annual Conference Program.* Washington, DC: AAMFT.
Arenberg, D. (1993). Memory and learning do decline in late life. In N. Shock, R. C. Greulich, R. Andres, D. Arenberg, P. T. Costa, E. G. Lakatta, & J. D. Tobin (Eds.), *Normal human aging: The Baltimore longitudinal study of aging.* Washington, DC: U.S. Department of Health and Human Services.
Arling, G. (1987). Strain, social support, and distress in old age. *Journal of Gerontology, 42,* 107-113.
Baillie, V., Norbeck, J. S., & Barnes, L. E. (1988). Stress, social support, and psychological distress of family caregivers of the elderly. *Nursing Research, 37,* 217-222.
Baltes, P. B., Smith, J., & Staudinger, U. M. (1991). Wisdom and successful aging. *Nebraska Symposium on Motivation, 39,* 123-167.
Baron, R. S., Cutrona, C. E., Hicklin, D., Russell, D. W., & Lubaroff, D. M. (1990). Social support and immune function among spouses of cancer patients. *Journal of Personality and Social Psychology, 59,* 344-352.
Blenkner, M. (1965). Social work and family relationship in later life with some thoughts on filial maturity. In E. Shanas & G. J. Streib (Eds.), *Social structure and the family: Generational relations* (pp. 46-59). Englewood Cliffs, NJ: Prentice-Hall.
Boss, P. (1988). *Family stress management.* Newbury Park, CA: Sage.
Boss, P., Caron, W., & Horbal, J. (1988). Alzheimer's disease and ambiguous loss. In C. Chilman, F. Cox, & E. Nunnally (Eds.), *Families in trouble* (pp. 123-140). Beverly Hills, CA: Sage.
Bossé, R., Aldwin, C. M., Levenson, M. R., Workman-Daniels, K., & Ekerdt, D. J. (1990). Differences in social support among retirees and workers: Findings from the Normative Aging Study. *Psychology and Aging, 5,* 41-47.
Bray, J. H., Williamson, D. S., & Malone, P. E. (1986). An evaluation of an intergenerational consultation process to increase personal authority in the family system. *Family Process, 25,* 423-436.
Burr, W. R. (1991). Rethinking levels of abstraction in family systems theories. *Family Process, 4,* 435-452.
Burr, W. R., Hill, R., Nye, F. I., & Reiss, I. L. (1979). Metatheory and diagramming conventions. In W. R. Burr, R. Hill, F. I. Nye, & I. L. Reiss (Eds.), *Contemporary theories about the family* (pp. 17-24). New York: Free Press.
Butler, R. N., Lewis, M., & Sunderland, T. (1991). *Aging and mental health: Positive psychosocial and biomedical approaches.* New York: Macmillan.
Carter, B., & McGoldrick, M. (1988). *The changing family life cycle: A framework for family therapy.* New York: Gardner Press.
Cartwright, A. (1990). Medicine taking by people aged 65 or more. (review). *British Medical Bulletin, 46,* 63-76.

Cattell, H. (1988). Elderly suicide in London: An analysis of coroners' inquests. *International Journal of Geriatric Psychiatry, 3,* 251-261.

Cerella, J. (1990). Aging and information-processing rate. In J. E. Birren & K. W. Schaie (Eds.), *Handbook of the psychology of aging* (pp. 201-221). New York: Academic Press.

Christozov, C., Predov, N., & Petrov, I. (1987). Suicidity and euthanasia in old age: Victimological and rehabilitation aspects. *European Journal of Psychiatry, 1,* 41-44.

Cicchetti, D. (1990). A historical perspective on the discipline of developmental psychopathology. In J. Rolf, A. Masten, D. Cicchetti, K. Nuechterlein, & S. Weintraub (Eds.), *Risk and protective factors in the development of psychopathology* (pp. 2-28). Cambridge, England: Cambridge University Press.

Col, N., Fanale, J. E., & Kronholm, P. (1990). The role of medication noncompliance and adverse drug reactions in hospitalizations of the elderly. *Archives of Internal Medicine, 150,* 841-845.

Conwell, Y., Rotenberg, M., & Caine, E. D. (1990). Completed suicide at age 50 and over. *Journal of the American Geriatrics Society, 38,* 640-644.

Costa, P. T., Jr., & McCrae, R. R. (1984a). Concurrent validation after 20 years: The implications of personality stability for its assessment: In N. Shock, R. C. Greulich, R. Andres, D. Arenberg, P. T. Costa, Jr., E. G. Lakatta, & J. D. Tobin (Eds.), *Normal human aging. The Baltimore longitudinal study of aging* (pp. 105-128). Washington, DC: U.S. Department of Health and Human Services.

Costa, P. T., Jr., & McCrae, R. R. (1984b). Personality as a lifelong determinant of well-being. In N. W. Shock, R. C. Greulich, R. Andres, D. Arenberg, P. T. Costa, Jr., E. G. Lakatta, & J. D. Tobin (Eds.), *Normal human aging: The Baltimore longitudinal study of aging* (pp. 129-164). Washington, DC: U.S. Department of Health and Human Services.

Costa, P. T., Jr., McCrae, R. R., & Norris, A. H. (1984). Personal adjustments to aging: Longitudinal prediction from neuroticism and extraversion. In N. W. Shock, R. C. Greulich, R. Andres, D. Arenberg, P. T. Costa, Jr., E. G. Lakatta, & J. D. Tobin (Eds.), *Normal human aging: The Baltimore longitudinal study of aging* (pp. 215-222). Washington, DC: U.S. Department of Health and Human Services.

Croog, S. H., Levine, S., Testa, M. A., Brown, B., Bulpitt, C. J., Jenkins, C. D., Klerman, G. L., & Williams, G. H. (1986). The effects of antihypertensive therapy on the quality of life. *New England Journal of Medicine, 314,* 1657-1664.

Cummings, S. R., Phillips, S. L., Wheat, M. E., Black, D., Goosby, E., Wlodarczyk, D., Trafton, P., Jergesen, H., Winograd, C. H., & Hulley, S. B. (1988). Recovery of function after hip fracture: The role of social supports. *Journal of the American Geriatrics Society, 36,* 801-806.

Decker, S. D., & Schulz, R. (1985). Correlates of life satisfaction and depression in middle-aged and elderly spinal cord-injured persons, Special Issue: Spinal cord injury. *American Journal of Occupational Therapy, 39,* 740-745.

Depner, C. E., & Ingersoll-Dayton, B. (1988). Supportive relationships in later life. *Psychology and Aging, 3,* 348–357.

Doane, J. A., Hill, L. W., & Diamond, D. (1991). A developmental view of therapeutic bonding in the family: Treatment of the disconnected family. *Family Process, 30,* 155–175.

Doherty, W. J., & Colangelo, N. (1984). The family FIRO model: A modest proposal for organizing family treatment. *Journal of Marital and Family Therapy, 10,* 19–29.

Doherty, W. J., Colangelo, N., & Hovander, D. (1991). Priority setting in family change and clinical practice: The family FIRO model. *Family Process, 30,* 227–240.

Doherty, W. J., Schrott, H. G., Metcalf, L., & Iasiello-Vailas, L. (1983). Effect of spouse support and health beliefs on medication adherence. *Journal of Family Practice, 17,* 837–841.

Dura, J. R., Stukenberg, K. W., & Kiecolt-Glaser, J. K. (1990). Chronic stress and depressive disorders in older adults. *Journal of Abnormal Psychology, 99,* 284–290.

Eisen, S. A., Miller, D. K., Woodward, R. S., Spitznagel, E., & Przybeck, T. R. (1990). The effect of prescribed daily dose frequency on patient medication compliance. *Archives of Internal Medicine, 150,* 1881–1884.

Eisen, S. A., Woodward, R. S., Miller, D., Spitznagel, E., & Windham, C. A. (1987). The effect of medication compliance on the control of hypertension. *Journal of General Internal Medicine, 2,* 298–305.

Emmerson, J. P., Burvill, P. W., Finlay-Jones, R., & Hall, W. (1989). Life events, life difficulties and confiding relationships in the depressed elderly. *British Journal of Psychiatry, 155,* 787–792.

Engel, G. (1977). The need for a new medical model: A challenge for biomedicine. *Science, 196,* 129–136.

Engel, G. (1980). The clinical application of the biopsychosocial model. *American Journal of Psychiatry, 7,* 535–544.

Erikson, E. H. (1950). *Childhood and society.* New York: Norton.

Erikson, E. H. (1968). *Identity, youth and crisis.* New York: Norton.

Erikson, E. H., Erikson, J. M., & Kivnick, H. Q. (1986). *Vital involvement in old age: The experience of old age in our time.* New York: Norton.

Falicov, C. J. (1988). *Family transitions: Continuity and change across the life cycle.* New York: Guilford Press.

Farmer, M. E., Locke, B. Z., Moscicki, E. K., Dannenberg, A. L., Larson, D. B., & Radloff, L. S. (1988). Physical activity and depressive symptoms: The NHANES I epidemiologic follow-up study. *American Journal of Epidemiology, 128,* 1340–1351.

Field, D., & Minkler, M. (1988). Continuity and change in social support between young-old and old-old or very-old age. *Journal of Gerontology, 43,* P100–P106.

Flori, D. (1989). The prevalence of later-life family concerns in the marriage and family therapy journal literature (1976–1985): A content analysis. *Journal of Marital and Family Therapy, 15(3),* 289–297.

Framo, J. L. (1992). *Family of origin therapy: An intergenerational approach.* New York: Brunner/Mazel.
Franks, P., Campbell, T., & Shields, C. G. (1992). Social relationships and health: The relative roles of family functioning and social support. *Social Science and Medicine, 34,* 779-788.
Franks, P., Campbell, T., Shields, C. G., Harp, J., McDaniel, S., & Botelho, R. (1992). The relationship of family factors to depression: Testing an alternate to social support. *Journal of Family Psychology, 6,* 49-59.
Gallagher, D., Rose, J., Rivera, P., Lovett, S., & Thompson, L. W. (1989). Prevalence of depression in family caregivers. *Gerontologist, 29,* 449-456.
Gallagher, D., Wrabetz, A., Lovett, S., Del Maestro, S., & Rose, J. (1989). Depression and other negative affects in family caregivers. In E. Light & B. Lebowitz (Eds.), *Alzheimer's disease treatment and family stress: Directions for research* (pp. 218-244). Rockville, MD: NIMH.
Gatz, M., Pedersen, N. L., Plomin, R., Nesselroade, J. R., & McClearn, G. E. (1992). Importance of shared genes and shared environments for symptoms of depression in older adults. *Journal of Abnormal Psychology, 101,* 701-708.
Gelfand, E. G. (1982). *Aging: The ethnic factor.* Boston: Little, Brown.
Goldstein, M. (1990). Family relations as risk factors for the onset and course of schizophrenia. In J. Rolf, A. Masten, D. Cicchetti, K. Nuechterlein, & S. Weintraub (Eds.), *Risk and protective factors in the development of psychopathology* (pp. 408-423). Cambridge, England: Cambridge University Press.
Goodman, C. C., & Pynoos, J. (1990). A model telephone information and support program for caregivers of Alzheimer's patients. *Gerontologist, 30,* 399-404.
Gottesman, I. I., & Shields, J. (1972). *Schizophrenia and genetics: A twin study vantage point.* New York: Academic Press.
Gottman, J. (1979). *Marital interactions: Experimental investigations.* New York: Academic Press.
Gottman, J. M. (1994). *What predicts divorce: The relationship between marital processes and marital outcomes.* Hillsdale, NJ: Erlbaum.
Hanson, B. S., Isacsson, S. O., Janzon, L., & Lindell, S. E. (1989). Social network and social support influence mortality in elderly men: The prospective population study of "men born in 1914," Malmö, Sweden. *American Journal of Epidemiology, 130,* 100-111.
Heston, L. L. (1991). Genetics of geriatric psychopathology. In J. Sadavoy, L. W. Lazarus, & L. F. Jarvik (Eds.), *Comprehensive review of geriatric psychiatry.* Washington DC: American Psychiatric Press.
HHS. (1991). *Aging America: Trends and projections.* Washington, DC: U.S. Department of Health and Human Services.
Hill, R. (1958). Generic features of families under stress. *Social Casework, 49,* 139-150.
Hopkinson, N., & Doherty, M. (1990). NSAID-associated gastropathy—A role for misoprostol? (review). *British Journal of Rheumatology, 29,* 133-136.
House, J. S., Landis, K. R., & Umberson, D. (1988). Social relationships and health. *Science, 241,* 540-545.

House, J. S., Robbins, C., & Metzner, H. L. (1982). The association of social relationships and activities with mortality: Prospective evidence from the Tecumseh Community Health Study. *American Journal of Epidemiology, 116,* 123-140.

Hughston, G. A., Christopherson, V. A., & Bonjean, M. J. (1989). *Aging and family therapy: Practitioner perspectives on Golden Pond.* New York: Haworth Press.

Jacob, T. (1987). Family interaction and psychopathology: Historical review. In T. Jacob (Ed.), *Family interaction and psychopathology* (pp. 3-22). New York: Plenum Press.

Kendler, K. S., Kessler, R. C., Heath, A. C., Neale, M. C., & Eaves, L. J. (1991). Coping: A genetic epidemiological investigation. *Psychological Medicine, 21,* 337-346.

Kennedy, G. J., Kelman, H. R., & Thomas, C. (1990). The emergence of depressive symptoms in late life: The importance of declining health and increasing disability. *Journal of Community Health, 15,* 93-104.

King, D. A., Bonacci, D. D., & Wynne, L. C. (1990). Families of cognitively impaired elders: Helping adult children confront the filial crisis. *Clinical Gerontologist, 10,* 3-15.

Kirsling, R. A. (1986). Review of suicide among elderly persons. *Psychological Reports, 59,* 359-366.

Krause, N. (1987). Chronic financial strain, social support, and depressive symptoms among older adults. *Psychology and Aging, 2,* 185-192.

Lavee, Y., McCubbin, H., & Patterson, J. (1985). The double ABCX model of stress and adaptation: An empirical test by analysis of structural equations with latent variables. *Journal of Marriage and the Family, 47,* 111-125.

Leff, J., & Vaughn, C. (1985). *Expressed emotion in families: Its significance for mental illness.* New York: Guilford Press.

Lieberman, M. A., & Peskin, H. (1992). Adult life crises. In J. E. Birren, R. B. Sloane, & G. D. Cohen (Eds.), *Handbook of mental health and aging.* San Diego: Academic Press.

McCrae, R. R., & Costa, P. T., Jr. (1984). Aging, the life course, and models of personality. In N. W. Shock, R. C. Greulich, R. Andres, D. Arenberg, P. T. Costa, Jr., E. G. Lakatta, & J. D. Tobin (Eds.), *Normal human aging: The Baltimore longitudinal study of aging* (pp. 292-303). Washington, DC: U.S. Department of Health and Human Services.

McCubbin, H., & McCubbin, M. (1987). Family stress theory and assessment: The T-double ABCX model of family adjustment and adaptation. In H. McCubbin & A. Thompson (Eds.), *Family assessment for research and practice.* Madison: University of Wisconsin.

McDaniel, S. H., Hepworth, J., & Doherty, W. J. (1992). *Medical family therapy: A biopsychosocial approach to families with health problems.* New York: Basic Books.

McGoldrick, M., Pearce, J. K., & Giordano, J. (1982). *Ethnicity and family therapy.* New York: Guilford Press.

Niederehe, G., & Fruge, E. (1984). Dementia and family dynamics: Clinical research issues. *Journal of Geriatric Psychiatry, 27,* 21-56:

Niederehe, G., & Funk, J. (1987). *Family interaction with dementia patients: Caregiver styles and their correlates.* Houston, TX: University of Texas Mental Sciences Institute.

Noller, P., & Fitzpatrick, M. A. (1988). *Perspectives on marital interaction.* Clevedon, England: Multilingual Matters.

Norris, V. K., Stephens, M. A., & Kinney, J. M. (1990). The impact of family interactions on recovery from stroke: Help or hindrance? *Gerontologist, 30,* 535-542.

Olson, D. H., Sprenkle, D. H., & Russell, C. S. (1979). Circumplex model of marital and family systems, 1: Cohesion and adaptability dimensions, family types, and clinical applications. *Family Process, 18,* 3-28.

Pagel, M. D., Erdly, W. W., & Becker, J. (1987). Social networks: We get by with (and in spite of) a little help from our friends. *Journal of Personality and Social Psychology, 53,* 793-804.

Palinkas, L. A., Wingard, D. L., & Barrett-Connor, E. (1990). The biocultural context of social networks and depression among the elderly. *Social Science and Medicine, 30,* 441-447.

Pearlin, L. I., Mullan, J. T., Semple, S. J., & Skaff, M. M. (1990). Caregiving and the stress process. An overview of concepts and their measures. *Gerontologist, 30,* 583-594.

Pearlin, L., & Schooler, C. (1978). The structure of coping. *Journal of Health and Social Behavior, 19,* 2-21.

Pedersen, N. L., Gatz, M., Plomin, R., Nesselroade, J. R., & McClearn, G. E. (1989). Individual differences in locus of control during the second half of the life span for identical and fraternal twins reared apart and reared together. *Journal of Gerontology, 44,* P100-P105.

Pillemer, K., & Finkeher, D. (1989). Causes of elder abuse: Caregiver stress versus problem relationships. *American Journal of Orthopsychiatry, 59,* 179-187.

Plomin, R., & McClearn, G. E. (1990). Human behavioral genetics of aging. In J. E. Birren & K. W. Schaie (Eds.), *Handbook of the psychology of aging* (pp. 67-79). New York: Academic Press.

Raffoul, P. R. (1986). Drug misuse among older people: Focus for interdisciplinary efforts. *Health and Social Work, 11,* 197-203.

Reiss, D., Gonzalez, S., & Kramer, N. (1986). Family process, chronic illness, and death: On the weakness of strong bonds. *Archives of General Psychiatry, 43,* 795-804.

Reiss, D., Plomin, R., & Hetherington, E. M. (1991). Genetics and psychiatry: An unheralded window on the environment (see comments). *American Journal of Psychiatry, 148,* 283-291.

Revicki, D. A., & Mitchell, J. P. (1990). Strain, social support, and mental health in rural elderly individuals. *Journal of Gerontology, 45,* S267-S274.

Richters, J., & Weintraub, S. (1990). Beyond diathesis: Toward an understanding of high-risk environments. In J. Rolf, A. Masten, D. Cicchetti, K. Nuechterlein, & S. Weintraub (Eds.), *Risk and protective factors in the development of psychopathology* (pp. 67-96): Cambridge, England: Cambridge University Press.

Rolf, J., Masten, A. S., Cicchetti, D., Nuechterlein, K. H., & Weintraub, S. (1990). *Risk and protective factors in the development of psychopathology.* Cambridge, England: Cambridge University Press.

Rolland, J. S. (1987). Chronic illness and the life cycle: A conceptual framework. *Family Process, 26,* 203-221.

Rook, K. S. (1984). The negative side of social interaction: Impact on psychological well-being. *Journal of Personality and Social Psychology, 46,* 1097-1108.

Rook, K. S. (1990). Stressful aspects of older adults' social relationships: Current theory and research. In M. A. Stephens, J. H. Crowther, S. E. Hobfoll, & D. L. Tennenbaum (Eds.), *Stress and coping in later-life families* (pp. 173-192). New York: Hemisphere.

Rutter, M. (1990). Psychosocial resilience and protective mechanisms. In J. Rolf, A. Masten, D. Cicchetti, K. Nuechterlein, & S. Weintraub (Eds.), *Risk and protective factors in the development of psychopathology* (pp. 181-214). Cambridge England: Cambridge University Press.

Salthouse, T. A. (1990). Cognitive competence and expertise in aging. In J. E. Birren & K. W. Schaie (Eds.), *Handbook of the psychology of aging* (pp. 311-319). New York: Academic Press.

Sameroff, A. J., & Seifer, R. (1990). Early contributions to developmental risk. In J. Rolf, A. S. Masten, D. Cicchetti, K. H. Nuechterlein, & S. Weintraub (Eds.), *Risk and protective factors in the development of psychopathology.* Cambridge, England: Cambridge University Press.

Scharlach, A. E. (1989). A comparison of employed caregivers of cognitively impaired and physically impaired elderly persons. *Research on Aging, 11,* 225-243.

Schooler, C. (1990). Psychosocial factors and effective cognitive functioning in adulthood. In J. E. Birren & K. W. Schaie (Eds.), *Handbook of the psychology of aging* (pp. 347-358). New York: Academic Press.

Schulz, R., & Fritz, S. (1987). Origins of stereotypes of the elderly: An experimental study of the self-other discrepancy. *Experimental Aging Research, 13,* 189-195.

Seeman, T. E., Kaplan, G. A., Knudsen, L., Cohen, R., & Guralnik, J. (1987). Social network ties and mortality among the elderly in the Alameda County study. *American Journal of Epidemiology, 126,* 714-723.

Shields, C. G. (1986). Critiquing the new epistemologies: Toward minimum requirements for a scientific theory of family therapy. *Journal of Marital and Family Therapy, 12,* 359-372.

Shields, C. G. (1992). Family interaction and caregivers of Alzheimer's disease patients: Correlates of depression. *Family Process, 31,* 19-33.

Shields, C. G., King, D. A., & Wynne, L. C. (1995). Interventions with later-life families. In R. H. Mikesell, D. Lusterman, & S. H. McDaniel (Eds.), *Interacting family therapy handbook of family psychology and systems theory* (pp. 141-158). Washington, DC: American Psychological Association.

Simonton, D. K. (1990). Creativity and wisdom in aging. In J. E. Birren & K. W. Schaie (Eds.), *Handbook of the psychology of aging* (pp. 320-329). New York: Academic Press.

Steinglass, P., Bennett, L., Wolin, S., & Reiss, D. (1987). *The alcoholic family.* New York: Basic Books.

Stoller, E. P., & Pugliesi, K. L. (1989). Other roles of caregivers: Competing responsibilities or supportive resources. *Journal of Gerontology, 44,* S231–S238.

Tollefson, G., & Hughes, E. (1982). Evaluation of depression (letter). *Journal of Family Practice, 16,* 23.

Vitaliano, P. P., Katon, W., Maiuro, R. D., & Russo, J. (1989). Coping in chest pain patients with and without psychiatric disorders. *Journal of Consulting and Clinical Psychology, 57,* 338–343.

Walker, A. (1987). Enlarging the caring capacity of the community: Informal support networks and the welfare state. *International Journal of Health Services, 17,* 369–386.

Walsh, F. (1982). *Normal family processes.* New York: Guilford Press.

Walsh, F. (1989). The family in later life. In B. Carter & M. McGoldrick (Eds.), *The changing family life cycle* (pp. 312–327). New York: Gardner Press.

Walsh, F., & McGoldrick, M. (1991). *Living beyond loss: Death in the family.* New York: Norton.

Ware, J. E., Jr. (1987). Standards for validating health measures: Definition and content. *Journal of Chronic Diseases, 40,* 473–480.

Ware, J. E., Jr., & Sherbourne, C. D. (1992). The MOS 36-item short-form health survey (SF-36), I: Conceptual framework and item selection. *Medical Care, 30,* 473–483.

Weddell, R. A. (1987). Social, functional, and neuropsychological determinants of the psychiatric symptoms of stroke patients receiving rehabilitation and living at home. *Scandinavian Journal of Rehabilitation Medicine, 19,* 93–98.

Weintraub, M. (1990). Compliance in the elderly. *Clinics in Geriatric Medicine, 6,* 445–452.

Williams, A. K., & Schulz, R. (1988). Association of pain and physical dependency with depression in physically ill middle-aged and elderly persons (see comments). *Physical Therapy, 68,* 1226–1230.

Williamson, D. (1981). Personal authority via termination of the intergenerational hierarchical boundary: A "new" stage in the family life cycle. *Journal of Marital and Family Therapy, 7,* 441–452.

Williamson, D. (1982a). Personal authority in family experience via termination of intergenerational hierarchical boundary: Part III—personal authority defined and the power of play in the change of process. *Journal of Marital and Family Therapy, 8,* 309–323.

Williamson, D. (1982b). Personal authority via termination of the intergenerational heirarchical boundary: Part II—the consultation process and the therapeutic method. *Journal of Marital and Family Therapy, 8,* 23–37.

Williamson, D. (1991). *The intimacy paradox.* New York: Guilford Press.

Williamson, G. M., & Schulz, R. (1990). Relationship orientation, quality of prior relationship, and distress among caregivers of Alzheimer's patients. *Psychology and Aging, 5,* 502–509.

Wynne, L. C. (1984). The epigenesis of relational systems: A model for understanding family development. *Family Process, 23,* 297–318.

Wynne, L. C., Shields, C. G., & Sirkin, M. (in press). Illness, family theory and family therapy, I: Historical and conceptual issues. *Family Process, 31,* 3-18.

Wynne, L. C., Sirkin, M., & Shields, C. G. (in press). Illness, family theory and family therapy, II: Clinical issues. *Family Process.*

Zarit, S. (1990). The emerging role of theory in caregiving research. Paper given at Gerontological Society of America Conference, Boston.

Zarit, S., & Zarit, J. (1982). Families under stress: Interventions for caregivers of senile dementia patients. *Psychotherapy Theory, Research and Practice, 19,* 461-471.

Zubin, J., & Spring, B. (1977). Vulnerability—a new view of schizophrenia. *Journal of Abnormal Psychology, 86,* 103-126.

III

SPECIAL ISSUES

☜ 7 ☞

Changing Roles and Life-Cycle Transitions

Mary A. Erlanger, Ph.D.
Athens Associates for Counseling and Psychotherapy
Athens, Georgia

Adaptation to the needs of the oldest generation is often complicated by the family's need to accommodate to the life-cycle changes taking place in other generations at the same time. As some members are moving into old age, others are contending with the empty nest and younger members face career and relationship tasks of young adulthood. The very youngest are just becoming part of the system. Indeed, a multigenerational family system is always in transition, and the transitional tasks of individual family members become dynamic forces affecting family equilibrium. The events at each level have an effect at every other level.

With the aging of parents, family issues of entitlement, loss, reciprocity, and fairness affecting all generations provide an agenda that must be dealt with for the family to function in a way that takes care of the needs of all its members. This may be seen by the family as a dynamic challenge—or as a temporary disturbance requiring "Band-Aid" solutions. At worst, the pressures may create family splits that outlast the transition itself. When the family is the client and the problems are viewed as the normal result of transition, the goal for therapy becomes finding ways to help the family support individual growth and development of members of all generations. However, this can be difficult in the face of multiple competing demands on assets, energy, time, labor, and emotional resources.

FACTORS AFFECTING FAMILY RESPONSE

A number of factors affect the family's response to transitional challenges since its ability to accommodate change evolves from earlier family patterns developed for stability and integration (Walsh, 1988). If previous transitions have been stormy, such as the "empty nest" having been complicated by an unsatisfactory marital relationship or overattachment to a child, the family may need considerable help in developing adult–adult relationships that facilitate adjustments necessary for changes in later life.

The family's own myths and beliefs about aging, transmitted down through the generations, also play a part in how it adapts to transition and loss. Societal myths, stereotypes, and ageism play a role as well. Sprenkle and Piercy (1992) point out the devaluation of our aging population as one of the major dimensions of contemporary family life that work against their definition of a healthy family. The pervasive expectation of inevitable decline in the elderly may contribute to fears on the part of the elder generation and the adult children, and can promote responses of overreaction or extreme denial and avoidance. Here, again, the life-cycle view that fosters the ability to see change as normal, capable of producing growth, rather than as a destructive life force presaging decline, can help families set about the task of making life the best it can be for all generations.

Recent studies that have looked at the meaning of aging for the elderly themselves have emphasized the importance of a sense of identity that maintains continuity despite the physical and social changes that come with old age (Kaufman, 1986). The older person draws meaning from the past, interpreting and recreating it as a resource for being in the present. The family is a major source of this continuity—the repository of values, ideals, and expectations—and as such plays a central role in the adaptation of its older members.

It must not be forgotten that members of the older generation have already experienced multiple transitions, sometimes having been "sandwiched" themselves. Their own expectations and fears are based on earlier crises, and they may tend to anticipate the repetition of a previous cycle or even collaborate in its occurrence. Looking at earlier patterns through family history and the genogram can help uncover latent strengths and resources, as well as prevent recurrences of earlier, destructive patterns.

CHANGES IN HELPING ROLES

One of the major aspects of the later-life transition is the change in the helping relationship shown by numerous studies to exist between parents and children throughout life (Cicirelli, 1983). Even in old age, parents continue to help their children in many ways, but the balance often begins to shift and roles change when illness or physical decline sets in. As parents give up their central role in caregiving and guiding the family, they turn to their children for more care (Brubaker, 1983). Having to cope with the physical and emotional needs of dependent parents has become a pervasive phenomenon, defined by Brody (1985) as a normative stress for the middle, or "sandwich," generation, which must respond simultaneously to the needs of both aging parents and their own children.

Although physical and mental decline do create dependence, Brody (1990) considers the idea of a role reversal between aging parents and adult children to be an inaccurate and destructive concept. Because of the long emotional history of the relationship, it is not possible to transform these feelings: "People cannot become children to their children and children cannot become parents to their parents" (p. 17).

Adaptation to new roles does involve many complex feelings, often including considerable grief, as older parents and their adult children deal with a sense of loss for their roles as they were previously experienced. Family therapy can help family members to express this grief appropriately, and also to accept that family identity, like individual identity, is not static. It is constantly evolving from experiences of the past, with values, beliefs, and symbols being formulated and reformulated to create a viable present.

Although some events, such as a stroke or sudden death, have immediate and dramatic effects, most changes in the older generation that affect family functioning occur gradually, over a period of time. Retirement is often the first marker that tests the later-life family's ability to adapt to life-cycle change.

RETIREMENT

Because of the centrality of the work role in virtually every stratum of our society, retirement has become the major normative life event in the later years of life. It presents both unique challenges and opportunities; it represents monumental loss—loss of identity, status, structure, and often of a sense of meaning and purpose in life. On the other hand, it offers new freedom from responsibility and time constraints, and creates opportunities to develop new leisure and work roles, as well as new relationships.

As a naturally occurring life event, retirement may be seen by the individual from either perspective—it may be dreaded or eagerly anticipated. It clearly requires changes of role, social network, economic base, management of time, and self-image. Atchley (1982) states that adjustment depends on having a secure income, good health, meaningful activities, and high marital satisfaction. Support of family can play a key role during this transition.

Retirement is inevitably a significant milestone for a married couple, and the roles of husband and wife may become even more important when work roles are lost (Vinick & Ekerdt, 1989). Most couples experience increased marital satisfaction after adjusting to the launching of children and throughout their later years together (Atchley, 1982). Olson (1988) found that good marital communication and compatibility of the partners were the most important resources characteristic of low-stress families at this stage. However, for couples without those resources, relationship problems may be inevitable. The sudden availability of large amounts of free time can be a personal challenge to the retired person, and for a couple may mean long hours together without the structure of work to manage time and emotional distance. It may provide fertile ground for the reemergence of old issues and conflicts, or dramatically point up the lack of shared interests and values.

Walsh (1988) states that the major task facing traditional couples once the husband retires is the incorporation of the husband into the home, with the resulting "impingement" on the wife's territory. Retirement does bring changes in role expectations (Dobson, 1983), and there is some increased participation by husbands in household tasks (Vinick & Ekerdt, 1989).

The effect of retirement on adult children may be powerful as well, if less obvious. Retirement opens the way for increased help to children, such as with chores, transportation, or child care. The freedom to travel may make possible more frequent contact with children and grandchildren. On the other hand, resentment may result if retired parents turn to their adult children to fill empty hours at a time when the children are attempting to meet their own life-cycle needs, such as launching a new career or consolidating a marriage.

Retirement sometimes involves a geographical move, which may result in family stress. Often a subject of disagreement between married partners (Vinick & Ekerdt, 1989), it may also pose a problem for the adult children, who may feel abandoned at the loss of the family home or the accustomed proximity of the parents.

A decline in health can seriously affect retirement life; one spouse may take on the care of the other and the plans and expectations of both partners are disrupted. Similar disruption can occur among couples responsible for the care of elderly parents. This situation can provide a new "job" for a retiree whether it is desired or not; some studies have confirmed that women often time their retirement according to family needs, such as having to care for a husband or parent (McClusky, 1989). The result may be reward or resentment: The caregiver may feel glad to be able to devote more time and concern to the parent's needs, or may be resentful that the time for travel and paying attention to long-postponed desires is slipping away. For many, it may be a mixture of both.

GRANDPARENTHOOD

The transition to grandparenthood can take place at an early or late time in the family's life cycle, but by age 65 it is a pervasive state: at least three quarters of all people over this age are grandparents, and some 40 percent are great-grandparents (Troll, 1983). The four-generation family is now commonplace, and five- and six-generation families are not unheard of.

In writing about "the modernization of grandparenthood," Cherlin and Furstenberg (1986) point out numerous changes in this role that have occurred in recent years; a primary factor is that life expectancy has greatly increased the number of years most people experience this role. Additionally, technological advances have made it easier for grandparents and grandchildren to see and talk to each other, and, at the same time, they may have contributed to the decline of grandparents as mentors, role models, and caretakers.

Troll (1983) describes grandparents as a latent source of support—the "family watchdogs," ever on the lookout for trouble and ready to provide assistance if a family crisis occurs. Research suggests that the grandparent role facilitates an older person's developmental process; through grandchildren, older people can feel a sense of biological renewal (Neugarten & Weinstein, 1964) and experience themselves as a central link between the past and the future.

Grandparenthood is clearly a systemic, life-cycle transition that alters relationships and offers a variety of role possibilities and opportunities for meaningful interaction (Walsh, 1988). However, except for stereotypes, there are few educational or informational supports for the transition to this new role (Cherlin & Furstenberg, 1986). Responses cover a wide spectrum, from the rocking chair nurturer to the family tyrant. Clinical accounts are filled with stories of grandparenting, and run the gamut from "Grandma was the only one who was there for me," to "I was always terrified of her!"

Predictably, geographical distance has been found to be the most powerful factor in the relationship between grandparents and grandchildren (Cherlin & Furstenberg, 1986): "Grandparents are at the mercy of their children's mobility" (p. 110). Additionally, grandparenthood builds on the relationship with the adult children; in enmeshed families, grandparents may create or be drawn into marital conflicts, especially around parenting issues, and the grandchildren may become triangulated. In other families, the children may provide a scapegoat or a buffer between conflicting generations. At worst, adult children and their parents may use the grandchildren in a struggle for power in the family system.

Several studies have documented the increased importance of the grandparent role in cases of divorce (Cherlin & Furstenberg, 1986). Grandparents are often asked for material assistance, a place to live, help in child rearing, guidance, and advice. This can lead to rewarding relationships, but also can cause resentment over having to forfeit other activities as well as *forgoing* the popular grandparents' role of having "all the fun and none of the responsibility."

Divorce can also penalize the noncustodial grandparents by curtailing access to the grandchildren, and hostile divorces may make grandparenting difficult or even impossible. A marital situation that results in grandparents being cut off from their grandchildren can be extremely painful and result in dysfunction of family relationships at all levels. Helping a family accept and grieve for the loss of these relationships can be an important goal of family therapy.

The initiative for redefining family roles and relationships may come from the grandchild's generation, as the following case illustrates.

> Kay C. was only eight years old when her grandfather committed suicide. Her mother, Ann, was devastated, and blamed *her* mother, Kathryn B., for the marital problems that she felt contributed to his violent death. In the aftermath of the death, Kathryn lavished attention and affection on her only granddaughter, Kay, while Ann became increasingly withdrawn and unresponsive as a parent. Furthermore, the interaction between Ann and Kathryn remained highly conflictual, and Kay began to function as mediator and communicator. When she came for therapy at the age of 30, she was still acting as the peacemaker and interpreter, and was angry and frustrated by her central role in the family turmoil. After individual therapy sessions, based on family-of-origin work, in which Kay learned to set boundaries for herself, she participated in sessions with her mother and grandmother where new patterns of direct communication were developed and practiced. Considerable heal-

ing took place between Ann and *her* mother, who was now dealing with a terminal illness, and Kay was freed to work on a more meaningful relationship with both her mother and grandmother.

LOSS AS A LIFE-CYCLE ISSUE

Loss occurs during all phases of the family life cycle, but it assumes a central role in the influences on later-life families. The developmental task of grieving for losses and moving on dominates much of the therapy in this stage of life. Despite vast clinical research on the issue of loss, Walsh and McGoldrick (1991) point out that the focus has been primarily on the individual and that the mental health field has failed to appreciate the impact of loss on the family as an interactional system.

Bowen's (1978) pioneering ideas included the concept of the "emotional shock wave" that occurs in a family around an important death, such as that of a grandparent. He theorized that the symptoms in a "shock wave" can be any human problem in any generation, including the whole spectrum of physical illness, emotional breakdown, and social dysfunction, such as drinking problems or school failure. Any member of the family system may be affected, often in an unpredictable and hidden manner.

An example is Hyland's (1981) case history of a 15-year-old child brought for treatment because she refused to attend school and was failing in all her high school subjects. Her family history and treatment revealed a connection between her symptoms and the death of three of her four grandparents within the past three years, and the surfacing of unresolved grief feelings with the recent death of a family pet.

> Judy's symptoms became more understandable as the family history was taken and explored. Judy's parents had been unprepared to become the oldest surviving members in their family. Painful unresolved feelings around the loss of Judy's grandparents, particularly for (the) parents, could be avoided by Judy's developing symptoms. Dealing with these unresolved grief reactions allowed Judy's parents to again allow Judy to attend school. She was no longer needed to help her parents with their grief work. (p. 11)

In cases where the parent hierarchy has been confused due to long-term disability or dementia, the loss of the elder may serve to reclarify roles and greatly improve the family's functioning. Beels (1977) reports a case of confused hierarchy/double bind, in which the patient "miraculously" recovered from a deep depression, stopped having disabling seizures, successfully took over the family business, and achieved a vastly improved relationship with his wife, all within a very short time after his father died.

Problems of Dependency

Although few reactions to loss are as extreme as in Beels' (1977) example, the issue of dependence/independence pervades the agendas of families in later life. In a normal family, handling increased dependency of aging parents does not involve the much mythologized "role reversal" (Brody, 1990; Walsh, 1988). The adult child remains in the emotional relationship of child to parent, even though their instrumental roles have changed dramatically.

Many aspects of the past relationships can influence a family's ability to handle changes smoothly. For example, when the emotional relationship between parent and child is already strained, problems around control are likely to arise. Old hurts among siblings may be resurrected, and ancient hostilities and rivalries revived around caregiving issues. Unfinished business of the past may need to be resolved before the family can address the tasks of the present in an effective way (Hargrave & Anderson, 1992).

Family style also influences response; enmeshed families may be especially susceptible to the tendency to overgeneralize the dependency needs of the elderly (Neidhardt & Allen, 1993). When the younger person takes control by "doing for" a parent and makes decisions alone rather than in consultation, the elder's feelings of helplessness may be exacerbated, as well as the younger person's feelings of burden.

Other problems occur when disengaged families tend to deny or avoid the problems and needs of their older members. Both realistic acceptance of functional loss and dependency needs by the older person and the acceptance of appropriate responsibility by the younger one(s) are necessary for successful resolution of these intergenerational issues.

Loss of a Spouse

The loss of a spouse is a virtually universal experience of the later years—the median age for widowhood is 68 for women and 71 for men (Lopata, 1973). Being widowed appears to be among the most difficult of all losses experienced in life, and the need for younger family members to understand and accept the parent's need to grieve is crucial to healthy family functioning (Walsh & McGoldrick, 1991). Adult children may attempt to protect parents from painful memories, or try to keep them from dwelling on the past, when what the parent needs to do is express the normal feelings of sadness, anger, and loss.

The profound social changes that occur after the loss of a spouse have been well studied (Lopata, 1973); they include loss of self-esteem, companionship, income, home, and, often, independence. Death of either parent always has many implications for the family: a widowed parent may experience new dependency needs, both physical and emotional, and the adult children may not have the time or inclination to meet these needs. Marital stress may result when a couple disagrees about how to respond; because caregiving is primarily "women's work," it may be the reluctant daughter-in-law who feels pressured into providing care that deprives the children of her time and energy. Acceptance by all generations of what is feasible and appropriate becomes a family task—not always easy to negotiate, and sometimes calling for therapeutic help.

In many cases, concerns around illness and dependence precede the death of either parent by several years. Loss of physical and mental functioning, chronic pain, and progressive dependency all bring changes to the family system, interacting with the differing needs and problems of the life-cycle stages of the younger members. The depression, feelings of helplessness, and loss of control that accompany physical and mental decline can result in anxiety that affects all the generations. The family's ability to deal openly with these painful losses may be the key to its capacity for accepting death when it comes and finding its own healthy ways to adapt and move on.

Mourning processes and family expectations around death vary widely and are not well documented (Walsh & McGoldrick, 1991). Whatever a family's unique rules and processes, these writers and others (Bowen, 1978; Friedman, 1985) agree that death, with its high emotional content, holds great potential for producing problems in a family *and* for opening up new possibilities for individual and family growth.

Friedman (1988) cites examples from his experience as a therapist that point up the fluidity of a family system around the time of death, and the potential for a funeral, its preparations, and its "celebration" to be a crystallizing experience for the family. He suggests that some major opportunities become available to families at this time, including the chance to take or shift responsibility, the opportunity to reestablish contact with relatives, the chance to learn family history, and the opportunity to shift energy directions in the family triangles.

CLINICAL IMPLICATIONS

The family-life-cycle framework has increasingly been demonstrated to be useful as a foundation for clinical intervention (Carter & McGoldrick, 1988; Liddle, 1988; Walsh, 1988). It provides a perspective that can incorporate both the historical approaches, emphasizing working through past conflicts and losses, and ahistorical approaches, focusing on current, ongoing interaction problems that make the family dysfunctional. In the life-cycle view, both past and present are taken into account, as therapeutic change is viewed as developmental adaptation over the course of the life span. It offers the opportunity for therapists to build on the needs and strengths of families in respectful, empowering ways.

Although the life-cycle paradigm appears to "have found its way into the clinical mainstream of family therapy" (Liddle, 1988, p. 450), it has been limited in the specific prescriptions for therapy (Liddle & Saba, 1983) and may be most useful as a framework for understanding and assessment. It has particular relevance for families in the later stages with its emphasis on human behavior as a developmental process and the more appropriate focus of therapy on normalcy rather than pathology.

The genogram is an especially useful tool for assessment of life-cycle patterns (Wachtel, 1982; Walsh, 1988) and offers special advantages for older clients, such as providing a natural framework for life review (Erlanger, 1990). Therapists with various approaches, strategies, and techniques may utilize the process of developing a genogram and the information obtained from it differently. For example, a Bowenian approach might focus extensively on past issues, such as a family "cutoff"; a brief therapy approach would attempt to address the current impasse and use life-cycle information to look for family strengths in past crises. An integrative approach would begin with the present and draw on the relevant past for bringing a new perspective to the problem, facilitating disposition of unfinished business, and fostering a new feeling of family solidarity and competence.

Liddle and Saba (1983) caution that in applying family-life-cycle concepts, therapists must take into account the family's own views and interpretations of its own family life cycle. They note that therapists may have a tendency to apply their personal assumptions about family-life-cycle theory and events; Liddle and Saba stress the importance of the therapist's recognition of his or her own value-laden templates, and the need to respect a family's unique ways of developing.

The genogram and life review appear to be especially suited to deal with the issue of family uniqueness; they can be invaluable in reinforcing a sense of family identity, placing positive and negative aspects of the past in perspective, and providing access to strengths that have helped the family cope with other crises.

The following case, using an integrative model, illustrates the use of the genogram and life review, as well as other standard tools of family therapy—structural interventions, behavioral directives, and educational processes.

Case History: The Saxon Family

Mabel Saxon and her husband Howard, both 70 years old, were referred for marital counseling after Mabel was hospitalized for depression complicated by her psychotic reaction to an antidepressant medication. The couple revealed that they had been in a great deal of conflict over the past several years, but not until Mabel's breakdown and hospitalization did they consider that psychotherapy might be helpful.

Mabel attributed her depression to her physical problems with severe arthritis, and her feelings associated with her retirement from elementary school teaching. She reported that "things just didn't work out the way I thought they would after I retired." Howard also spoke of problems—feelings of uselessness, boredom, physical decline—associated with his retirement from over 40 years of work as a supervisor in the maintenance department of a local appliance factory. Both described their marriage as "happy" up until these last years, and their family as "loving" and "close." Both expressed great respect and love for their children, grandchildren, and their families of origin.

In exploring how the couple had dealt with the transition from retirement, it became clear that they had replaced the old roles with new ones. Mabel had taken on the virtually full-time role of invalid—since her pain came and went she could be more active on some days than on others—and she and Howard both organized their lives around how Mabel felt. Howard became caregiver on the "bad days" and "go-fer" and chore doer for most of their needs. Much of their interaction centered around his questions about Mabel's health and her defensive responses; the result was misery for both. Mabel felt scrutinized, judged, and pressured, and Howard felt manipulated and imposed upon. The typical pattern was for Mabel to respond to Howard's questions with hurt feelings and tears, and Howard to withdraw and sulk.

It also became apparent that the couple was enmeshed with their two daughters, Martha and Jane. Mabel and the eldest, Martha, formed a close dyad, and Howard and Jane another. Mabel and Martha talked every day, usually about Mabel's arthritis and Martha's husband, Brad, who was suffering from recurring back pain due to a recent car accident. Howard's daily conversations with Jane also dealt with these issues, but from a different perspective—Howard and Jane believed that Mabel could do more than she did and reinforced each other's views that she used her illness to manipulate. Resentful feelings on both sides were interfering with the family's ability to communicate openly with each other, and appeared to be damaging the relationship with the grandchildren. This was yet another loss for Mabel and Howard as they had provided considerable child care during their early retirement years and missed the duties and companionship that came with the grandparent role.

The family genogram revealed that all three generations of the family were in transition, with Mabel and Howard entering their old age, Martha and Jane entering midlife, and their children in the early stages of adolescence. Martha and Jane were clearly the "generation in the middle," with pressures to provide emotional support and help with the parents' transition (while beginning to acknowledge their mortality), while dealing with their own career pressures. Further complications related to the concerns around Brad's injuries and the need to give their children support and understanding as they dealt with the crucial developmental tasks of adolescence.

An early family meeting addressed the issue of boundaries, and Martha and Jane warmly embraced the therapist's directive that Mabel and Howard had to find ways to talk to each other about their problems, rather than to their daughters. It was the beginning of an uneven and rocky road toward recovery of a once-satisfying marital—and family—relationship.

Further work with the genogram, used as a framework for life review, brought up many issues for the therapy. A major stressor was the illness of Mabel's oldest sister, Ruth, now in a moderately advanced stage of Alzheimer's disease. For Mabel, this brought back painful memories of her father's devastating experience with this illness and her own fears that this fate might be ahead for her. A series of psychological tests, which revealed no signs of dementia, helped free Mabel from her excessive worry and enabled her to grieve appropriately for the impending loss of her sister, whom she dearly loved.

During the life review work, both Mabel and Howard gained new insights into their family patterns, and into ways in which these old patterns were being played out in their present relationships. Mabel had been the youngest in her family, with two older sisters, who, along with her mother, both babied her and "bossed her around." Her parents were loving but strict and highly judgmental—"God had a ledger, and was keeping score!" was the way Mabel described it. When Howard criticized her, she heard her father's stern judgment and felt guilty, resentful, and devalued.

Howard's self-esteem as a "good son" had meant being at his mother's beck and call. He was an only child; his father was largely absent, and his mother had many physical ailments—Howard remembered how she would faint in a stressful situation and the terror and helplessness he felt. Howard's life had been regulated by her needs, and his new role as caretaker brought back old feelings of frustration, as well as his lifelong resentment (never expressed to his mother) of being manipulated by illness.

As the interpretation of the genogram began to facilitate a self-focus for both Howard and Mabel, they each began to find new ways to play out roles that had given them satisfaction in years past. Instead of trying to "teach" Howard (by insisting things be done her way), Mabel began to volunteer in a tutoring program where she could use her skills and experience to help children with reading difficulties. Howard began to use his impressive talents as a "fixer," honed by his years of maintenance supervision, for his church's maintenance program, thereby easing his frustration at not being able to "fix" Mabel. The spouses were able to talk openly about the decline of their sexual relationship, which had been one of the strengths of their marriage, and to express what a loss this was for both of them. This opened the way for them to explore new ways to express affection, comfort, and appreciation for each other.

In the therapy sessions, they continued to practice actually *listening* to each other and responding in ways that were respectful of themselves as well as of each other. After several months, they were able to take a mountain vacation with both daughters and their families to celebrate their 50th wedding anniversary and to express the belief that both family and marital ties had been healed and strengthened.

SPECIAL CONSIDERATIONS

As in all cases of working with older people, therapists must be especially sensitive to the possibilities of countertransference. Older clients can stimulate the therapist's own memories of parents and grandparents—both positive and negative—as well as activate fears about his or her own aging. In the case of life-cycle issues, the therapist may be especially at risk if he or she happens to be in a life stage where needs are in conflict with those of the older generation. Alertness to this possibility and, when it occurs, consultation with another clinician or aging specialist are essential to providing effective treatment.

Furthermore, therapists may tend to apply their own assumptions about family life cycles to a situation without giving sufficient thought to the client family's own, idiosyncratic ways of developing. The factors of ethnicity and culture are highly important, especially in light of the significance of continuity of identity in the aging process (Kaufman, 1986), noted earlier in this chapter. The ethnic, racial, and cultural context of the family clearly has a powerful role in the quest for continuity. McGoldrick's (1988) work is particularly helpful in providing a perspective for family therapists on the differing norms and roles of diverse ethnic groups and the importance of this issue for developmental transitions.

Any life cycle transition can trigger ethnic identity conflicts since it puts families more in touch with the roots of their family traditions. How the rituals of transition are celebrated can make an important difference in how well the family will adjust to the changes. ... All situational crises ... can compound ethnic identity conflicts, causing people to lose a sense of who they are. The more a therapist is sensitive to the need to preserve continuities, even in the process of change, the more he or she can help the family to maintain maximum control of the context and build upon it. (p. 86)

CONCLUSION

The life-cycle perspective offers family therapists a solid framework for normalizing transitions and crises and for reinforcing family strengths, competence, and resilience. With its emphasis on change as healthy and loss as opportunity, it has particular meaning for families in later life. It can help to offset the negative stereotyping of older people by therapists and promote the idea that elders and their families can indeed be helped to deal with loss and transition and move on to more fulfilling lives. Family therapy tools, such as the genogram and life review, are uniquely suited to help older adults and their families integrate past and present and find new strengths to meet the future.

REFERENCES

Atchley, R. C. (1982). Retirement: Leaving the world of work. *Annals, American Academy of Political and Social Science, 464,* 120-131.

Beels, C. C. (1977). The identified patient. In P. Papp (Ed.), *Family therapy: Full length case studies* (pp. 35-46). New York: Gardner Press.

Bowen, M. (1978). *Family therapy in clinical practice.* New York: Jason Aronson.

Brody, E. (1985). Parent care as a normative family stress. *The Gerontologist, 25*(1), 19-29.

Brody, E. (1990). Role reversal: An inaccurate and destructive concept. *Journal of Gerontological Social Work, 15,* 15-22.

Brubaker, T. (1983). *Family relationships in later life.* Beverly Hills, CA: Sage.

Carter, B., & McGoldrick, M. (1988). *The changing family life cycle.* New York: Gardner Press.

Cherlin, A. J., & Furstenberg, F. F. (1986). *The new American grandparent.* New York: Basic Books.

Cicirelli, V. G. (1983). Adult children and their elderly parents. In T. Brubaker (Ed.), *Family relationships in later life* (pp. 31-46). Beverly Hills, CA: Sage.

Dobson, C. (1983). Sex role and marital-role expectations. In T. D. Brubaker (Ed.), *Family relationships in later life* (pp. 109–127). Beverly Hills, CA: Sage.
Erlanger, M. A. (1990). Using the genogram with the older client. *Journal of Mental Health Counseling, 12*(3), 321–331.
Friedman, E. (1985). *Generation to generation.* New York: Guilford Press.
Friedman, E. (1988). Systems and ceremonies: A family view of rites of passage. In B. Carter & M. McGoldrick (Eds.), *The changing family life cycle* (pp. 119–148). New York: Gardner Press.
Haley, J. (1973). *Uncommon therapy.* New York: Norton.
Hargrave, T., & Anderson, W. (1992). *Finishing well.* New York: Brunner/Mazel.
Hyland, C. A. (1981). *A death in the family: Long-term impact on the life of the family.* Unpublished paper.
Kaufman, S. R. (1986). *The ageless self: Sources of meaning in late life.* Madison: University of Wisconsin Press.
Liddle, H. A. (1988). Developmental thinking and the family life cycle. In C. J. Falicov (Ed.), *Family transitions* (pp. 449–465). New York: Guilford Press.
Liddle, H. A., & Saba, G. W. (1983). Clinical use of the family life cycle: Some cautionary guidelines. In J. C. Hansen & H. A. Liddle (Eds.), *Clinical implications of the family life cycle* (pp. 161–176). Rockville, MD: Aspen Systems.
Lopata, H. Z. (1973). *Widowhood in an American city.* Cambridge, MA: Schenkman.
McClusky, N. G. (1989). Retirement and the contemporary family. In G. Hughston, V. Christopherson, & M. Bonjean (Eds.), *Aging and family therapy* (pp. 211–224). New York: Haworth Press.
McGoldrick, M. (1988). Ethnicity and the family life cycle. In B. Carter & M. McGoldrick (Eds.), *The changing family life cycle* (pp. 70–90). New York: Gardner Press.
Neidhardt, E. R., & Allen, J. (1993). *Family therapy with the elderly.* Newbury Park, CA: Sage.
Neugarten, B., & Weinstein, K. (1964). The changing American grandparent. *Journal of Marriage and the Family, 26,* 199–204.
Olson, D. H. (1988). Family types, family stress and family satisfaction: A family development perspective. In C. J. Falicov (Ed.), *Family transitions* (pp. 55–80). New York: Guilford Press.
Sprenkle, D. H., & Piercy, F. P. (1992). A family therapy informed view of the current state of the family in the United States. *Family Relations, 41*(4), 404–407.
Troll, L. E. (1983). Grandparents: The family watchdogs. In T. Brubaker (Ed.), *Family relationships in later life* (pp. 63–74). Beverly Hills, CA: Sage.
Troll, L. E., Miller, B. J., & Atchley, R. C. (1979). *Families in later life.* Belmont, CA: Wadsworth.
Vinick, B. H., & Ekerdt, D. J. (1989). Retirement and the family. *Generations, 8* (2), 53–56.
Wachtel, E. F. (1982). The family psyche over three generations: The genogram revisited. *Journal of Marital and Family Therapy, 8,* 335–343.
Walsh, F. (1988). The family in later life. In B. Carter & M. McGoldrick (Eds.), *The changing family life cycle* (pp. 311–332). New York: Gardner Press.
Walsh, F. & McGoldrick, M. (1991). *Living beyond loss.* New York: Norton.

8

Marriage in Middle and Later Life

Richard B. Miller, Ph. D.
Kansas State University
Manhattan, Kansas

Karla Hemesath, Ph. D.
Kansas State University
Manhattan, Kansas

Briana Nelson, Ph. D.
Texas Tech University
Lubbock, Texas

One consequence of the increased longevity of adults is that more and more couples are having the opportunity to enjoy marriage into later life. In previous years, it was common for one of the spouses to die in early adulthood or midlife, ending the marriage before the couple reached old age. Now, unless the marriage ends in divorce, most couples can anticipate being married for four or five decades.

In order to help couples in later life, it is necessary to first understand the characteristics of these marriages. How are they different from marriages in the early years? How do marriages typically change over time? How do health problems affect the marital relationship? What are common characteristics of the sexual relationships among older couples? Finally, what are the trends and effects of divorce in later life? By addressing these questions, marital therapists will have a better understanding of how best to help these couples.

In addition to the research that has been done to help us understand later-life marriages, clinicians need information concerning specific treatment issues with this population. How is treating a couple that has been married 50 years different from helping one that has been married only five years? What approaches and therapeutic models have been developed to work specifically with older couples?

CHANGES IN MARRIAGE OVER TIME

The question of how marriages change over time is most often addressed by examining marital satisfaction. Research studies generally have found that most spouses experience a decrease in marital satisfaction when children are born and an increase when the children leave home (Glenn, 1990; Miller, 1994). The evidence from research in recent years has led to a general acceptance that this curvilinear pattern is characteristic of most marriages.

There is evidence that change over the family life cycle may be different for different couples. One study followed a group of 17 couples for over 50 years (Weishaus & Field, 1988). These couples had been studied at several points during their marriage, allowing for an examination of how levels of satisfaction had changed during that time. Using qualitative methodology, the researchers found that there was some variation among couples in the course of their marriages.

Based on their analyses, they developed a taxonomy of the course of long-term marriages. They found that some of the marriages were *stable/ positive*. These marriages were stable over time, and the spouses maintained a fairly high level of satisfaction and affect throughout the marriage. Other marriages were *stable/neutral*, indicating that the partners experienced overall satisfaction with the marriage, but that they never had very high satisfaction or affect. The *stable/negative* marriages generally had negative affect throughout the marriage, which was demonstrated by either conflict and hostility or indifference. Finally, there were some marriages that were characterized as *curvilinear*. These couples experienced a decline in satisfaction and affect during the middle years of the marriage, but then a rise during the later stages.

Although there was some variation, most of the couples in the study had a high level of marital satisfaction. Other studies of older marriages have also found that couples report fairly high levels of marital satisfaction (Johnson, 1985; Troll, 1986). For example, in one study, 62 percent of married elderly respondents reported that their marriage was very satisfying, and 29 percent felt that their marriage was mostly satisfying (Connidis, 1989).

Changing the focus from marital satisfaction to other aspects of the marriage, there is evidence that attitudes toward marriage change over time. In a study that examined changes in marriage over a 40-year period, Holahan (1984) found that attitudes toward marriage changed as the couples got older. Both men and women developed more egalitarian attitudes concerning gender-role relationships, with both men and women feeling more strongly that women should have equality in the marriage—although this change toward egalitarianism was more pronounced among the women. Also, after 40 years, the men felt that they should be more emotionally involved in the relationship.

Patterns of interaction in the marriage also tend to change over time. In part, these changes may be due to the maturational process of the relationship, but some of the changes are attributable to changes in life circumstances. Swensen, Eskew, and Kohlhepp (1984) comment that:

> Older couples are different from other married couples. They have had an intimate relationship for a longer period of time. They are past the pressures of raising children and of earning a living, so that they have more time available to devote to activities of choice and personal preference rather than of necessity. However, eventually they face the problems of accumulating losses. Friends and siblings die, and the marriage itself may be stressed, first by serious illness, and finally by death. (pp. 71–72)

As a result of maturation and contextual changes, relational dynamics shift. Older couples tend to become less involved with friends (Ade-Ridder, 1985) and other outside activities; instead, they become more interdependent (Greenbaum & Rader, 1989; Zube, 1982). This is largely due to a loss of outside activities and careers, as well as the loss of friends and family members through illness and death. In addition, their own health problems make it more difficult to participate in outside activities. Consequently, they spend more time with each other.

In addition to these changes, how love is felt and expressed alters as couples age. In most cases, emotional intensity between husband and wife declines. Johnson (1985, p. 171) refers to love among older couples as having a "muted quality," where there is less positive affect experienced in the marriage. However, older couples still share in positive interactions together and enjoy each other. In fact, Levenson, Carstensen, and Gottman (1993) found that older couples engaged in more enjoyable activities than did middle-aged couples. But the relationships are characterized by being comfortable with each other and enjoying each other's companionship, rather than experiencing intense romantic feelings.

There are changes in values concerning love. Reedy, Birren, and Schaie (1982) found that older couples view love differently than do younger couples. Older couples rate sexual intimacy as less important than younger couples do, and they view emotional security and loyalty as more important.

Although the intensity of the positive affect decreases over time, there is also a decrease in negative interaction. Older couples experience less conflict than do middle-aged couples (Levenson, Carstensen, & Gottman, 1993) and younger couples (Swensen, Eskew, & Kohlhepp, 1981). There is less conflict about children, money, religion, recreation, intimacy, and relatives. Johnson (1985) not only found less conflict among older couples in her study, but she also reported that the couples handle conflict differently in later life than they did when they were younger. Instead of overt arguments, they were more likely to tease, make sarcastic remarks, and joke about the conflict.

The increase in positive interactions and decrease in negative ones over the course of the marriage can be summarized in a study by Gilford and Bengtson (1979). In their cross-sectional study of three-generation families, they divided marital interaction into two separate dimensions. Negative interaction referred to such marital behaviors as arguing and being sarcastic, and positive interaction consisted of such behaviors as laughing together and working together on a project. Their data suggest that negative interaction decreases over the life course and that positive interaction, on the other hand, is curvilinear.

THE CONTINUITY OF RELATIONSHIPS OVER TIME

Patterns have generally become established in a later-life marriage that determine how the spouses live their life together and adjust to new transitions. Cole (1984) reports that the strongest predictor of marital satisfaction in later life is the couple's level of satisfaction in the early stages of the marriage. Moreover, after finding few differences between mid-life and later-life marriages, Ade-Ridder (1985, p. 233) concluded that "patterns established during the middle years are likely to persist into the later years."

CLINICAL IMPLICATIONS

These themes of change and continuity in later-life relationships can serve as helpful guideposts for therapists working with older couples. On the one hand, therapists must remember that marriages change over time. Working with a 30-year-old couple married for just five years is different from helping a couple that has just celebrated a 50-year wedding anniversary.

On the other hand, therapists must also respect the history and heritage that have been established by the couple. Although some aspects of the marriage change over time, many dynamics in the marriage remain remarkably stable. Rather than expecting quick, dramatic changes within the relationship, therapists are wise to build on the positive patterns long-established in the relationship.

ISSUES AMONG OLDER COUPLES

Major Illness

The Effect of Health on Marriage

Because many older people experience health problems, physical health is a significant issue for many couples in later life. Changes in both physical and mental health often disrupt the normal day-to-day functioning of couples and frequently require lifestyle and role alterations after many years of marriage.

Having a spouse suffer a major illness does not usually affect the overall marital satisfaction of the couple (Field & Weishaus, 1984; Johnson, 1985), and sometimes the process of caring for an ill spouse may actually increase the marital bond (Weishaus & Field, 1988). The caregiver often experiences more strain, but it does not usually negatively affect feelings toward the spouse (Johnson, 1985).

Although feelings for one's spouse usually do not change during major illnesses, there is often a shift in the power structure of the relationship (Johnson, 1985). With the ill spouse temporarily or permanently disabled, the caregiving spouse must assume more responsibility and make more decisions.

An exception to the general finding that major illness has but a minimal effect on marital satisfaction is found in the case of Alzheimer's disease. These caregivers generally report lower levels of marital satisfaction than do spouses in other later-life marriages (Wright, 1991). This decrease in marital satisfaction is primarily due to a substantial decline in companionship that is experienced during the course of the illness.

The Effect of Marriage on Health

The marital relationship can have an influence on partners' physical and mental health (Burman & Margolin, 1992). Changes in health status may serve an adaptive function in later-life marriages in that health problems may appear or intensify during or after significant changes in the marriage. Greenbaum and Rader (1989) suggest that health problems may be exaggerated at later-life transition points in an unconscious attempt to rebalance power within a relationship and maintain a sense of focus. Similarly, Ouslander (1982) suggests that depression is often masked in older individuals. He argues that today's generation of elderly persons were taught to inhibit expression of feelings at all times, even in times of stress. To compensate for this, they sometimes develop a more acceptable means of expression through bodily symptoms or the exaggeration of physical symptoms from preexisting conditions.

Greenbaum and Rader (1989) suggest that health issues may play a role in a couple's negotiation of the role shifts that occur in later life. To accomplish a shift and compromise less (covertly), the man may indirectly express role reversal or a tendency toward androgyny through hypochondria or illness. In this way, he is able to relinquish some of his dominant role and power in a way that allows him to save face.

A woman's depression may serve a number of functions in the marital relationship. The symptoms can protect the marriage by diverting attention from unresolved marital issues and directing it toward the wife's difficulties with mood and functioning (Braverman, 1986). These symptoms may also serve to establish distance between wife and husband, or they may serve to get the husband more involved in helping his wife, thereby increasing the closeness in the relationship.

Recognizing the role that physical symptoms can play in marriages in later life, therapists must be mindful of possible functions that the physical complaints have in the marriage. By examining possible payoffs of the symptoms for the relationship, therapists can better assess whether the physical problem has a systemic etiology. In these cases, marital therapists can be instrumental in providing psychosocial solutions to these problems.

Sexuality

There is a frequent misconception that a couple's sexual interest and activity wane or cease to exist as the partners grow older. Several studies have shown that sexual relations are, in fact, an important factor in middle and later life (Ade-Ridder, 1990; Marsiglio & Donnelly, 1991; Renshaw, 1988). Although a decline in frequency tends to occur with age, sexual activity usually continues throughout later life (Ade-Ridder, 1990; Marsiglio & Donnelly, 1991). In fact, 66.7 percent of the couples (ranging in age from 61 to 92 years) in Ade-Ridder's (1990) study remained sexually active. Marsiglio and Donnelly (1991) found that 53 percent of the couples in their study reported sexual intercourse an average of about four times per month. Thus, sexuality remains an important component of marriage for most couples in later life.

Problems with sexuality in later life are generally a function of either physical problems or negative attitudes toward sex. A symptom of some health problems is a decrease in sexual desire or a lessened ability to become sexually aroused (Comfort, 1980). For example, diabetes can have a negative effect on sexual functioning, but appropriate treatment of the condition often helps to restore it. In addition, a side effect of some of the medications that are prescribed for medical problems is diminished sexual functioning. Mellaril, for instance, causes erectile disorders among many men (Comfort, 1980). Because the probability increases in later life that sexual problems will have a medical etiology, it is important that therapists make sure that older clients who have such problems visit a physician for a medical consultation.

Sexual problems can also be the result of negative stereotypes about the elderly. Unfortunately, some elderly share these opinions that sexuality is not normal or appropriate in later life. Whitlatch and Zarit (1989) suggest that sexual problems may result from "misunderstandings, negative beliefs, expectations, and behavior patterns surrounding sexual behavior" (pp. 44–45).

Education is a critical component of therapy with later-life couples, including providing information about sexual alternatives, physiological and normal changes, and disease and drug effects (Ade-Ridder, 1990; Renshaw, 1988; White & Catania, 1982; Whitlatch & Zarit, 1988). Education not only increases knowledge about sexuality, but may foster modifications of attitudes and beliefs (White & Catania, 1982). Such rethinking may allow later-life couples to experience greater sexual enjoyment.

Divorce

Although divorce among the elderly is still rare, the divorce rate of those over age 65 has increased in recent years (Hammond & Muller, 1992). In 1985, only 1.3% of the 2.4 million divorces in the United States involved a person over the age of 65. Conversely, 74 percent involved couples under 40 years old (Uhlenberg, Cooney, & Boyd, 1990). However, there is evidence that the rate of divorce among the elderly is increasing. Between 1970 and 1980, the divorce rate among the elderly in the United States increased by 0.7 percent, and between 1980 and 1985, it increased by 2.7 percent. In comparison, the divorce rate between 1980 and 1985 actually decreased for couples under the age of 34 (Uhlenbeg, Cooney, & Boyd, 1990).

Unfortunately, virtually no empirical research has been conducted on the cause of the increase in divorces among the elderly. Among the reasons suggested by scholars is the increase in the proportion of elderly persons who are in their second or third marriages, which are more prone to end in divorce (Hennon, 1983); newer cohorts entering old age who are more accepting of divorce (Uhlenberg & Meyers, 1981); and the increase in the number of older women who are not economically dependent on their husbands (Uhlenberg & Meyers, 1981).

Not only is the divorce rate increasing, but it is expected that there will be an increase in the number of elderly persons who have been divorced. (For most, the divorce will have happened earlier in life.) Today, people reaching the age of 65 are about twice as likely to be widowed as divorced. However, Uhlenberg and his associates (1990) estimate that, as the baby boom generation enters old age (over 65), more of them will be divorced than widowed.

Research has shown that women who divorce later in life experience poorer adjustment following the divorce than do younger women who divorce (Bogolub, 1991; Cain, 1988). There may be several explanations for their problems with postdivorce adjustment. The elderly divorcee may have certain attitudes toward marriage along with a taboo against divorce that inhibits adjustment. The women in Cain's (1988) study saw divorce as a "shameful life event" (p. 565). Also, these women may feel more responsible for the divorce than do their younger counterparts (Cain, 1988). In fact, because of the stigma of divorce in later life, it is a more stressful transition experience than is widowhood. Finally, the stress of divorce may be greater for older women, which makes adjustment more difficult (Bogolub, 1991; Campbell, 1984).

Later-life divorce presents several specific consequences, with psychological and social/relational aspects. A decline in self-esteem among women who divorce in later life has been reported (Bogolub, 1991; Cain, 1988). As with divorce at any age, there is a deep sense of loss; however, these feelings may be more pervasive and have greater personal impact for those in later life (Bogolub, 1991; Cain, 1988; Campbell, 1984). Enhancing self-esteem and competence are important factors that reduce the stress in later life and allow for successful aging following a major life transition, such as divorce (Campbell, 1984).

Divorced parents may depend on children for emotional and economic support (Bogolub, 1991; Shamoian & Thurston, 1986). Later-life divorce can put stress on the parent-child relationship, forcing a new relationship to be negotiated. Dependence on adult children is often a struggle for women who divorce (Bogolub, 1991), as they experience the termination of a relationship they may have once depended on for their identity.

Later-life divorce also produces changes in interpersonal relations outside the family. A decline in friendship networks is found to be a consequence of divorce (Bogolub, 1991; Cain, 1988; Shamoian & Thurston, 1986). These changes often increase loneliness among persons experiencing later-life divorce.

A final consequence of divorce is the economic fallout. Researchers have shown that divorce is economically more devastating for women (Wallerstein, 1986), and this is certainly true for women who experience later-life divorce. According to Uhlenberg and colleagues (1990), older women "who are divorced, experience much lower standards of living than married women" (p. S10). Many later-life women who divorce suddenly find themselves without economic support and have to find employment. They may never have been employed before or they may not have held a job for many years (Bogolub, 1991). Thus, they may find themselves in jobs that are uninteresting, low-paying, and stressful (Bogolub, 1991; Campbell, 1984), adding to the difficulty in adjusting to later-life divorce.

Although the available research on later-life divorce often paints a bleak picture, Cain (1988) found various coping methods among women. The support of friends and family, community involvement, and participation in a support group were among the strategies. Realizing the value of these resources in facilitating the coping and adjustment process, therapists should work with divorced older adults to activate such social networks.

MARITAL THERAPY WITH OLDER COUPLES

There are relatively few publications that address marital therapy with older couples. However, in many ways, therapy with older couples is similar to therapy with couples of other ages (Knight, 1992). Approaches that have been developed for working with couples in general can be applied to working with older couples, if certain adjustments are made. Special considerations need to be appended to existing approaches when joining with the couple, assessing their marital relationship, and implementing strategies to help them change.

Joining with Older Clients

There is generally a mistrust of marital therapy among older couples (Gafner, 1987a; Greenbaum & Rader, 1989). Many were raised with the value that they should be self-reliant, and that only "crazy people" received psychotherapy (Stone, 1987). These couples are also often uncomfortable when dealing with emotional or intimate issues. Consequently, for older couples to feel comfortable enough in therapy to facilitate growth, marital therapists must particularly emphasize the joining process.

Therapists must be sensitive to fears that the couple may bring to therapy. For example, some couples fear that marital therapy will lead to involuntary institutionalization (Stone, 1987). It is important to socialize these couples to therapy, and to reassure them that they have control of the therapy sessions. Validating self-determinism will help them to feel safer in the therapy environment.

As a way to deal with the challenges of joining with elderly couples, Gafner (1987a) suggests the use of "exaggerated engagement." The styles used by therapists working with younger couples in which assessment and intervention take place early in the therapeutic process are less effective with older couples. Therefore, he suggests that unless there is a marked degree of distress or other problems requiring urgent attention, it is advisable to delay interpersonal work during the initial sessions of therapy (p. 309). This is done by exaggerating issues of *time*. The therapist should take the needed amount of time for the joining process. The process includes learning about the couple's sense of time and the historical periods that were important in their lives. The therapist demonstrates that there is time for the couples to have someone listen to them.

The therapist must also accentuate *interest* in the couple. Exaggerated interest might include questions about World War II or about their children and grandchildren. By exaggerating time and interest, the therapist is able to establish credibility, which facilitates the process of developing a therapeutic relationship. Robison, Smaby, and Donovan (1989) outline special strategies that enhance the therapeutic relationship with older adults. Such interventions as therapist self-disclosure, reflective listening, communication at the client's level of understanding, and minimizing direct confrontation are all attempts to work with an older client's reluctance to participate in therapy.

A helpful therapeutic stance to employ might be a gentler, nonauthoritarian, not-knowing stance, such as that described by Hoffman (1990). When dealing with resistance, she advocates the use of a collaborative approach to therapy rather than a power-based stance in which the therapist is viewed as expert. This idea is wonderful for older couples and younger therapists because of the tremendous amount of life experience and expertise that couples bring to therapy.

Compounding the difficulties in joining with older couples is the negative attitude that many marital therapists themselves have toward working with this population (Gafner, 1987a). This uneasiness with aging on the therapist's part may affect the therapeutic process. Reactivity or discomfort with issues of dependence, disability, and powerlessness may be strong factors that may influence the therapeutic relationship. An awareness of these issues when working with older clients is important since one's own anxiety will probably be reflected in the therapeutic process.

The joining process is often complicated by the likelihood that there may be notable sensory impairments for one or both of the spouses (Stone, 1987). This often makes it difficult to communicate effectively with elderly couples. The aging process typically affects the ability of the elderly to articulate (Dreher, 1987). They often experience changes in pronunciation, pitch, and timing of speech. In addition, many elderly have hearing impairments. Consequently, therapists must make a special effort to ensure effective communication.

Assessment Issues

Older couples bring a tremendous marital history to therapy. Most of these couples have been married to each other for four or five decades, and they have established long-standing attitudes and patterns of interaction and affect in their relationships. To adequately understand current difficulties, it is important to assess prior coping styles and patterns. A look back to earlier difficulties and stresses and how the couple managed these situations can shed light on a current situation. Many couples possess significant resources and strengths. The identification of these attributes can be an important assessment technique that can later be used during the treatment phase of therapy.

A small number of diagnostic aids and assessment tools are mentioned in the literature for use with older couples. Most of those indicated have been used for research purposes. When using standardized assessment tools, it is important to consider the couple's stage in the family life cycle. Some of these may have been developed for and tested with couples at earlier stages in the family life cycle, who have experienced a different societal climate than older couples.

An example of a current assessment tool used in research is the dyadic adjustment scale (DAS) (Spanier, 1976). Ade-Ridder (1985), in a study of marital satisfaction in couples married 50 or more years, used the DAS with one modification because of the age of the respondents. This modification was not specified by the author. Lauer and Lauer (1986) modified the DAS with additional questions assessing commitment for use with older couples. The first 32 items of the DAS were used and seven Likert items were added to tap respondents' attitudes toward their spouses and toward marriage. The spousal attitude items inquired about appreciation of the spouse's achievements, viewing the spouse as a best friend, liking the spouse as a person, and believing that the spouse had grown more interesting over time. Attitudes toward marriage in this measure were assessed with the following inquiries: viewing marriage as a long-term commitment, a sacred obligation, and an important factor in societal stability.

Gafner (1987a, 1987b) has developed a more informal approach to marital assessment, using a visual tool called the discouragement meter. This pictorial representation of a thermometer lists in ascending order some of the problems, or discouragements, that older couples face. Among the areas assessed by this device are somatic complaints, sensory loss, life adjustments, death of family and friends, moves, lack of money, symptoms of depression and anxiety, difficulties in cognitive functioning, and symptoms of severe depression, such as hopelessness and despair. With this visualization, couples are able to identify some of the discouragements that they are experiencing, as well as to understand the cumulative effect that several discouragements can have on their lives.

The employment of an assessment method such as this seems useful because many of the difficulties that older couples bring to therapy or to the attention of professionals, such as physicians, relate directly or indirectly to aging-related changes in functioning. The traditional methods of assessment used with younger couples often overlook those areas that are quite significant in the lives of their older counterparts.

A genogram may be a useful assessment tool when working with older couples (Erlanger, 1990). The genogram is particularly suited to help organize information about the system, especially given that family events and processes can often be complex in an extended family. By creating a genogram, the family dynamics that might have an influence on the marriage can be identified. The process of creating the genogram also widens the frame and context of current difficulties. Recall of past adjustments helps to reveal the resources and strategies that were used previously. Within an intergenerational and family system context the solutions may not be readily apparent, but laying out the forces at work in this way is often a liberating experience in which clients may come to feel that the problems "are not all my fault."

The genogram process might also make the clients feel more comfortable as they reminisce, changing the atmosphere so that the interaction seems less like a mental health interview. Also, this information gathering about the rest of the family helps to take some of the focus off the identified patient and puts the difficulties in the wider context of a family problem. Of importance here is that the stance of the therapist is changed to a one-down position by making the client an expert. This is particularly helpful for the elderly in that often life stresses and losses, such as physical decline, retirement, and widowhood, make the client feel devalued. In a sense, the therapist becomes a learner.

In addition to the usual assessment process, therapists who work with older couples should look for assessment issues that are a result of aging. The two areas that are most salient to the assessment process are mental and physical functioning. Changes in mental acuity are often precursors to marital discord. Dementia that is in its early stages may be undetected, yet may be disrupting the normal patterns of interaction in the marriage (Stone, 1987). With the source of the disruption undetected, negative attributions as to the cause of the changes in the marriage may intensify marital conflict. For example, a spouse may make the attribution, "He forgot to pick me up from my friend's house because he doesn't care about me." On the other hand, if memory loss is correctly attributed as the cause for this husband's not picking his wife up, she will be less negative about his actions.

It is critical, then, that memory impairments be properly assessed during treatment. In most cases, marital therapists are not adequately trained to make specific assessments regarding dementia. Instead, a specialist who is trained in geriatric diagnostics should be called in to provide the diagnosis.

Physical functioning should also be evaluated (Stone, 1987). Changes in physical functioning can have a dramatic impact on the roles that the couple has assumed for decades. Although most couples are able to negotiate these role changes successfully, the disruption of roles and lifestyles may be a significant contributor to marital discord. The accurate assessment of these physical changes helps to place the presenting problem of the older couple in a more meaningful context.

Finally, a consideration of the losses older couples have undergone, as well their adaptation to them, is important to the process of assessment. Deaths of friends and family members, chronic disease and disability, sensory losses, and decreasing cognitive and mental abilities all represent significant losses in the marriage. The accumulation of losses, especially if they are unresolved, may have a negative impact on the couple's ability to interact effectively. Consequently, the presence of losses needs to be determined in order to fully understand the marital relationship.

Treatment Issues and Strategies

Although any of the intervention strategies of general marital therapy can be applied to older couples, some of the unique aspects of elderly couples must be taken into consideration. One such consideration is the inability of many older couples to come to a clinic for therapy. Because one or both of the spouses may be homebound due to health problems, it may be necessary for the therapist to make home visits (Greenbaum & Rader, 1989; Stone, 1987). This not only makes the services more accessible for the couple, but provides an atmosphere that is less threatening than an office. Health factors may also limit the stamina of the couple, requiring the therapist to reduce the length of the session from the traditional "therapeutic" hour.

Stone (1987) has experienced in his work a reluctance of many older couples to work in the arena of feelings. Although there are exceptions, he has found that many older couples find the exploration of emotions threatening. They are more comfortable focusing on specific patterns of behaviors and interactions that can be changed to better adapt to their current life circumstances. However, this general resistance to exploring feelings among the elderly is likely to decrease in the future as new cohorts of couples enter old age.

Paradoxical Interventions

Paradoxical interventions may be particularly suited for many older couples (Frey, Swanson, & Hyer, 1989). Because of their long marital history, these couples have "negotiated elaborate, interdependent relationships" (Brubaker & Kinsel, 1985, p. 246), and their patterns of interaction have become very entrenched. Moreover, the "world view" (Minuchin & Fishman, 1981) of the couples' reality is also very stable and resistant to change. Consequently, it is often difficult to induce change through the use of straightforward techniques. Because of this, paradoxical interventions may be an effective approach to change.

Gilewski, Kuppinger, and Zarit (1985) illustrate the use of paradox in marital therapy with an older couple that had long-standing conflict. Outside of therapy, they spent very little time together. During therapy, the couple had a pattern of arguing and blaming each other for their marital problems, rather than focusing on ways to improve the marriage. They were resistant to in-session interventions, and they were noncompliant with homework. The couple, when they were asked what they wanted out of therapy, stated that they wanted to spend more time together. Based on this, the therapist introduced a paradoxical intervention, whereby he instructed the couple to spend *less* time together. At the next session, the husband reported that they had complied with the homework, but that he missed spending more time with his wife. This response surprised his wife, who then softened her stance in the marriage. After that, they were able to work together better in therapy, and they began to experience some improvement in their relationship.

Models of Marital Therapy with Older People

Many of the existing models of marital therapy can be applied to working with older couples, as long as adjustments are made to fit the circumstances associated with aging. For example, Beckham and Giordano (1986) suggest a behavioral approach for such work. Training the couple to develop communication and problem-solving skills is the major focus from this perspective. These enhanced skills can then be used to solve the couple's specific problems. As Stone (1987) suggests, the behavioral perspective is often less threatening to older couples, and it fits many of their desired goals in therapy—to find solutions to specific problems.

Long and Mancini (1985) use the Bowen model as a conceptual framework for viewing the marital issues in later life. This model lends itself nicely to a historical perspective that is useful in examining difficulties of older couples. Bowen's intergenerational focus is also a good fit with the context of older couples residing in complex multigenerational families.

For example, emotional cutoff is a Bowenian concept that is commonly found in mid- and later-life marriages. Cutoff is a means of dealing with intensity or differences of feelings and opinions with family members by eliminating emotional closeness and/or physical contact. With the stresses of life, people may cut off from significant others, such as siblings or adult children, as a means of dealing with intense differences and feelings. The result is an increase of intensity within the marriage, which exacerbates and magnifies problems between the spouses. As the emotional cutoff is reduced with the family member, the intensity of the marital relationship decreases, and the marriage becomes less stressful.

Developmental Marital Therapy

Although most therapy with older couples involves the adaptation of existing marital therapy models to their particular circumstances, one model has been developed specifically for working with this population. Wolinsky (1986, 1990) has developed the developmental marital therapy model, which integrates developmental-stage theory, psychodynamic theory, and grief counseling to deal with the unique challenges that face older couples. The model consists of four stages. In the evaluation stage, the presenting problem is discussed, appropriate testing is conducted, and a marital history is taken. She calls this marital history process a marital-life review. The treatment stage consists of an eclectic range of interventions, including continuing marital-life review, insight-oriented therapy, supportive therapy, and grief counseling.

The task- and action-oriented stage helps the couple make the transition to the appropriate life stages in their marriage, and in their individual lives. Therapy is used to identify and utilize appropriate resources to facilitate these transitions. Finally, the termination stage reviews therapeutic progress, as well as individual and marital strengths.

CASE STUDY

Background

George (age 65) and Jane (age 64) came to marital therapy on the recommendation of their family physician, Dr. Williams. The presenting complaint was that George, who recently retired from his job as a foreman in a factory, was voicing more physical complaints, particularly complaints of chest pain. After rigorous testing yielded nothing out of the ordinary, Dr. Williams questioned George regarding his adjustment to his recent retirement. George responded, "I retired in the hopes that Jane and I would be able to spend more time together and do the things we always planned to do. Now Jane is gone spending most of her time with her friends or caring for her dad. That old man has taken most of Jane's time for too long. Now it is my turn to enjoy having my wife around, doing things with me." Dr. Williams suggested that George and Jane seek marital therapy. The couple, though somewhat reluctant, agreed.

Joining

George and Jane came to the first session somewhat warily, embarrassed by "needing to see someone to work out our problems." But Jane admitted, "We have been married 43 years and always worked things out before, but this time we need help." Although they realized they were having difficulty, they were worried about what it meant to seek therapy. Both were concerned about what people, particularly their children and their extended families, would think. The therapist assured them of the confidentiality of the process, and that their children and families would find out only if George and Jane decided to tell them. Not only were they concerned about what others would think, but they worried that they were "crazy" or "sick" because they were in therapy. Their fears were acknowledged, and the success they had over the course of their lives and their marriage was discussed. When their current difficulties were framed as a temporary problem due to a big change in their lives, George and Jane were both visibly relieved and expressed hope about the therapy process.

Using Gafner's (1987a) "exaggerated engagement," problem definition was deliberately slowed down to increase the joining phase of therapy. In an effort to join with this couple, the therapist questioned them in depth about their family, and they took great delight in telling about their three children and five grandchildren. They talked about the history of their married life and what they were doing when they first were married. They described their courtship and the early years of their marriage when George was in the army during the Korean conflict. They shared with the therapist the struggles that they overcame during the separation and the difficult times of the war. Both remarked about how different life was for couples today, particularly the lives of their children and their children's spouses.

Assessment

When asked about what brought them to therapy, George and Jane both described feeling angry, let down, and disappointed by each other since George's retirement. When asked to describe to each other how they felt about the situation, both Jane and George had a difficult time clearly expressing their anger and disappointment with the other. At numerous points during the sessions, they would make sarcastic remarks about one another, but they refused to overtly express their anger at each other. When asked if this behavior was similar to what went on at home, both reluctantly agreed.

A central issue for George and Jane was, as Jane described it, "We have led separate lives for so long that it is very hard to get used to having the other around most of the time." George, however, disagreed in that he felt much of the problem centered around Jane's involvement with the care of her aging father, John (age 87). John had required a great deal of care since the death of Jane's mother 12 years earlier. A diabetic, he was finally placed in a nursing facility two years ago after Jane and her siblings could no longer provide care for him in his home or in their homes. George expressed a great deal of resentment about Jane's extensive care of her father, and he described feeling left out because Jane spent a great deal of time focused on her father. He also expressed concern for Jane's well-being as he was well aware of the strain, both physical and emotional, that Jane has endured while caring for her father. George felt resentful about Jane not sharing his idea that now that he had retired, it was *their* time.

In working with this couple, many family-life-cycle issues were presented and needed to be addressed. It was important to emphasize to the couple the multitude of strengths they possessed that enabled them to successfully manage many transitions throughout the years. The current transition point of retirement was identified as a "stuck spot" that was complicated by individual issues of loss and aging. Juxtaposing the couple's strengths with their current struggles framed the present difficulties in a manageable context.

Treatment Issues

When discussing the situation of her father, Jane became quite tearful. Jane was slowly and gently questioned; she described her feelings of guilt about not being better able to care for her father in her home or in his own home: "He hates it in the nursing home, and I feel responsible for his misery. If only I would have tried harder." Surprisingly, George supportively defended Jane, "Honey, you did what you could; you don't owe him any more." It took several sessions to discuss each's feelings about this painful situation. The therapist worked hard in the area of Jane's issues of guilt, and she began to set limits around how much time she would spend with her father.

In conjunction with Jane's discussion of issues about caring for her father, George discussed his feelings of loss and inadequacy around his being a "good son" to his parents. His ability to reflect on his own feelings concerning his parents and their deaths lessened his reactivity to Jane's struggles with her dad. Jane was surprised to hear George speak of his feelings of sadness and loss regarding his parents. She had assumed from his reaction to her relationship with her father that George didn't have the same type of feelings that she did. This realization narrowed the differences between them and both understood something about the other that they had not previously understood.

After some of their reactivity and anger lessened, George and Jane began to negotiate the tasks around the house and yard. Behavioral strategies, such as caring days and quid pro quo negotiation, were used to help each feel cared for by the other. Jane and George began to negotiate the time they spent together, and they developed a plan to go on an outing together at least once a week. Although both felt that this overt process was awkward and bothersome initially, they complied. As Jane and George began to give and reciprocate, they felt less awkward and reported that they felt like spending more time with each other. As George put it, "We are now starting to do the things we had hoped to do during our retirement."

REFERENCES

Ade-Ridder, L. (1985). Quality of marriage: A comparison between golden wedding couples and couples married less than fifty years. *Lifestyles: A Journal of Changing Patterns, 7,* 224-237.

Ade-Ridder, L. (1990). Sexuality and marital quality among older married couples. In T. H. Brubaker (Ed.), *Family relationships in later life* (pp. 48-67). Newbury Park, CA: Sage.

Anderson, S. A., Russell, C. S., & Schumm, W. R. (1983). Perceived marital quality and family life-cycle categories: A further analysis. *Journal of Marriage and the Family, 45,* 127-139.

Atchley, R., & Miller, S. (1983). Types of elderly couples. In T. H. Brubaker (Ed.), *Family relationships in later life* (pp. 77-90). Newbury Park, CA: Sage.

Beckham, K., & Giordano, J. A. (1986). Illness and impairment in elderly couples: Implications for marital therapy. *Family Relations, 35,* 257-264.

Bogolub, E. B. (1991). Women and mid-life divorce: Some practice issues. *Social Work, 36,* 428-433.

Braverman, L. (1986). The depressed woman in context. In M. Ault-Riche (Ed.), *Women and family therapy.* Rockville, MD: Aspen Systems.

Brubaker, T. H., & Kinsel, B. I. (1985). Who is responsible for household tasks in long-term marriages of the "young-old" elderly? *Lifestyles: A Journal of Changing Patterns, 7,* 238-247.

Burman, B., & Margolin, G. (1992). Analysis of the association between marital relationships and health problems: An interactional perspective. *Psychological Bulletin, 112,* 39-63.

Cain, B. S. (1988). Divorce among elderly women: A growing social phenomenon. *Social Casework: The Journal of Contemporary Social Work, 69,* 563-568.

Campbell, S. (1984). The fifty-year-old woman and midlife stress. *International Journal of Aging and Human Development, 18,* 295-307.

Cole, C. (1984). Marital quality in later life. In W. Quinn & G. Hughston (Eds.), *Independent aging: Family and social systems perspectives* (pp. 72-90). Rockville, MD: Aspen Systems.

Comfort, A. (1980). Sexuality in later life. In J. E. Birren & R. B. Sloan (Eds.), *Handbook of mental health and aging* (pp. 885-892). Englewood Cliffs, NJ: Prentice-Hall.

Connidis, I. A. (1989). *Family ties and aging.* Toronto: Butterworths.

Dreher, B. B. (1987). *Communication skills for working with elders.* New York: Springer.

Erlanger, M. A. (1990). Using the genogram with the older client. *Journal of Mental Health Counseling, 12,* 321-331.

Field, D., & Weishaus, S. (1984, November). *Marriages over half a century: A longitudinal study.* Paper presented at the meeting of the Gerontological Society of America, San Antonio, TX.

Frey, J., Swanson, G. S., & Hyer, L. (1989). Strategic interventions for chronic patients in later life. *The American Journal of Family Therapy, 17,* 27-33.

Gafner, G. (1987a). Engaging the elderly couple in marital therapy. *The American Journal of Family Therapy, 15,* 305-315.
Gafner, G. (1987b). Paradoxical marital therapy and the discouragement meter. *Clinical Gerontologist, 6,* 67-70.
Gilewski, M. J., Kuppinger, J., & Zarit, S. (1985). The aging marital system: A case study in life changes and paradoxical intervention. *Clinical Gerontologist, 3,* 3-16.
Gilford, R., & Bengtson, V. L. (1979). Measuring marital satisfaction in three generations: Positive and negative dimensions. *Journal of Marriage and the Family, 41,* 387-398.
Glenn, N. D. (1990). Quantitative research on marital quality in the 1980s: A critical review. *Journal of Marriage and the Family, 52,* 818-831.
Greenbaum, J., & Rader, L. (1989). Marital problems of the old elderly as they present to a mental health clinic. *Journal of Gerontological Social Work, 14,* 111-126.
Hammond, R. J., & Muller, G. O. (1992). The late-life divorce: Another look. *Journal of Divorce and Remarriage, 17,* 135-150.
Hennon, C. B. (1983). Divorce and the elderly: A neglected area of research. In T. H. Brubaker (Ed.), *Family relationships in later life.* Beverly Hills, CA: Sage.
Hoffman, L. (1990). Constructing realities: An art of lens. *Family Process, 29,* 1-12.
Holahan, C. K. (1984). Marital attitudes over 40 years: A longitudinal and cohort analysis. *Journal of Gerontology, 39,* 49-57.
Johnson, C. L. (1985). The impact of illness on late-life marriages. *Journal of Marriage and the Family, 47,* 165-172.
Knight, B. G. (1992). *Older adults in psychotherapy: Case histories.* Newbury Park, CA: Sage.
Lauer, R. H., & Lauer, J. C. (1986). Factors in long-term marriages. *Journal of Family Issues, 7,* 382-390.
Levenson, R. W., Carstensen, L. L., & Gottman, J. M. (1993). Long-term marriage: Age, gender, and satisfaction. *Psychology and Aging, 8,* 301-313.
Long, J. K., & Mancini, J. A. (1985). Aging couples and the family system. In T. H. Brubaker (Ed.), *Later life families* (pp. 29-47). Beverly Hills, CA: Sage.
Marsiglio, W., & Donnelly, D. (1991). Sexual relations in later life: A national study of married persons. *Journal of Gerontology, 46,* S338-S344.
Miller, R. B. (1994, November). *A re-examination of the U-shaped curve of marital satisfaction over the life course: A review of longitudinal evidence.* Paper presented at the Theory Construction and Research Methodology Workshop at the annual meeting of the National Council of Family Relations, Minneapolis, MN.
Minuchin, S., & Fishman, H. C. (1981). *Family therapy techniques.* Cambridge, MA: Harvard University Press.
Ouslander, J. (1982). Physical illness and depression in the elderly. *Journal of the American Geriatric Society, 2,* 593-598.
Qualls, S. H. (1991). Resistance of older families to therapeutic intervention. *Clinical Gerontologist, 11,* 59-68.
Reedy, M. N., Birren, J. E., & Schaie, K. W. (1982). Age and sex differences in satisfying love relationships across the adult life span. *Human Development, 24,* 52-66.

Renshaw, D. C. (1988). Sexual problems in later life: A case of impotence. *Clinical Gerontologist, 8,* 73-75.

Robison, F. F., Smaby, M. H., & Donovan, G. L. (1989). Influencing reluctant elderly clients to participate in mental health counseling. *Journal of Mental Health Counseling, 11,* 259-272.

Shamoian, C. A., & Thurston, F. D. (1986). Marital discord and divorce among the elderly. *Medical Aspects of Human Sexuality, 20,* 25-34.

Spanier, G. B. (1976). Measuring dyadic adjustment: New scales for assessing the quality of marriage and similar dyads. *Journal of Marriage and the Family, 38,* 731-738.

Stone, J. D. (1987). Marital and sexual counseling of elderly couples. In G. R. Weeks & L. Hof (Eds.), *Integrating sex and marital therapy: A clinical guide* (pp. 221-245). New York: Brunner/Mazel.

Swensen, C. H., Eskew, R. W., & Kohlhepp, K. A. (1981). Stage of family life cycle, ego development, and the marriage relationship. *Journal of Marriage and the Family, 43,* 841-853.

Swensen, C. H., Eskew, R. W., & Kohlhepp, K. A. (1984). Five factors in long-term marriages. *Lifestyles: A Journal of Changing Patterns, 7,* 94-106.

Troll, L. E. (1986). *Family issues in current gerontology.* New York: Springer.

Uhlenberg, P., Cooney, T., & Boyd, R. (1990). Divorce for women after midlife. *Journal of Gerontology, 45,* S3-S11.

Uhlenberg, P., & Myers, M. P. (1981). Divorce and the elderly. *The Gerontologist, 21,* 276-282.

Wallerstein, J. S. (1986). Women after divorce: Preliminary report from a ten year follow-up. *American Journal of Orthopsychiatry, 56,* 65-77.

Walsh, F. (1989). The family in later life. In M. McGoldrick & B. Carter (Eds.), *The changing family life cycle: A framework for family therapy* (2nd ed.) (pp. 311-332). Boston: Allyn & Bacon.

Weishaus, S., & Field, D. (1988). A half century of marriage: Continuity or change? *Journal of Marriage and the Family, 50,* 763-774.

White, C. B., & Catania, J. A. (1982). Psychoeducational intervention for sexuality with the aged, family members of the aged, and people who work with the aged. *International Journal of Aging and Human Development, 15,* 121-138.

Whitlatch, C. J., & Zarit, S. H. (1988). Sexual dysfunction in an aged married couple: A case study of a behavioral intervention. *Clinical Gerontologist, 8,* 43-62.

Wolinsky, M. A. (1986). Marital therapy with older couples. *Social Casework: The Journal of Contemporary Social Work, 67,* 475-483.

Wolinsky, M. A. (1990). *A heart of wisdom: Marital counseling with older and elderly couples.* New York: Brunner/Mazel.

Wright, L. K. (1991). The impact of Alzheimer's disease on the marital relationship. *The Gerontologist, 31,* 224-237.

Wright, L. K. (1993). *Alzheimer's disease and marriage.* Newbury Park, CA: Sage.

Zube, M. (1982). Changing behavior and outlook of aging men and women: Implications for marriage in the middle and later years. *Family Relations, 31,* 147-156.

9

Gender Issues and Elder Care

Nancy L. Kriseman, M.S.W.
Kennesaw State College
Atlanta, Georgia

Jacalyn A. Claes, Ph.D.
University of North Carolina at Greensboro
Greensboro, North Carolina

Contemporary society offers a variety of family configurations. This diversity affects how older people are cared for as they become frail. Think of the following as snapshots of dilemmas in caretaking.

- A single parent, an only child with few financial resources: She is challenged to find the time and money needed to provide quality care for her 82-year-old mother, a stroke victim.
- A lesbian daughter in a family of three other siblings who are married with children: The siblings expect her to care for their aging parents because she is single and appears to have fewer family obligations or responsibilities.
- A married son, an only child, with children and work obligations: Living in a different state than his mother has left him torn by multiple responsibilities since his mother has begun showing signs of dementia.
- An adult daughter, estranged from her mother: As her mother becomes frail, she wonders what her responsibility is.

- A woman who has established an affectionate relationship with her stepmother: Since her stepmother has no other living family, she feels pulled between wanting to care for her own mother and wanting also to meet the needs of her stepmother.

These family members have roles in their families of origin as well as in their families of choice. Midlife brings many new tasks that relate to the different stage of each type of family. Within the context of these later-life families, generational patterns of maleness and femaleness become evident.

GENDER PATTERNS AND CAREGIVING

In a society that has traditionally separated economic and instrumental tasks from nurturing and expressive tasks, care of the elderly is a task that has been set aside for women. Since women have been trained not only to nurture those whom they love but to be invested in the continuation of these relationships over their lifetime, their position as the ideal caregiver of elders was assured. Within this societal paradigm, females have been expected to take on caregiving tasks with the same enthusiasm as mothering (Chodorow, 1978; Gilligan, 1982; Pruchno & Resch, 1984).

On the other hand, men were expected to direct their energy into careers. Investing long hours in their work was seen as a way for them to get ahead and become better providers. As priorities were established, career came first, children came second, and the spouse sometimes competed with friends and personal time (Pruchno & Resch, 1984).

A number of factors now make the earlier pattern of female caregiving impractical for families. First, women can no longer provide full-time nurturing to their families. Time demands have changed as more women are employed outside the home. More than half of all women ages 45 to 64 are working full-time. With most women still responsible for household management and meal preparation, the demands for their time provide a setup for elder caregiving to be unfairly burdensome (Lang & Brody, 1983; Baruch & Barnett, 1983).

Second, the skills required to care for a frail adult are different from the skills necessary to care for a small child. Some theorists believe that the skills needed are management and instrumental skills, such as scheduling, organizing resources, and overseeing tasks. Therefore, what is needed for the caregiving of elders goes beyond nurturing and expression.

Finally, some theorists believe that learned gender roles are not stagnant throughout the life cycle, but are cyclically complementary. Gutman (1987) postulates that as men and women reach mid- and later life, the shadow or unexpressed side of their being longs for expression. As they age, women become more attracted to developing instrumental and assertive skills. Men are more interested in expanding their expressive and nurturant capacities. Thus, these life-cycle changes can provide an opportunity to broaden traditional patterns of caregiving, since the caregiving of elders is dominated by women.

Some research shows 72 percent of all caregivers are women (Stone, Cafferata & Sangi, 1987). Women often feel a sense of duty and obligation in caring for loved ones. Caregiving is often an incremental process with wives, daughters, and daughters-in-law' gradually stepping in to help. Before long, they are providing day-to-day care. Often the process and ownership are never discussed by the family. Family members may assume that the women in the family will assume caregiver roles without giving thought to a different possibility. The women of the family, having internalized caregiver roles with their gender, feel guilty in challenging male family members to assume custodial and nurturing functions (Aronson, 1992).

> Mrs. Phillips is an 86-year-old woman who has been widowed for the past 10 years. She has been living alone in her own apartment since the death of her husband. She has two children, Mark, 54 years old, and Joan, 52 years old. Joan sought therapy when her mother began showing serious signs of dementia. The therapist recommended a joint session with the mother and her son and daughter. In the first session, the effect of unfinished business from childhood was revealed. Joan expressed anger at her brother for being the "favorite child" and for expecting her to assume responsibility for their mother's care. Her anger increased as her mother gave reasons and excuses as to why Mark was never involved. Mark did not disagree with his sister's interpretation. In fact, he said, "My sister should take care of my mother, she knows more about what Mom needs." In exploring this attitude with Mark, it became evident that he wanted nothing to do with his mother's care, except to help out with finances. He was given power of attorney for his mother upon his father's death. This infuriated Joan. "I know all the responsibility of care will fall on me, and then I will be in the position of begging for my money from my brother."
>
> This is the case Joan stated: "I need to place my mother in a personal care home and my brother is saying that Mom doesn't need that kind of care. He says that kind of care is too expensive. I know that Mom has money to cover her care for quite some time. I think he just wants to inherit her money. The more that is left, the more he will inherit." Mark clarified his intention. He explained

that he just wanted his mother to live out as much of her life in her own home as possible. When the therapist asked him how he intended to arrange care for his mother in her apartment, he said he did not know and did not have time to find someone to supervise her. He mentioned that he was a pharmacist and worked odd hours, whereas his sister did not work at all. "So why can't she be responsible for her?" he asked.

This case illustrates well gender expectations in caregiving, where women may be expected to assume significant responsibility without corresponding power. The therapist in this case mobilized the children in two ways. First, she recognized the importance of having the mother tested neuropsychologically, since the testing would help define her physical and psychological strengths and weaknesses. Second, the therapist addressed the unfinished business between the children. She helped them see that although their unfinished business was real and uncomfortable, it stood in the way of their mother's receiving the care that she needed. The therapist asked if they could attempt to lay aside their conflicts until they addressed all of the caregiving choices. Both siblings agreed. Upon reaching agreement, the therapist gave both siblings a homework assignment to find out what resources were available to their mother for care at home and out of the home. The therapist directed each on the quest.

The siblings and therapist met again after the homework was completed. Resources were examined for advantages and disadvantages and for the effort required in carrying out the plan. There was arguing and disagreement, but the therapist helped them overcome these obstacles. Eventually, both agreed to place their mother in a personal care home that provided independence while being accessible to both children and which was moderately priced. The entire process lasted six sessions. The therapist followed up with the family a month later. Mrs. Phillips was doing well in the personal care home and her children were satisfied with their decision. When asked if they would like to work on their unfinished business, Mark declined. Joan chose to see the therapist individually to work through some of her feelings around her brother and her mother.

Without therapeutic intervention, the daughter would likely have done all the caregiving and (more likely than not) have been very angry with her mother and brother. Although the siblings were unable to work through their unfinished business, they were able to cooperate to provide the *care*. Acknowledging the unfinished business prevented a roadblock, even though the issues remained unresolved.

In addition to the duty and obligation that women often feel regarding caregiving, they also personally help the older adult with activities of daily living and personal hygiene. These activities may include grocery shopping, meal preparation, bathing, grooming, toileting, and house cleaning. Because of gender-role socialization, many women feel that they should provide these tasks themselves rather than rely on paid or volunteer help from community agencies. These are the tasks that a "good woman" provides without complaint (Aronson, 1992). They can be quite tiring for an adult daughter, especially when she has conflicting demands on her time from work, partner, children, or friends.

Adult daughters also face a continual struggle around changes in roles as their parent becomes more frail. Daughters find it difficult to make decisions for a parent. The roles of mother and daughter change rather than reverse in later life. A parent always remains a parent, even when he or she becomes more dependent. It is this change of role that may evoke emotion and stress for the adult child.

As the role of the daughter changes, many women also shift more time and attention toward their loved one, particularly if the patient is their mother. In a study of caretaking patterns, Aronson found that the daughters included their mothers in their thoughts of everyday activities and future plans. They also spent a lot of energy anticipating what caregiving assistance their mothers might need next, so as to minimize their mothers' awareness of being dependent (Aronson, 1992).

> Susan is a 42-year-old married woman with two young children. She is an only child. She works as a lawyer in a midsize law firm. Greta is 78 years old and has been widowed for one year. She has been showing signs of dementia for the past three years and has been alcoholic for most of her adult life, although "dry" since her husband's death. Susan moved her mother to a retirement community about six months after her father died, because her mother was not taking care of herself. She states that there is not a day that goes by when she is not worried about how her mother is doing. She visits her at least four times a week and is the only one her mother will let take care of her. She does all of her mother's laundry and grocery shopping. Greta eats one meal a day in the retirement community, where she is beginning to make friends. Susan feels "tugged" in many different directions and is very angry at her mother for having been a drunk most of her adult life. Susan always had to be "the responsible one," even as a child, and now that her dad is gone she feels stuck "picking up the pieces." Susan reports being depressed and having very little patience when dealing with her own children. Her children have been misbehaving more recently, which has put stress on her marriage. Stress has affected

her physically manifesting in high blood pressure and gastrointestinal problems.

In working with this daughter, the therapist quickly found that Susan always felt responsible for Greta's happiness. Since Susan was adopted, she thinks she should be available for Greta, regardless of personal sacrifice. Several sessions were spent using a genogram to help Susan develop a different perspective on her relationship with her mother. Susan explored the responsibilities she felt as a daughter and examined where she might let go, ask others for help, and set priorities for the energy that she was willing to expend. Susan's husband was included so that his help could be secured. Finally, several sessions were held with Susan and Greta to begin to air their unfinished business.

Even with her dementia, Greta was able to express herself well. She was afraid of being abandoned, as she had been when she was three years old when her mother died and she was placed in an orphanage. Now that her husband was deceased, she was afraid of being left alone with no one to care for her. She admitted to having high and often unrealistic expectations of her daughter. As the emotional honesty in the session rose, Greta told her daughter for the first time how much she loved her and what she really meant to her. Susan accepted her mother's honesty and was able to express some of her anger and disappointment. She did this in a very caring and loving way. As the sessions progressed, a door was opened for healing in their relationship. In addition, Susan was able to set boundaries with her mother around the physical care that she was willing to provide. As this happened, she found that she worried less about her mother and was able to accept help from others, especially her husband.

Women also extend the quality of life for spouses by providing care for them in later life. The majority of elderly men can look to their spouses to tend to their needs, and to provide consistent and dependable care. Elders being cared for by their spouses have significantly less chance of being removed from their homes and placed in an institutional setting, regardless of their level of disability, than are elders whose spouses are not the primary caretakers (Barusch & Spaid, 1989; Cantor & Little, 1985; George & Gwyther, 1986; Horowitz, 1985; Poulshock & Demling, 1984).

MALE CAREGIVING PATTERNS

Although the majority of elderly women do not have access to spousal caretaking by their male partners, men do participate in this activity. In a survey of 2.2 million caregivers of noninstitutionalized elderly, husbands accounted for 32 percent of the care given by spouses. Unfortunately, this level of male involvement does not generalize to brothers, sons, or other male relatives (Stone, 1987).

When husbands provide care, their experience is different from that reported by women. Male caregivers are usually older than their female counterparts. But despite their age, the demands of the caregiving role appear to be more in harmony with the needs of men. Male caregivers are in better health, and report less dissatisfaction with their role. Husbands also are more invested in their marital relationship than are their female caregiving peers, and are more likely to report that the care that they were giving was *due* their spouse for all the care she had given throughout her life (Chang & White-Means, 1991; Fitting & Rabins, 1985; Miller, 1987; Pruchno & Resch, 1984; Zarit & Zarit, 1982).

> Harry is an 83-year-old man who had been married to his wife, Sara, for 50 years. Sara had Parkinson's and Alzheimer's diseases. They first met when he was in the hospital and she was his nurse. He was quick to comment, "Sara took care of me from the very beginning. I felt it was my responsibility to take care of her now." He added, with tears in his eyes, "I was so busy with my work that I felt bad that I did not spend more time with her. I have to make it up to her." Harry cared for Sara in their home as long as he physically could. He had a heart condition. As she became worse, he was afraid that if something happened to him, she would be stranded. With much trepidation, he decided to place her in a nursing home. He went to the nursing home every day to feed her and visit. He loved taking care of her. She became wheelchair bound and did not know when he was there. However, he said that, in his heart, he felt that she knew of his presence. When she finally died, he was sad, but said, "I know that I did everything I could to make her last years comfortable. I still feel some guilt about not being there when we were younger, but I must admit I felt closer to her than ever when I was taking care of her. It felt real good."

Husbands like Harry who care for their wives are more likely to have help with caregiving duties. Their wives tend to continue with housework and cooking while frail. When she is no longer capable of doing these tasks, her husband seeks help from others rather than increasing his burden and stress. Male spousal caregivers are more likely to allow outside assistance with meals, cleaning, and personal care than are female caregivers. Men may engage help more readily because they are traditionally used to paying for help when they need it. Since it is not *expected* of men to care for their wives when they become frail, families and friends are more willing to help out (Pruchno & Resch, 1984; Snyder & Keife, 1985; Westbrook & Viney, 1985).

CAREGIVER WELL-BEING

The experience of caregiving for women is more negative than for men. Women experience more stress exhibited as depression, and they report higher levels of burden (Barusch & Spaid, 1989; Cantor, 1983; Cicirelli, 1981; Fitting, Rabins, Lucas, & Eastham, 1986; Horowitz, 1985; Johnson, 1983; Noelker & Poulshock, 1982; Pruchno & Resch, 1984; Robinson & Thurnher, 1979; Zarit & Zarit, 1982). Many have questioned the reason for this difference. One theory is that since women have been in the position of caregiving for their entire lives, they experience burnout in later life when caregiving demands are increased in meeting the physical, emotional, and spiritual needs of a frail elder. Men, on the other hand, have not been expected to assume the nurturing role in their relationships, whether as father, husband, or son. Men in spousal caretaking positions, however, seem to thrive in the role (Barusch & Spaid, 1989). Another explanation might be that men have been conditioned to be stoic and not to complain, and, thus, such gender-role conditioning may skew their responses (Vinick, 1982).

There are a number of reasons why caregiving may be a perfect fit for men in the life-cycle stage of postretirement. Upon retiring, many men feel a lack of usefulness, which is detrimental to their sense of a competent self. Caregiving provides a means for them to demonstrate their competence through tasks that are life-enhancing for their partner. Since women are less likely to rely solely on their primary caregivers for support, actively maintaining their social networks despite their illness, the emotional demands that they place on their spouse may be manageable (Westbrook & Viney, 1985).

CONCLUSION

While the number of male spousal caregivers is growing, this same trend is not evident in male adult children caregivers. If it is important for both men and women to be nurturing caregivers, more education and instruction must be provided to men in the skills necessary to care for their relatives. The assumption that women are best suited to care for the frail elderly negatively affects men and places an unjust burden on women. Finley (1989) suggests that as long as society does not expect emotional input from males, they will remain distant and less involved in the caregiving experience. Little behavioral change will occur in caregiving by sons until society changes its view of how men should contribute to caregiving. However, as family constellations and work demographics change, more men will either be asked or be expected to become so involved. It is important for family therapists to take a closer look at preparing and supporting men in this role while helping women to transfer the caregiving tasks that sap their energy and spirit.

REFERENCES

Aronson, J. (1992). Women's sense of responsibility for the care of old people: But who else is going to do it? *Gender and Society, 6,* 8-29.

Baruch G., & Barnett, R. C. (1983). Adult daughters' relationships with their mothers. *Journal of Marriage and the Family,* August, 601-606.

Barusch, A., & Spaid, W. (1989). Gender differences in caregiving: Why do wives report greater burden? *The Gerontologist, 29,* 667-676.

Cantor, M. H. (1983). Strain among caregivers: A study of experience in the United States. *The Gerontologist, 23,* 597-608.

Cantor, M., & Little, V. (1985). Aging and social care. In R. Binstock (Ed.), *Handbook of aging and the social sciences.* New York: Van Nostrand Reinhold.

Chang, C. F., & White-Means, S. (1991). The men who care: An analysis of male primary caregivers who care for frail elderly at home. *The Journal of Applied Gerontology, 10*(3), 343-358.

Chodorow, N. (1978). *The reproduction of mothering.* Berkeley: University of California Press.

Cicirelli, V. (1981). *Helping elderly parents: The role of adult children.* Boston: Auburn House.

Finley, N. J. (1989). Theories of family labor as applied to gender differences in caregiving for elderly parents. *Journal of Marriage and the Family, 51,* 79-86.

Fitting M., & Rabins, P. (1985). Men and women: Do they give care differently? *Generations,* Fall, 23-26.

Fitting, M., Rabins, P., Lucas, M. J., & Eastham, J. (1986). Caregivers for dementia patients: A comparison of husbands and wives. *The Gerontologist, 26,* 248-252.

George, L., & Gwyther, L. (1986). Caregiver well-being: A multidimensional examination of family caregivers of demented adults. *The Gerontologist, 26,* 253-259.

Gilligan, C. (1982). *In a different voice: Psychological theory and women's development.* Cambridge, MA: Harvard University Press.

Gutman, D. L. (1987). *Reclaimed powers: Towards a new psychology of men and women in later life.* New York: Basic Books.

Horowitz, A. (1985). Family caregiving to the frail elderly. In C. Eisdorfer, *Annual review of gerontology and geriatrics, Vol. 5.* New York: Springer.

Johnson, C. L. (1983). Dyadic family relations and social support. *The Gerontologist, 23,* 377-383.

Lang, A. M., & Brody, E. M. (1983). Characteristics of middle-aged daughters and help to their elderly mothers. *Journal of Marriage and the Family, 45,* 193–202.

Miller, B. (1987). Gender and control among spouses of the cognitively impaired: A research note. *The Gerontologist, 27,* 447–453.

Noelker, L. S., & Poulshock, S. W. (1982). *The effects on families of caring for impaired elderly in residence.* Washington, DC: Administration on Aging.

Poulshock, S. W., & Demling, G. T. (1984). Families caring for elders in residence: Issues in the measurement of burden. *Journal of Gerontology, 39,* 230–239.

Pruchno, R., & Resch, N. (1984). Husbands and wives as caregivers and antecedents of depression and burden. *The Gerontologist, 29,* 159–165.

Robinson, B., & Thurnher, M. (1979). Taking care of aged parents: A family life cycle transition. *The Gerontologist, 19,* 586–593.

Snyder, B., & Keife, K. (1985). The unmet needs of family caregivers for frail and disabled adults. *Social Work in Health Care, 10,* 1–4.

Stone, R., Cafferata, G. L., & Sangi, J. (1987). Caregivers of the frail elderly: A national profile. *The Gerontologist, 27,* 616–626.

Vinick, B. (1982). *Elderly men as caregivers of wives.* Paper presented at the 35th Annual Scientific Meeting of the Gerontological Society of America, Boston.

Westbrook, M. T., & Viney, L. (1985). Age and sex differences in patients' reactions to illness. *Journal of Health and Social Behavior, 24,* 313–324.

Zarit, S. H., & Zarit, J. (1982). Families under stress: Interventions for caregivers of senile dementia patients. *Psychotherapy: Theory, Research and Practice, 19,* 461–471.

❧ 10 ✦

Alzheimer's Disease and the Family: Working with New Realities

Janie Long, Ph.D. *
University of Georgia
Athens, Georgia

Studies suggest that nearly four million people in the United States have Alzheimer's disease or other forms of dementia (Cohen & Eisdorfer, 1986). Among persons 85 years and older, now the fastest growing age bracket in the U.S. population (Siegel & Taeuber, 1986), 10 percent to 20 percent are believed to have senile dementia of the Alzheimer's type (SDAT) (Niederehe & Fruge, 1984). The National Institute on Aging projects that unless a preventative discovery is made or a cure is found, an estimated 12 to 14 million Americans will be affected by the year 2040 (Alzheimer's Association, 1989).

It is important to consider individuals who have SDAT in the context of their families. Alzheimer's is certainly a joint experience, as the entire family system is perturbed by its reality. Visions of a happy retirement may be erased, and family members are often called on to perform new tasks and to

---

*This chapter is written in memory of my father, Harold Benjamin Long, who taught me about his own reality of Alzheimer's disease.

take on new responsibilities (Famighetti, 1986). Because relationships of family members are usually based on family roles that have been maintained over many years, changes in these roles can lead to conflict and stress for all concerned (Long & Mancini, 1990).

Family therapists and other helpers who intend to provide a formal support system for families in the midst of shifting roles are moving into uncharted territory. The helping professions are being called on to help families confront situations and circumstances for which there are no role models (Long & Mancini, 1990). Despite the efforts of gerontologists, geriatricians, and organizations such as the Alzheimer's Association to educate the public, many care providers are uninformed and untrained to work with these families.

PHYSICAL CHANGES IN THE BRAIN

The cause of Alzheimer's disease and the dementing process it activates is as yet unknown. For this reason, there is currently no cure, no aids for prevention, and no easily accessible treatment other than the use of medications to help in controlling symptoms (Hutton & Kenny, 1985). Some of the changes to the brain found with Alzheimer's disease are also changes that are common with aging. One of the most conspicuous alterations, which comes both with aging and with dementia, is the loss of neurons from the nervous system. The brain consists of at least 10 billion nerve cells, with 10 times as many "supporting" cells. The nerve cells are interconnected. The loss of neurons or the death of nerve cells occurs in several locations in the brain of persons with SDAT, but is usually more prominent in the cerebral cortex (outer layers of nerve cells that cover the brain), the hippocampus (a large curved accumulation of nerve cells near the underside of the brain), and the nucleus basalis of Meynert (part of a circuit of nerves that communicate with one another and are involved with the physiological processes that perform memory and other complex brain functions) (Cook-Deegan, 1988).

The two major microscopic changes associated with Alzheimer's are neurofibrillary tangles in the nerve cells and the presence of neuritic (senile) plaques. The disease manifests "a typical pattern of neuron degeneration which is masked microscopically by the presence of neurofibrillary tangles (abnormal nerve cell bodies with accumulations of the paired helical filaments, that is, filaments twisted around each other in a helical fashion) and neuritic plaques (focal accumulations of degenerating nerve terminals surrounding a core of amyloid protein)" (Katzman, 1987, p. 71). Even though

Alzheimer's Disease and the Family

these changes are not uniform to any particular area of the brain, the hippocampus and frontal cortex are usually more severely affected.

The presence of neuritic plaques and neurofibrillary tangles does not, however, constitute sufficient evidence for a diagnosis of Alzheimer's. Neurons with fibrillary changes and plaques are also common in normal persons 65 years of age and older. The difference between the normal aged brain and the brain affected by SDAT appears to be based on the number of plaques and diseased neurons present. Because it is not yet clear how many plaques and tangles are too many to be labeled normal aging of the brain, neuropathologists usually do not diagnose Alzheimer's on this basis alone.

DIAGNOSIS

Alzheimer's disease has unfortunately become a catchall description for dementia in the elderly for the general public. The clinical indications of SDAT are also found in several other conditions, including depressive pseudodementia, multi-infarct dementia, brain tumors and subdural hematomas, Parkinson's disease, syphilis, viral encephalitis, and nutritional deficiency. Thus, it is crucial that clinicians explore all possibilities when formulating a diagnosis. Currently, it is impossible to verify the diagnosis of Alzheimer's before postmortem examination of brain tissue (Lyman, 1989). Therefore, clinicians use a multilevel assessment approach in order to rule out all other known possibilities for the changes in affect, behavior, and cognitive abilities that indicate the possibility of SDAT.

The clinician can initiate the diagnosis process by utilizing the criteria* of the *Diagnostic and Statistical Manual of Mental Disorders, Fourth Edition (DSM-IV)*, pp. 142–143 for dementia of the Alzheimer's type, including:

A. The development of multiple cognitive deficits manifested by both

   (1) memory impairment (impaired ability to learn new information or to recall previously learned information)
   (2) one (or more) of the following cognitive disturbances:
      (a) aphasia (language disturbance)
      (b) apraxia (impaired ability to carry out motor activities despite intact motor function)
      (c) agnosia (failure to recognize or identify objects despite intact sensory function)

---

*Reprinted with permission from the *Diagnostic and Statistical Manual of Mental Disorders, Fourth Edition*. Copyright 1994, American Psychiatric Association.

(d) disturbance in executive functioning (i.e., planning, organizing, sequencing, abstracting)
B. The cognitive deficits in Criteria A1 and A2 each causes significant impairment in social or occupational functioning and represents a significant decline from a previous level of functioning.
C. The course is characterized by gradual onset and continuing cognitive decline.
D. The cognitive deficits in Criteria A1 and A2 are not due to any of the following:
(1) other central nervous system conditions that cause progressive deficits in memory and cognition (e.g., cerebrovascular disease, Parkinson's disease, Huntington's disease, subdural hematoma, normal-pressure hydrocephalus, brain tumor)
(2) systemic conditions that are known to cause dementia (e.g., hypothyroidism, vitamin B_{12} or folic acid deficiency, niacin deficiency, hypercalcemia, neurosyphilis, HIV infection)
(3) substance-induced conditions
E. The deficits do not occur exclusively during the course of a delirium.
F. The disturbance is not better accounted for by another Axis I disorder (e.g., Major Depressive Disorder, Schizophrenia).

In the early stages, the symptoms of Alzheimer's are difficult to distinguish from those of normal aging (Khachaturian, 1985). Taking a history from a member of the person's family may be crucial in uncovering early signs of Alzheimer's in the affected individual, whose own account may be unreliable due to the propensity to deny the existence of Alzheimer's. As previously noted, there are many types of dementia with varying consequences, and for this reason a thorough examination should be carried out to differentiate the type of dementia present. Cohen and Eisdorfer (1986) suggest that the following examinations and tests should be performed: a complete physical exam, including urine and blood analysis; x-rays; an electrocardiograph (ECG), personal and family medical histories; an accurate history of recent medications and alcohol use; a neurological exam; a comprehensive psychiatric exam; psychological testing; an electroencephalogram (EEG), a computed tomography (CT) scan; and, when possible, a positron emission tomography (PET) scan or magnetic resonance imaging (MRI). If clinicians base their diagnosis on the results of only a few of these areas, they risk overlooking a significant indicator of the problem and making a diagnostic error.

COMMON CHANGES IN THE PERSON WITH ALZHEIMER'S DISEASE

Global Description

Alzheimer's disease is generally insidious in onset with progressive deterioration. The course of SDAT is characterized by the incremental loss of cognitive and functional capacities with the additional complication of neuropsychiatric problems (Freels et al., 1992). The clinician must keep in mind that the course of the illness in any individual may be quite variable. Persons with SDAT face many transitions. Not only is their comfortable way of life often thrown into pandemonium, but they also eventually perceive life differently because of the physical changes going on within the brain. Behaviors that would normally be labeled as "inappropriate" can be seen as the consequence of neurological disease and not simply as willful, rude, or childish behavior (Ronch, 1989). Following are some of the components that bring about and make up this altered reality.

Behavioral Changes

When Chenowith and Spencer (1986) asked families, "What was the main symptom that first caused you, your relative with Alzheimer's, or someone else to look for help?," *memory-related problems* were mentioned most often. In SDAT, memory for more recent life experiences may be more impaired than memories of the distant past, especially in the early and middle stages of the progression of the disease. Learning new information, therefore, will be difficult and at times impossible. The person with SDAT tends to forget things quickly. "For the person with a memory impairment, life may be like constantly coming into the middle of a movie: one has no idea what happened just before what is happening now" (Mace & Rabins, 1981, p. 35). Often the person with SDAT will conceal memory loss in the early stages and thus delay the diagnosis. Some persons seek to conceal their memory loss by keeping lists; to cover their forgetfulness, others respond by using such comments as, "Of course I know that."

The person with SDAT experiences two types of *problems with communication:* problems in expressing themselves to others and problems in understanding what is being said to them (Cohen & Eisdorfer, 1986). Some persons with SDAT only have occasional difficulty in finding the "right" words, whereas others may speak quite fluently but one is unable to make sense of what they are saying. One should not, however, assume that the person is simply "babbling." Such communication may be clear in their reality. Speech impairments such as dysarthria (speech that is slow and slurred) are common in persons with SDAT.

Some persons with SDAT exhibit *wandering behavior*. Once they have wandered off, they may panic when they realize that they do not recognize their surroundings. Mace and Rabins (1981) suggest that there are different reasons for SDAT-related wandering behavior: sometimes it is the result of getting lost or moving into an unfamiliar environment; other times it appears to be aimless. When the behavior is questioned, however, persons with SDAT may reveal, for instance, that they are trying to find their way home even though they may actually be at home. Teri, Borson, Kiyak, and Yamagishi (1989) report that only 5 percent of a sample that was mildly to moderately impaired reported wandering behavior. Even though not as prevalent as other behavioral disturbances, this particular behavior is especially anxiety producing in caregivers, who fear that they will be unable to find the person.

Confusion and disorientation are also common in persons with SDAT. Some persons become afraid of leaving their homes, worried that they will become lost. A memory-impaired person will have difficulty in finding his or her way around a new setting, so many choose to isolate themselves in a reality that is more comfortable for them. This isolation is often difficult for family members to accept. They may still want the individual to participate in all former activities. Due to the loss of memory, many persons with SDAT are prone to losing things. They cannot recall where they last placed the object and their short-term memory loss prohibits the retrieval of such information. For instance, persons with SDAT who wear dentures may repeatedly forget where they left them.

Perseveration or the tendency to repeat certain actions may develop, particularly in the moderately impaired (Volicer, Fabiszewski, Rheaume, & Lasch, 1988). For instance, the person may repeatedly stand up, pace around the room, and sit back down. This action will be repeated over and over again. This type of activity is also more unnerving for family members than for the person with SDAT, who is unaware of the repetition or is unaffected by it.

Persons with Alzheimer's may *exhibit behaviors that are considered inappropriate,* such as exposing their genitals in public. Some persons will undress completely and wander into public places oblivious to their behavior. Urination in public places may also occur. Some persons with SDAT will make frequent demands for sexual intercourse or will propose sexual intercourse in the company of visitors. These behaviors would be considered highly unlikely for these persons under normal circumstances, and they may feel very ashamed later if they become conscious of their actions.

The person with SDAT will often complain even when the family is doing all that it can to help. Persons may become more *critical* and *demanding* as the disease progresses. The person may lose the ability to behave in a tactful manner. Because brain-impaired persons cannot accurately filter all of the activity around them, they may not be able to understand or accept all of the family's behaviors but may perceive them as being harmful or cruel.

Changes in Mood

Wragg and Jeste (1989), in a review of 30 studies on Alzheimer's disease, report that *depressed mood* occurs in 40 percent to 50 percent of those persons with SDAT and that an additional 10 percent to 20 percent exhibit the symptoms of actual major depressive disorders. Persons with SDAT will generally exhibit depressive symptoms in the early stages of the disease when they are trying to come to terms with the many changes that evolve as a result of the degenerative process (Reifler, Larson, & Hanley, 1982). The person with Alzheimer's is dealing with multiple losses, which may include loss of a job, loss of the ability to be independently mobile, loss of control of personal finances, possible loss of the home, loss of control of bodily functions, and literally loss of self.

Symptoms of depression that have been identified in persons with SDAT include loss of interest or pleasure in usual activities, feeling overly tired, feeling worthless, irritability for at least two weeks, sad mood for at least two weeks, lack of energy, disturbances in sleep, and thoughts of death (Mackenzie, Robiner, & Knopman, 1989). Depression that is left untreated can increase the functional limitations of the brain-impaired person (Pearson, Teri, Reifler, & Raskind, 1989). Several approaches to treatment of the depression have been suggested, including cognitive interventions, behavioral interventions, and the use of antidepressants (Teri & Gallagher-Thompson, 1991; Thompson, Davies, Gallagher, & Krantz, 1986). Care should be taken when using any form of medication with an older adult. The body of the elderly person is less efficient in metabolizing drugs. This phenomenon is increased with the presence of Alzheimer's or other illnesses. Most psychotropic drugs are drawn to the fatty tissues in the body and are absorbed by them, leaving less of the drug to circulate to the brain. Cohen and Eisdorfer (1986) report that the brain of the person with SDAT is more sensitive to medication than the brain of the average older adult so that the person with SDAT may need lower doses of a drug than would normally be prescribed.

Persons with Alzheimer's sometimes become *apathetic*. They want to isolate and not engage in any form of activity. Sometimes the person uses this response as a coping mechanism to cover his or her inability to perform certain tasks. Persons with SDAT may also fear getting lost or confused. Mace and Rabins (1981) suggest that it is important to keep such persons as active and involved as possible in order to help maintain their spirits and to help ward off other potential illnesses. Encouraging participation in activities in which they can succeed and feel useful will increase their desire to participate.

Persons with Alzheimer's may become *agitated* as a result of attempts to get them more involved or to draw them out. The person may begin to pace, fidget, strike the arm of a chair, turn up the television volume, or cry. Attempts to calm persons exhibiting these behaviors or to get them to explain why they are agitated may increase their anxiety. Agitation may also be the result of boredom, a reaction to medication, a response to tension present in the family, or a reaction to whatever is happening in the brain (Mace & Rabins, 1981). The best response is to remain calm and to try to reduce the level of activity going on around the person.

A *catastrophic reaction* is a sudden outburst of physical or verbal aggression that under normal circumstances would be considered an overreaction (Volicer et al., 1988). Catastrophic reactions usually occur when the brain-impaired person is attempting to perform a task that involves several thought processes at the same time. It is important to remember that the brain-impaired person can be easily overwhelmed by situations that most people consider routine. For instance, taking a bath may be a major undertaking because it requires the ability to coordinate several tasks at the same time—finding the bathroom, turning on faucets, unbuttoning and/or unzipping clothing, finding a towel, getting into the tub, etc.

Persons who are forgetful also can become *suspicious* of others. They may become convinced that others are stealing their money or hiding things from them. For example, a family member recently complained that the toilet tissue started to disappear after her mother, who had Alzheimer's disease, moved into her home. Each time she bought new toilet tissue and put it in the cabinet at home, it would disappear within two days. She quickly learned to look in her mother's dresser drawer where she would find the tissue hidden beneath the clothing. When she questioned her mother about the toilet tissue, her mother reported that someone had been hiding it from her so she decided to put it in her room where it would be safe (author's personal files).

Persons with Alzheimer's have been known to experience *hallucinations*. They may believe that they see, hear, feel, or smell things that are not there.

The person may become scared, angry, or even joyful upon experiencing the hallucination (Mace & Rabins, 1981). Family members often become frightened when these episodes take place and may fear that others will see the behavior as "crazy" rather than understand that the hallucinations are a result of the atrophy process in the brain. Persons with SDAT who are hallucinating may also need to have their medication levels checked due to the possibility of toxicity. Physicians, in an attempt to keep the person's behaviors manageable, may prescribe dosages that are too high or may prescribe medications that should not be taken simultaneously.

Physical Changes

Loss of coordination often severely limits the person's ability to maneuver and remain independently mobile. It is also common for the person with Alzheimer's to develop *myoclonus*, or rapid jerking movements of individual body parts. Some persons with SDAT begin to develop a *stooped posture* or to *shuffle* when they walk. All of these conditions increase the likelihood that the person will fall. Persons with Alzheimer's may not be aware of feelings of pain and may even suffer a broken bone without realizing what has happened. It is important to check the person frequently to ensure that he or she is not bruised, cut, or blistered (Mace & Rabins, 1981).

Incontinence of urine or of feces in persons with Alzheimer's is often reported by caregivers. Mace and Rabins (1981) offer several reasons why this condition might develop, including bladder infections, a fecal impaction, medications, problems with mobility, and weakening muscles. Caregivers should carefully examine the circumstances around the incontinence to be sure that treatable aspects have been addressed.

Certain conditions are not the direct result of Alzheimer's but may cause further difficulties in the ability of the person with SDAT to communicate with others. Problems with hearing often develop in the aged. Because the person with SDAT is already brain impaired, it is important to make sure that the person does not suffer from loss of hearing. Hearing aids or surgery may be required. Problems with vision also often increase with age. The person with SDAT should be checked periodically for changes in vision or the development of cataracts. It is important that persons who are experiencing difficulty in maintaining their balance have clear vision. Cohen and Eisdorfer (1986) also note that blurred vision can be a side effect of the four major classes of psychotropic medications—antipsychotics, antidepressants, antianxiety drugs, and hypnotics—all of which are often used with persons with SDAT. Dental problems may also be ignored or unrecognized by persons with Alzheimer's. They become less concerned with personal hygiene as the disease progresses and neglect the teeth and dentures. They may also be unaware of ill-fitting dentures or of pain related to problems with the teeth, tongue, or gums. In the areas of hearing, vision, and oral hygiene, the person should be monitored on a regular basis in order to ensure good health and adequate ability to communicate.

Psychological Changes

Very little research has been conducted to learn the perceptions of persons with Alzheimer's regarding how the disease process and the accompanying losses affects them (Long, 1993). Most of the research has focused on the caregiver, and the research that is available on persons with SDAT focuses on cognitive abilities and behavioral management (Cotrell & Lein, 1993). Cotrell and Schulz (1993) point out that the person with SDAT is often treated as an object rather than as a significant and valued contributor to knowledge about the illness and its course. Lyman (1989) has suggested that this restricted approach to studying Alzheimer's has resulted in a more biomedically oriented understanding of the disease, thus placing the person with SDAT in the role of victim of the disease process. Several studies suggest, however, that individuals' coping styles prior to the onset of Alzheimer's may have a lot to do with their adaptation to the disease (Shoemaker, 1987; Snyder, Rupprecht, Pyrek, Brekhus, & Moss, 1978). "The inherent message is that individuals with dementia are important actors responding and adapting to the disease, rather than passive individuals who are succumbing to its deficits" (Cotrell & Schulz, 1993, p. 206).

Cohen, Kennedy, and Eisdorfer (1984) outline six psychological reactions or stages that the person with SDAT may experience during the progression of the disease: prediagnosis, during diagnosis, postdiagnosis, coping, maturation, and separation from self. Not all people will experience all of the stages, and the stages may not appear in the same order for all people. The delineation of these stages was developed following clinical interviews with several hundred people.

During the *prediagnosis stage,* the person recognizes that something is wrong and becomes concerned about mild cognitive deficits, such as difficulty with telling time, difficulty with remembering names, and getting lost on trips. During this phase, the person must be assisted in finding professional help and in making sense of the cognitive changes.

Once the *diagnosis* has been made, those with SDAT may feel a sense of relief or may deny the presence of the disease. Family members and professionals are encouraged to be honest with the person and to give him or her as much information as possible about the progress of the disease. The earlier in the progression of the disease patients are told, the more easily their intact cognitive abilities can be utilized to accept the reality of the condition and the more they can be involved in planning for the future and in saying goodbye to loved ones (Ronch, 1989).

Individuals' response to the diagnosis stage will be influenced by their personality type, prior coping skills, amount of cognitive impairment, amount and effectiveness of their social support system, and the competency of the professionals with whom they are working. It is important that the family offer reassurance to the person with SDAT that they will work together in facing the difficulties that lie ahead.

Postdiagnosis encompasses the period in which the person with SDAT and the family begin to come to terms with the reality of the disease. The person with the disease and family members will experience a broad range of emotions, including anger, guilt, sadness, shock, and confusion. This stage is also the appropriate time to begin discussing concerns about finances, death and dying, institutionalization, and others. Cohen and associates (1984) emphasize the importance of the involvement of the person with SDAT in decision-making processes as much as possible. Family therapy can be particularly helpful during this phase (Long, 1993).

The fourth phase is the *coping* phase. "Living with an irreversible dementia requires a major effort to face each day and maintain an activity level that provides satisfaction, pleasure, and meaning, minimizes stress, and optimizes function" (Cohen, Kennedy, & Eisdorfer, 1984, p. 13). As in the previous phase, it is important that the person with SDAT have as much input as possible in the development of coping strategies. Including the person in the process fosters a better sense of self-control and promotes self-esteem (Cohen, 1991).

The fifth phase is the *maturation* phase. Those who experience rapid deterioration often will not reach this phase and others may live in this phase for several years. During this phase, the person develops an attitude of living each day as it comes until death. Cohen, Kennedy, and Eisdorfer (1984) point out that the needs of the person during this stage include the following: to feel worthwhile; to maintain mastery of something; to accept the need for others; to have intimacy; to have mobility; and to maintain basic biological functioning. In this phase, the individual develops what Charmaz (1987) has identified as a salvaged self. Such persons attempt to define themselves as positive and worthwhile in spite of their decreased ability to function. Charmaz stresses that it is important not to allow chronically ill persons to become so preoccupied with loss that they lose their ability to integrate the changes and form a new concept of self.

The last phase is known as *separation from self* or *loss of self*. The loss of self is a slow process and one that is faced by many who are chronically ill

(Charmaz, 1983). Persons with Alzheimer's will often experience their former self-image being chipped away as the disease progressively takes away parts of self (Cohen & Eisdorfer, 1986). Assisting the person to successfully navigate the coping and maturation phases will help to minimize feelings of (1) burdening others, (2) leading restricted lives, (3) social isolation, and (4) being discredited (Charmaz, 1983, 1987). Persons who reach this stage are often described as a "different person" by family members (Orona, 1990). Those with SDAT may react to things in the environment but have lost the ability to be an active participant in the environment and are often unable to communicate in an understandable way. We have no way of knowing how a person experiences this stage because of the inability to communicate. Cohen (1991) proposes that the major needs of the individual here are to be as comfortable and secure as possible.

As summarized in this section, the person with SDAT experiences many different changes on many different levels. The changes outlined are presented in order to offer an overview of some of the changing reality faced by those with Alzheimer's. Alzheimer's does not affect any two people in exactly the same way. No one will exhibit all of the changes described, and neither will all persons with SDAT follow the various phases or stages in the exact sequence presented.

PERTURBATIONS WITHIN THE FAMILY SYSTEM

As previously stated, the entire family system is affected by the diagnosis of one of its members with Alzheimer's disease. The implications of the disease process for the family are multiple, often beginning before the diagnosis is made and continuing for years after the death of the loved one. Families will live with the disease process and the often extended loss of a family member in varied ways, depending on such factors as prior relationships of family members; the family's financial status, ethnic or cultural norms, ability to work within the social service system, religious beliefs, and coping strategies; length of the illness; and the accessibility of outside resources.

Much has been written about the influence of Alzheimer's on the family (Blieszner & Shifflett, 1990; Boss, 1993; Cohen & Eisdorfer, 1988; Famighetti, 1986; Henderson & Gutierrez-Mayka, 1992; Rabins, Mace, & Lucas, 1982; Zarit, Orr, & Zarit, 1985). A review of the literature reveals six major challenges faced by the family: communication problems, financial and legal concerns, the question of institutionalization, the issue of power and the renegotiation of roles, dealing with grief, and unresolved family-of-origin issues. The partner must also deal with adjustments in the sexual relationship.

Communication Problems

Communication with a person who is brain impaired can be challenging, especially as the disease progresses into the middle and late stages. Several contributing factors to problems in communication exist. In the prediagnosis stage of Alzheimer's, partners and other family members often report conflictual relationships with the person with SDAT. Family members do not understand the changing personality and behaviors of the person with undiagnosed dementia who has become suspicious, overly critical, or demanding.

The person with Alzheimer's may be experiencing and trying to hide memory problems. Such persons often fabricate stories to cover the fact that they are uncertain about what they have been doing. For example, when asked by her partner where she was during the afternoon, the woman with SDAT may invent an answer to hide the fact that she does not remember. Partners may become suspicious and mistrustful of the person with SDAT. They may suspect that the person with Alzheimer's is having an affair and trying to cover it up (author's personal files).

Another memory-related communication problem is repetition in conversation. A topic may be discussed over and over within a short time span without awareness. This behavior can become unnerving for family members.

Other problems in communication were previously discussed including difficulty in generating words and difficulty in comprehending what is being communicated by others. Family members are encouraged to slow down communication and not give too much information at one time to the person with SDAT. Simplify tasks and directions and watch for signs that the person is unsure about what is being said.

Family members often avoid communication in this situation in order to evade responses involving suspiciousness, criticism, or catastrophic reactions. The person with Alzheimer's may also choose to stop communicating owing to confusion or disorientation. Many persons in the early stages of Alzheimer's know that they have difficulty with communication and feel embarrassed by their inability to carry on conversations as they did in the past. They begin to withdraw from the family and from friends. Family members are encouraged to continue to engage the person in conversation, remembering to keep it simple and direct. Because long-term memory is functional for a longer time than is short-term memory, the person with SDAT is often more comfortable with discussing the past rather than the present.

Financial and Legal Concerns

Families should plan in advance for handling the many financial and legal concerns that can arise when a family member has Alzheimer's. Laws vary from state to state, so all families must become familiar with the laws of their state and seek the advice of legal counsel. The person with SDAT should be included in making legal and financial decisions as much as possible; therefore, addressing these issues early in the progression of the disease is imperative. The wishes of the person with SDAT should be considered if at all feasible. Due to the complicated strategies that are sometimes necessary to protect a family's finances, attorneys and family members may have to struggle with the ethical and moral dilemma of whose rights are being protected (Dubler & Strauss, 1988). Attorneys are often first contacted by a family member on behalf of the person with Alzheimer's. The attorney may ask for clarification concerning the client because of the potential for conflict between the rights of the person with SDAT and the rights of the family. These issues are particularly difficult when there is reason to believe that the person with Alzheimer's is responding with unwarranted suspiciousness or paranoia (Dubler & Strauss, 1988).

The establishment or revision of wills is a significant first step. If the person with SDAT is married, it is important that the spouse understand the ramifications of leaving large assets to the person with SDAT. Substantial monetary inheritance can negate one's eligibility for certain government entitlements that the person with Alzheimer's may need later in the progression of the disease (Gilfix, 1988). Family members should discuss the question of to whom financial assets should be distributed in order to best provide long-term care for the family member with SDAT.

A legal issue that is sometimes difficult for families to negotiate is the decision of who will have the *power of attorney* to manage both the personal and business affairs of the person with SDAT when and if the person becomes incapacitated. Again, this decision is best made early in the progression of the disease while the person still has legal capacity and can provide input into the use of the document. Because of the possibility of suspiciousness on the part of the person with SDAT, this process can be complicated. Families often report that persons with SDAT believe that family members are stealing their money and can become very upset and angry. Individual family members then have to deal with their own anger and frustration. Difficulties can arise in families when an adult child must take over these responsibilities and not everyone agrees as to who the guardian should be. Other related issues include the possibility of establishing a living trust, conservatorship, or guardianship. Families must make decisions regarding bank accounts and should seek legal counsel on the pros and cons involved in joint bank accounts.

Families often feel overwhelmed by the complicated Medicare and Medicaid systems. In most cases, Medicare is not applicable to the person with Alzheimer's because it is set up to be an acute-care system rather than a long-term chronic-care system. Many families encounter difficulties in meeting the qualifications for Medicaid assistance. Those dealing with SDAT are faced with many financial strains, including loss of the salary of the person with SDAT; denial of disability or retirement income due to the person's being fired, being forced to take an early retirement, or quitting a job when unable to perform adequately; loss of the caregiver's salary; the costs of home or respite care; and, for some, the costs of nursing-home care (Mace, 1987).

Families can quickly deplete their financial resources. Under considerable financial strain, they must often rely on the Medicaid program to help cover the costs of care. This assistance is unobtainable unless the person with SDAT has nominal assets or has transferred assets through gift giving at least two years prior to the application for Medicaid (Dubler & Strauss, 1988). Nursing-home care is rarely covered by private insurance policies or Medicare (Long, 1992), so the person with Alzheimer's must rely on the assistance provided by the family and by Medicaid. Because the Medicaid law is a combination of both federal and state statutes and varies from state to state, it can be confusing. In addition, families may be given inaccurate information by nursing home staff (Mace, 1987) and should be encouraged to seek correct information through their local department of social services. Unfortunately, overburdened caregivers do not always have the time to deal with social service agencies and may feel so dehumanized by the experience that they do not pursue these avenues of support.

Institutionalization

Studies suggest that older adults fear the possibility of moving into a nursing home (Long & Mancini, 1989; Stein, Linn, Slater, & Stein, 1984). Orona (1990) reports that 80 percent of those with Alzheimer's disease are cared for in a family setting, and the majority are cared for by female family members (Dillehay & Sandys, 1990). However, placement in a nursing home is an option that many families consider, especially as the disease progresses and the role of caregiver becomes too demanding. The increased likelihood of nursing home placement has been related to such variables as living alone, being poor, being unable to perform activities of daily living, being female, the number of medical conditions, the presence of incontinence, and the amount of caregiver burden or strain (Colerick & George, 1986; Dolinsky & Rosenwaike, 1988; Knopman, Kitto, Deinard, & Heiring, 1988; Pruchno, Michaels, & Potashnik, 1990). Cohen and Eisdorfer (1986) point out several reasons why the decision about nursing home placement is so difficult for families to make:

1. It is a major life change that disrupts the relationships established over many years of being together.
2. Moving into a nursing home is not considered a natural part of the family life cycle.
3. Institutionalization confuses and strains the ties of loyalty, commitment, justice, and kinship among partners, parents, children, and siblings. Family members often feel guilty and view the transition as a tragic event rather than as a natural step in providing help for the person with Alzheimer's. Family therapists can help families negotiate these decisions and come to terms with their feelings.

Power and Role Renegotiation

The issue of power is very important to older adults (Long & Mancini, 1990), who contend with the possible loss of power on many levels, including retirement, a decrease in their financial status, declining physical health, and loss of the caregiver role for their children. In addition, families that deal with Alzheimer's at times feel very powerless over the disease process and its effects on the family (Cohen & Eisdorfer, 1988). These families must often renegotiate roles as the person with Alzheimer's deteriorates. The ability of the person with SDAT to drive and his or her ability to handle finances are often two of the first areas that have to be addressed. Also, activities related to daily living, such as cooking, can be problematic for someone who has memory problems. Role changes can be stressful for family members, who report having to assume additional responsibilities (Blieszner & Shifflett, 1990; Famighetti, 1986; Rabins, Mace, & Lucas, 1982). Many families struggle with how to renegotiate roles without undermining the power of the person with Alzheimer's and without overburdening any one individual.

Grief

Persons with Alzheimer's disease often live for several years after they first start exhibiting symptoms. The pattern of progression of the disease is uncertain, with some persons deteriorating more rapidly than others. As Cohen and Eisdorfer (1986) note, "Family members share a life of emotional turmoil as they witness the disintegration of someone they love" (p. 22). In the later stages of the disease, families must cope with the loss of someone who is physically present but does not respond to them in any coherent way. This sort of ambiguous loss can be very stressful and painful. Boss (1993) proposes that families are more stressed by the uncertainty of Alzheimer's than by the severity of the illness. She notes that a high degree of uncertainty can cause the family to become stuck and unable to move forward. When a family is stuck, family members may quit communicating with each other and with the person with SDAT. This inability to move forward can inhibit the grief process for all involved and prevent closure. Blieszner and Shifflett (1990) report that caregivers expressed a need to reach closure on their relationship with the person with Alzheimer's, but many of their respondents lost communication with the person before closure was achieved. Family therapists can aid families in dealing with these issues at any stage of the progression of the disease, but should encourage them to deal with their grief and establish closure before the brain-impaired person's reality is too far from their own to communicate successfully.

Family-of-Origin Issues

Families do not enter into the many facets of dealing with Alzheimer's without relational interaction patterns and family-of-origin issues already established. It is, therefore, imperative that the family therapist working with these families gain some sense of how each particular family system operates, including the role of boundaries, the existence of triangles, and the possibility of fusion or emotional cutoff. Ory et al. (1985) suggest that family members who have poorer relationships with the person with SDAT prior to the onset of the disease will experience greater feelings of burden in dealing with the consequences of Alzheimer's. Also, Shields (1992) has examined the relationship between primary caregivers and other family members and found that these relationships can also become stuck, with the primary caregiver seeking empathy from other family members while those family members instead want to focus their energies on trying to problem solve rather than act as listeners. The result is that caregivers become depressed, feeling that others do not understand them. Family members then respond negatively to the depressed caregiver. He observes that the rigidity of this particular pattern is influenced by the relationships established throughout the family's history.

Adjustments in the Sexual Relationship

Cohen and Eisdorfer (1986) cite five major areas in which the person with SDAT may have sexual difficulties: those resulting from destruction of the brain tissue; those associated with physical illnesses; those that are the side effects of medications; those brought on by psychological conflicts; and those resulting from social pressures and attitudes (p. 178). Persons with SDAT may have difficulty with sexual arousal, but they also may desire an increase in sexual activity. Whatever the nature of the problem, partners should be encouraged to seek professional advice to ascertain to what extent the difficulties are treatable. Partners who are no longer able to enjoy intercourse may still enjoy manual or oral stimulation.

This section has concentrated on challenges encountered by the family facing SDAT. We often do not prepare aging families for "finishing well" (Hargrave & Anderson, 1992). Even though the areas presented are potential problem areas for all aging families, the presence of Alzheimer's presents its own unique aspects. It is important that the therapist who is working with the family understand these nuances in order to help its members deal effectively with their areas of concern.

A THERAPEUTIC APPROACH FOR WORKING WITH FAMILIES

When working with older couples and families it is important that the clinician be aware of the needs and difficulties experienced by the family and also of the therapeutic tools necessary for working with these families. Family therapists can choose from many therapeutic approaches, most of which are based on systems theory. Systems theory directs attention to relationships and relationship issues as opposed to the individual and individual issues. The focus of family therapy approaches is on patterns of interaction with an emphasis on reciprocity, recursion, and shared responsibility (Becvar & Becvar, 1993).

Case Example

"I Didn't Mean to Be This Way": A Psychodynamic Approach

A 52-year-old woman (Anne) called to request therapy for depression. In the initial session, Anne shared with the therapist that she was having trouble sleeping, had no appetite, and had difficulty getting out of bed in the mornings. A genogram was utilized in order to gather information related to current family status and to family history.

While gathering information for the genogram, the therapist discovered that Anne owned and operated her own landscaping company, had never been in a long-term relationship, and was the primary caregiver for her 78-year-old mother, who had been tentatively diagnosed with Alzheimer's disease four years previously. Anne had been living with her mother for eight years since her father's death. Some of her mother's behaviors and reactions related to the disease were challenging, particularly her mother's much impaired ability to communicate and her incontinence. Anne's mother was often repetitive in her speech and told Anne over and over again, "I didn't mean to be this way."

Anne had two older siblings. Her brother, Doug, was the oldest and lived six hours away. Doug had not interacted with the family, except for sending an annual Mother's Day card, since leaving home at the age of 18. Anne's sister, Diane, lived three hours away. Diane had a spouse and two children and was a loan officer in a bank. She visited her mother about six times a year and called every two weeks.

The Goal of Therapy and the Role of the Therapist

According to Bowen, the goal of therapy is self-differentiation. To be successful, the impetus for differentiation of self must come from the client and not the therapist (Becvar & Becvar, 1993). The role of the therapist is to serve as a consultant or coach to move the client into a mode of intellectual processing. The therapist teaches the client about systems and the intergenerational transmission process (Becvar & Becvar, 1993).

Clinical Interventions

The therapist continued to develop and utilize the genogram in early sessions with Anne. Through their mapping of the genogram, Anne was able to identify patterns of emotional functioning that had passed down through the generations in her family. For example, she was able to identify several youngest children on both sides of her family who had been the family caretakers. She also became aware of her own triangulation between her father and her mother. She had been very ill as a child, and her parents' attention had focused on her. She felt a tremendous sense of obligation to care for her mother who had taken such good care of her when she was a child.

As Anne became aware of her own fusion with her mother, she understood more fully how trapped she felt by her mother's dependency and how angry she was at her siblings for not offering more assistance. She wanted an opportunity to live on her own again. Anne's relationship with her brother was distant and she felt her relationship with her sister was superficial. She wanted to end the emotional cutoff with her brother and strengthen her relationship with her sister.

Encouraged by her therapist, Anne contacted her siblings to ask to spend some time with each of them. She was coached by her therapist on how to interview them about their experiences of growing up in their family. Anne also would be sharing what she was learning about herself in therapy. She was able to visit with both her brother and sister who then agreed to come into therapy with Anne to discuss the situation with their mother.

Because of the distance traveled by Doug, sessions were extended to three hours and were held on Saturdays. The initial session focused once again on the genogram, adding the perspectives of both Doug and Diane. The siblings were able to address the triangles in the family and to discuss their own levels of differentiation. Both Diane and Doug expressed an interest in becoming more involved in their mother's care. They visited their mother for extended periods over the weekend and gained more insight into her difficulties. All three siblings also spent time together getting to know each other again.

The second session was held a month later and focused on how the three siblings could work together as a unit to better care for their mother. Nursing home placement was finally considered to be the best option for providing optimal care. All three admitted a high level of guilt associated with this conclusion. The therapist suggested that they hold the next session in their mother's home in order to discuss their conclusion with her and to give her an opportunity to express her desires and concerns.

The session in the home of the mother was very meaningful. Diane volunteered to explain to the mother their concerns about their continued ability to care for her at home. She shared concerns with her mother one at a time and asked that her mother squeeze her hand if she understood each concern. The mother was able to communicate to her children that she was ready to move to a nursing home even though it frightened her. The children assured her that they would take extra care in choosing a nursing home and that they would visit as often as possible. When Doug explained the options of nursing homes to his mother, she indicated her preference. Even though the mother was not able to communicate verbally with her children for any length of time, she was able to convey her wishes through physical contact with limited verbal responses. She was very intent on having physical contact with each of her children before leaving the room.

After their mother left the room, Anne, Diane, and Doug agreed that they had never faced a more difficult decision. However, they felt that their mother had taken part in the decision-making process; they agreed that her mood was much better on this day than it had been during all of their recent visits. Anne speculated that on some level their mother was aware of having all of her children together again and found comfort in that awareness.

The case, of course, was more complicated than presented in this scenario. However, the family was able to navigate a very difficult process with the guidance of a therapist who utilized a Bowenian approach to therapy. In a follow-up session, Anne reported that she was not experiencing her previous symptoms of depression and was very excited about settling into her new house. She revealed that she still struggled with her new, differentiated position but also enjoyed her new sense of freedom.

SUGGESTIONS FOR CLINICIANS

The following is a brief list of possible topics to be explored and practical suggestions for working with families that include a member with Alzheimer's disease.

Changing Family Roles

1. Unresolved family-of-origin conflicts can exacerbate the tension that often accompanies the redefining of family roles.
2. Issues of loyalty, entitlement, justice, and legacy often need to be explored.
3. Clinical interventions that capture the role of family history can be very effective (genograms, family reconstruction, reminiscence).

Difficult Discussion Topics

1. Decisions related to guardianship and handling family finances
2. Issues of sexuality
3. The need to stop isolated caregiving before exhaustion takes over
4. How to handle violent outbreaks by the person with SDAT or by the caregiver
5. The possibility of nursing home placement
6. Death and dying

Logistics of the Therapy Session

1. Provide in-home sessions when possible to lower the confusion level of the person with SDAT. Therapists may also need to hold sessions in nursing home settings.
2. Both the therapist and the family need to have an assessment of the cognitive, functional, affective, and behavioral status of the person with SDAT prior to the beginning of therapy.
3. Consider 30-minute sessions twice a week to allow for a decreased attention span.
4. Provide the person with SDAT a tape of the session to facilitate memory and learning.
5. Provide a pad of paper for note taking during the session for people in the early stages.
6. Speak slowly and sit facing the person with SDAT. Keep communication simple. Do not introduce too many topics at the same time.
7. Touch the arm of the person with SDAT to help him or her stay focused. Some persons may become distracted or scared when touched, so caution should be exercised. Check out this possibility with the caregiver before beginning the session.
8. Begin discussion of termination about two months before the termination date. The caregiver and the person with SDAT often feel very dependent on the therapist because of their feelings of isolation.

CONCLUSION

Family therapists face the increasing possibility of working with persons with Alzheimer's disease and their families due to the increased identification of Alzheimer's disease among the growing population of older adults. Clinicians must become more informed about the disease itself and the possible effects on the family, especially since most persons with Alzheimer's disease are cared for in the home. The burdens of the primary caregiver are well documented. Much of the research related to Alzheimer's focuses on the stresses faced by the caregiver and the family. Overall, the literature neglects the changing reality of the person with SDAT. Family therapists who operate out of a systemic perspective have a unique opportunity to begin to help bridge the gap between the reality of the person with Alzheimer's disease and the reality of the family, the therapist, and society in general. These families live in a delicate balance, facing and responding to the many changes among and within one another. Finding ways to help families and others have a better understanding of this altering reality and an opportunity to create new realities is the challenge that lies ahead.

REFERENCES

Alzheimer's Association. (1989, Winter). Research on Alzheimer's disease holds here for the future. *Alzheimer's Association: Someone to stand by you*, p. 1.

American Psychiatric Association. (1994). *Diagnostic and statistical manual of mental disorders* (4th ed.). Washington, DC: Author.

Becvar, D. S., & Becvar, R. J. (1993). *Family therapy: A systemic integration* (2nd ed.). Boston: Allyn & Bacon.

Blieszner, R., & Shifflett, P. A. (1990). The effects of Alzheimer's disease on close relationships between patients and caregivers. *Family Relations, 39*, 57-62.

Boss, P. G. (1993). The reconstruction of family life with Alzheimer's disease: Generating theory to lower family stress from ambiguous loss. In P. G. Boss, W. J. Doherty, R. LaRossa, W. R. Schumm, & S. K. Steinmetz (Eds.), *Sourcebook of family theories and methods: A contextual approach* (pp. 163-166). New York: Plenum Press.

Charmaz, K. (1983). Loss of self: A fundamental form of suffering in the chronically ill. *Sociology of Health and Illness, 5*, 168-195.

Charmaz, K. (1987). Struggling for a self: Identity levels of the chronically ill. *Research in the Sociology of Health Care, 6*, 283-321.

Chenowith, B., & Spencer, B. (1986). Dementia: The experience of family caregivers. *The Gerontologist, 26*, 267-272.

Cohen, D. (1991). The subjective experience of Alzheimer's disease: The anatomy of an illness as perceived by patients and families. *American Journal of Alzheimer's Care and Related Disorders and Research, 6*, 6-11.

Cohen, D., & Eisdorfer, C. (1986). *The loss of self*. New York: NAL Penguin.

Cohen, D., & Eisdorfer, C. (1988). Depression in family members caring for a relative with Alzheimer's disease. *Journal of the American Geriatrics Society, 36*, 885-889.

Cohen, D., Kennedy, G., & Eisdorfer, C. (1984). Phases of change in the patient with Alzheimer's dementia: A conceptual dimension for defining health care management. *Journal of the American Geriatrics Society, 32*, 11-15.

Colerick, E. J., & George, L. K. (1986). Predictors of institutionalization among caregivers of patients with Alzheimer's disease. *Journal of the American Geriatrics Society, 34*, 493-498.

Cook-Deegan, R. M. (1988). *Confronting Alzheimer's disease and other dementias*. Philadelphia: Lippincott.

Cotrell, V., & Lein, L. (1993). Awareness and denial in Alzheimer's disease victims. *Journal of Gerontological Social Work, 19*, 115-132.

Cotrell, V. C., & Schulz, R. (1993). The perspective of the patient with Alzheimer's disease: A neglected dimension of dementia research. *The Gerontologist, 33*, 205-211.

Dillehay, R. C., & Sandys, M. R. (1990). Caregivers for Alzheimer's patients: What we are learning from research. *International Journal of Aging and Human Development, 30,* 263-285.

Dolinsky, A., & Rosenwaike, I. (1988). The role of demographic factors in the institutionalization of the elderly. *Research on Aging, 10,* 235-257.

Dubler, N. N., & Strauss, P. J. (1988). Ethical dilemmas facing caregivers and attorneys in dealing with legal, financial, and health-care decision making. In M. K. Aronson (Ed.), *Understanding Alzheimer's disease: What it is, how to cope with it, future directions* (pp. 276-292). New York: Scribner's.

Famighetti, R. A. (1986). Understanding the family coping with Alzheimer's disease: An application of theory to intervention. *Clinical Gerontologist, 5,* 363-384.

Freels, S., Cohen, D., Eisdorfer, C., Paveza, G., Gorelick, P., Luchins, D. J., Hirschman, R., Ashford, J. W., Levy, P., Semla, T., & Shaw, H. (1992). Functional status and clinical findings in patients with Alzheimer's disease. *Journal of Gerontology: Medical Sciences, 47,* M177-M182.

Gilfix, M. (1988). Legal planning for Alzheimer's disease. In M. K. Aronson (Ed.), *Understanding Alzheimer's disease: What it is, how to cope with it, future directions* (pp. 276-292). New York: Scribner's.

Hargrave, T. D., & Anderson, W. T. (1992). *Finishing well: Aging and reparation in the intergenerational family.* New York: Brunner/Mazel.

Henderson, J. N., & Gutierrez-Mayka, M. (1992). Ethnocultural themes in caregiving to Alzheimer's disease patients in Hispanic families. *Clinical Gerontologist, 11,* 59-74.

Hutton, J. T., & Kenny, A. D. (1985). *Senile dementia of the Alzheimer type.* New York: Alan R. Liss.

Katzman, R. (1987). Alzheimer's disease: Advances and opportunities. *Journal of the American Geriatrics Society, 35,* 69-73.

Khachaturian, Z. S. (1985). Diagnosis of Alzheimer's disease. *Archives of Neurology, 42,* 1097-1105.

Knopman, D. S., Kitto, J., Deinard, S., & Heiring, J. (1988). Longitudinal study of death and institutionalization in patients with primary degenerative dementia. *Journal of the American Geriatrics Society, 36,* 108-112.

Long, J. K. (1992). Families and long-term care for the elderly. Interview with Joan Rachel Goldberg (Ed.), *Family Therapy News,* 3.

Long, J. K. (1993, October). *Helping families cope with the reality of Alzheimer's.* Paper presented at the meeting of the American Association for Marriage and Family Therapy, Anaheim, CA.

Long, J. K., & Mancini, J. A. (1989). The parental role and parent-child relationship provisions. In J. A. Mancini (Ed.), *Aging parents and adult children* (pp. 151-165). Lexington, MA: D.C. Heath.

Long, J. K., & Mancini, J. A. (1990). Aging couples and the family system. In T. H. Brubaker (Ed.), *Family relationships in later life* (2nd ed.) (pp. 29-47). Newbury Park, CA: Sage.

Lyman, K. A. (1989). Bringing the social back in: A critique of the biomedicalization of dementia. *The Gerontologist, 29*, 597-605.

Mace, N. (1987). The family. In Office of Technology Assessment (Ed.), *Losing a million minds.* Washington, DC: U.S. Government Printing Office.

Mace, N. L., & Rabins, P. V. (1981). *The thirty-six hour day.* New York: Warner Books.

Mackenzie, T. B., Robiner, W. N., & Knopman, D. S. (1989). Differences between patient and family assessments of depression in Alzheimer's disease. *American Journal of Psychiatry, 146*, 1174-1178.

Niederehe, G., & Fruge, E. (1984). Dementia and family dynamics: Clinical research issues. *Journal of Geriatric Psychiatry, 17*, 21-56.

Orona, C. J. (1990). Temporality and identity loss due to Alzheimer's disease. *Social Sciences Medicine, 30*, 1247-1256.

Ory, M. G., Williams, T. F., Emr, M., Lebowitz, B., Rabins, P., Salloway, J., Sluss-Radbaugh, T., Wolff, E., & Zarit, S. (1985). Families, informal supports, and Alzheimer's disease. *Research on Aging, 7*, 623-644.

Pearson, J. L., Teri, L., Reifler, B. V., & Raskind, M. A. (1989). Functional status and cognitive impairment in Alzheimer's patients with and without depression. *Journal of the American Geriatric Society, 37*, 1117-1121.

Pruchno, R. A., Michaels, J. E., & Potashnik, S. L. (1990). Predictors of institutionalization among Alzheimer disease victims with caregiving spouses. *Journal of Gerontology, 45*, S259-S266.

Rabins, P. V., Mace, N. L., & Lucas, M. J. (1982). The impact of dementia on the family. *Journal of the American Medical Association, 248*, 333-335.

Reifler, B. V., Larson, E., & Hanley, R. (1982). Coexistence of cognitive impairment and depression in geriatric outpatients. *American Journal of Psychiatry, 139*, 623-626.

Ronch, J. L. (1989). *Alzheimer's disease.* New York: Continuum.

Shields, C. G. (1992). Family interaction and caregivers of Alzheimer's disease patients: Correlates of depression. *Family Process, 31*, 19-33.

Shoemaker, D. (1987). Problematic behavior and the Alzheimer patient: Retrospection as a method of understanding and counseling. *The Gerontologist, 27*, 370-375.

Siegel, J. S., & Taeuber, C. M. (1986). Demographic perspectives on the long-lived society. *The Aging Society, 115*, 77-118.

Snyder, L., Rupprecht, P., Pyrek, J., Brekhus, S., & Moss, T. (1978). Wandering. *The Gerontologist, 18*, 272-280.

Staff. (1989, Winter). Research on Alzheimer's disease holds hope for the future. *Alzheimer's Association: Someone to stand by you,* p. 1.

Stein, S., Linn, M. W., Slater, E., & Stein, E. M. (1984). Future concerns and recent life events of elderly community residents. *Journal of the American Geriatrics Society, 32*, 431-434.

Teri, L., Borson, S., Kiyak, H. A., & Yamagishi, M. (1989). Behavioral disturbance, cognitive dysfunction, and functional skill: Prevalence and relationship in Alzheimer's disease. *Journal of the American Geriatrics Society, 37*, 109-116.

Teri, L., & Gallagher-Thompson, D. (1991). Cognitive-behavioral interventions for treatment of depression in Alzheimer's patients. *The Gerontologist, 31,* 413–416.

Thompson, L. W., Davies, R., Gallagher, D., & Krantz, S. (1986). Cognitive therapy with older adults. In T. Brink (Ed.), *Clinical gerontology* (pp. 245–279). New York: Haworth Press.

Volicer, L., Fabiszewski, K. J., Rheaume, Y. L., & Lasch, K. E. (1988): *Clinical management of Alzheimer's disease.* Rockville, MD: Aspen.

Wragg, R. E., & Jeste, D. V. (1989). Overview of depression and psychosis in Alzheimer's disease. *American Journal of Psychiatry, 146,* 577–587.

Zarit, S. H., Orr, N. K., & Zarit, J. M. (1985). *The hidden victims of Alzheimer's disease: Families under stress.* New York: New York University Press.

ॐ 11 ॐ

Family Systems and Nursing Home Systems: An Ecosystemic Perspective for the Systems Practitioner

Wayne A. Caron, Ph.D.
University of Minnesota
Minneapolis, Minnesota

No one wants to think about living in a nursing home. Neither is it comfortable to consider placing a loved one there. However, nursing homes are increasingly part of family life and likely will be part of the future. While about 5 percent of the over-65 population live in a nursing home facility, the risk over the life span is much higher. Of those who turned 65 years old in 1990, 35 to 45 percent will live in nursing homes before they die. Most long-term care continues to be provided by family and friends at home, but approximately one and a half million elderly are cared for in long-term care facilities. By the year 2030, this number is projected to rise to 5.3 million (Pepper Commission Report, 1990).

Nursing home care deserves the attention of systems therapists for several reasons. First, as the population ages, greater numbers will live in long-term care facilities. For the systems therapist working with later-life issues, contact with nursing home care is inevitable. Second, many will face nursing home life either personally or in their families. Working with clients in later life forces family therapists to face their possible futures. Third, nursing homes are of central importance to the health care system. Nursing home care accounts for 8 percent of the total health care budget of the United States (Lamy, 1993). Nursing homes represent the largest component of the elders' health care system. Although only about 20 percent of disabled elders live in nursing homes, 82 percent of the money spent in health care for chronic conditions in the aged go to these facilities. Finally, nursing homes represent a model of health care in desperate need of a systemic perspective. The evidence indicates widespread and entrenched difficulties in nursing homes for the residents, their families and the staff. At the heart of these difficulties lie dysfunctional patterns of interaction and relationships, which a systems therapist is uniquely qualified to address.

In this chapter, the long-term care experience is examined from different perspective: the elders living in nursing homes, the staff providing care, the families of nursing home residents. The relationship patterns among these groups are also discussed. Building in this way from the particular to the general, a picture of the nursing home context emerges, reflecting the multiple relationships connecting these principal subsystems.

TAKING A DEVELOPMENTAL AND ECOSYSTEMIC PERSPECTIVE

What distinguishes system therapists from other helping professionals involved with nursing homes is their theory base. Two theoretical frameworks in particular are useful—the developmental and the ecosystemic. The developmental framework calls attention to temporal characteristics of social processes. Placement of an elder is not a singular event but rather part of a process. It stands as a transition between two periods—the end of home care and the beginning of professional care. Understanding this process as a part of what came before the actual transfer event and what comes after helps the clinician appreciate the experience of those involved.

The developmental framework also suggests that living in a nursing home is only one phase in the life span of an individual. It comes at a specific time of life, a period with unique issues and challenges. Most patients in nursing homes are over 65 years old. But as nursing homes increasingly become places of care for younger populations (e.g., those with AIDS), the nature of these issues and challenges will inevitably change. Work with older clients requires awareness of the life experiences they bring into the setting and sensitivity to the developmental processes alive in their final years.

Finally, marrying the developmental perspective and the family systems framework broadens the therapist's task beyond simply attending to the issues of the elderly. The entire family system is involved with the experience of nursing home care. There must be sensitivity to the developmental issues of all family members: the elder in the later stages of life, the adult children in their middle years, the grandchildren in their young adulthood, and the great-grandchildren in the beginning stages of life. The genius of the family system is its ability to tap into the strengths of different ages and stages. Appreciating this power offers new possibilities for useful interventions.

The ecosystemic framework also provides concepts that are useful in work with nursing home care. The basic principles of the ecosystemic framework are familiar to all systems thinkers—individuals' behaviors are organized in response to those around them such that groups can be thought of as forming systems. These systems in turn organize their behaviors in response to other systems to form even larger systems.

It is useful to think of the people involved in nursing homes as organized into subsystems aggregating into a larger system. Some of these subsystems are organized around professional groupings—the nursing staff, the social services staff, the administrative staff, and so on. Other subsystems have less coherence. For example, each family can be thought of as constituting a separate subsystem, but rarely do families in a facility organize strongly enough to form a coherent subsystem. Identifying and characterizing each of the subsystems provides a powerful means for identifying critical issues and mapping strategies for effective interventions. Each subsystem in a long-term care setting must be appreciated in terms of its own structure, its own issues, and the unique personalities from which it is made up. Each nursing home has its own structure consisting of the individuals interacting in groups to form the whole.

The ecosystemic framework also focuses on the relationships among the subsystems. The level of organization achieved is understood by examining how regular or predictable the patterns of interaction are. These interactions are characterized in terms of their qualities—either highly connected or disengaged, cooperative or competitive, protracted or intermittent.

With a grounding in each of these foundations—the developmental and ecosystemic—family therapists can gain a view of nursing home care that allows both a wide-angle perspective and a focused view. The discussion that follows is predicated on these ideas.

1. The recipients of nursing home care and their families must be understood in terms of their developmental context—a view that takes into account their unique history, their current developmental issues, and their future.
2. The long-term care context comprises separate and identifiable social systems that interact in patterned ways to constitute a larger

ecosystem. Looking at the total human ecosystem allows us to see patterns and opportunities we would miss if we focused solely on the elder and the family as the unit of analysis and intervention.
3. The family is a unique subsystem within the ecosystem. It has unique features and stands outside the internal structure of the long-term care facility. This uniqueness provides opportunities for working through families to make a positive impact on the entire nursing home ecosystem.
4. Focusing attention on the ecosystemic perspective allows attention to be given to the strengths and qualities of relationships that develop among families, elders, nursing care staff, and administration. These relationships create a context that has a direct impact on the quality of life for residents and their families.

NURSING HOME RESIDENTS

It is dangerous to generalize toward a group of people. Generalizations about persons who live in nursing homes are especially problematic as residents come from all walks of life. However, the context of long-term care creates a powerful environment. The response of the diverse population of elders to this environment creates a homogeneity among them. Generally we think of nursing home residents as old and physically frail. Most are in later years, with 88 percent over the age of 65 (Pepper Commission, 1990). However, physical frailty is no longer the defining characteristic of nursing home residents. Although nursing homes were designed to treat and manage medical problems, increasingly psychiatric illness is the defining feature of residents' issues.

Research has shown that 94 percent of nursing home residents have a condition that is diagnosable according to the revised third edition of the *Diagnostic and Statistical Manual of Mental Disorders* (DSM-III-R) (Rovner, Kofenek & Fillipp, et al., 1986). Of this number, 32 percent suffer from a depressive disorder, with 16 percent showing symptoms of severe depression (Parmelee, Katz, & Lawton, 1992). This means that approximately a million Americans living in nursing homes are in need of mental health treatment (Larson, et.al., 1989). Elderly people who live in the community have lower rates of psychiatric illness than the general population, making the higher rates seen in long-term care even more alarming (Myers, Weissman, Wischler, et al., 1984; Robins, Helzner, Weissman, et al., 1984; Weissman, Myers, Tischler, et al., 1985). Even though mental disorders are the rule rather than the exception in long-term care facilities, they are often undetected, misdiagnosed, and mistreated (Sabin, Vitug, & Mark, 1982; Ernst, Badash, & Beran, 1977; National Institute on Aging Consensus Task Force, 1980).

Why is there such a high incidence of psychiatric disorders among elders in long-term care? Many of those entering nursing homes are doing so with mental illness already in place. German, Rovner, Burton, Brant, and Clark (1992) found that 80 percent of new admissions suffered from psychiatric illness. Some of these are lifelong disorders. Approximately 30 percent of elderly living in state mental institutions were placed in nursing homes during the period of deinstitutionalization (Mercer, Garner, & Leon, 1991). A substantial portion suffer from organic conditions, such as Alzheimer's disease (German et al., 1992; Donnelly, Compton, Devany, Kirk, & McGuigan, 1989; Ineichen, 1990; Aronson et al., 1992). Another factor contributing to the psychological problems of nursing home residents is chronic pain and disability, which often result in depression (Cohen-Mansfield & Marz, 1993).

Although these factors together can provide some explanation for the ubiquity of mental disorders among elders living in nursing homes, to understand the persistence of such difficulties we must look to the environmental context nursing homes create. Nursing homes were developed and continue to be organized around provision of care of physical illness. The characteristics of long-term care facilities that make them efficient providers of medical care make them less well suited for dealing with psychological problems.

Nursing homes claim from their residents their autonomy (Kane, Freeman, Caplan, Aroskar, & Urv-Wong, 1990). The majority (60 percent) of nursing home residents report having had no say in the decision to be placed in a long-term care facility—the decision was made primarily by physicians and family members (Reinardy, 1992). Researchers have documented the progressive loss of an elder's sense of autonomy and efficacy over the course of time in a nursing home, regardless of the elder's level of physical or cognitive disability. Decreases in sense of control over life result in decreased life satisfaction and level of activity in those who live in nursing homes (Arling, Harkins, & Capitman, 1986).

One indication of the lack of personal autonomy is the widespread use of restraints. Concerned over the potential abuses in using physical and chemical restraints (in the form of psychotropic medications) to make residents easier to manage, Congress set forth stringent regulations for nursing homes receiving Medicare and Medicaid reimbursement in the Omnibus Budget Reconciliation Act of 1987. These regulations state that physical and chemical restraints may only be used with a physician's order and only for the purpose of protecting the health and well-being of the nursing home resident. Nevertheless, the use of restraints continues. Burton, German, Rovner, and Brant (1992) found that almost half of nursing home residents had physical restraints (defined as mechanical means to restrict or restrain action), including trunk restraints (such as Posey vests), waist restraints, reclining chairs with tables designed to prevent rising (commonly called gerichairs), and extremity restraints (such as mitts or wrist or ankle straps) applied to them within their first month of admission. Two thirds had restraints applied within the first year of their stay. Almost a third (27 percent) of the new residents in their study were tied down at all times. The use of restraints was correlated with the severity of mental illness but also varied a great deal from nursing home to nursing home. The homes with the least use of restraints restricted 25 percent of their residents within the first month and 46 percent within the first year. By contrast, the homes with the highest use confined 68 percent within the first month of stay and 79 percent by the end of the first year. Results for psychotropic medications are somewhat more encouraging. Garrard et al. (1992) found that 38 percent of nursing home residents were prescribed psychotropic medications upon admission. However, possibly in response to regulations mandating the periodic review of psychotropic use, the majority were taken off their medications over time, with only 7 percent consistently on neuroleptics and 5 percent consistently on benzodiazapines over a 12-month period.

Use of restraints is often defended as necessary. It is argued that the behavior problems of elders in nursing homes are so severe that drastic efforts are needed to manage them. However, there is good evidence that nursing home residents respond positively to various forms of psychotherapeutic intervention (Lomranz, 1991; Santmyer & Roca, 1991; Frey, Kelbley, Durham, & James, 1992). Very few mental health professionals work in long-term care environments (Santos & Vandenbos, 1982), meaning that an estimated 80 percent of elderly persons in nursing homes who might benefit from treatment receive none (Levenson & Felkins, 1979).

With respect to nursing home residents as a group, the picture emerges of a population disempowered and disenfranchised. They enter long-term care facilities physically ill and frail and suffering from mental disorders caused by both neurological disease and emotional distress. As Lomranz (1991) writes:

> One basic problem may be evidenced by the fact that most institutions adopt the concept of "home" (nursing home, home for the aged, etc.). The very nature of any "institution" seems incompatible with the nature, requirements and expectations from home. The efforts to combine the two forms of living may constitute an ongoing dilemma reflected in the work of the staff, as well as in the

quality of the resident's psychological well-being ... [Nursing home residents share] the effects of institutionalization, without which it is impossible to comprehend the experience of the elderly in homes for the aged ... Inevitably (these effects) include loss of self-esteem, estrangement, isolation, deindividuation and disculturation. (p. 50)

Just as institutional context affects nursing home residents individually, so it also affects them as a group. A review of primarily ethnographic and participant observation research shows that (1) nursing home residents rarely talk with each other; (2) the pattern of communication most often noted among residents was casual conversation, usually limited to short remarks about disruptions of normal routines; and (3) residents who do converse frequently are evaluated negatively by other residents. In-depth interviews with nursing home residents indicate consensus around the following rules of communication: (1) do not complain; (2) do not talk with the opposite sex, and if you do, keep it to formalities; (3) do not talk about loneliness or dying; and (4) do not talk too much (Kaakinen, 1992).

The nursing home context seems to offer few resources for elders to deal with the challenges of their lives—their physical and emotional difficulties. However, lest we become too pessimistic, it is important to note that the residents of nursing homes not only bring with them enormously complex and serious problems, but they also bring enormous resources. These are life's survivors and they bring with them their life histories of both good and bad times. The challenge for the therapist is to help elders tap into this strength. This is true for both the cognitively intact and cognitively impaired.

Counseling persons in nursing homes requires attention not only to the internal struggles of the clients but also to their social context. By attending to the emotional context of the lives of the person in a nursing home, the therapist can have significant impact. The nursing home care context may emphasize elders' disabilities and dependencies, but the therapist should bring a sensitivity to and appreciation of the strengths and resources of the client. This can often be found in the life history of the resident. Nursing home residents have often lived full lives with struggles, triumphs, and accomplishments. Seen in this light, they offer many resources for enriching the lives around them.

THE NURSING HOME STAFF

The next important system within the long-term care context is the nursing home staff. Nursing homes are generally rigidly structured, both along professional lines (separate departments to attend to nursing, social work, activities, dietary provisions, and housekeeping) and along lines of authority (direct care staff, supervisory staff and administrative staff).

Direct care staff members are at the heart of any long-term care system. Eighty percent of the care in nursing homes is provided by nurses' aides, who are likely to have the least training and education, be the poorest paid, and have the least power and influence within the system. Because of their central role in the nursing home, they have received much attention from researchers and analysts.

The evidence indicates that the nursing care staff as a group has many difficulties. Studies have shown staffs plagued by poor morale and low job satisfaction (Chappell & Novak, 1992; Mullins, Nelson, Bosciglio, & Weiner, 1988; Hare & Skinner, 1990). The most telling sign and one with direct impact on the well-being of residents is the high turnover rate. One recent study found the average annual turnover rate for nurses' aides to be 65 percent, with a range from 55 percent to more than 400 percent (Wagnild, 1988). With such high turnover, the ability of the staff to develop relationships with residents and families is severely limited. In investigating the reasons for staff problems, Chappell and Novak (1992) identified poor training, low pay, and lack of rewards.

A study by Bowers and Becker (1992) found that the primary challenge for nursing care staff is time management. Through the course of a shift, nurses' aides must constantly balance and manage multiple care demands that occur simultaneously. Staff members receive little training in necessary time-management skills. Those who do not quit within the first month develop strategies for managing the workload, which involve cutting corners and "rounding" as a way to organize work.

The researchers found that aides cut corners by decreasing their work quality in "private" (when they are alone with the resident) rather than in public (when they can be observed by nursing supervisors and other staff). The private interactions between nurses' aides and residents suffer. The difference between "good aides" and "bad aides" was revealed not in *whether* they cut corners but in *how* they cut corners. Good aides cut corners in areas they knew were not critical. Good aides were also reported by the researchers to feel remorse over the corners they cut.

Rounding means setting up an order for working with each resident during the shift and moving systematically from task to task. It requires stability and predictability in meeting work demands. Interruptions are the major threat to this strategy. Not surprisingly, residents with dementia or other forms of mental illness are more likely to cause interruptions through either direct demands or disruptive behaviors that require attention. Families also cause interruption with questions and demands that necessitate immediate response. Aides feel frustrated and angry on these occasions, making their interactions tense and unpleasant.

The systems therapist needs to understand the operations of administrative staff as a part of the operation of the nursing home facility. Although not as directly involved in the moment-to-moment care of residents, the administrative staff sets the emotional tone of the facility and through this has enormous impact on the quality of life for both residents and staff.

One important function of the administrative staff is boundary maintenance, serving as the buffer between the home and the outside world. The administration manages complaints from families and residents. If the home is part of a chain, the administrators must be responsive to their central office in matters of policy and operations. Administrators have primary responsibility for interacting with regulators from the many agencies that regulate nursing home operations.

The last function is especially important. The nursing home industry is the most heavily regulated in the United States (Mercer, Garner, & Leon, 1991). These regulations and the regulators who enforce them create inevitable constraints on behavior. The administration must pay careful attention to avoiding citations. Citations result in fines, threats of license revocation, and bad public relations. There are no rewards for excellence built into the regulatory environment. This creates *conservative pressures* to be cautious and avoid mistakes.

Fortunately, administrators can do more than just handle complaints and deal with regulators. They serve as leaders, establishing the character of the facility. This role is crucial. The kind of organizational climate administrators create has a more powerful impact on the quality of care than the size and type of facility, or even the quality of direct supervision received by the care staff (Sheridan, White, & Fairchild, 1992). As Pattee and Otteson (1991) note in their guide for nursing home medical directors:

> Successful organizations possess a clear and explicit philosophy about how they aim to conduct their business. They pay a great deal of attention to shaping and fine-tuning their values and communicating them to all individuals in the organization. Values vary from organization to organization, but the leadership ability to preserve and promote the values of the organizational members is a central source of leadership power ... The organization's culture is considered strong when its core values are intensely held and widely shared. The more universal these understandings among organizational members, the stronger the culture. Weak cultures lack such common themes; beliefs held by members are more diffuse.... The stron-

ger the organization's culture, the less it requires formal rules and regulations to guide members' behavior. A strong culture lessens the propensity for individuals to leave the organization. The terms management and leadership are often considered synonymous and are used interchangeably. The skills often reside in the same individual. But management and leadership skills are distinct attributes and one set of skills is not necessarily accompanied by the other.... Leaders embody the values of the group.... The leader creates a vision, inspires loyalty and helps foster a climate that encourages organizational change and revitalization. (pp. 86-92)

For the systems therapist, understanding the culture of the facility is essential. The role of administration in providing leadership for the facility is central. The systems therapist working with the family around placement issues, or dealing with behavior problems in a nursing home resident, may never come into direct contact with the administrative staff, but understanding the culture of the facility, and the means by which this culture is created through leadership (or lack of leadership), is crucial for determining ways of effectively working with the system.

THE FAMILY

While it is important to understand the systemic context in nursing homes as created by the elders-in-residence, the direct care staff, and administrators, the family deserves special attention. Families often serve as the entry point for the systems therapist—they more often seek out services of a counselor than do nursing home residents or staff. The family has special strengths and legitimacy in dealing with issues that affect all parts of the larger system. It is often the unique features of family systems that are targeted as points for the most effective interventions. Nevertheless, as noted earlier, the systems therapist must beware of being connected primarily with the family system and having the family as the primary client. To do so is to ignore the other strengths and resources in the human ecosystem.

Still, the family has unique features and strengths that can be of service to the systems therapist. From the perspective of the family system, it is important to understand nursing home care as a process. The process has a history which begins earlier as the family tries to care for the elder and faces the limits of their coping resources. This process of finding the limits of caregiving is a negotiation, which in the case of a chronic illness, such as Alzheimer's disease or Parkinson's disease, may take years. In other situations, the family may abruptly come face to face with its limitations when a catastrophic medical event occurs, such as a stroke or traumatic injury. In either situation, the decision to place the elder in a nursing home is part of a process through which the family arrives at a consensus that says, "There is no other alternative." For families, then, nursing home placement symbolizes their limitations and their failure. The family places at the point of exhaustion. Placement is an admission that they cannot go further (Smallegan, 1985).

The placement decision is never an easy one. Placement is often a time of crisis. Rather than being an orderly transition from one type of care to another, it more often occurs when there is a breakdown in the family's capacity to cope. Some families pull together during this time and support one another, but many others respond to the stress and strain with conflict and acrimony. Not only are family adaptive resources often exhausted by years of home caregiving, but the nature of nursing home care itself immobilizes family coping resources.

A prime factor in this immobilization is boundary ambiguity. This term, coined by Boss and Greenberg (1984), refers to situations of ambiguous loss where a family member is not clearly present or absent from the family system. Chronic dementing illness (from which 60 percent of nursing home residents suffer) represents one situation that creates boundary ambiguity (Boss, Caron, & Horbal, 1988; Boss, Caron, Horbal, & Mortimer, 1990). Nursing home placement also creates boundary ambiguity. While caring for a frail elder with chronic illness, the family's energies increasingly become centered around the caregiving task. This work often fills the days of the primary caregiver. With nursing home placement, the caregiver goes from being central to the care of the elder to becoming peripheral to that care. Not only are the day-to-day tasks now taken over by nursing home staff, but the nature of care and its language change. Whereas care in the family context is carried out in the realm of personal relationships, intimate knowledge, and familial obligation, care in nursing homes is embedded in professional relationships, technical knowledge, and contractual or regulatory obligations. Nowhere is the difference more noteworthy than in quarterly "family meetings" that many nursing homes are obligated to hold under federal regulations. These meetings are better characterized as medical meetings to which the family is invited. Information flow is generally one way—from the professional staff to the family. The language of the meetings is medical and problem solving is organized around discipline (e.g., nursing, social work, nutrition, occupational therapy). The family is marginalized, often becoming defined as part of the problem rather than part of the support network.

Following the placement of a relative, the family must find their niche in the system of care represented by the nursing home. The success with which the family establishes a stable role in the nursing home helps determine how quickly the family system can recover from the crisis of placement.

The type of role the family develops with the nursing home determines the quality of interactions with the elder and the staff. In general, four types of role commonly emerge along a continuum. At one extreme are those families that become *disengaged*. They seem to disappear once nursing home placement occurs. They rarely visit, they do not attend care conferences, and they often fail to respond to attempts by staff to contact them. It is as if they give over their elder entirely to the nursing home, extruding the person from the family.

A less extreme level of distancing is reflected by those families we can call *consultants*. These families generally attend care conferences and respond to requests from the home; however, they fail to maintain a personal relationship with the resident, rarely visiting the resident or involving him or her in family gatherings. Again, the process appears to be one of extruding the elder from the family system. Although we may be tempted to judge such families harshly for their apparent abandonment of their relative, we can understand this behavior as adaptive from the perspective of the theory of boundary ambiguity (Boss & Greenberg, 1984). With placement, the elder belongs to two systems—the nursing home and the family. "Sharing" the elder creates ambiguity for the family, requiring a constant process of accommodation and negotiation of boundaries with the home staff. Extruding the elder resolves this ambiguity. By sacrificing the relationship with the elder, the family attempts to move on.

For families that remain emotionally involved with their elder, there is the challenge of developing a role in the caregiving process. For some families, the role is *competitive* with the nursing home staff; that is, they seek to establish control over the way in which care is delivered. These families are often seen as complainers by staff members, spending time each visit checking on the staff's care and searching out errors or omissions. They describe themselves as advocates and often see their role as protecting their elder against poor care, implying that without their efforts their relative's well-being would surely suffer. This stance does not contribute to positive relations with the staff. Even in situations where families pursue legitimate grievances, the approach leads the staff to become defensive, suspicious, and closed. This adversarial dynamic can also affect the relationship between the staff and the resident.

Finally, some families stay involved in the daily care of their elder while negotiating a clear role of *collaborating* with the staff. These families identify themselves as partners in care and are generally supportive of the staff's efforts even when aware of shortcomings in the care provided. Their interactions with the staff are positive, and both sides feel valued and supported. It is important to understand the family's role in nursing home care. The systems therapist is concerned with families not simply because they suffer distress in the placement process, but because families have the potential for exerting a powerful influence on the quality of the nursing home experience for everyone.

CHARACTERIZING THE CONTEXT OF CARE

We have examined each of the major subsystems in turn—the residents, the nursing home staff (both direct care staff and administration), and the families. The challenge remaining is to characterize the interactions among these groups. It is the pattern of these interactions, the way in which each part of the nursing home ecosystem influences the others, that determines the outcomes of care and provides resources and opportunities for changing outcomes.

One means of assessment looks at shared versus conflicting interests among groups. It is easy to find examples of conflicting interests. The nursing home resident's need for autonomy can be in direct conflict with the care staff's need for efficiency and organization. Family members' desires to protect and promote an elder's personal interests can come into conflict with the administration's need to balance out the interests of all residents in the facility. There are also areas of shared interests. These center on ameliorating problems, minimizing disruptions, and avoiding incidents. An essential task for the systems therapist involved with nursing homes is the identification of shared and conflicting interests that arise in a given situation.

A second means of assessment focuses on the use of power and control. Interactions may be either constraining or empowering. Unfortunately, most interactions are far more constraining than liberating. These are the overt examples of constraints, for example, the use of physical and chemical restraints. However, the very structure of the organization has built-in patterns of constraint and control. These come with a reliance on defined and delineated disciplines, externally imposed and rigidly enforced regulations and rules, and strict hierarchical lines of authority.

Interactions among these groups also draw on a process of individuation versus depersonalization. Interactions can serve to support and promote the expression of each participant's uniqueness and individuality or can serve to limit and suppress this expression. Nursing home care is generally depersonalizing. Both residents and staff experience this. For direct-care staff, the emphasis is on completing predefined care tasks, with little room left for creativity or self-direction. Resident assignments for the staff are changed from shift to shift and staff members may be rotated from floor to floor, making it difficult to develop and sustain close, intimate relationships with residents. When the resident shows symptoms of mental illness (usually dementia), there is a tendency to label, to objectify, and even to infantalize the person.

Thus, the structure of nursing homes and their operation seem to foster conflicts of interest, controlling and constraining interactions, and depersonalized approaches to care. Admittedly, this view is disheartening. It is important to remember that these problems do not arise because of uncaring attitudes, greed, or ill will on the part of those who work in the long-term care industry. Rather, nursing homes are fulfilling roles in our society for which they were not originally intended. Nursing homes are organized to provide medical care, and they do this well. Through the middle part of this century, they provided transitional care, serving as a more cost-efficient means for managing long-term care than hospitals. They were the bridges from the acute medical centers back to the community. Now, with our population living longer and increased numbers of frail elderly straining the resources of caregiving families, nursing homes are the places where people go to live until they die. Elders may spend decades in a long-term care facility. Nursing homes are no longer simply the context in which medical care is provided—they are the context in which people live and die. They are *home* for the elder residents, and in our approach to working with issues related to nursing homes, family therapists should always focus on those aspects of long-term care facilities that support the definition of home.

PRINCIPLES FOR SYSTEMIC INTERVENTION

The systems therapist may come into contact with nursing home care via different avenues—through families referred for help with placement issues, through requests for consultations in managing behavior problems in residents, through contracts to provide training and/or organizational consultation and support. A special consideration is whether one should work on the inside or outside of the nursing home, that is, as part of the nursing home team or separate from the nursing home staff. Modes for providing mental health services for both residents and families from within the nursing home organization have been proposed and demonstrated to be helpful. However, one must be cautious when working from within the system. In a context in which rigid distinctions are made between who gives care and who receives it, the family is often relegated to the latter. This happens early in the nursing home placement process, with many nursing homes assigning a staff social worker during intake to provide support and to address family issues. Clearly, there are many practical difficulties for families during the time of placement; however, relegating the family to the role of service recipients from the earliest point of involvement undercuts their ability to relate to the staff from an equal and collaborative stance. They become clients rather than partners in care.

When a systems therapist is hired to help a family deal with nursing home placement, she or he runs the risk of contributing to the marginalization of the family. The "problem-saturated" view of the family should be complemented at every turn with the "opportunity-immersed" perspective.

One means of accomplishing this shift in perspective involves using the unique features of the family system as the foundation for the therapist's work. The family stands apart, distinct and special, by virtue of five characteristics. First, the family is *generationally diverse*. The family system contains a range of generations, from the very young to the very old. There is an emotional energy that comes from the convergence of these diverse generations, as anyone who has watched the eldest member of a family interact with the youngest can often attest. This positive energy is an important resource and it behooves the systems therapist to find ways of bringing the different generations together whenever possible.

A second characteristic of family systems is that they are *temporally situated*. Families have a history and a destiny. There is a connection across time from the family's past, its present, and its future. The life experiences of the elder teaches and guides the younger generation and provides a sense of continuity.

Third, families are *relatively stable* systems. Compared with nursing home staffs, families have a low turnover rate. This means that relationships have a stability and weight based on existence over time and through multiple life experiences.

Fourth, family relations are *intimate* both in what family members know of each other and in what they feel toward each other. Family relations are unique and individual. Family members are not interchangeable. Each member has a distinctive relationship with every other family member. The sum of these relationships constitutes the emotional environment of the family.

Finally, family relations have a *special legitimacy* reflected in our legal doctrines, our cultural beliefs, and our religious customs. The support and protection society places on the elder's relationship with the family are without peer. The legitimacy of family lends weight to elders whose families are close and involved. These elders are clearly connected with a community through their relationships with family, no matter how mentally impaired the elders maybe. Elders without families are more likely to be seen as alone, disconnected, and disenfranchised.

USING FAMILY STRENGTHS: THE BIOGRAPHY PROJECT

There are challenges for therapists taking a systems approach to work effectively in nursing homes. The structure of the nursing home ecosystem creates interactional patterns that can be constraining, depersonalizing, and inflexible. Limited reimbursement and organizational resistance present obstacles to any therapist seeking to provide mental health services to nursing home residents. But perhaps the major barrier for systems therapy in nursing homes has been lack of interest on the part of family therapists in working in long-term care facilities. It is easy to understand why therapists may be more comfortable working within familiar and comfortable contexts, such as private practices and clinics. However, therapists cannot offer much more than palliative responses to nursing home clients unless they find ways of working directly with long-term care systems.

Several models for dealing with mental health issues in nursing homes have been proposed. Some have favored providing special training for the nursing staff to help them become more sensitive and effective in their responses to psychosocial issues (Heiselman & Noelker, 1991; Spore, Smyer, & Cohn, 1991). Special care units have been developed to provide environments better fitted to the needs of demented elders (Chafetz, 1991; Peppard, 1991). Cox and Ephross (1989) describe how a group program for both families and residents was useful in easing the transition into the facility. Santmyer and Roca (1991) show how a psychiatric nurse can help intervene in behavior problems. Lomranz (1991) discusses a model for psychotherapeutic programming that provides a range of mental health services for the staff, the residents, and the families. What is missing in the literature are examples of systems-based models that focus interventions on the interactional, contextual, and organizational factors contributing to problems for residents, staff, and families. Such models would address the boundary issues between family and facility that are inherent in long-term care. Conflicting interests among residents, staff members, and families would be deemphasized in favor of identifying shared purpose. Interventions would seek to liberate individuals in the system rather than constrain their creativity and flexibility. Finally, such models of intervention would promote the uniqueness of each person in order to balance depersonalization resulting from emphasis on regulations, procedures, and medical diagnostic classifications.

The Biography Project of the University of Minnesota* provides one example of a systems intervention approach. The program aims to accomplish three major objectives. The first is to engage families in a positive growth-oriented activity to balance the experience of loss, failure, and sense of disloyalty that often accompanies nursing home placement. The second is to build a relationship between the staff and families that is based on equal status, collaborative activities, and clearly defined complementary roles. The third objective is to foster the development of positive relations between direct-care staff members and elders by providing the staff with information and personal perspectives on the individual. This last objective serves as the central organizing feature of the intervention based on research that has shown the salutary effects of life history information about residents on staff attitudes and perceptions (Learman, Avorn, Everitt, & Rosenthal, 1990; Pietrukowicz & Johnson, 1991).

The Biography Project centers on multiple family groups with a focus on constructing materials that capture the life history and personal characteristics of the resident. Such information is developed to present to the staff as a means to help them understand and appreciate the life of the elder before illness led to the nursing home. The development of the biography organizes the activities of families and serves as the core around which the staff and family can build a relationship. This working relationship is based not on the biomedical model with the resident seen as ill and dependent, but rather on a textured narrative of life experiences of the elder. The biography thus serves to create a new type of conversation between the family and staff. The biography allows the development of a "binocular view," melding the perspectives of the elder as he or she is now with a view of that person through the course of his or her life.

For the family, creation of the biography accomplishes three things. First, it gives the family a positive activity around which to organize their interactions. At the time of nursing home placement, family emotional and physical resources are often exhausted. Placement often feels like a failure—failure to stop the illness and failure to keep the elder within the family. For some, it may feel like an act of disloyalty and betrayal. The biography process does not so much distract the family from such feelings as it places them within a larger context. The last decade or so of the elder's life may be a story of illness and deterioration, but seen within the context of a life history or a family history spanning several generations, the story is only one

---

*Development of the Biography Project was funded by grants from the Alzheimer's Association and the National Institute of Aging.

chapter among many. In the biography process, the family reclaims some of what has been lost. Especially when there has been a progressive dementing illness where the distinct character of the elder is lost, the gathering of materials representing life and individuality helps the family to recapture symbolically the elder's personhood. Most families create some sort of object in the group—a book of stories and photos, a videotape, or a box filled with favorite possessions—which is kept as a legacy. Often the materials gathered into stories and photos are copied and sent to other family members, even those in other locations. Thus, the biography process can be used by family members to reconnect with each other, as well as with the elder who has been placed.

In leading the groups, the therapist has a specific role, serving as an expert on the process of constructing a biography. However, the group leader claims no expertise as to the content of the presentation. Only the family knows the elder's life and only the family can lay claim to expertise in this area. The family members' expertise provides them with the stature and legitimacy that is crucial to taking the role of teacher to the nursing home staff. The group leader not only suggests directions for the process, but also acts as a student, allowing the family to teach him or her about the elder. Similarly, families in the groups serve as both teachers and students to each other.

With multiple members from the family involved, different perspectives, memories, and feelings become available. Sometimes memories and interpretations of family members are diametrically opposed to one another. The group leader does not try to mediate these disputes or resolve the conflicts. Instead, each perspective is accepted and valued. Leaders discuss the inevitability of different perceptions within the family. Each family member's unique contribution to the biography adds texture and dimensionality to the view of the elder, making it more realistic.

The final product, the biography presentation, deserves special attention. Often nursing homes already obtain biographies through social histories and the like. There are important distinctions between what biography groups develop and what social histories obtain. In the biography process, families are directed to spend less time on the facts of a person's life and more time on capturing the essence of the person.

Three approaches are emphasized to capture the person: stories, pictures, and objects. Stories and narratives fixed in time and place that illuminate something about the person have an immediacy and concreteness. If a family member describes an elder as fastidious or gregarious, we ask the person to tell us a story to illustrate this feature. Pictures have a similar directness in what they communicate about a person. Photos of the elder across the life span from infancy to adulthood powerfully illustrate growth and development. We encourage family members to examine familiar photos in new ways, to try to see them as if for the very first time. In this way, they gain some insight into how the nursing staff members, who are new to the photos, might react. It also helps family members break through their own habitual perceptions of the elder, allowing a note of discovery and surprise to become part of the process. We encourage each family to bring in meaningful objects from the elder's life. Sometimes these are favorite possessions—a book, a sculpture, a special pipe. Sometimes it is an object the elder created—a painting, a quilt. Other objects may represent accomplishments—a mounted fish that grandmother caught, a recipe that won an award and was published in the paper, a commendation for excellence at work.

Much of the material developed by families relates to positive aspects of the elder's life. This seems appropriate since the biography process is in part a celebration of the elder's life by the family, an act of loyalty and regard that helps balance out the disloyalty of nursing home placement. However, each group also deals with some darker material—past family conflicts, personal failings in the elder, and even issues of abuse and neglect. We rely on group wisdom to advise families on how to present this material in terms of the staff. We are guided by the desire to help the staff appreciate the elder as an individual. The problem of shameful or negative memories in families is a potentially difficult issue. However, in our experience to date, families, with help from the group and group facilitator, have been able to come to comfortable resolutions of these issues every time they arose.

Within the family groups, we seek to capture and express something of *the essence of the elder*. Families serve as teachers and students to each other. The multiple-family group works together in focusing the material developed over several months into a reasonable and meaningful presentation for the staff. The group also decides the manner in which they will present the material. Some groups have videotaped their presentation and then shown the tape to the staff. Others have made direct presentations, either family by family or all together as a group. By relying as much as possible on group wisdom for determining issues of content and format, we are promoting the development of *relationships among the families*. These relationships appear to last beyond the formal program, with some groups continuing the meet many months after the completion of the biographies.

The actual presentation to the staff is, in many ways, a ritual of transition and gathering together. In sharing the stories, photos, and objects, families not only teach but symbolically invite staff into intimate regions of their lives. The personal nature of the material shared during these meetings creates the foundation for further exchanges between family and staff. In one case, for example, the staff was frustrated by a wife's insistence that her demented husband be cleanly shaved even though he became quite upset and combative when this was done. When she shared with them her husband's past pride in his appearance, his fastidiousness, and the shock he would feel were he aware of how he looked, the staff could appreciate her pain and understand her wishes.

The Biography Project provides an alternative to the problem-saturated formulations upon which the biomedical model of care is based. It incorporates the unique strengths of family systems. At its best, it draws on material from multiple generations. It situates present events within the family history and in so doing implies a family future. It explicitly values intimate domains of knowledge and affect. It is firmly centered in the legitimacy of the family as the "owners" of the elder's story and experts in his or her life history.

Further research and development continue in the Biography Project. The efficacy of the program in achieving its goals of helping families cope and bringing families and staff closer together are being evaluated. We are studying the process by which biographies are constructed and the types of discourses that result.

Two major issues will be the subject of future studies. First is the place of the elder in the biography process. Up to this time, we have applied the program in cases where the elder was severely demented and unable to tell his or her own story. The family's construction of the biography was intended to replace what the elder could not do. In bringing cognitively intact elders into the process, it would seem important to not allow their voices to dominate the narrative. It would be more difficult to follow through on the principle that each perception within the family is valid and adds to the whole if this happened. Given the weight that would normally be accorded a person's perceptions of his or her own life, how to balance out contributions of elders and their families to the creation of life history materials will require further study as we work in this way with nondemented or moderately demented populations.

The second important question concerns how the infusion of personal material into the nursing home narrative affects care. Will the staff use elements of the personal history in constructing care plans? Will the stories be shared when training new aides? Will the experience of the biography change the ways in which the nursing staff interacts with the resident?

CONCLUSION

When working with elders, we are simultaneously involved with our past and our future. The available evidence suggests that our reliance on the model of care that has evolved through the long-term care industry fails to meet our obligation to our aged. Solutions do not come easily. We must remember, however, that nursing homes not only serve the aged of today, but will doubtless serve the aged of tomorrow—us. As systems therapists, our contribution is especially crucial. Our background and understanding of family strengths give us a model for how to best contribute to the betterment of long-term care—by the infusion of intimacy, increased cooperation and collaboration, and support for individuality and empowerment. The Biography Project is offered as only one example of this type of approach. It is hoped that this becomes just one alternative among many contributed by systems-trained therapists.

More than any other institution, nursing homes are repositories of our history—the rich life experiences contained within their walls create a resourse of incalculable value. People come to work in the nursing home industry because of a commitment to an important part of our culture and community. A systemic perspective views the problems in the long-term care industry as a result of misguided or narrowly focused attempts at solutions. Positive interventions in nursing home care do not require the infusion of additional resources. They encompass the essential resources. Positive interventions come by removing barriers to connection among family, staff, and residents and fostering sharing and collaboration among all.

REFERENCES

Arling, G., Harkins, E., & Capitman, J. (1986). Institutionalization and personal control: A panel study of impaired older people. *Research on Aging, 8*(1), 38–56.

Aronson, M., Cox, D., Guastadisegni, P., Frazier, C., Sherlock, L., Grower, R., Barbera, A., Sternberg, M., Breed, J., & Koren, M. (1992). Dementia and the nursing home: Association of care needs. *Journal of the American Geriatrics Society, 40,* 27–33.

Boss, P. (1986). *Family stress management.* Newbury Park, CA: Sage.

Boss, P., Caron, W., & Horbal, J, (1988). Alzheimer's disease and ambiguous loss. In C. Chillman, E. Nunnally, & F. Cox (Eds.), *Chronic illness and disability: Volume II in Families in Trouble series.* Newbury Park, CA: Sage.

Boss, P., Caron, W., Horbal, J., & Mortimer, J. (1990). Predictors of depression in caregivers of dementia: Boundary ambiguity and mastery. *Family Process, 29,* 245–254.

Boss, P., & Greenberg, J. (1984). Family boundary ambiguity: A new variable in family stress theory. *Family Process, 23,* 535–546.

Bowers, B., & Becker, M. (1992). Nurses' aides in nursing homes: The relationship between organization and quality. *The Gerontologist, 32*(2), 360–366.

Burton, L., German, P., Rovner, B., & Brant, L. (1992). Physical restraint use and cognitive decline among nursing home residents. *Journal of the American Geriatrics Society, 40,* 811–816.

Chafetz, P. (1991). Behavioral and cognitive outcomes of SCU care. *Clinical Gerontologist, 11*(1), 19–38.

Chappell, N., & Novak, M. (1992). The role of support in alleviating stress among nursing assistants. *The Gerontologist, 32*(2), 351–359.

Cohen-Mansfield, J., & Marz, M. (1993). Pain and depression in the nursing home: Corroborating results. *Journal of Gerontology: Psychological Sciences, 48,* 96–97.

Cox, C., & Ephross, P. (1989). Group work with families of nursing home residents: Its socialization and therapeutic functions. *Journal of Gerontological Social Work, 13* (3/4), 61–73.

Donnelly, C., Compton, S., Devany, N., Kirk, S., & McGuigan, M. (1989). The elderly in long term care: 1—Prevalence of dementia and levels of dependency. *International Journal of Geriatric Psychiatry, 4,* 299–304.

Ernst, P., Badash, D., & Beran, B. (1977). Incidence of mental illness in the aged: Unmasking the effects of a diagnosis of chronic brain syndrome. *Journal of the American Geriatrics Society, 25,* 371–375.

Frey, D., Kelbley, T., Durham, L., & James, J. (1992). Enhancing the self-esteem of selected male nursing home residents. *The Gerontologist, 42* (4), 552–557.

Garrard, J., Dunham, T., Makris, L., Cooper, S., Heston, L., Ratner, E., Zelteman, D., & Kane, R. (1992). Longitudinal study of psychotropic drug use by elderly nursing home residents. *Journal of Gerontology: Medical Sciences, 47*(6), M183–M188.

German, P., Rovner, B., Burton, L., Brant, L., & Clark, R. (1992). The role of mental morbidity in the nursing home experience. *The Gerontologist, 32*(2), 152–158.

Hare, J., & Skinner, D. (1990). The relationship between work environment and burnout in nursing home employees. *The Journal of Long-Term Care Administration,* Fall, 9–12.

Heiselman, T., & Noelker, L. (1991). Enhancing mutual respect among nursing assistants, residents, and residents' families. *The Gerontologist, 31*(4), 552–555.

Ineichen, B. (1990). The extent of dementia among old people in residential care. *International Journal of Geriatric Psychiatry, 5,* 327–335.

Kaakinen, J. (1992). Living with silence. *The Gerontologist, 32*(2), 258–264.

Kane, R., Freeman, I., Caplan, A., Aroskar, M., & Urv-Wong, E. (1990). Everyday autonomy in nursing homes. *Generations,* supplement, 69–71.

Lamy, P. (1993). Institutionalization and drug use in older adults in the United States. *Drugs and Aging, 3*(3), 232–237.

Larson, D., Lyons, J., Hohmann, A., Beardsley, R., Huckeba, W., & Rabins, P. (1989). A systemic review of nursing home research in three psychiatric journals 1966–1985. *International Journal of General Psychiatry, 4,* 129–134.

Learman, L., Avorn, J., Everitt, D., & Rosenthal, R. (1990). Pygmalion in the nursing home: The effects of caregiver expectations on patient outcomes. *Journal of the American Geriatrics Society, 38,* 797–803.

Levenson, A., & Felkins, B. (1979). Prevention of psychiatric recidivism. *Journal of the American Geriatrics Society, 27,* 536–540.

Lomranz, J. (1991). Mental health in homes for the aged and the clinical psychology of aging: Implementation of a model service. *Clinical Gerontologist, 10*(3), 47–72.

Mercer, S., Garner, J., & Leon J. (1991). *Geriatric case practice in nursing homes.* Newbury Park, CA: Sage.

Mullins, L., Nelson, C., Busciglio, H., & Weiner, H. (1988). Job satisfaction among nursing home personnel: The impact of organizational structure and supervisory power. *The Journal of Long-Term Care Administration,* Spring, 12–18.

Myers, J., Weissman, M., Wischler, G., et al. (1984). Six month prevalence of psychiatric disorders in three communities. *Archives of General Psychiatry, 41,* 959–967.

National Institute on Aging Consensus Task Force. (1980). Senility reconsidered: Treatment possibilities for mental impairment in the elderly. *Journal of the American Medical Association, 244,* 259–263.

Parmelee, P., Katz, I., & Lawton, M. P. (1992). Incidence of depression in long-term care setting. *Journal of Gerontology: Medical Sciences, 47*(6), M189–M196.

Pattee, J., & Otteson, O. (1991). *Medical direction in the nursing home: Principles and concepts for physician administrators.* Minneapolis, MN: North Ridge Press.

Peppard, N. (1991). Special care units for dementia: The next generation. *The Journal of Long-Term Care Administration,* Spring, 10–16.

Pepper Commission Report. (1990). *A call for action,* Washington, DC: U.S. Government Printing Office.

Pietrukowicz, M., & Johnson, M. (1991). Using life histories to individualize nursing home staff attitudes towards residents. *The Gerontologist, 31*(1), 102–106.

Reinardy, J. (1992). Decisional control in moving to a nursing home: Postadmission adjustment and well-being. *The Gerontologist, 32,* 96–101.

Robins, L., Helzner, J., Weissman, M., et al. (1984). Lifetime prevalence of specific psychiatric disorders in three sites. *Archives of General Psychiatry, 41,* 949–958.

Rovner, B., Kakoneck, S., Fillipp, L., et al. (1986). Prevalence of mental illness in a community nursing home. *American Journal of Psychiatry, 143,* 1446–1449.

Sabin, T., Vitug, A., & Mark, V. (1982). Are nursing homes' diagnosis and treatment adequate? *Journal of the American Medical Association, 248,* 321–322.

Santmyer, K., & Roca, R. (1991). Geropsychiatry in long term care: A nurse-centered approach. *Journal of the American Geriatrics Society, 39,* 156–159.

Santos, J., & Vandenbos, G. (Eds.). (1982). *Psychology and the older adult: Challenges for training in the 1980s.* Washington, DC: American Psychological Association.

Sheridan, J., White, J., & Fairchild, T. (1992). Ineffective staff, ineffective supervision or ineffective administration?: Why some nursing homes fail to provide adequate care. *The Gerontologist, 32,*(3), 334–341.

Smallegan, M. (1985). There was nothing else to do: Needs for care before nursing home admission. *The Gerontologist, 25*(4), 364-369.

Spore, D., Smyer, M., & Cohn, M. (1991). Assessing nursing assistants' knowledge of behavioral approaches to mental health problems. *The Gerontologist, 31*(3), 309-317.

Wagnild, G. (1988). A descriptive study of nurse's aide turnover in long term care facilities. *The Journal of Long-Term Care Administration*, Spring, 19-23.

Weissman, M., Myers, J., Tischler, G., et al. (1985). Psychiatric disorders (DSM-III) and cognitive impairment among elderly in a U.S. urban community. *Acta Psychiatrica Scandinavia, 71*, 366-379.

❧ 12 ✥

Reconciling with Unfulfilled Dreams at the End of Life

Wayne E. Oates, Ph.D.
University of Louisville
Louisville, Kentucky

Much is made of the burden of aging as it applies to the younger and middle generations of the family. Caregiving responsibility, economic stress, and impingement on normal life-cycle activities are consistently lamented by the younger generations as this burden of aging is considered. But the older generation is very often the most stable of the family and often experiences the caregiving obligation, economic responsibility, and denial of time to devote to their own interests and desires because of the burden of the younger generations. This is a special type of burden that elders face when their posterity is unwilling or unable to care for themselves and provide responsible care for the family. In such situations, the elders have to deal not only with the normal grief and stress associated with aging and loss but also with grief over their unfulfilled dreams of a healthy family that will carry on the loving commitment that the elder provided.

An early marriage and family therapist, Ernest Groves (1940), said that the need for perpetuity is a distinctly human craving. As the end of life approaches, one of the fundamental efforts of older individuals is to overcome the stagnation to which modern life relegates them so that they might continue their involvement in life in their old age (Erikson, 1994). Successful involvement in this last stage of life often results in the elder's seeking *ego transcendence* (Peck, 1978), as he or she focuses on passing down elements of his or her wisdom and family strength to the younger generations (Hargrave & Anderson, 1992). Thus, the need for and effort toward transcendence, emotional and spiritual contribution to the family, is invested by aging persons in their children and grandchildren. It expresses itself in their dreams for their children's and families' futures, their achievements and contributions to the community at large. In the Old Testament, the prophet Joel says, "Your old ones shall dream dreams and your young ones shall see visions" (Joel 2:28).

EXAMPLES OF DEATHS OF DREAMS IN AGING FAMILIES

Today, the efforts toward transcendence and dreams of many older persons languish because their children and grandchildren have no vision of responsible creativity for their own lives. Older people are more conscious of the shortness of life and easily despair as they see their children and grandchildren waste time and opportunity. More traumatic collapses of dreams and posterity occur when children's or grandchildren's lives are lost to accident, suicide, or murder, or to such diseases as AIDS. Consider the following cases as evidence of the many situations in which older people experience the loss of their "normal" lives and the deaths of their dreams for "normal" families.

Case One

A 70-year-old couple have a 40-year-old daughter, who is single and still lives at home with them. She is chronically depressed and repeatedly attempts suicide. They are somewhat affluent and have sought psychiatric treatment for her. She is a borderline personality or a stably unstable person who is developmentally immature and suffers social invalidism (Millon, 1981). She has difficulty keeping a job, and consistently takes menial jobs not in keeping with her college education. Her parents have made many attempts to enable her to live independently, but her inability to pay her own basic expenses causes her to return to the family home as a refuge. This pushes the parents into codependency–dependency as they grieve that she cannot make something out of herself.

They have a son who is 35 years old and highly successful as an investment broker. In their conversations with friends, in which everyone extols the successes of their respective children, the parents omit references to their daughter and focus on the successes of their son. The son is married and has two small children, three and five years old. When the grandchil-

Reconciling with Unfulfilled Dreams at the End of Life 261

dren visit, the couple is overjoyed to see them but remain restrained in the presence of the daughter, who is not married and shows no interest in being so, or having children herself.

The parents wonder if the daughter will ever amount to anything, and recognizing that they are nearing the end of their lives, they worry about what will become of her after their deaths.

Case Two

A 79-year-old widow, this woman was married twice and outlived both of her husbands. She and her first husband had adopted two infant daughters, who are now ages 38 and 36. The younger daughter has a 15-year-old son and 18-year-old daughter, both with whom all seems to be well. The widow's older daughter, however, has a very different story. She has been on drugs since the age of 15, and she was in prison for two years on drug and forgery charges. She moves from one place to another with different men, and she has AIDS. Her mother rarely knows where she is or how to get in touch with her. Nevertheless, the daughter lists her mother's home and phone number as her own. The police show up at the door and call to ask about the daughter's whereabouts. Department store officials call wanting to speak to the daughter about bad checks she has written.

The mother is under constant stress related to her older daughter's well-being. This prompts many physiological symptoms, which undermine her own health and alarm her even further. Her dreams for her daughter have long since died. The mother wishes the daughter could stay in prison so that at least she would have some stability—a place to live with a bed and three meals a day. She repeatedly refers to her own age and the possibility of her own death.

But the mother has some hope in that the drug-addicted daughter has a 21-year-old daughter herself. The grandchild is a stunningly beautiful person, a junior in college with a 4.0 average. She finances her college tuition by working at up-scale restaurants and receiving grants from women's organizations and scholarships from the university on the basis of her grades. She and her grandmother had a very positive relationship. The grandmother's dreams for her granddaughter somewhat assuage her grief over her smashed and broken dreams for her daughter.

Case Three

Sometimes the death of a dream for elderly persons is not a metaphor. In this case, a 75-year-old couple had an only daughter. At age 40, she was divorced, and the mother of 10-year-old son. She had been severely ill with schizophrenia for several years but was well enough to work as long as she took her medications. She and her son lived with her parents. During a severe episode of her illness, she became convinced of a conspiracy involving two or three men who were going to kidnap her son. One evening the delusion became so overpowering that to prevent it from actually happening she shot her son to death while he slept and then killed herself.

The murder/suicide was a sudden traumatic event for the parents/grandparents. The illness of their daughter had caused perpetual sorrow for them. The deaths put an end to their hopes and dreams that the daughter would recover and to their aspirations for the young grandson. They suffered from shock even after several months. With each trip to the rural cemetery, they were forced to confront the despair of the situation.

Case Four

This couple, in their early 60s, are the parents of two daughters and a son, who was their second child. The younger daughter and the son have fulfilled the hopes of their parents vocationally and maritally. However, tragedy struck with the older daughter. She married before she became established vocationally and moved 600 miles away with her husband. The marriage was an unhappy one from the start for the daughter, and it became progressively worse after two children were born.

The daughter decided to get a divorce in the small southern town in which she and her husband lived. After a brutal divorce hearing and incompetent legal assistance, the judge granted her husband custody of their two young children. She was allowed to see them only every other weekend and had to vacate the home. The husband was the custodial parent and was able to decide whether it was in the best interests of the children to be seen by their mother. The daughter lived in the area for a month with friends, with no job and no money to pay rent. When she did see the children, they both were so ill at ease that she had to ask their father to come pick them up.

The daughter called her parents and asked if she might live with them. They consented and she moved her clothing and a bedroom set to her parents' home. Four years have passed since she has seen her children. In this time, the husband has not allowed telephone contact, her letters remain unanswered and her gifts unacknowledged. The grandparents receive the same treatment. All contact between them and the grandchildren has been severed. After they supported their daughter for two years of professional training, she finally left the program, found a job, rented an apartment, and moved out of the house. She is angry with her parents because of her dependency on them. The grandparents bear the loss of access to the grandchildren mostly in silence, talking only to a few very close friends about it. Their dream of being able to express their love to their grandchildren is, for all practical purposes, dead. And their dream for their daughter to have a self-sustaining and fulfilling vocation is yet to be realized.

EFFECTS OF THE DEATH OF DREAMS ON AGING PERSONS AND THERAPEUTIC RESPONSES

Aging people certainly do not all respond alike to the deaths of their dreams for their children and grandchildren. Nevertheless, they do have several responses in common with varying degrees of intensity. The marriage and family therapist can devise effective therapeutic responses that will lessen the load of sorrow that the elderly suffer.

The Shortness of Life Remaining

The elderly hope against hope that they will live long enough to see their sons, daughters, and grandchildren straighten out. They feel the shortness of life bearing in on them. They wonder what will happen to their loved ones after their own deaths. As one parent said to a chronically alcoholic son, "This stuff is killing you a little bit at a time. I want you to bury me. I don't want to have to bury you." Over and beyond this anxiety about the shortness of life, those persons who have any measure of affluence spend considerable time and money in writing their wills and forming trusts to care for their surviving, but impaired, loved ones. Furthermore, these elderly parents cannot depend on their offspring to take care of their funerals and burials. They have to plan them themselves. While still alive, they may experience disabling diseases or accidents and find that they must fend for themselves in nursing homes, wondering where their son or daughter is and what, if anything, he or she can do to help.

The therapist can be of special help to the elderly person who is being forced to confront plans for his or her own impairment or death when there is no reliable child or grandchild to help. The therapist can be a sounding board for the testing of plans for a will, a trust, or a funeral. In many cases, the therapist may be asked to conduct or assist in the aging person's funeral so that his or her wishes and plans are implemented. These interactions with the therapist can put the elderly person's mind at ease.

Nevertheless, the therapist needs to be careful not to handle his or her own anxiety about death and dying by reassuring the person to the point of disregarding the reality. It is essential that the therapist realize that aging persons see many friends die and need to be taken seriously. An elderly therapist knows the concern about the shortness of life. A younger therapist may take the issue more lightly, neglecting the older client in the process. A better approach is to let the older person teach the younger therapist what facing the impending end of life is like.

The therapist can also provide real support to elderly parents and grandparents with respect to issues around dying by leading group therapy sessions. If the therapist has a group of elderly persons in treatment, he or she can bring the issue of life and time remaining back into clear focus and explore how each participant handles this concern. Some philosophize, while others seek consolation for their life-threatening diseases.

Embarrassment

The condition of a son or daughter who has shattered an aging parent's dream is often an embarrassment to the parent. In social conversations, it is customary for friends—especially casual ones—to ask about each other's children. What are they doing now? Are they married? Do they have children? In many cases, these questions are openers for the acquaintance whose grown sons and daughters are doing well to boast about their accomplishments. If the parent has one or more successful children and one who is impaired, the parent will discuss the successful ones only. They are too embarrassed to talk about an impaired child, sometimes to the point of not discussing any of their children, except in generalities.

This situation, which I call "show and tell," can become one of devious innuendo. However, when real friendships develop between aging individuals, the sharing of unfulfilled expectations can be a healing experience. It becomes a profound expression of friendship and caring when people actually know the story of impaired sons or daughters and can share each other's broken dreams. Such friendships become mutual burden-bearing pilgrimages through which aging persons discover that they are not alone.

The therapist can provide a safe place for people to explore the death of their dreams without embarrassment. This experience can mark the beginning of the older person's acceptance—with some degree of serenity—of a situation that has not changed despite all of their efforts and investments of time, money, and energy. Alternatives, such as reinvesting their time and love in younger disadvantaged children, may foster a renewal of energy and hope for them. Such meaningful activity may even extend life, whereas giving up and giving in to adversity may well shorten it. They can be gently led away from using checkbook therapy, squandering money in the hope of changing the behavior of an impaired or irresponsible son or daughter.

Reconciling with Unfulfilled Dreams at the End of Life 265

Isolation

Embarrassment may prompt aging persons to isolate themselves by withdrawing from conversation with other people. Disengagement is a natural part of retirement and aging. Disability may increase this isolation. Despair is a very common reaction to the collapse of one's dreams for sons, daughters, and grandchildren. All of these influences can converge to perpetuate social isolation among the aged and aging.

Again, informal groups led by a therapist can help prevent isolation. As older persons interact with one another, there is potential for acceptance, trust, and hope. However, older people who are isolated often do not wish to participate in groups. Depression can squelch any initiative toward involvement. It is often advisable and necessary to enlist the help of an internist or psychiatrist to prescribe medication to mitigate the immobilizing effects of depression. An expansion of therapy into community institutions will often accomplish the goal of getting the aged to join groups. The therapist, for instance, can contract with a nursing home to conduct groups on a regular basis. Also, more and more churches and synagogues are being pressured by their constituency to form therapeutic groups. The spectrum of what can be found includes divorce recovery groups, widows' and widowers' bereavement groups, and blended family groups. What is often lacking is a professionally skilled leader. A therapist working as a trained consultant can be of immeasurable help. To form a consultantship with the church or synagogue to do this would be well within the budget of the larger, more affluent religious institutions. The therapist's entrepreneurial skills can be put to work here. Another possible alternative would be adult gatherings held in the evening at a local high school. Getting older persons out at night is not an easy task, but if this were done early, before dark, in better weather, it could have real possibility. A likely side effect of such efforts is that older individuals, having met the therapist in a group session, are more likely to seek individual therapeutic assistance in the therapist's office. One reason therapists may lack for clients is that they themselves may be isolated, not mingling with people of the community in settings other than their private offices.

Codependency–Dependency

Many times aging parents actually contribute to the dissolution of their own dreams by being a codependent-dependent with impaired loved ones. The widow in Case Two is an example. Her drug-addicted daughter found an excellent job in a hospital laboratory. She was trained for the work and was good at it. But the mother insisted that the daughter *and* the granddaughter spend the summer with her in her apartment. She drove the daughter to work each day and picked her up at the bus stop at the end of the workday. She provided room and board free to her daughter and granddaughter. This met the grandmother's need to do something about her daughter's plight. However, it also freed up the daughter's income to buy drugs, which she did. The daughter became so inefficient and undependable at her job that she was fired. Prior to her relapse, she had been a valuable employee. If the mother had encouraged her daughter to get an apartment near her work and to make a place for her own daughter, there would have been less chance of exploitation—the codependence-dependence of grandparents promotes their exploitation and confirms the children or grandchildren in their deviant behaviors. For this reason, therapeutic 12-step approaches put as much responsibility on the members of the family system as they do on the identified patient. Even so, 12-step programs do not involve the entire system of the family, for instance, a high-achieving sibling or several such siblings. The more functional members may give money to the aging parent or grandparent, who then gives it to the dependent family member.

The Long-Term Patterns of Life

The responses of the parent or grandparent to the stresses caused by the death of a dream are shaped by his or her long-term ways of handling the emergencies of life. For example, a dependent person may crumple up in helplessness. The histrionic person may overdramatize the grief to the despair of the whole family system. The narcissistic person may feel that he or she should to have been an exception to having to face dreams unrealized.

To help in dramatizing these patterns for the family, the therapist may create a genogram. The use of the genogram provides an understanding of the global context of disappointment and what to anticipate in caring for the aged person who feels betrayed by life. Diagnostically, the degree of flexibility the person has in moving from one mode of coping to another is an important capacity to encourage. For example, codependent-dependents may need to do things for themselves. Dependent persons can be encouraged to believe in themselves and their futures.

THERAPEUTIC ATTITUDES AND RESOURCES

The therapist needs a certain frame of mind to be aware of the grief the elderly feel as they watch their dreams disappear. They often are so filled

Reconciling with Unfulfilled Dreams at the End of Life

with hopelessness they cannot see any use in talking about it. Overcome by the finiteness of life, they struggle with the inevitability of death, of mortality. Many people who are over 50 years of age have a secret sense of how long they will live. Those who are hemmed in by the death of their dreams can often find a real reason for talking about it to the therapist, assuming he or she asks at an appropriate time and under the right circumstances: As you face the loss of this dream, what do you think about in terms of how long you will live? The therapist's own consciousness of finitude and the shortness of life creates empathy for the aging person.

The therapist who is a loner is not likely to understand the aged person at this crossroads. And as areas of specialization are increased, with people often being cared for by several other professionals—physicians, internists, neurologists, cardiologists, urologists, and podiatrists, or, in cases where money is scarce, social agencies, social workers, and welfare or disability administrators—the therapist may be inadvertently locked out of the interdisciplinary team. In the process, therapists can become isolated.

On the other hand, seeking access to information that can be provided by these other professionals and conferring with them reduces the isolation of the therapist. It may turn out that these professionals are trained and certified as therapists themselves. This approach also has spinoff value. These professionals can become sources of referral to the family therapist; in addition, their contributions can lessen the possibility of litigation, and they can share the responsibility of litigation should it occur.

The therapist can supplement his or her individual and family therapy by making use of the services of self-help groups in the community. For example, the aged parents of the murder/suicide in Case Three could have found help in Survivors of Suicide sponsored by Comprehensive Mental Health Centers. Compassionate Friends is a highly responsible and well-led community group for parents and grandparents who have lost a son, daughter, or grandchild to death. It would not be a waste of the therapist's time to accompany the couple in Case Three to their first meeting. In addition to being a support to the couple, the therapist becomes acquainted with the leadership of the group and in it finds a potential source of friendship and referral.

GENERAL THERAPEUTIC STRATEGIES IN DEALING WITH DEATH OF DREAMS

Bereavement is a process—from shock through mourning to living again. The process of grief most congruent with life from the author's rather long experience with many bereaved persons is as follows:

(1) **Shock.** A daze of unbelief characterizes this stage. The person may think and act as if nothing has really happened and function that way. For example, a man told that his son has been killed continues to work in his garden as if nothing has changed.

(2) **Numbness.** Here the person realizes what has happened, but cannot *feel* its reality. This is nature's anesthetic, allowing the person gradually to absorb the pain of the loss.

(3) **A struggle between fantasy and reality.** With the gradual dissipation of numbness, the realization of loss, the client may weep, express anger, and verbalize tender feelings about the person on whom he or she had pinned his or her hopes. Other times, fantasy takes over and the client acts as if there has been no loss. The widow in Case Two would immerse herself in community work and dissociate her grief over her daughter's imprisonment for several days. Then the harsh reality would hit and she would become very agitated when at home alone.

(4) **Mourning and catharsis.** The person hits bottom and pours out his or her sorrow. This is the crisis of dereliction, or what Marty (1993) calls the cry of absence—absence of the loved one and even of God. Once the person's healing has taken root, he or she begins to live life in peace for spans of time.

(5) **Selective memories and stabbing pain.** This happens periodically when events occur that trigger all of the unpleasant emotions again. Then for 24 to 96 or more hours, the person fast-cycles back through the process again. Over the course of the next two or three years this happens less and less frequently.

(6) **The formation of new attachments and the discovery of a new purpose in life.** The loss exists as a real memory, but it is now located in the past—out of the way of constructive living.

The therapist will see the client more often from stage 1 through stage 4, less often during stage 5, and on request when stage 6 is reached. The therapist's main task is to keep the sense of hope alive and to support the person through this definable process.

As Charles Bugg (1993) writes regarding the severe pineal cancer of his 10-year-old son, death seemed to be certain. However, the child eventually recovered, although his growth was stunted. He is now 22 years of age. But the parents of this child were in midlife. They *had* time. The *grandparents* would be in their 70s or 80s. Their grief would be complicated by a sense of their time being short. This awareness would make their grief very different. Would they have the opportunity to learn to live again?

People caring for this family would likely not notice the grandparents. But the therapist who considers the whole system of generations would consider them even if they were inaccessible.

CONCLUSION

The central theme of this chapter has been finitude—the inherently limited amount of time that the elderly have to find ways to come to grips with the death of their dreams. This fixed parameter leads to a unique form of grief, which requires the design and implementation of specific therapeutic strategies. The therapist's perspective must encompass insight into this population's distinct circumstances and be built on empathy, patience, and wisdom.

REFERENCES

Bugg, C. (1993). *Learning to dream again: From grief to gratitude.* Macon, GA: Smyth & Helwys.
Erikson, E., et al. (1994). Vital involvement in old age. New York: Norton.
Groves, E. (1940). *The social functions of the family.* New York: J. B. Lippincott.
Hargrave, T. & Anderson, W. (1992). *Finishing well: Aging and reparation in the intergenerational family.* New York: Brunner/Mazel.
Marty, M. (1993). *The cry of absence.* New York: HarperCollins.
Millon, T. (1981). *Disorders of personality: DSM-III, Axis II.* New York: Wiley.
Peck, M. S. (1978). *The road less traveled.* New York: Simon & Schuster.

13

Dying and Death in Aging Intergenerational Families

William T. Anderson, Ed.D. [*]
Texas Woman's University
Denton, Texas

Dying and death have been with humankind as long as pregnancy and birth. These key themes related to family loss and family gain have played themselves out across the centuries, since the beginning of recorded history. When Moses, the great leader of the Jews, came to the end of his life, the scripture writer (Deuteronomy, 34, 7) noted that "he was a hundred and twenty years old when he died, his eye undimmed, his vigor unimpaired." This seems to be the source of the Jewish festive greeting, "May you live to be 120." How many current Americans will reach 80, let alone 120, with their eyes undimmed, their vigor unimpaired?

Dying and death are obviously not new issues. Every culture has made attempts to deal with the ending of life, in ways consonant with prevailing societal belief systems. Boyle and Morris (1987) clearly trace the images of aging and dying used in varying cultures and differing centuries. Different peoples and races have made "Promethean attempts to defeat time, to arrest aging, and to conquer death.... It is the unfolding of a tale about time, aging

---

[*]The author wishes to acknowledge the clinical input of William Whalen, hospital chaplain in Olympia, Washington. His suggestions for this chapter, based on many years of working with the dying and their families, have been invaluable.

and dying in the lives of certain people who, like jewels in a setting, reflect in their philosophies, not only themselves and their thoughts, but the tapestry of their culture as well" (p. xi). As we approach the end of the 20th century, we Americans also attempt to defeat time (our youth-centered culture), to arrest aging (through modern miracles of medicine), and to conquer death. Yet, the reality remains: one is born, one lives, and one dies.

DYING AND DEATH IN MODERN AMERICA

The Aging of America

In 1900, the U.S. Census Bureau noted that there were about 76 million people in the United States. Of that number, only 3 million were 65 or older. This 4 percent of the total population was divided equally between men and women. In 1987, the U.S. Census Bureau indicated that the U.S. population had reached 243 million; 30 million of that number were age 65 or older. That number represented 12 percent of the population. Sixty percent of this number were women. Present projections indicate that by the year 2010 (only 15 years away), the elderly will represent about 14 percent of the population of the United States. These trends point to the gradually increasing number of aging intergenerational families; this population will undoubtedly need the assistance of family therapists in the years to come.

Lebowitz (1985) has argued strongly that American "families go to extraordinary lengths to care for their elderly" (p. 457). However, due to progress in medicine, the elderly live much longer, sometimes in a physical or mental condition that requires more care than the family can continue to provide. As a result, dying and death often take place in impersonal settings, such as hospitals or nursing homes.

Denial of Death

At the beginning of this century, it was quite common for people to die in their own home, surrounded by members of the extended family. Today, the picture is radically different. Marshall (1980) reviewed the literature on where older people die. He concluded "that although only about 5 percent of the older population live in nursing homes at any one time, about 25 percent of older people who die in a given year die in a nursing home. Another 50 percent die in hospitals and 25 percent die at home or in the community" (Atchley, 1991, p. 245). Currently, then, the majority of Americans who die will do so surrounded by hired caregivers, not members of their extended family.

A prevailing belief is that hospital caregivers tend to avoid the dying patient; in many hospitals, however, the opposite is true. One hospital caregiver wrote: "When a patient is dying and there are no family members or friends present, the nursing staff will frequently make it a point to sit in the patient's room while they do their charting. Social workers and chaplains will also pay more frequent visits to the dying patients. Compassionate people do not lose their compassion simply because someone is dying" (personal communication). Nevertheless, in the present health care system, there is a high probability that most of us will suffer the ultimate loss, death itself, without the presence and comfort of our loved ones.

This "hiding" of the death of aging family members from the normal experience of the younger generations colludes with the emphasis on youth in the American culture. Youth is our defense against the existential anxiety that we are all aging and that we are all approaching our own death, day by day. As Kubler-Ross (1969) noted:

> We use euphemisms, we make the dead look as if they were asleep, we ship the children off to protect them from the anxiety and turmoil around the house if the patient is fortunate enough to die at home, we don't allow children to visit their dying parents in the hospitals, we have long and controversial discussions about whether patients should be told the truth.... (p. 7)

Murray Bowen (1976) put it this way:

> In 20 years of family practice, I have had contact with several thousand families, and I have been in the background "coaching" families through hundreds of deaths and funerals. I urge family members to visit dying family members whenever possible and to find some way to include children if the situation permits. I have never seen a child hurt by exposure to death. They are hurt only by the anxiety of the survivors. (p. 345)

One hospice worker recalls that she was present when an 85-year-old man was dying. Four generations were present around the bed of the dying man as the family shared their prayers with him. "The great-grandson (two years old) climbed up on the bed, and began to talk and to shake the legs of his dying great-grandfather. Although this upset the wife a bit, the grandchildren allowed the boy to 'be with his great-grandfather.' It all seemed so natural that the young boy would share this powerful moment of death in the family" (personal communication).

The lack of literature in the family therapy field goes hand in hand with our own culture's denial of death (Walsh & McGoldrick, 1991). American society avoids death by focusing on youth, a supposed defense against mortality; family therapists avoid asking about anticipatory or actual loss, thus colluding with their clients, who also fear dying and death. Death is a very uncomfortable topic.

It is common knowledge that many people die without a will. Recent attempts to encourage older people to complete living wills have met with limited success. These are reminders to each of us of our own mortality, something many of us would rather not consider. This fear of our own mortality keeps many from discussing, even with their loved ones, that which is most obvious: we shall all die.

The family therapist working with aging intergenerational families thus faces several tasks: assisting the dying person, helping family members deal with their own anticipatory or actual loss of the dying person, and coming to grips with their denial or reluctance to accept their own death, the ultimate loss. As Paul and Paul (1982) have put it so aptly, "While there exists a constant shadow of death in everybody's life, everybody is entertaining notions of his or her own immortality" (p. 229).

This author has participated in the funerals of his parents and of three siblings. Given these experiences, it is much harder to maintain this illusion of immortality. A friend recently wrote: "When my father died (three years after my mother), I can vividly remember walking up to the coffin, looking at his body, and saying to myself, 'Well, I'm up at the plate now. It is my turn at bat and then I, too, will leave.'"

DYING AND DEATH IN AGING FAMILIES

In their review of the literature about the elderly and death, Wass and Myers (1982) have observed that *theorists* "concerned with the psychology of aging have concentrated on the awareness of death, its increasing certainty and its nearness as central to their formulations" (p. 131). However, *empirical studies* have not necessarily been based on these abstract views. What these two reviewers found were elderly studies that touched on such areas as talking about death, death fears, dying, suicide, attitudes toward death, and bereavement. Some findings (Wass & Myers, 1982) that could be helpful for therapists follow.

- Old persons not only were willing to talk about their death, but actually welcomed the opportunity (p. 131).
- Aged persons seem to be less fearful of death than younger persons (p. 132).
- Four of every five people would prefer to die in their homes (p. 132).

- The large majority of elderly wish to be allowed to die "naturally," rather than be maintained by artificial or heroic means (p. 133).
- And this additional finding powerfully reinforces the preceding: Suicide rates are higher in the elderly than in any other age group (Butler, Lewis, & Sunderland, 1991).

Facing Death: The Dying Person

There are probably as many ways of dying as there are of living. Each one of us seizes life in our own manner. Kubler-Ross (1969) reported that when her young, hospitalized patients learned of their terminal illness, they typically went through five stages:

1. Denial and isolation. *Not me!*
2. Anger. *Why me?*
3. Bargaining. *What if?*
4. Depression. *I'm very sad.*
5. Acceptance. *I'm ready to go.*

Weisman (1972), however, studied dying people who averaged 60 years of age and found that acceptance of death without denial occurred in this cohort. Kalish (1985) contended that there are little empirical research data to support Kubler-Ross's five stages. Not all who are dying pass through these stages, nor is there any natural progression. He concludes that it is paramount to recognize that people face death in their own manner. Following the client, not the model, seems to be most appropriate in therapy with the dying. The key is a willingness to be present with the person wherever he or she may be on the journey, especially if it is not where you would want the client to be.

The paradigm of life stages has been a very useful one for family therapists as they work with families and their members proceeding through normal stages of birth, growth, development, and aging. Each stage presents a person or a family with appropriate tasks specific to that period of life for the individual or for the group. Now, at the end of life, the elderly dying person is faced with some final tasks. In dealing with these, the person begins to experience his or her anticipatory grief (Rando, 1986, p. 27). Time is limited as death approaches.

Some of the tasks confronting the elderly dying include:

1. Arranging affairs, such as making a will, arranging for one's funeral, leaving last messages for friends, and taking care of any surviving loved ones.

2. Coping with his or her impending loss of loved ones. These last days and hours can be times of great healing, or continued distance in the family. Butler (1963) notes that the older person "may reveal to his wife, children, and other intimates unknown qualities of his character and unstated actions of his past; in return, they may reveal heretofore undisclosed or unknown truths. Hidden themes of great vintage may emerge, changing the quality of a lifelong relationship. Revelations of the past may forge a new intimacy"(p. 75).
3. Coping with the loss of life itself. After a long lifetime of dealing with various losses, he or she is now faced with the ultimate loss, that of life itself.
4. Deciding whether to speed up or slow down the process of death itself. If the dying elderly has completed personal unfinished business, he or she is now free to let go of life.

The anticipatory grief of the client is intimately connected with the anticipatory grief experience of the family members. Montalvo (1991) observes that the elderly patient's choice to die may only appear to be independent of the family choices. His experience indicates that when some clients choose to die, they do so because of "a desire to avoid conflict with the caregivers, or a wish to avoid being a burden to them." One caregiver told me that the most common expression by the elderly is that they do not wish to be a burden; they are willing to accept nursing home placement, rather than be a bother to their children.

Bowen (1976) relates a powerful consultation that he did in a medical center with a terminally ill woman, who was married and the mother of an emotionally disturbed daughter. This dying client was indeed facing her tasks of coping with the loss of her husband and her daughter, as well as accepting her own impending death. The doctor had told the husband and the family therapist about the woman's cancer, but he did not tell the client. This was a good example of a closed emotional system. Early in the consultation, Bowen asked the client why she thought she was not told about her terminal illness. She replied that they were afraid to tell her. "I know I have cancer. I have known it for some time.... This is the loneliest life in the world. Here I am, knowing that I am going to die, and not knowing how much time I have left. I can't talk to anyone. When I talk to my surgeon, he says it is not cancer. When I try to talk to my husband, he makes jokes about it.... I am cut off from everyone.... I wish I could die soon and not have to pretend any longer" (Bowen, 1976, pp. 343-344). At the end of the consultation, the mother mentioned to Bowen: "We sure have spent an hour walking around on my grave, haven't we? When you go home tonight, thank Washington for sending you here today."

In his comments on this consultation, Bowen points out the essential issue with this family: "to permit the mother to talk, to keep the father's anxiety from silencing her, and to hope the regular therapist could continue the process later.... It illustrates the intensity of a closed relationship system between the patient, the family and the medical staff" (p. 344). Thus, one of the major tasks of a family therapist working with a closed relationship system in an intergenerational family is to assist in helping to open up the system, at least partially, for the interfamilial communication so urgently needed when an elder member is dying.

One of the great needs of people is to talk about their illness with those who can understand. Facilitators of cancer support groups, for example, have noted that participants have many times expressed how important it was for them to talk about their cancer to someone who would listen. This improved communication enables the family to cope better with the impending death and loss.

David (1987), a family therapist dying from leukemia, stated in a very powerful way the desire of the dying to communicate deep needs and feelings to significant others:

> During the first seven and a half weeks I was hospitalized, I became painfully aware of the sense of isolation and abandonment that dying patients feel as they approach death. I am not talking simply about the sense of aloneness that comes from having no people about one, but from being unable to communicate the things that are important to oneself, or from having certain feelings that others find inadmissible. This stems from the fear that if one communicates one's deep and often painful feelings, this will stir up so much anxiety in the other that he or she will distance all the more—which is the last thing the patient wants. (p. 280)

Facing Death: The Family Survivors

As the client experiences grief at the approach of death, so, too, do the surviving family members. Rando (1986) notes three interrelated processes affecting the family members. First of all, each family member is affected intrapsychically. Everyone becomes aware of the threat of imminent death of the elderly family member. Each survivor gradually accommodates to the impending loss to the family through the approaching death. The feelings and thoughts of the loved ones are deeply perturbed, as they plan for a future without the dying elderly. Second, the family members deal with their anticipatory grief by interacting with the dying person. This occurs when they devote attention and energy to the dying. It also gives them an opportunity to resolve any unfinished business. This interactional process can preclude premature detachment from the dying person before death; otherwise, the older person will feel increased isolation. Finally, the family begins to reorganize itself as the roles and responsibilities of the dying are reassigned to surviving family members.

NORMATIVE GUIDELINES FOR GRIEF

The Individual

Human beings learn to attach soon after their exit from the womb. The most profound attachments are usually those made in the context of the family: husband–wife, mother–child, sibling–sibling. Thus, it is not surprising that when a person suffers the loss of such a significant attachment, as in the death of an elderly parent or spouse, the homeostasis developed over many years is deeply disturbed. The experience of grief is a departure from this state of homeostatic connections. A grieving person, thus, is going through a normal process of healing, analogous to physiological healing of the body. Grief after the loss of a significant relationship is normal and indeed healthy.

Therapists need to know that coping with grief is very idiosyncratic. Difficulties in therapy can arise when we want the family or the individual to grieve in a way that is comfortable for us, not necessarily helpful to them. Grief at the death of an elderly parent or spouse can manifest in screaming, laughter, pacing, smashing the wall, talking, crying, or a number of other actions. Men often apologize for their tears.

In writing about individual grief following the death of a loved one, Worden (1982) claims that completed bereavement involves four basic tasks:

1. To accept the reality of the loss in death. It is normal right after a death, even an expected one, to believe that it really has not happened. Thus, "the first task of grieving is to come full face with the reality that the person is dead, that the person is gone and will not return" (p. 11).
2. To experience the pain of grief. "It is necessary to acknowledge and work through this pain, or it will manifest itself through some symptom or other form of aberrant behavior" (p. 13). Perhaps our death-phobic American culture can hinder this task of the mourner, especially by subtle messages that grief feelings are not comfortable or acceptable in our society.
3. To adjust to an environment in which the deceased is missing. For

an elderly widow or widower, the loss of the spouse after many years of communal living can make this adjustment very stressful. One hospital caregiver told me of an incident where the elderly husband was dying in an intensive care unit. Each day, his elderly wife would visit for most of the day. When the husband did die, the wife turned to the caregiver and asked: "What am I going to do? What do I do now?" This elderly woman, now suddenly a widow, was totally immobilized, sitting in a chair, and completely lost.
4. To withdraw emotional energy from the relationship with the deceased and reinvest it in other relationships. For many elderly bereaved, this may be the most difficult task of all. For them, it feels as though life stopped when the spouse died.

However, sometimes grief after the death of a loved one can take on abnormal aspects. Horowitz (1980) states that abnormal grief is "the intensification of grief to the level where the person is overwhelmed, resorts to maladaptive behavior, or remains interminably in the state of grief without progression of the mourning process towards completion" (p. 1157).

These abnormal grief reactions can become manifest in different ways (Worden, 1982). First of all, they can be *chronic,* such as when the grief has continued for several years and the client cannot seem to bring an end to the sadness. A second form of abnormal grief is *delayed* or *suppressed,* manifesting some time after the initial, profound loss, often in response to a subsequent, less significant loss. The third type of abnormal grief reaction is *exaggerated,* when the survivor believed that he or she cannot live without the dead loved one, thus leading to hopelessness and despair. Finally, there is *masked* grief, which often shows itself in symptoms or behaviors that the client cannot consciously connect with the loss of the loved one. Persons who do not allow themselves to experience normal grief will often develop disabling somatic problems, seemingly unconnected with the masked grief.

Clients can present this unresolved or abnormal grief very directly and consciously; the clients know that they are not handling the grief well and so directly ask for professional help. However, some clients present nongrief issues that can serve to hide the unresolved sorrow. Lazare (1979) has suggested some clues that can alert the therapist to unresolved grief. One clue is when the client cannot speak of the dead loved one without showing intense grief in the present, even though the loss may have happened years earlier. Another clue is when, during therapy, there is a repeated theme of loss, thus hinting at unresolved grief. A third clue is the client's physical symptoms similar to those experienced by the loved one before death. Last, a radical change in one's lifestyle may be a tip off to unresolved grief in response to the loss of a loved one.

The Family

When an elderly family member dies, the grief reaction permeates the entire intergenerational family system. Healthy individuals coping with the grief of a loved one can and do resolve this grief over time, without the help of professional therapists. In the same vein, healthy families that have adapted to their varied losses over the course of the life span are usually able to deal with the profound grief at the loss of a beloved elderly family member. They will normally not seek out family therapists to help them with tasks that are already being handled in a functional manner.

What Worden (1982) posits for the individual survivor can also be said of the surviving intergenerational family. The family adaptational tasks after the loss of a loved one are twofold:

1. Shared acknowledgment of the reality of death and shared experience of loss. Clear information about the death of an elderly family member facilitates this shared acknowledgment. When this does not happen, there is a high risk of continued familial conflicts or emotional cutoffs. Rituals, such as funerals, provide the family with an opportunity to experience the loss together as a family.
2. Reorganization of the family system and reinvestment in other relationships and life pursuits. When an elderly family member dies, the family members need to realign important roles and relationships; if this does not occur, there may be a move back to rigid, dysfunctional patterns that no longer work for the family. If the family reorganizes, then there is an openness to invest in other relationships the energy that was once focused on the departed elderly member (Walsh & McGoldrick, 1991).

Various factors can influence the family's adaptation to loss: the manner of the death, the quality and nature of the family system, family flexibility, family communication patterns, the familial role of the departed in the family system, and the life-cycle timing of the death. Thus, family therapists working with grieving families do well to assess the total family context in which the death of the elderly occurred.

Families with a closed emotional system, however, often have great difficulty in dealing with the death of a significant elderly member. Family therapists are aware of the interconnectedness of the family system; a drastic change (such as a death) in one part of the system reverberates throughout the family constellation.

Bowen (1976) wrote about the "emotional shock wave" he observed in families months or years after significant losses, especially death:

The "Emotional Shock Wave" is a network of underground "aftershocks" of serious life events that can occur anywhere in the extended family system in the months or years following serious emotional events in a family. It occurs most often after the death or the threatened death of a significant family member.... It operates on an underground network of emotional dependence of family members on each other. (p. 339)

Because of this interconnectedness in the family, the therapist working with grieving aging families needs to consider at least three areas: the total family configuration, the functioning position of the dying person in the family, and the overall family level of life adaptation. Direct language helps to open up a closed emotional system and to deal with the denial so common in such family systems (Bowen, 1976).

Wide Variations in Grief

One of the pitfalls in grief work with individuals and families is the belief that grief following the loss of a loved one must go through certain stages, or must possess specific qualities, if it is not to become abnormal. Wortman and Silver (1989) examined four common myths about coping with loss:

1. Depression is inevitable following loss. The popular myth is that after a major loss (e.g., death or severe spinal injury), the normal reaction is intense distress. Some clinical studies, however, have not substantiated that view. Depression after a severe loss is not necessarily inevitable. Although it is normal for the grieving person to be sad, to be down, or to have the blues, these moods are not the same as clinical depression.
2. Failure to experience distress is indicative of pathology. The popular myth is that the absence of depression after a powerful loss indicates abnormal or delayed grief. Present studies, however, do not support such a view. Absence of grief does not necessarily indicate insufficient attachment to the departed beloved; in addition, delayed grief is relatively rare.
3. It is necessary to "work through" or process a loss. Once again, the available research does not support this popular myth.
4. Recovery and resolution are normal expectations following a loss. People expect a bereaved person to return to normal functioning after a relatively brief time. One woman whose son had died suddenly was expected to be back at work two days after the funeral. Six months after the death, the woman was still angry at her em-

ployer for requiring her to resume "normal life" so quickly after such a devastating loss. Present evidence indicates that "a substantial minority of individuals continue to exhibit distress for a much longer period of time than would commonly be assumed" (Wortman & Silver, 1989, p. 353).

Wortman and Silver discovered that available empirical research sometimes even contradicts these four traditional beliefs. They conclude that those working with grieving persons should be open to a wide variability of responses to loss. "As Zisook and Shuchter (1986) have indicated, at the present time 'there is no prescription for how to grieve properly for a lost spouse, and no research-validated guideposts for what is normal vs. deviant mourning ... We are just beginning to realize the full range of what may be considered "normal" grieving.' Recognition of this variability is crucial in order that those who experience loss are treated nonjudgmentally and with the respect, sensitivity and compassion they deserve" (Wortman & Silver, 1989, p. 355).

INTERVENTIONS WITH GRIEVING FAMILIES

Family therapists often have developed a high degree of empathy for their families, since they, too, have experienced in their own lives many of the difficulties that clinical families present in counseling. Counseling with the dying elderly, however, is normally possible only through second-hand experience, since the counselor has not yet experienced the process of dying. While true in all forms of therapy, the role of the therapist as learner is of utmost importance in working with the elderly dying. Kubler-Ross (1969) emphasized this role for *professionals as learners,* when she described the *dying as teachers* for caregivers. Indeed, she learned about the five stages from her dying clients, who showed her how they were coping with terminal illness.

Life-Review Therapy

Such therapy is an effective intervention strategy in working with older people, both with those who are dying and with those who survive. Butler (1963) viewed life review as "a naturally occurring, universal mental process, characterized by the progressive return to consciousness of past experiences, and particularly the resurgence of unresolved conflicts; simultaneously, and normally, these revived experiences and conflicts can be surveyed and reintegrated" (p. 66).

Westcott (1983) points out how the life-review technique with the elderly can help to improve their self-esteem, to resolve intergenerational conflict, to continue living, and to prepare them for their approaching death. Hargrave and Anderson (1992) claim that in contextual family therapy, life review with elderly clients can be used by family therapists to discover still-unresolved transgenerational issues and to credit family members for entitlement and obligations in the family ledger. This approach can help elderly family members to conclude unfinished family business and finish their life well.

Being, Not Doing

Family therapists are primarily action-oriented persons. Yet, with the dying elderly, "being" rather than "doing" seems more appropriate. Paterson (1989), working with individuals, developed four basic principles:

1. **Simply be there.** "The most valuable thing we have to offer the older person facing death is our own caring presence" (p. 230). *Being there* means to be fully present to the dying person, even if the visit lasts only five minutes. Any one visit to the dying may be the last one.
2. **Be yourself.** When we are aware of our own feelings and those of the dying person, we can be truly present to the client.
3. **Listen actively.** As dying clients reach out to us, we can use well our therapeutic skills of listening, letting them know that we are indeed *with* them. Words of comfort and a gentle touch can convey this sense of active listening.
4. **Try to understand the thoughts and feelings of the dying person.** Understanding means that the therapist accepts and respects the feelings of the dying, validating them by acceptance, yet not intruding.

Family therapists can model these behaviors for families of the dying, encouraging them to do the same. In this way, individual and systemic isolation is transformed into connectedness.

Therapist as Listener

Kemp (1984) observes that it is the counselor who is the student; the dying elderly "are the most reliable source of information about the experience of dying and death" (p. 270). He suggests that those who counsel with the dying elderly may benefit from the following lessons he learned in his work with elderly persons over a five-year period.

1. The counselor needs to accept his or her own mortality; giving up life is a process, just as living life is.
2. The counselor needs to help the dying elderly deal with death *as the elderly perceives it,* not as the counselor does. The counselor is alive and well; the client is ill and dying. The perspective of the client is what counts.
3. The counselor merely helps the elderly person do what he or she was going to do anyway, that is, to die. The client deserves all the credit!
4. Older people decide when they are going to die. When the elderly know that they have completed their "unfinished business," then they let go of life and allow death to happen.

Many caregivers working with the dying would not agree with Kemp. One hospice worker stated: "Older people die when it is their time, not necessarily when they want to. On many occasions, I have waited with people who wanted to die, but physiologically were not able to do so."

In a brief, but powerful chapter entitled "Unfinished Business," Kubler-Ross (1984) expressed the hope that "we raise a generation of children who learn about their natural emotions in such a way that they have no grief work" (p. 2). To do this, we need to examine our own lives, especially our own unfinished business. "What we have not finished in our lives will be passed on as unfinished business to our children" (p. 2). The dying elderly are faced with this task of completing unfinished business; when they do, they are ready to let go and move on to the last stage of life on earth, that of dying.

Death for many is considered the greatest loss, something to be avoided at all costs. Yet, birth, life, and death are all part of one's life journey. Thus, we can consider death as the last natural event in life. Jones (1993) comments that in the past, "death was a ritual, a part of life" (p. 89). Today, the health care system wages medical war against death, which is considered a failure of curative interventions. Jones described a single case of a terminally ill cancer patient who chose the manner and place in which she finally let go of life. Patients need to "be allowed spiritual freedom and independence of mind to experience life and death in ways that are right for them" (p. 93). Thus, one person's dying experience can be a personal expression of health, since in this context, dying is a part of life. Once again, the client is the teacher; the counselor is the learner.

Expansion of Family Emotional System

Family therapists sometimes encounter in their usual therapy practice individuals or families who are struggling with the dying or death of a beloved elderly family member. Little or nothing can be done about such factors as the ethnicity of the family, their history of dealing with previous losses, or the nature or timing of the death of the family member. The one factor that "the family or the family therapist has the ability to shift is the openness of the system" (Herz Brown, 1989, p. 474). Herz Brown makes several suggestions about how to expand the family emotional system:

1. Use open, factual terms. If the therapist uses direct factual terms (such as dying or dead), this gives the therapist and the family an opportunity to deal openly with the data presented to the family.
2. Establish at least one open relationship in the family system. The therapist can facilitate family members' ability to talk to each other, not to the therapist, about the toxic issues of dying and death. Other techniques include relevant reading material, family viewing of films such as *I Never Sang for My Father*, and participation in multiple family groups to normalize the family's grief over loss and death.
3. Be sensitive to rhythms of the family, as they avoid and then face the painful topics of the dying and then the death of one of their loved members.
4. Remain connected but nonreactive to the family pain. It is not helpful for the therapist to avoid the toxic issues, or to remain "professional" (that is, cold and distant) with these grieving families. The therapist should show the family warm empathy, not sympathy nor apathy. One caregiver remembers a situation in a hospital emergency room when an older patient, brought in by the local rescue service, died. When the doctor, nurse, and caregiver went to tell the wife of his death, the woman became hysterical. The caregiver just let the woman scream and cry, as her grief exploded. Later, the caregiver held the sobbing woman as she began to process this tremendous loss. Empathy was needed, but not at the price of stifling the pain.
5. Keep the focus on the family stress. Grieving families will often develop "sideshow" symptoms, such as acting out by a child. Therapists need to deal with the sideshow symptom and then return to the family's dealing with the major stresses brought about by the dying or death.
6. Encourage the family to use their own coping customs and rituals.

Dying and Death in Aging Intergenerational Families 285

Learning how the family has dealt with losses in the past reveals how they have coped with stress. Open discussion in the family about how to handle this impending or actual death is another way to expand closed systems, while honoring that which the family considers is "right" for their own system.

FAMILY THERAPISTS AND LOSS

No matter what therapeutic model is being followed, family therapists bring into the therapy room their own history and coping style. This becomes most evident when the therapist needs to address the toxic topics of dying and death with the grieving intergenerational family. Therapists who have not dealt well with their own losses in the past will be unable to hide that completely from the grieving family. After 20 years of academic interest and clinical experience in dying and death, Rosen (1988) observes that "the therapist's own grief history and attitudes about death will be a factor in his/her ability to approach this topic with a client" (p. 193). In much the same vein, Katz and Genevay (1987) state that working with the elderly and the dying gives the professional caregiver "an extraordinary opportunity to look at his or her own distance from potential and real loss, disability and death, in order to be a more competent helper" (p. 32). We would do well to examine our own denial, fears, anger, need for control, and need to be needed. Therapists who are willing to face these powerful issues in themselves will be greatly enriched in their work with the elderly and the dying.

When grief counselors explore their own history of losses, this process can help them in at least three ways (Worden, 1982).

1. They can better understand the process of mourning, as they review how they themselves have mourned their own losses.
2. They become more aware of what resources are available to the grieving persons. In addition, they become aware of their own coping style, which will have impact on the progress of therapy.
3. They recognize their own personal limitations, which usually arise when the grief therapy touches the therapist's own issues in this emotionally powerful area. One hospital social worker recalls how she stayed with a family while they were waiting to see the body of a grandmother who had just died. The professional went to see if everything was ready for the family to view the body. When she saw the body for the first time, she was stunned. It reminded her of her own ailing, beloved grandmother. She realized that she could

not continue to work with this family, due to her own emotional reactions. She requested that another colleague take over.

Three Personal Testimonies

Carter (1991) described her experiences with the dying and eventual death of her own father in 1973. After a cutoff of 13 years from her family of origin, she reconnected with them, only to face the impending death of her father. When she organized an anniversary party for her parents, she resumed ties with important members of her family in a warm but differentiated manner. Tension in her own family of procreation decreased, as did some of her own somatic symptoms. This enabled her to adjust much better to the death of her father six weeks after the party. Finally, Carter noted that in doing the hard work of family therapy: "Lately I don't find it as difficult to avoid taking sides emotionally within families" (p. 283).

In a powerful chapter entitled "The Use of Terminal Candor," David (1987) writes about her own struggle with leukemia, to which she finally succumbed. While ill with the cancer, she did family therapy with the terminally ill and their families. At the same time, she continued to communicate openly with her own husband and children about her cancer and impending death. This stance raised the level of anxiety in her own family.

> No one is immune to death anxiety. By confronting these anxieties, taking a differentiated position, and learning to control my own reactivity, there has been, I believe, a vital release of energy, creativity, thoughts and feelings for myself, my family, and others who ultimately face death, separation, loss and change (p. 298).

Three years ago, I had a powerful experience with my oldest brother. After our parents and his wife died, my brother withdrew for about 15 years from regular contact with most of his siblings, including me. When I heard that he was dying, I flew to my hometown, to reconnect with him before he died. The three days I spent with him in the nursing home were bittersweet. His mind drifted in and out; when he was lucid, we shared many memories of our childhood during the Great Depression, of his life work in the military and police force, and of our losses—our parents, his wife, a brother and a sister—and now he himself was approaching death. When he drifted off to sleep, I just sat at his bedside and gave thanks for such a wonderful, caring brother.

A few minutes before I had to leave for the airport, my brother struggled to free his arm from under the bed sheets; in a hoarse voice, he whispered,

"Bill, hold my hand. You, your wife, and I are all going on a long journey. But I am going first. And I am scared." We both shed long, hard brotherly tears. As I took leave of my only remaining brother, I held his hand, kissed him, and whispered in his ear: "I love you and I will miss you." I left the room in tears, never to see him again. One week later, almost to the hour, he died. My brother and I had forged a new intimacy; I shall carry this treasured memory with me to my own death (Hargrave & Anderson, 1992, p. 113).

Stress for Family Therapists

Working with differing groups of clients (e.g., wife-batterers, sex addicts, violent persons) normally affects therapists in different ways. In the same vein, working with dying and death in aging families tends to bring forth in family therapists certain issues (Sprung, 1989). These include the arousal of death anxiety in the therapist, unresolved conflicts that the therapist has with his or her own parents, the need to make things better for clients who suffer multiple losses, and partiality by the therapist for the adult children during family therapy sessions.

Lattanzi (1984), a family therapist and a hospice worker, remarks that "death and grief force family members into uncharted territory. A family therapist who is challenged to explore this unknown area with the family must be an approachable, secure guide with a good sense of timing for the journey" (p. 96). Family therapists need to understand the major stressors that they will confront when they begin to work with families facing dying and death. As a result of her experience in hospice work, Lattanzi emphasizes that the family therapist will often have to cope with these stressors.

1. **Realistic expectations of self and the family.** The family needs to set the goals and the pace in the dying and grieving processes; these are rarely tidy experiences.
2. **Situational limitations.** Crises occur frequently and normally in the dying process. Family therapists may feel that they are never off duty, since crises can and do occur at any time.
3. **Proximity to death.** This powerful experience is bound to affect the family therapist deeply. It is something like standing near a fire: "The stress of caregiving is in experiencing the heat without running away and without getting burned" (p. 101).
4. **Availability of support.** While true for all therapists, it is especially important to have supportive supervisors and colleagues who understand the stresses of working with families facing death.

CULTURAL VARIATIONS

In the United States, there is a wide spectrum of cultural groups. Each of these cultural groupings deals with dying and death in its own ways. The modern family therapist needs to be sensitive to these differences in working with grieving families. "Helping family members deal with a loss often means showing respect for their particular cultural heritage and encouraging them actively to determine how they will commemorate the death of a loved relative" (Walsh & McGoldrick, 1991, p. 178). They suggest that the family therapist working with culturally different grieving families ask the following questions about the family's traditions.

1. What are the prescribed rituals for the disposal of the body and for commemorating the loss?
2. What are the beliefs about what happens after death?
3. What do they believe about appropriate emotional expressions?
4. What are the gender rules for handling the death? (p. 179)

When working with a family from a culture different from that of the caregiver, a family therapist can find that it is helpful right at the start to identify who is the family spokesperson. It is not always the oldest or the most educated. This spokesperson is the gateway to the rest of the family and to the culture itself.

In addition to the above areas, Rosen (1990) believes that the therapist working with families facing death should consider these points.

1. How are pain, suffering, and grief expressed in this specific family?
2. How much help will the family seek from nonfamily sources when a family member faces death?

From a nursing perspective, Pickett (1993) considered cultural awareness in the context of terminal illness. She points out that human care is a universal element in human survival across all cultures: "Care is largely derived from culture and requires culturally based knowledge and skills to be effective, legitimate and relevant to people of diverse cultures" (p. 105). She proposes that caregivers become "cultural brokers" who can serve to translate messages, instructions, and belief systems among cultural groups.

A CASE STUDY

The following is a true case study provided by a family therapist who works in the western part of the United States. As you read this case, consider what might be your own responses and interventions with this family. The family is still in therapy.

The Brown Family

Ray and Susan Brown were married soon after World War II. They settled down in their hometown, a medium-sized urban community in the western United States. Over the years, they had four children: two sons and two daughters. Their family life was routine, rigid, and largely isolated from outside social influences. Both parents were overly protective. Ray was very involved with his children, usually in a very patriarchal manner. Susan nurtured the children as best she could, although she, too, exerted much control over their lives. The family members rarely spoke to one another directly; the familial emotional system was both closed and constipated.

As the children grew to adulthood, they had great difficulty separating from their parents in a healthy manner. The older daughter finally left home by marrying an older divorced man with two children; the rest of the family then cut her off completely. The younger daughter became pregnant before her marriage to a truck driver. This marriage was barely tolerated by Ray and Susan. Neither son married, although both finally moved to their own apartments when they turned 30 years old. The sons remained in daily, close contact with both parents, who had an emotionally distant and often conflictual marriage.

A few years after the younger son moved out, Susan developed breast cancer; she died within a year. The months just before her death were very difficult for the family. Susan wanted to reconcile with her older daughter, but Ray remained adamant that she did not belong in their family. When Susan finally did die, Ray relented and allowed his older daughter to attend the funeral. Although they all loved Susan deeply, the family members shed few tears at the wake and the funeral. All of them seemed to turn their deep grief inside. Both sons were very upset with their father over his treatment of their older sister; however, neither had the courage to confront him. Ray, now 74, has begun to show signs of depression that have become chronic; he drinks daily, sometimes to excess.

Exactly one year after the death of the mother, the older daughter suffered a severe heart attack. The family physician, who had treated all the family members for many years, indicated that he felt that the heart attack was directly related to the severe family tensions and to recent family losses; he suggested family therapy. The four adult children, in varying degrees, want to deal with the many unresolved issues from the past, as well as the present family divisions. Ray, in turn, blames his older daughter for contributing to his wife's cancer, due to the stress over her marriage to the divorced man. Ray refuses to attend the family sessions, but all four adult children are willing to participate in family therapy.

The first two sessions were spent joining with the adult children, listening to the family story, and gently encouraging each sibling openly to express repressed grief and to support one another in confronting family and individual pain. The family therapist has also encouraged the younger son, Ray's favorite child, to share with his father what has occurred during the family sessions; the other three siblings are supportive of this connection with their remaining parent.

Eventually, the family therapist plans to follow the suggestions of Herz Brown (pp. 474 ff) about expanding the family emotional system. In addition, he plans to assist the adult children (and Ray, when he starts to attend the sessions) to move toward forgiveness of self and of one another in this family (Hargrave, 1994).

REFERENCES

Atchley, R. (1991). *Social forces and aging* (6th ed.). Belmont, CA: Wadsworth.

Bowen, M. (1976). Family reaction to death. In P. Guerin (Ed.), *Family therapy: Theory and practice* (pp. 335-349). New York: Gardner Press.

Boyle, J., & Morris, J. (1987). *The mirror of time: Images of aging and dying.* New York: Greenwood Press.

Butler, R. (1963). The life review: An interpretation of reminiscence in the aged. *Psychiatry, 26,* 65-76.

Butler, R., Lewis, M., & Sunderland, T. (1991). *Aging and mental health: Positive psychosocial and biomedical approaches* (4th ed.). New York: Macmillan.

Carter, B. (1991). Death in the therapist's own family. In F. Walsh & M. McGoldrick (Eds.), *Living beyond loss: Death in the family* (pp. 273-284). New York: Norton.

David, L. (1987). The use of terminal candor. In P. Titelman, (Ed.), *The therapist's own family* (pp. 179-300). London: Jason Aronson.

Hargrave, T. (1994). *Families and forgiveness: Healing wounds in the intergenerational family.* New York: Brunner/Mazel.

Hargrave, T., & Anderson, W. (1992). *Finishing well: Aging and reparation in the intergenerational family.* New York: Brunner/Mazel.

Herz Brown, F. (1989). The impact of death and serious illness on the family life cycle. In B. Carter & M. McGoldrick (Eds.), *The changing family life cycle* (2nd ed., pp. 457-482). Boston: Allyn & Bacon.

Horowitz, M. (1980). Pathological grief and the activation of latent self-images. *American Journal of Psychiatry, 137,* 1157-1162.

Jones, S. (1993). Personal unity in dying: Alternative conceptions in the meaning of health. *Journal of Advanced Nursing, 18,* 89-94.

Kalish, R. (1985). *Death, grief and caring relationships* (2nd ed.). Monterey, CA: Brooks/Cole.

Katz, R., & Genevay, R. (1987). Older people, dying and countertransference. *Generations, 11*(3), 28-32.
Kemp, J. (1984). Learning from clients: Counseling the frail and dying elderly. *Personnel and Guidance Journal, 26*(5), 270-272.
Kubler-Ross, E. (1969). *On death and dying*. New York: Macmillan.
Kubler-Ross, E. (1984). Unfinished business. In T. Frantz (Ed.), *Death and grief in the family* (pp. 1-10). Rockville, MD: Aspen.
Lattanzi, M. (1984). Professional stress: Adaptation, coping, and meaning. In T. Frantz (Ed.), *Death and grief in the family* (pp. 95-106). Rockville, MD: Aspen.
Lazare, A. (1979). Unresolved grief. In A. Lazare (Ed.), *Outpatient psychiatry: Diagnosis and treatment* (pp. 498-512). Baltimore: Williams & Wilkins.
Lebowitz, R. (1985). Family caregiving in old age. *Hospital and Community Psychiatry, 36,* 457-458.
Marshall, V. (1980). *Last chapters: A sociology of aging and dying*. Monterey, CA: Brooks/Cole.
Montalvo, B. (1991). The patient chose to die: Why? *The Gerontologist, 31*(5), 700-703.
Paterson, G. (1989). Death, dying and the elderly. In W. Clements (Ed.), *Ministry with the aging* (pp. 220-234). New York: Haworth.
Paul, N., & Paul, B. (1982). Death and changes in sexual behavior. In F. Walsh (Ed.), *Normal family processes*. New York: Guilford.
Pickett, M. (1993). Cultural awareness in the context of terminal illness. *Cancer Nursing, 16,* 102-106.
Rando, T. (1986). *Loss and anticipatory grief*. New York: Lexington Books.
Rosen, E. (1988). Family therapy in cases of interminable grief for the loss of a child. *Omega, 19*(3), 187-201.
Rosen, E. (1990). *Families facing death*. New York: Lexington Books.
Schefft, B., & Lehr, B. (1990). Psychological problems of older adults. In K. Ferraro (Ed.), *Gerontology and issues* (pp. 283-293). New York: Springer.
Sprung, G. (1989). Transferential issues in working with older adults. *Social Casework, 70*(10), 597-602.
Walsh, F., & McGoldrick, M. (1991). *Living beyond loss: Death in the family*. New York: Norton.
Wass, H., & Myers, J. (1982). Psychosocial aspects of death among the elderly: A review of the literature. *Personnel and Guidance Journal, 61*(3), 131-137.
Weisman, A. (1972). *On dying and denying*. New York: Behavioral Publications.
Westcott, N. (1983). Application of the structured life-review technique in counseling elders. *Personnel and Guidance Journal, 62*(3), 180-181.
Worden, J. (1982). *Grief counseling and grief therapy*. New York: Springer.
Wortman, C., & Silver, R. (1989). Myths of coping with loss. *Journal of Consulting and Clinical Psychology, 57,* 349-357.
Zisook, S., & Shuchter, S. (1986). The first four years of widowhood. *Psychiatric Annals, 15,* 288-294.

IV

IMPLICATIONS FOR THE FUTURE

14

Future Directions for Family Therapy with Aging Families

Suzanne Midori Hanna, Ph.D.
University of Louisville
Louisville, Kentucky

Terry D. Hargrave, Ph.D.
Amarillo College
Amarillo, Texas

Richard B. Miller, Ph.D.
Kansas State University
Manhattan, Kansas

As can be seen with the array of thinking presented in this book, family therapists are developing new applications to address later-life issues. However, there is much more to do. As the nation ages, the culture of aging crosses paths with other cultures that are affected by these trends. Minority groups will influence the aging process as they become a larger voice in American life. Local social services and adult protective services already feel the impact of dilemmas related to elder abuse and neglect. Marriage and family therapy training programs are exploring ways to incorporate gerontological training, and many "cutting edge" models of family therapy have yet to be applied to elders. In this chapter, recommendations for further work in these areas are offered. It is our belief that systemic thinking will effectively address these challenges as the 21st century begins.

SERVING MINORITY ELDERS

It is estimated that by the year 2050, nonwhite ethnic groups will constitute 49.2 percent of the general population and 20 percent of the elderly in this country (U.S. Bureau of the Census, 1991). For these elderly, poverty, morbidity, and stress-related psychological disturbances occur at a higher rate than in whites (Grant, 1995). With this population, where kinship ties are important and multiple challenges exist, family therapy ought to be the treatment of choice. However, as mentioned in Chapter 1, service providers for the aging rarely have solid family therapy training. For the field at large, the challenge is to recruit those service providers into the ranks of family therapists. Why is family therapy the treatment of choice for minority elderly? The answer lies, in part, in its flexibility. This group is most likely to need an understanding of diversified systems and contexts, and such understanding is the element most often missing when professionals feel unsuccessful with them. The following example illustrates this point.

> Martha is a 70-year-old, African-American woman. After having both legs amputated due to chronic vascular problems, it was necessary to place her in a nursing home where her unique physical needs could be addressed more easily. Her daughters, struggling to raise their own families at the time, were unable to care for her. After several months in a nursing home, Martha ceased social and recreational activities, slumped into a deep depression, and refused to eat. Her daughters also stopped visiting. Despite several interventions, her condition worsened over several months. Eventually her caseworker referred her to Project Support (see Chapter 5).
>
> A social work field placement student was assigned to the case and was encouraged to work systemically, even though Martha's daughters refused to be involved in sessions. Through conducting a life review and constructing a detailed genogram, the student was able to stimulate conversation with Martha that had a positive impact on her condition.
>
> Martha's depression was affirmed as a natural and understandable response to a series of losses—her amputations the most recent, but not the most tragic. As the student became an empathic and interested audience to her pain and her survival, Martha looked

forward to her visits. It was obvious these conversations were rare, or possibly nonexistent, with other service providers, yet they represented the most significant parts of Martha's lived experience. Before long, Martha began to eat and eventually reported that her daughters were visiting more often since her depression had lifted.

This case illustrates the power of process and the significance of recognizing context. The student was never able to gain more information about why Martha's daughters had refused involvement or what their historical issues might have been. However, armed with the essentials of gerontological family therapy, she used a genogram and life review as vehicles to explore context in a manner most meaningful for the client. Martha was able to grieve her many losses and reclaim the wholeness of her life, rather than remain stuck in her immediate circumstances.

In African-American life, the saying "Your blues ain't my blues" acknowledges that adversity is both universal and unique. Everyone has "blues," but each person has them differently. Models of family therapy that focus on an affirmation of personal experience coupled with the celebration of survival incorporate systemic thinking in ways that are affirming to minority elders, who may have been marginalized, first because of race, and second because of age. Particularly with elders, their sense of difference from other people increases with age—it is experience that makes each person unique. Thus, family therapy, with its circular questions and narratives, has the capacity to acknowledge difference and affirm strengths while turning hopeless thoughts into hopeful action. However, for such services to be more available, contemporary models of family therapy will have to be applied more frequently in elderly settings.

APPLYING NEW TREATMENT MODELS

Family therapists are beginning to focus on older families. However, integrations that incorporate constructivist thinking are still underdeveloped with elders. Bonjean's work (Chapter 4) is a good example of what is needed from more recent schools of thought. In any population, there are those families who need services but who present challenges to traditional models of family therapy. Contemporary models based on social construction theory or narrative practice are often more effective in such cases (Todd & Selekman, 1991). For the field of family therapy fully to mature, interventions with difficult populations must also be developed for the elderly. Examples of approaches commonly associated with the constructivist movement in family therapy are those of the Milan Team and Michael White

(Nichols & Schwartz, 1995). The following are suggestions for how models based on their work can be useful with later-life families.

The Milan Team

The Milan Team, while noted for paradoxical interventions and circular questions, is credited by Nichols and Schwartz (1995) for turning the field of family therapy toward an emphasis on belief systems and cognitive process within the family (psychodynamics). Various members of the early team integrated political concepts, behavioral intervention, and phenomenological analysis into their work with families. Their circular questions directed attention to historical evolutions in family life, while also providing empathy for dilemmas faced by family members. Although they are often categorized within a strategic model of family therapy, they added a psychodynamic emphasis in understanding individual members.

For aging families, the contributions of the Milan Team can be significant. By avoiding traditional psychoanalytic interpretation, its members are respectful of a culture that is often uncomfortable with the traditions of psychotherapy. They have a curiosity for the unusual and an optimism in the face of pain. They understand the influence of legacies and loss. They compliment family members for their good intentions. Although they developed much of their model from work as child psychiatrists dealing with psychosis and anorexia (Selvini Palazzoli, Boscolo, Cecchin, & Prata, 1978), they provide an example of how integrative models can accommodate unusual populations.

Aging families often feel unusual, some never having been faced with these kinds of challenges before. They may be confused or in a state of medical emergency. They may be addressing issues of life and death, which are more pressing than issues in younger families. Perhaps it is the transitional confusion experienced by most aging families that is best addressed by Milan strategies. They developed many innovations with families who were in a great deal of pain and learned to bypass the shame that often brings on a family's resistance to change (Selvini Palazzoli, 1986).

Michael White

Michael White has developed an integrative approach to family therapy, which also incorporates political, behavioral, and psychodynamic elements. Although adopting a structural-strategic approach early in his career (White, 1979), his perspective evolved into something called a transgenerational system approach as he worked with families facing anorexia (White, 1983).

This shift represented a focus on the development of cognitive processes in the family that were generally overlooked in traditional structural-strategic work. Eventually, he added a focus on the politics of society, which influenced the politics of the family, paying attention to the oppression of alternative views that could aid in problem resolution. These other views were termed "subjugated knowledge."

With aging families, their experience in general can easily be thought of as subjugated knowledge. Very often, their voices are ignored or overlooked by society. Marginalized by the dominant views of the culture, older people are often neglected as sources of wisdom and knowledge. The problems of elders can be addressed in many creative ways, using the ideas of Michael White. He often incorporates attention to legacy and loss by searching for the family's "history of struggle and protest." He develops playful and pragmatic interventions that focus on behavioral competence and future possibilities. He is interested in knowing a family's story, in helping them to claim authorship of their own growth, and in creating an audience from the informal support system that will help to solidify new patterns of progress. Most of all, he demonstrates an acceptance of uniqueness and avoids thinking that would impose a common standard on families in oppressive ways.

For families with medical crises, Michael White's model might help them to challenge the oppressive elements in traditional medical thinking. For families going through losses, his model might take a paradoxical view, helping them to "hold on" to deceased loved ones, rather than to "let go" (White, 1989). When aging families are going through role transitions, this model has the flexibility to pursue pragmatically the influence of behavioral sequences (landscape of action) while also pursuing important beliefs that have a bearing on the situation (landscape of meaning) (White & Epston, 1990).

Other constructivist approaches to family therapy have elements similar to those attributed to the Milan Team and Michael White. The common denominators include an acknowledgment of unique experience, the use of nonadversarial interventions, and a depathologizing of family members. As Caron (Chapter 11) has illustrated in his discussion of nursing homes, constructivist interventions have rewarding utility in the most challenging environments. Such analysis and application are also needed in the realm of elder abuse and neglect.

ADDRESSING ELDER ABUSE AS A LARGER SYSTEMIC ISSUE

One of the frustrations of an aging society is the increase in cases of elder abuse and neglect. Community adult protective services are often faced with numerous reports of concern or complaint related to the mistreatment or neglect of elders. A common scenario involves those cases where an investigation yields no available legal course of action, but neighbors or relatives remain concerned. Sometimes abuse by a family member is suspected and has been disclosed to a neighbor or friend, but when caseworkers investigate, the elder is hesitant to make a formal complaint. Other times, elders may be isolated and refuse help to better care for themselves.

Service providers are often those who first suspect elder abuse; however, they frequently do not address the issue directly with the elder for fear of further alienating him or her from accepting services. These cases, whether the suspected abuse is financial, physical, psychological, or self-neglect, are often the subject of repeated reports to authorities until conditions finally deteriorate enough to warrant legal action. These "revolving door" interactions are a common source of frustration for those who serve elders. At-risk families are often beyond the reach of interventions that can prevent more serious problems.

More systemic thinking is needed to effect change in these overlapping systems. At the microlevel, service providers are often untrained to involve other family members in the delivery of their services. In a game without end where recurring interaction patterns continue with progressive deterioration, second-order change involves a change in the nature of the relationship of the parties involved. For example, where a service provider suspects someone in the household as an abuser, training must take place that enables the provider to develop a collaborative rather than an adversarial relationship with the suspect. In cases where the elder may be in serious danger but does not take steps on his or her own behalf, interventions must work within the elder's reality. In contrast, interventions aimed at convincing or persuading the elder to take action are rarely effective because the provider is unable to grasp the complexity of the situation from the elder's point of view.

At the macrolevel, service organizations typically follow policies and procedures that restrict their access to the informal support system of the elder (i.e., family, neighbors, friends). Although many agencies have conditions for service, few have any conditions that include permission to collaborate with informal supports. For example, many housing facilities have an application that requests detailed financial and medical information, but does not require any family information. As Caron (Chapter 11) has illustrated, the agency pursues one agenda and the family another, and the potential for conflict escalates. These situations often deteriorate because policies do not address the levels of relationship that exist among agency and employees, family and agency, and employees and family. Many cases of abuse and neglect persist to the frustration of helpless bystanders. Just as Caron employed an ecosystemic analysis in nursing home systems, so must the ecosystem of elder abuse be reviewed before more effective interventions will be developed.

Caron's ecosystemic analysis is the positive result of integrating theory, research, and practice. It is hoped that this ecosystemic approach will serve as a model for more family therapists to follow. However, to further these efforts in gerontological family therapy, education and training programs must integrate later-life issues more fully into the academic and clinical components of their programs.

ETHICS AND GERONTOLOGY

Technology has forced more and more ethical dilemmas into the therapeutic context in dealing with aging. Primary in this debate are the timing, place, and conditions of death. The President's Commission for the Study of Ethical Problems in Medicine and Biomedical and Behavioral Research (1983) concludes that with the medical controls that are now in place, the issues of how and when to die are more of a deliberate decision. Issues regarding pain and suffering of the older persons and families are increasingly being addressed. Dilemmas regarding the quality versus quantity of life as a person ages are also difficult to deal with as economic resources of the family and community become more scarce. The medical profession will be increasingly faced with problems of when to withhold treatment from the elderly or perhaps even when to participate in ending a person's suffering—such as with physician-assisted suicide.

Although there are no clear answers for these ethical considerations, family therapists are well situated to assist the family in making informed decisions that address individual needs, as well as those affecting the intergenerational health of the family. Models such as the ones suggested by Hargrave and Anderson (Chapter 3) and Hanna (Chapter 5) utilize various considerations for the value of the older person's life in the intergenerational family. The biopsychosocial model suggested by McDaniel, Hepworth, and Doherty (1992) offers an excellent model for elements of collaboration from various fields that provide the family with resources in facing the hard ethical dilemmas that aging and illness force on our society.

Another ethical issue that is increasingly moving to the forefront of the aging debate is one of values and spirituality. Oates (Chapter 12) and Anderson (Chapter 13) touch on this issue, but by and large the field of family therapy, and psychotherapy as a whole, has been fairly resistant to the idea of addressing spiritual issues in therapy. As death approaches, there is clearly movement by a large percentage of elders to consider the transcendent qualities of their lives. It indeed seems neglectful on the part of the therapist not to deal openly with the older person's need and desire to confront the spiritual issues they face. Integration of this dimension will require new models of treatment and guidelines of incorporation as therapists learn to help lead clients in spiritual and value definition without becoming dogmatic or imposing their own belief systems on aging individuals.

INCLUDING GERONTOLOGY IN TRAINING PROGRAMS

Myers and Blake (1986) have investigated training counselors who work with older clients, and they have suggested that there are four possible training models.

Integrated Model

This model calls for the infusion of gerontological curricula into the standard clinical curricula that are stipulated by the accrediting organization (Myers, 1989). For example, the integration of gerontological training into the marriage and family therapy curriculum that is required by the Commission on Accreditation for Marriage and Family Therapy Education (COAMFTE) could be accomplished by including articles and discussion in the standard curriculum that are relevant to working with older adults and their families.

Theoretical Foundations of MFT: What examples from the lives of the elderly and their families can be used to illustrate systems theory's concepts and principles?

Assessment and Treatment in MFT: Are there issues with validity and reliability when using common MFT assessment instruments with older families? What special considerations need to be made in arranging the physical setting for therapy with older persons? How can the major MFT theories be applied to address some of the problems faced by elderly clients and their families? What are some common triangles among aging family members? How do the ages of the therapist and clients affect the course of therapy?

Human Development and Family Studies: How do marital and parent–child relationships change throughout the aging process? How do changes in individual development affect the family system? What are the common significant individual and family transitions in later life? What are the important issues in later life regarding gender and ethnicity? How does the aging process affect the sexual lives of the elderly?

Ethics and Professional Studies: What are some of the legal and ethical issues associated with doing therapy with the elderly? What are the state laws regarding mandating reporting of elderly abuse and neglect? What constitutes neglect? How should a family therapist go about receiving the informed consent of a disoriented elderly family member (Agresti, 1992)?

Research: What are some issues in conducting research with older individuals and their families? What special methods have been developed to research this special population?

The main advantage of the integration model is that everyone in the training program would receive training to work with older adults and their families. Because a substantial percentage of therapists will work with at least one elderly client during their career (Gatz, Karel, & Wolkenstein (1991), it is important that all therapists receive some preparation to work effectively with them. The disadvantage is that the integrated model requires the commitment of all members of the training faculty to make the model work. Even those faculty who do not specialize in gerontology would have to be motivated to include aging issues in class readings and discussions.

Separate Course Model

The second model utilizes a separate therapy course to train clinicians to work with older adults and their families. The course would cover general background information about issues of aging, such as common dynamics found in aging families and mental health issues among the elderly. The goal would be for students to gain an understanding of and sensitivity to the elderly. The second goal would be to train students to use the systemic perspective of marriage and family therapy to treat their elderly clients. The course could be either required or offered as an elective.

The main advantage of this model is that only one faculty member needs to have an interest in gerontology to train students to work with the elderly. The only involvement needed from the other faculty members would be their cooperation in approving a new course in the curriculum. Another advantage is that a separate course would allow the instructor the opportunity to introduce therapeutic approaches that have been developed specifically to help the elderly population and their families. It is unlikely that these specialized approaches would be included in existing courses as part of the integrated model. The main disadvantage is that the curriculum in most clinical training programs is already "full," making it difficult to find room for a new course.

Area of Concentration Model

An MFT program could offer an area of concentration or specialization in MFT with the elderly and their families. The specialization curriculum would include two or more didactic courses related to clinical gerontology. Course topics could include MFT models for working with the elderly, mental health disorders among the elderly, and family dynamics and functioning among aging families. The specialization likely would offer a practicum opportunity in a setting that primarily treats elderly clients.

The main advantage of this model is that students would obtain a high level of competence in providing marriage and family therapy to the elderly population and their families. The depth of didactic and experiential training would provide outstanding preparation for students to work with this population. The main disadvantage would be the amount of resources that would be required of the program to provide such a specialization. In addition, with relatively few marriage and family therapists currently working in gerontology settings, it often would be difficult to find adequately trained supervisors to work with the students in their field placements. It is likely that MFT faculty would need to help with the supervision responsibilities until additional gerontologically trained MFT supervisors become available in gerontology settings (Duffy, 1992).

Interdisciplinary Model

The final model utilizes courses and faculty from other departments in the university to teach MFT students about gerontology. Students would have the opportunity to take gerontology courses in such departments as sociology, psychology, biology, literature, and economics. Such a range of options promotes a rich variety of perspectives on the aging experience and the challenges associated with old age. Many universities have a multidisciplinary Center for Aging that coordinates gerontology instruction across the university. These centers could be used as a resource for MFT programs seeking to develop an appropriate selection of aging courses. In addition, these Centers for Aging often offer a graduate certificate in gerontology for students who take several gerontology courses in more than one department. This certificate could be a helpful credential for MFT students wishing to market themselves as specialists in gerontology.

The main advantage of the interdisciplinary model is that it does not require any resources from the MFT program. It simply utilizes existing university courses, and possibly the university's Center for Aging, to provide gerontology instruction to MFT students. The disadvantage is that it does not provide specific MFT clinical training to help students apply the gerontological literature from other disciplines to the practice of MFT. For example, a knowledge of social gerontology and the economics of aging may help students understand the elderly, but it does not necessarily suggest clinical interventions to help the elderly and their families as they face specific challenges.

Combining Models

It is possible to combine elements of several models to develop a curriculum that fits the circumstances of each individual program. The curriculum that was developed by the Kansas State University doctoral MFT program to train MFTs to work with the elderly and their families is a good example. This specialization, which combined elements of the area of concentration model and the interdisciplinary model, required students to earn the graduate certificate in gerontology from the university's Center for Aging. This called for students to take at least three courses from outside the department and to write their dissertation on a gerontology-related topic. In addition, the students took a course within the program on MFT and aging. Finally, the primary practicum placements of the students were at the Veterans Administration Medical Center, where they worked with elderly veterans and their families. On-site supervision was provided by a gerontological social worker who had extensive training and experience in marriage and family therapy.

Postgraduate Training

It is common for MFTs to not become interested in working with older families until many years after they graduate from school, perhaps following some personal experience. They may have experienced the death of a close relative, have had a parent become disabled, or have become heavily involved in the role of a caregiver to a family member. Or they may have become aware of their own aging process. Whatever the reason, many therapists become interested in working with the elderly and their families during the middle of their career. There are training opportunities for them, as well.

A good opportunity for training exists at the annual conferences of the professional therapy organizations. For example, the selection of workshops available at the American Association for Marriage and Family Therapy (AAMFT) conference includes a number of sessions related to gerontology. By attending the sessions in the aging track, a conference participant can learn about MFT with the older population from the leading experts in the field. Similarly, the American Counseling Association (ACA) and American Psychological Association (APA) offer workshops on clinical gerontology during their annual conferences. In addition, professional gerontological organizations also offer clinical workshops at their annual meetings. The American Society of Aging (ASA) offers excellent therapy workshops at its annual meetings; the organization also offers workshops across the country throughout the summer.

Therapists can also take appropriate gerontology courses at a local university. As non–degree-seeking students, they could take a few aging courses to provide them with valuable knowledge and training about working with older adults and their families. Finally, therapists can seek supervision from a marriage and family therapist who is skilled in working with the elderly population, which would provide practical help in learning the applied aspects of becoming a competent gerontologically trained MFT.

SUMMARY

As the field of marriage and family therapy continues to offer many avenues of creative application and integration, families at the turn of the next century will invite systemic practitioners to focus on those issues, unique and universal, that affect the culture of aging. Family therapists are well suited to improve the quality of life for elders and their offspring; however, the context of service delivery for older people and patterns of practice among clinicians have left family therapists in short supply where elders are served. In recent years, one noteworthy trend that signals progress has been the rise of interest in family systems medicine, that collaboration which exists among family therapists and family practice physicians (McDaniel, Hepworth, & Doherty, 1992). As these collaborations become more common, elders will greatly benefit from the best of both worlds.

Many of the chapters in this book reveal how difficult it is for family therapists to remain detached from their own later-life concerns, once they begin to address them at all. Such a transformation is sobering, but exhilarating. These voices invite us to view a different future than that viewed by young generations. It is a necessary shift if the field of family therapy is to remain vital.

As more effort is made to direct theory, research, and practice toward gerontological family therapy, the life cycle of our profession will finally make one complete round. We are not there, yet. However, this evolution is progressing, bringing perspective to our assessments and depth to our interventions by challenging realities developed with younger families. Having "come of age" during the adolescence and young adulthood of systemic thought, the field of family therapy continues to broaden its influence in society. With this next developmental step, it will be time to capitalize on the energy of our youth and the commitment of our adulthood as we "come of wisdom" and include those of every age in our dialogue about systems.

REFERENCES

Agresti, A. A. (1992). Counselor training and ethical issues with older clients. *Counselor Education and Supervision, 32*, 43-50.

Duffy, M. (1992). A multimethod model for practicum and clinical supervision in nursing homes. *Counselor Education and Supervision, 32*, 61-69.

Gatz, M., Karel, M. J., & Wolkenstein, B. (1991). Survey of providers of psychological services to older adults. *Professional Psychology: Research and Practice, 22*, 413-415.

Grant, R. W. (1995). Interventions with ethnic minority elderly. In J. Aponte, R. Y. Rivers, & J. Wohl (Eds.), *Psychological interventions and cultural diversity.* Boston: Allyn & Bacon.

McDaniel, S. H., Hepworth, J., & Doherty, W. J. (1992). *Medical family therapy: A biopsychosocial approach to families with health problems.* New York: Basic Books.

Myers, J. E. (1989). *Infusing gerontological counseling into counselor preparation: Curriculum guide.* Alexandria, VA: American Counseling Association.

Myers, J. E., & Blake, R. H. (1986). Preparing counselors for work with older people. *Counselor Education and Supervision, 26*, 43-50.

Nichols, M. P., & Schwartz, R. C. (1995). *Family therapy: Concepts and methods* (3rd ed.). Boston: Allyn & Bacon.

President's Commission for the Study of Ethical Problems in Medicine and Biomedical and Behavioral Research. (1983). *Deciding to forego life-sustaining treatment.* Washington, DC: U.S. Government Printing Office.

Selvini Palazzoli, M. (1986). Towards a general model of psychotic games. *Journal of Marital and Family Therapy, 12*, 339-349.

Selvini Palazzoli, M., Boscolo, L., Cecchin G., & Prata, G. (1978). *Paradox and counterparadox.* New York: Jason Aronson.

Todd, T., & Selekman, M. D. (1991). *Family therapy approaches with adolescent substance abusers.* Needham Heights, MA: Allyn & Bacon.

United States Bureau of the Census. (1991). 1980 and 1990 Censuses of the population. *General population characteristics.* PC80-1-B1. U.S. Department of Commerce.

White, M. (1979). Structural and strategic approaches to psychosomatic families. *Family Process, 18*, 303-314.

White, M. (1983). Anorexia nervosa: A transgenerational system perspective. *Family Process, 22*, 255-273.

White, M. (1989). Saying hullo again: The incorporation of the lost relationship in the resolution of grief. *Selected papers.* Adelaide, Australia: Dulwich Centre Publications.

White, M., & Epston, D. (1990). *Narrative means to therapeutic ends.* New York: Norton.

Name Index

Ackerman, R. J., 32
Ade-Ridder, L., 180, 181, 184, 188
Agresti, A. A., 303
Albert, M. S., 141, 142
Aldous, J., 55
Aldwin, C. M., 144
Allen, J., 170
Alzheimer's Association, 209
American Association of Retired People (AARP), 42
Anderson, W. T., 21, 24, 26, 31, 32, 62, 67, 68, 170, 226, 259, 282, 287
Anthony, C. R., 31
Arenberg, D., 141
Arling, G., 142, 146, 239
Aronson, J., 201, 203
Aronson, M., 239
Aroskar, M., 239
Asnes, D. P., 65
Atchley, R. C., 166, 271
Avorn, J., 251

Badash, D., 239
Baillie, V., 144
Baltes, P. B., 141
Banks, M. E., 32

Barber, C. E., 32
Barnes, L. E., 144
Barnett, R. C., 200
Baron, R. S., 144, 146
Barrett-Connor, E., 144, 146
Baruch, G., 200
Barusch, A., 204, 206
Bateson, G., 74
Becker, J., 144
Becker, M., 242
Beckman, K., 192
Becvar, D. S., 226, 227
Becvar, R. J., 226, 227
Beels, C. C., 169, 170
Benbow, S., 30
Bengtson, V. L., 51, 181
Bennett, L., 135
Bepko, R. A., 29
Beran, B., 239
Berg, I. K., 89
Bigner, J. J., 45, 46
Birren, J. E., 44, 181
Bischof, G. P., 20
Blake, R. H., 302
Blau, Z. S., 54
Blazer, D. G., 30, 32
Blenkner, M., 136
Blieszner, R., 22, 55, 220, 224, 225
Bodin, A., 28, 83, 102

Bogo, M., 29
Bogolub, E. B., 185, 186
Bonacci, D. D., 136
Bonjean, M. J., 30, 131, 297
Borson, S., 214
Bosciglio, H., 242
Boscolo, L., 124, 127, 298
Bosly-Craft, R., 51
Boss, P. G., 32, 132, 151, 220, 225, 245, 246
Bossé, R., 144
Boszormenyi-Nagy, I., 19, 27, 28, 30, 31, 61, 62, 63, 64, 67, 71, 72, 74, 106
Boutselis, M., 31
Bowen, M., 19, 27, 28, 169, 171, 192, 227, 272, 275, 276, 279, 280
Bowers, B., 242
Boyd, R., 185
Boyle, J., 270
Braithwaite, V. A., 51
Brant, L., 239, 240
Braverman, L., 183
Brekhus, S., 218
Brody, E. M., 23, 30, 51, 54, 165, 170, 200
Brody, H., 46

Name Index

Brown, J. H., 109, 111
Brubaker, T. H., 165, 191
Bugg, C., 268
Burman, B., 183
Burr, W. R., 145
Burton, L., 239, 240
Burvill, P. W., 144
Butler, R. N., 24, 31, 32, 48, 51, 53, 66, 136, 274, 275, 281

Cade, B. W., 83
Cafferata, G. L., 201
Cain, B. S., 185, 186
Caine, E. D., 142, 144
Calasanti, T. M., 51
Campbell, S., 185, 186
Campbell, T., 133
Cantor, M. H., 204, 206
Capitman, J., 239
Caplan, A., 239
Carni, E., 30
Caron, W., 32, 132, 245, 300, 301
Carrilio, T. E., 29
Carstensen, L. L., 181
Carter, B., 20, 22, 30, 53, 54, 105, 132, 135, 137, 171, 286
Cartwright, A., 146
Catania, J. A., 184
Cattell, H., 146
Cecchin, G., 124, 127, 298
Cerella, J., 142
Chafetz, P., 250
Chang, C. F., 205
Chappell, N., 242
Charmaz, K., 219, 220
Chenowith, B., 213
Cherlin, A. J., 167, 168
Chodorow, N., 200
Christopherson, V. A., 131
Christozov, C., 146
Cicchetti, D., 132, 137
Cicirelli, V. G., 54, 165, 206

Clark, E. O., 32
Clark, R., 239
Cohen, D., 209, 212, 213, 215, 217, 218, 219, 220, 224, 225, 226
Cohen, R., 143
Cohen-Mansfield, J., 239
Cohler, B., 31, 32
Cohn, M., 250
Col, N., 146
Colangelo, N., 151
Cole, C., 181
Colerick, E. J., 224
Comfort, A., 184
Compton, S., 239
Connidis, I. A., 180
Conwell, Y., 142, 144
Cook-Deegan, R. M., 210
Cooney, T., 185
Cooper, J. K., 71
Cooper, K., 31, 32
Costa, P. T., Jr., 141, 142
Cotrell, V. C., 218
Cox, C., 250
Croog, S. H., 146
Cummings, N., 99
Cummings, S. R., 143
Cutrona, C. E., 144, 146

Dannenberg, A. L., 146
David, L., 276, 286
Davies, R., 215
Davis, J., 29
Decker, S. D., 146
Deinard, S., 224
Del Maestro, S., 144
Demling, G. T., 204
Depner, C. E., 146
deShazer, S., 29, 82, 83, 90
Devany, N., 239
deVries, H. A., 45
Diamond, D., 139
Dillehay, R. C., 223
Doane, J. A., 139
Dobson, C., 166
Dobson, J. E., 30, 32, 54
Dobson, R. L., 30, 32, 54

Doherty, M., 146
Doherty, W. J., 32, 146, 151, 301, 306
Dolinsky, A., 224
Donnelly, C., 239
Donnelly, D., 184
Donovan, G. L., 187
Dowd, J., 54
Dreher, B. B., 188
Dubler, N. N., 222, 223
Duffy, M., 30, 304
Dura, J. R., 144
Durham, L., 240
Dysken, M., 31, 32

Eastham, J., 206
Eaves, L. J., 141, 146
Eisdorfer, C., 209, 212, 213, 215, 217, 218, 219, 220, 224, 225, 226
Eisen, S. A., 146
Eisenberg, D. M., 29
Ekerdt, D. J., 144, 166
Elliot, J., 32
Emmerson, J. P., 144
Engel, G. L., 32, 151
Ephross, P., 250
Epston, D., 103, 299
Erdly, W. W., 144
Erickson, M. H., 82, 83, 106, 126
Erikson, E. H., 24, 26, 47, 48, 52, 66, 72, 73, 133, 134, 141, 259
Erikson, J. M., 24, 26, 52, 72, 73, 133
Erlanger, M. A., 189
Ernst, P., 239
Eskew, R. W., 180, 181
Everitt, D., 251
Eyde, R., 90
Eye, A. V., 33

Fabiszewski, K. J., 214
Fairchild, T., 243
Falicov, C. J., 30, 132

Name Index

Falloon, I., 28
Famighetti, R. A., 210, 220, 224
Fanale, J. E., 146
Farmer, M. E., 146
Felkins, B., 240
Field, D., 144, 179, 182
Fillenbaum, G., 51
Fillipp, L., 238
Finkeher, D., 136
Finlay-Jones, R., 144
Finley, N. J., 206
Fisch, R., 28, 29, 127
Fisher, B. L., 32
Fishman, H. C., 27, 28, 102, 105, 191
Fitting, M., 205, 206
Fitzpatrick, M. A., 147
Flickinger, M. A., 31
Flori, D., 20
Foner, A., 55
Framo, J. L., 19, 30, 131
Franks, P., 133, 144
Freels, S., 213
Freeman, I., 239
Frey, D., 240
Frey, J., 191
Friedman, E., 171
Fritz, S., 145
Fruge, E., 132, 209
Funk, J., 132
Furstenberg, F. F., 167, 168

Gafner, G., 187, 188, 189, 194
Gallagher, D., 144, 215
Gallagher-Thompson, D., 215
Garfield, S. L., 99
Garner, J., 239, 243
Garrard, J., 240
Gatz, M., 142, 303
Gelfand, E. G., 133
Genevay, R., 285
George, L. K., 51, 204, 224
German, P., 239, 240

Gerson, R., 71
Gibson, D. M., 51
Gilewski, M. J., 191
Gilfix, M., 222
Gilford, R., 181
Gilleard, C. J., 20, 33
Gillespie, J., 111
Gilligan, C., 200
Giordano, J. A., 133, 192
Glenn, N. D., 179
Goldstein, M., 132
Gonzalez, S., 143
Goodman, C. C., 143
Gottesman, I. L., 138
Gottman, J. M., 144, 147, 181
Grant, R. W., 296
Greenbaum, J., 180, 183, 187, 191
Greenberg, J., 245, 246
Groves, E., 259
Guralnik, J., 143
Gutierrez-Mayka, M., 220
Gutman, D. L., 200
Gutmann, D., 23
Gwyther, L. P., 30, 32, 204

Haley, J., 27, 29, 74, 104, 105
Hall, W., 144
Hammond, R. J., 184
Hanley, R., 215
Hanna, S. M., 30, 102, 109, 111, 126, 301
Hanson, B. S., 143
Hare, J., 242
Hargrave, T. D., 21, 24, 26, 31, 32, 62, 67, 68, 170, 226, 259, 282, 287, 290, 301
Harkins, E., 239
Hartford, M. E., 32
Havinghurst, R. J., 49
Heath, A. C., 141, 146
Hedlund, J., 30
Heiman, M., 53

Heiring, J., 224
Heiselman, T., 250
Helzner, J., 238
Henderson, J. N., 220
Hennon, C. B., 185
Hepworth, J., 32, 301, 306
Herr, J. J., 20, 29
Herz Brown, F., 284, 290
Hess, B., 55
Heston, L. L., 142
Hetherington, E. M., 142
Hicklin, D., 144, 146
Hiebert, W., 111
Hill, L. W., 139
Hill, R., 145, 151
Hoffman, L., 111, 187
Hofland, B. F., 52
Holahan, C. J., 24
Holahan, C. K., 24, 180
Hooyman, N. R., 40, 41, 42, 43, 46, 53
Hopkinson, N., 146
Horbal, J., 32, 132, 245
Horowitz, A., 204, 206
Horowitz, M., 278
House, J. S., 147
Hovander, D., 151
Hughston, G. A., 131
Hutton, J. T., 210
Hyer, L., 191
Hyland, C. A., 169

Iasiello-Vailas, L., 146
Imber-Black, E., 127
Ineichen, B., 239
Ingersoll-Dayton, B., 146
Isacsson, S. O., 143

Jackson, D., 74
Jacob, T., 145
James, J., 240
Janzon, L., 143
Jarvik, L. F., 24
Jerrome, D., 30
Jeste, D. V., 215
Johnson, C. L., 180, 181, 182, 206

Name Index

Johnson, M., 251
Johnson, R. P., 23
Jones, S., 31, 283

Kaakinen, J., 241
Kakoneck, S., 238
Kalish, R., 274
Kaminsky, M., 31
Kane, R., 239
Kantor, D., 27
Kaplan, G. A., 143
Karel, M. J., 303
Kastenbaum, R., 24
Katon, W., 146
Katz, I., 238
Katz, R., 285
Katzman, R., 210
Kaufman, S. R., 164, 175
Keeney, B., 87
Keife, K., 206
Keith, D., 28
Kelbley, T., 240
Kelman, H. R., 142, 146
Kemp, J., 282
Kendler, K. S., 141, 146
Kennedy, G. J., 142, 146, 218, 219
Kenny, A. D., 210
Kessler, R. C., 141, 146
Khachaturian, Z. S., 212
Kiecolt-Glaser, J. K., 144
King, D. A., 136, 150, 151
Kinney, J. M., 144
Kinsel, B. I., 191
Kirk, S., 239
Kirsling, R. A., 146
Kiser, D., 89
Kitto, J., 224
Kivnick, H. Q., 24, 26, 52, 72, 73, 133
Kiyak, H. A., 40, 41, 42, 43, 46, 53, 214
Knight, B. G., 186
Knopman, D. S., 215, 224
Knudsen, L., 143
Kohlhepp, K. A., 180, 181
Kramer, N., 106, 143

Krantz, S., 215
Krasner, B., 61, 62, 63, 67, 71, 72, 74, 106
Krause, N., 144
Kronholm, P., 146
Kubler-Ross, E., 272, 274, 281, 283
Kuppinger, J., 191

Lamy, P., 236
Landis, K. R., 147
Lang, A. M., 200
Lankton, C., 107, 126, 127
Lankton, S., 107, 126, 127
LaRossa, R., 54
Larson, D. B., 146, 238
Larson, E., 215
Lasch, K. E., 214
Lattanzi, M., 287
Lauer, J. C., 189
Lauer, R. H., 189
Lavee, Y., 151
Lawton, M. P., 238
Lazare, A., 278
Lazarus, L. W., 31, 32
Leahey, M., 117, 123
Learman, L., 251
Lebowitz, R., 271
Lee, G. R., 54
Leff, J., 139, 147
Lehr, B. K., 50
Lehr, W., 27
Lein, L., 218
Leon, J., 239, 243
Levenson, A., 240
Levenson, M. R., 144
Levenson, R. W., 181
Levine, S., 146
Lewis, M. I., 24, 32, 51, 136, 274
Liddle, H. A., 171, 172
Lieberman, M. A., 24, 132, 141
Lieberman, S., 20, 33
Lindell, S. E., 143
Linn, M. W., 223
Lipchik, E., 83, 89

Little, V., 204
Livson, F., 49
Locke, B. Z., 146
Lomranz, J., 240, 250
Long, J. K., 192, 210, 218, 219, 223, 224
Longino, C. F., 42, 43
Lopata, H. Z., 170, 171
Love, D. W., 71
Lovett, S., 144
Lubaroff, D. M., 144, 146
Lucas, M. J., 206, 220, 224
Lyman, K. A., 211, 218

Mace, N. L., 213, 214, 216, 217, 220, 223, 224
Mackenzie, T. B., 215
Madanes, C., 28, 29
Maiden, R. J., 24
Maiuro, R. D., 146
Mancini, J. A., 22, 55, 192, 210, 223, 224
Manton, K. G., 42, 43
Margolin, G., 183
Mark, V., 239
Marshall, V., 271
Marsiglio, W., 184
Marz, M., 239
Masten, A. S., 137
Matlin, M., 49
McClearn, G. E., 142, 143
McClusky, N. G., 167
McCrae, R. R., 141, 142
McCubbin, H., 103, 151
McCubbin, M., 103, 151
McDaniel, S. H., 32, 301, 306
McEwan, E. G., 31
McGoldrick, M., 20, 22, 30, 53, 54, 71, 105, 131, 132, 133, 135, 137, 169, 170, 171, 175, 272, 279, 288
McGuigan, M., 239
McQuellon, R. P., 30
Mercer, S., 239, 243

Name Index

Metcalf, L., 146
Metzner, H. L., 147
Meyers, M. P., 185
Michaels, J. E., 224
Milkner, M., 53
Miller, B., 205
Miller, D. K., 146
Miller, R. B., 179
Miller, S., 99
Millon, T., 260
Minkler, M., 144
Minuchin, S., 27, 28, 69, 73, 102, 105, 191
Mitchell, J. P., 142, 146
Montalvo, B., 275
Morris, J., 270
Mortimer, J., 32, 245
Moscicki, E. K., 146
Moss, T., 218
Mullan, J. T., 146
Muller, G. O., 184
Mullins, L., 242
Myers, J. E., 23, 31, 52, 55, 238, 273, 302

National Center for Health Statistics, 41
National Institute on Aging Consensus Task Force, 239
Neale, M. C., 141, 146
Neidhardt, E. R., 170
Nelson, C., 242
Nesselroade, J. R., 142
Neugarten, B. L., 49, 167
Newman, B. M., 44
Newman, P. R., 44
Newmann, J. P., 24
Nichols, M. P., 298
Niederehe, G., 132, 209
Noelker, L. S., 206, 250
Noller, P., 147
Norbeck, J. S., 144
Norris, R. R., 141
Norris, V. K., 144
Novak, M., 242
Nuechterlein, K. H., 137

Nuttall, P., 23, 32
Nye, F. I., 145

Olson, D. H., 151, 166
Ornstein, R., 84
Orona, C. J., 220, 223
Orr, N. K., 220
Ory, M. G., 225
Osgood, N. J., 30
Otteson, O., 243
Ouslander, J., 183

Pagel, M. D., 144
Palinkas, L. A., 144, 146
Palmore, E., 51
Parmelee, P., 238
Parsons, R., 32
Pasley, B. K., 32
Paterson, G., 282
Pattee, J., 243
Patterson, J., 103, 151
Paul, B., 273
Paul, N., 273
Pearce, J. K., 133
Pearlin, L. I., 146
Pearson, J. L., 215
Peck, M. S., 259
Peck, R. C., 26, 48
Pedersen, N. L., 142
Peeler, R., 20, 33
Peller, J., 84
Penn, P., 111
Peppard, N., 250
Pepper Commission Report, 235, 238
Peskin, H., 132, 141
Peterson, P. G., 49
Petrov, I., 146
Pickett, M., 288
Piercy, F. P., 89, 164
Pietrukowicz, M., 251
Pillemer, K., 136
Plomin, R., 142, 143
Potashnik, S. L., 224
Poulshock, S. W., 204, 206
Prata, G., 124, 127, 298

Predov, N., 146
President's Commission for the Study of Ethical Problems in Medicine and Biomedical and Behavioral Research, 301
Pruchno, R. A., 200, 205, 206, 224
Przybeck, T. R., 146
Pugliesi, K. L., 144
Pynoos, J., 143
Pyrek, J., 218

Quigley, C., 31
Quinn, W. H., 55

Rabins, P. V., 205, 206, 213, 214, 216, 217, 220, 224
Rader, L., 180, 183, 187, 191
Radloff, L. S., 146
Raffoul, P. R., 71, 146
Rando, T., 274, 276
Raskind, M. A., 215
Rathbone-McQuan, E., 30
Ratna, L., 29
Ravicki, D. A., 146
Reedy, M. N., 181
Reichard, S., 49
Reifler, B. V., 30, 215
Reinardy, J., 239
Reiss, D., 135, 142, 143
Reiss, I. L., 145
Renshaw, D. C., 184
Resch, N., 200, 205, 206
Revicki, D. A., 142
Rheaume, Y. L., 214
Rich, J., 90
Richardson, C. A., 20, 32, 33
Richters, J., 132
Riley, M. W., 55
Rivera, P., 144
Robbins, C., 147

Name Index

Roberts, J., 127
Robertson, J., 52
Robiner, W. N., 215
Robins, L., 238
Robinson, B., 206
Robison, F. F., 187
Roca, R., 240, 250
Rockstein, M. J., 44
Rodway, M. R., 32
Roe, K., 53
Rolf, J., 137
Rolland, J. S., 32, 132, 133
Ronch, J. L., 213, 219
Rook, K. S., 145
Rose, J., 144
Rosen, E., 285, 288
Rosenthal, R., 251
Rosenwaike, I. A., 41, 224
Rotenberg, M., 142, 144
Rovner, B., 238, 239, 240
Rupprecht, P., 218
Russell, C. S., 151
Russell, D. W., 144, 146
Russo, J., 146
Rutter, M., 132

Saba, G. W., 172
Sabin, T., 239
Salthouse, T. A., 141
Sameroff, A. J., 132
Sandys, M. R., 223
Sangi, J., 201
Santmyer, K., 240, 250
Santos, J., 240
Satir, V., 28
Sawa, R. J., 32
Schaie, K. W., 181
Scharlach, A. E., 144
Schefft, B. K., 50
Schooler, C., 141, 143, 146
Schrott, H. G., 146
Schulz, R., 142, 144, 145, 146, 218
Schwartz, R. C., 298
Seeman, T. E., 143
Segal, L., 29
Seifer, R., 132

Seigler, I., 30
Selekman, M. D., 33, 123, 297
Seltzer, M. M., 23
Selvini Palazzoli, M., 124, 127, 298
Semple, S. J., 146
Shamoian, C. A., 186
Shanas, E., 54
Sheehan, N. W., 23, 32
Sherbourne, C. D., 133
Sheridan, J., 243
Shields, C. G., 32, 132, 133, 144, 145, 150, 151, 225
Shields, J., 138
Shifflett, P. A., 220, 224, 225
Shoemaker, D., 218
Shuchter, S., 281
Siegel, J. S., 209
Siegler, I., 32
Silver, R., 280, 281
Simonton, D. K., 141
Sirkin, C. G., 132
Sirkin, M., 133
Skaff, M. M., 146
Skinner, D., 242
Slater, E., 223
Smaby, M. H., 187
Smallegan, M., 245
Smith, G. C., 23
Smith, J., 141
Smith, M. F., 23
Smyer, M., 52, 250
Snyder, B., 206
Snyder, L., 218
Soldo, B. J., 42, 43
Spaid, W., 204, 206
Spanier, G. B., 188
Spark, G., 63
Spencer, B., 213
Spitznagel, E., 146
Spore, D., 250
Sprenkle, D. H., 20, 151, 164
Spring, B., 139

Sprung, G., 287
Stafford, B., 31, 32
Stahmann, R., 111
Staudinger, U. M., 141
Stein, E. M., 223
Stein, S., 223
Steinglass, P., 135
Stephens, M. A., 144
Stoller, E. P., 144
Stone, J. D., 187, 188, 190, 191, 192
Stone, R., 201, 205
Strauss, P. J., 222, 223
Stukenberg, K. W., 144
Sunderland, T., 32, 136, 274
Sussman, M., 44
Swanson, G. S., 191
Swensen, C. H., 180, 181

Taeuber, C. M., 209
Tagore, R., 1
Teri, L., 214, 215
Testa, M. A., 146
Thomae, H., 25
Thomas, C., 142, 146
Thompson, L. W., 144, 215
Thompson, R. F., 84
Thurnher, M., 206
Thurston, F. D., 186
Timberlake, E. M., 26
Tischler, G., 238
Tobin, S. S., 49
Todd, T., 33, 123, 297
Toseland, R. W., 23
Treas, J., 51, 54
Troll, L. E., 167, 180

Uhlenberg, P., 185, 186
Ulrich, D. N., 63, 64
Umberson, D., 147
United Nations Secretariat, 42
U.S. Bureau of the Census, 39, 41, 42, 43, 44, 271, 296

Name Index

U.S. Department of Health and Human Services (HHS), 134
U.S. Senate Special Committee on Aging, 42
U.S. Social Security Administration, 39, 42
Urv-Wong, E., 239

Vandenbos, G., 240
Vaughn, C., 139, 147
Viney, L., 206
Vinick, B. H., 166, 206
Vitaliano, P. P., 146
Vitug, A., 239
Volicer, L., 214, 216

Wachtel, E. F., 172
Wagnild, G., 242
Walker, A., 145
Wallerstein, J. S., 186
Walsh, F., 30, 51, 52, 53, 131, 132, 164, 166, 167, 169, 170, 171, 172, 272, 279, 288
Walter, J., 84
Ware, J. E., Jr., 133
Waring, J. M., 55
Wass, H., 273
Watzlawick, P., 28, 29, 83, 127
Weakland, J. H., 20, 28, 29, 74, 127
Weakland, T., 83
Weddell, R. A., 145
Weiner, H., 242
Weinstein, K., 167
Weintraub, M., 146
Weintraub, S., 132, 137
Weishaus, S., 179, 182
Weisman, A., 274
Weissman, M., 238
Westbrook, M. T., 206
Westcott, N., 282
Whitaker, C., 28
White, C. B., 184
White, J., 243
White, M., 103, 106, 115, 298–299
White-Means, S., 205
Whiting, R., 127
Whitlatch, C. J., 33, 184
Williams, F. R., 30
Williamson, D., 19, 28, 30, 131, 136, 142, 144, 146
Willott, J. F., 46
Wilson, L., 103
Windham, C. A., 146
Wingard, D. L., 144, 146

Wischler, G., 238
Wolin, S., 135
Wolinsky, M. A., 31, 74, 192
Wolkenstein, B., 303
Womphrey, J., 31
Wood, V., 52
Woodward, R. S., 146
Worden, J., 277, 278, 279, 285
Workman-Daniels, K., 144
Wortman, C., 280, 281
Wrabetz, A., 144
Wragg, R. E., 215
Wright, L. K., 117, 123, 182
Wynne, L. C., 132, 133, 135, 136, 150, 151

Yamagishi, M., 214

Zarit, J. M., 25, 44, 45, 47, 132, 205, 206, 220
Zarit, S. H., 25, 31, 33, 44, 45, 47, 132, 184, 191, 205, 206, 220
Zeig, J., 106
Zisook, S., 281
Zube, M., 180
Zubin, J., 139

✤ *Subject Index* ✤

Abuse, of elders, future directions, 299–301
Aging process, 19–38, 39–58
  biology of, 44–47
    cardiovascular system, 45
    musculoskeletal system, 45–46
    nervous system, 46–47
    respiratory system, 45
    sensory perception, 44
  chronic illness, 24–25
  culture and, 21–22
  demography, 39–43
  family roles and, 22–23
  family therapy and, 27–33
    behavioral approaches, 28
    developmental approaches, 30–31
    educational approaches, 31–33
    generally, 27
    political approaches, 27–28
    problem-solving approaches, 29–30
    psychodynamic approaches, 28–29
  intergenerational legacy, 25–27
  losses in, 23
  overview, 19–21
  psychological factors, 47–50
  social factors, 50–55
Alzheimer's disease, 209–234
  behavioral changes, 213–215
  brain functioning, 210–211
  diagnosis, 211–212
  family dynamics and, 1–15

  family system perturbations, 220–226
    communication, 221
    family-of-origin issues, 225
    financial and legal issues, 222–223
    generally, 220
    grief, 224–225
    institutionalization, 223–224
    power and role renegotiation, 224
    sexuality, 226
  global description, 213
  incidence of, 209
  mood changes, 215–217
  physical changes, 217–218
  psychological changes, 218–220
  stages of, 8
  suggestions for clinicians, 229–230
  therapeutic approach, 226–229

Behavioral approaches, family therapy and aging process, 28
Bereavement. *See* Grief
Biography Project, nursing home systems, 250–254
Biology, of aging process, 44–47. *See also* Aging process
Brain, Alzheimer's disease, 210–211
Brief therapy. *See* Solution-focused brief therapy

Cardiovascular system, aging process, 45
Chronic illness. *See* Physical illness

Subject Index

Codependency, death of dreams, 263–266
Communication
  Alzheimer's disease, 221
  contextual family therapy, 74
  strength–vulnerability model, 136
Contextual family therapy, 61–80
  applicability and case example, 75–79
  goals, 64–65
  overview, 61–62
  process, 65–75
    assessment, 70–75
    interventions, 67–68
    life review, 66–67
    life validation, 65–66
    therapist role, 68–70
  theory, 62–64
Culture
  aging process and, 21–22, 26
  death and, 288

Death, 270–291
  case example, 288–290
  cultural variations, 288
  demography and, 271
  denial of, 271–273
  family dynamics and, 273–277
  grief guidelines, 277–281
  interventions, 281–285
  life-cycle transitions, 169–171
  losses, aging process, 23
  overview, 270–271
  of spouse, life-cycle transitions, 170–171
  widowhood, social factors, 51–52
Death of dreams, 259–269
  case examples, 260–263
  effects and therapy, 263–266
  overview, 259–260
  therapeutic attitudes and resources, 266–267
  therapeutic strategies, 267–269
Demography
  aging, 39–43
  death and, 271
  marriage (late), 178
Dependency
  death of dreams, 263–266
  life-cycle transitions, 170

Developmental approaches
  family therapy and aging process, 30–31
  marital therapy (late), 192–193
Developmental factors
  aging process, 47–48
  strength-vulnerability model, 133–134, 136
Developmental-interactional model, 101–130
  assessment, 108–115
  background, 102–104
  evaluation of, 127–129
  overview, 101
  problem-solving, 115–127
    tasks, 115–126
    techniques, 126–127
  process overview, 107–108
  theoretical assumptions, 104–107
Diagnostic and Statistical Manual of Mental Disorders (DSM-III-R), 238
Diagnostic and Statistical Manual of Mental Disorders (DSM-IV), 211–212
Divorce
  grandparenthood, 168
  marriage (late), 184–186

Ecosystemic perspective, nursing home systems, 236–238
Educational approaches, family therapy and aging process, 31–33
Elder abuse, future directions, 299–301
Employment, aging and demographics, 42–43
Ethics
  future directions, 301–302
  relational, contextual family therapy, 63–64
Ethnicity
  aging trends and, 43
  minorities, future directions, 296–297

Family dynamics
  Alzheimer's disease and, 1–15
  contextual family therapy, 72–74
  diversity in, 199–200

Subject Index

family therapists and, 285–287
grief interventions, 284–285
nursing home systems and, 244–247
Family life cycle
life-cycle transitions, 163–164. *See also*
Life-cycle transitions
marriage (late), 179–181
strength–vulnerability model,
134–136
Family roles
aging process and, 22–23, 53–55
Alzheimer's disease, 224
gender issues, caregiving and, 200–206
Family therapy. *See also* Treatment
models; *Entries under specific
treatment models*
aging process and, 19–38. *See also* Aging
process
future directions, 295–307. *See also*
Future directions
Financial issues, Alzheimer's disease,
222–223
Future directions, 295–307
elder abuse, 299–301
ethics and gerontology, 301–302
minorities, 296–297
overview, 295–296
training programs, 302–306
treatment models, 297–299

Gender issues, 199–208
caregiver well-being, 206
caregiving and, 200–204
family diversity, 199–200
Genogram
Alzheimer's disease, 227
contextual family therapy, 71–72
developmental–interactional model,
110–111
life-cycle transitions, 172–175
Geography, demography, aging and, 43
Gerontology, future directions, 301–306
Grandparenthood
aging process, social factors, 52–53
life-cycle transitions, 167–169
Grief
Alzheimer's disease, 224–225

death of dreams, 267–269
guidelines for, death, 277–281

Health. *See* Physical illness

Illness. *See* Physical illness
Institutionalization, Alzheimer's disease,
223–224. *See also* Nursing home
systems
Intergenerational legacy, aging process,
25–27

Late marriage. *See* Marriage (late)
Legal issues, Alzheimer's disease, 222–223
Life-cycle transitions, 163–177
clinical implications, 171–175
factors affecting, 164
grandparenthood, 167–169
helping roles, 165
loss and death, 169–171
overview, 163–164
retirement, 165–167
special considerations, 175–176
Life expectancy
ethnicity, aging trends and, 43
marriage (late), 178
statistics, 39, 41
Life review
contextual family therapy, 66–67
grief interventions, 281–285
Life validation, contextual family
therapy, 65–66
Loss. *See also* Grief
aging process, 23
life-cycle transitions, 169–171

Males, gender issues, caregiving and,
204–206
Marriage (late), 178–198
clinical implications, 182
divorce, 184–186
family life cycle, 179–181
marital therapy, 186–195
assessment, 188–190
case examples, 193–195
generally, 186
joining, 187–188

Subject Index

Marriage (late), *(continued)*
    models, 192–193
    treatment, 191–192
  overview, 178–179
  physical illness, 182–183
  relationship continuity, 181
  sexuality, 183–184
Men, gender issues, caregiving and, 204–206
Mental Research Institute (MRI) approach
  family therapy and, 29–30
  solution-focused brief therapy, 83
Metaphor, developmental-interactional model, 113–115
Milan Team, 298
Minorities
  aging trends and, 43
  future directions, 296–297
Mortality rates, ethnicity, aging trends and, 43
Musculoskeletal system, aging process, 45–46

Nervous system, aging process, 46–47
Nursing home systems, 235–258. *See also* Institutionalization
  context of care, 247–248
  developmental and ecosystemic perspective, 236–238
  family and, 244–247
  family strengths utilization, 250–254
  overview, 235–236
  residents, 238–241
  staff, 241–244
  systemic intervention principles, 248–250

Omnibus Budget Reconciliation Act of 1987, 239
Outcomes
  developmental-interactional model, 127–129
  solution-focused brief therapy, 99

Paradoxical intervention
  developmental-interactional model, 126–127

  marital therapy (late), 191–192
Personality, aging process, 49–50
Physical illness
  aging process, 24–25
  Alzheimer's disease, diagnosis, 211–212. *See also* Alzheimer's disease
  contextual family therapy, 70–72
  marriage (late), 182–183
  retirement and, 166–167
  strength–vulnerability model, 132–133
Political approaches, family therapy and aging process, 27–28
Problem-solving approaches, family therapy and aging process, 29–30
Psychodynamic approaches, family therapy and aging process, 28–29
Psychological factors, aging process, 47–50

Relational ethics, contextual family therapy, 63–64, 74–75
Respiratory system, aging process, 45
Retirement
  aging process, social factors, 50–51
  life-cycle transitions, 165–167
Ritual, developmental-interactional model, 127

Seizures, Alzheimer's disease, 11–12
Sensory perception, aging process, 44
Sexuality
  Alzheimer's disease, 226
  marriage (late), 183–184
Social factors, aging process, 50–55
Solution-focused brief therapy, 81–100
  assessment, 90–91
  case example, 94–98
  overview, 81–82
  theory, 82–83
  therapeutic assumptions, 84–87
  therapeutic process, 87–90
  therapist role, 92–94
Spouse, death of, life-cycle transitions, 170–171
Strength–vulnerability model, 131–160
  case example, 147–150
  nursing home systems, 250–254
  overview, 131–132

research implications, 145–147
research utility, 150
theoretical background, 132–137
  developmental change, 136
  family life cycle, 134–136
  individual life cycle, 132–134
  interactions, 136–137
therapeutic applications, 137–145
  health-enhancing processes, 143–144
  propositions, 137–140
  risk processes, 144–145
  strength processes, 140–141
  vulnerability processes, 142–143
Suicide, Alzheimer's disease, 7–8

Training programs, future directions, 302–306

Treatment models
  contextual family therapy, 61–80. *See also* Contextual family therapy
  developmental–interactional model, 101–130. *See also* Developmental–interactional model
  solution-focused brief therapy, 81–100. *See also* Solution-focused brief therapy
  strength–vulnerability model, 131–160. *See also* Strength–vulnerability model

Widowhood
  aging process, social factors, 51–52
  death, grief guidelines, 277–281
  life-cycle transitions, 170–171

Terry D. Hargrave, Ph.D., is Associate Professor of Psychology at Amarillo College. His teaching and research focus on the psychology of marriage and family, highlighting intergenerational issues. Dr. Hargrave lectures internationally on issues of later life. He is the author of *Families and Forgiveness: Healing Wounds in the Intergenerational Family* and coauthor of *Finishing Well: Aging and Reparation in the Intergenerational Family.*

Suzanne Midori Hanna, Ph.D., is both Associate Professor and Program Director in the Family Therapy Program, Kent School of Social Work at the University of Louisville. She is coauthor of *The Practice of Family Therapy: Key Elements Across Models.* Dr. Hanna is also in private practice.